The Virgin
Directory of World
Music

The Virgin Directory of World Music

Philip Sweeney

An Owl Book

Henry Holt and Company

New York

This book is dedicated to Lizzie for her support and inspiration of every possible kind, not least in putting up continually with Mahlathini when she'd have preferred to be listening to Mahler.

Copyright © 1991 by Philip Sweeney
All rights reserved, including the right to reproduce
this book or portions thereof in any form.
First published in the United States in 1992 by
Henry Holt and Company, Inc., 115 West 18th Street,
New York, New York 10011.
Originally published in Great Britain in 1991 by
Virgin Books.

Library of Congress Cataloging-in-Publication Data
Sweeney, Philip.
The Virgin directory of world music / Philip Sweeney.—1st Owl
Book ed.
p.   cm.
"Originally published in Great Britain in 1991"—T.p. verso.
"An Owl book."
Includes discographies and index.
1. Popular music—History and criticism.   2. Popular music—
Developing countries—History and criticism.   3. Musicians—
Developing countries.   I. Title.
ML3470.S95   1992   92-9791
781.63'09—dc20   CIP
                                                                MN

ISBN 0-8050-2305-4 (An Owl Book: pbk.)

Henry Holt books are available at special discounts
for bulk purchases for sales promotions, premiums,
fund-raising, or educational use. Special editions
or book excerpts can also be created to specification.

For details contact: Special Sales Director,
Henry Holt and Company, Inc., 115 West 18th Street,
New York, New York 10011.

First American/Owl Book Edition—1992

Illustrations by Debbie Harter
Printed in the United States of America
Recognizing the importance of preserving
the written word, Henry Holt and Company, Inc.,
by policy, prints all of its first editions
on acid-free paper.   ∞

1   3   5   7   9   10   8   6   4   2

CONTENTS

THE FAR EAST AND PACIFIC

THE CARIBBEAN

SOUTH AMERICA

NORTH AMERICA

ACKNOWLEDGEMENTS

I should like to thank the hundreds of people who have been kind enough to take an interest in my enquiries and offer help, information and encouragement of various sorts, but particularly the following:

Lucy Duran, Jenny Cathcart, Charlie Gillett, Andy Kershaw, Thomas Brooman and all at the WOMAD organisation; Trevor Herman, Jumbo Vanrenen, Joe Boyd, Ben Mandelson, Roger Armstrong, Anne Hunt, Nick Gold, Stuart Lyon, Bintou Simporé, the producers and directors of the BBC TV *Rhythms of the World* and *Under African Skies* series, Don Alexander, David Stockley, Mike Hennessy, Pete Laurence, Mario Pachero, Ricardo Pachon, Tim McGirk, Ana Villacorta, Michael Collins, Luis Maio, Joao Lisboa, Helene Hazera, Angela Bognano, Robert Andrews, Peter Best, John Carr, Agi Pattalis, Pandelis Griadakis, Tasos Kotzanastassis, Ketty Avarlis, Akis Ladikos, Kim Burton, Martin Kiszko, Art Troitsky, Nidam Abdi, Bouziane Daoudi, Michel Levy, Rabah Mezouane, Sidi Seddiki, Ali Jihad Racy, Institut du Monde Arabe (Paris), the late Philippe 'Hummous', Al Kenzi, David Lodge, Mohamed Hijazi, Mohamed Maklouf, Hassan Erraji, Wagdy Soleiman, David Southall, Chris Davis, M. Ketroussi, Wahid Abohiga, Assem Naguib, 'Sam' from Spectrum Radio, Baria Alamuddine, Asem and Alaa, Mona Talib, Abdullah Al-Ruwaishid, Nessim Saroussi, Gilead Limor, Aris Gasparian, Nadir Sugur, Cyrus Khajavi, Kagan Ozerhan, Mehmet Gaygusuz, Najma Akhtar, Martin Stokes, Edward Fox, Simi Chowdhury, Sanjiv Kholi, Atlaf Shiekh Hussain, Steve Coe, Rohan and Chelian, Jaime Lim, Richard Lim, Jared Lim, Freddie Aguilar, Robin Jacob, Helen Lee, Maia Norman, Dr Keith Howard of Durham University, Chinami Nishimura, Tomoyo, Paul and Etsuko Montgomery, Wang Cong, Pi-Chu Wang, Dustin Wong, Shu-sheng Chen, Li Quiang, Win Lu, Neil Gibson, Len Alldis, Guo Yué, Phil Tripp, Liz Sweeney, Patsy Garrard, Rungnapa Sasitorn, Krai, Karyn Noles, Jan Ramsey, Casey Monahan, Paul Kitchin, Everyone at Sterns, London, especially Robert Urbanus and Lois Darlington, Iain Scott, Ronnie Graham, Chris Stapleton, Graeme Ewens, Kwabena Fosu-Mensah, Moussa Joh, Moawia Yassin, Alula Andeta, Salif and Daouda Keita, Toumani Diabate, Dembo Konte, Youssou N'Dour, Manu Dibango, Philippe Conrath, Laurent Viguié, Ibrahim Sylla, John Collins, Michel David, Ian Anderson, Martin Howell, Diapy Diawara, Gilles Sala, The Mighty Gabby, Lester Green, Smokey Joe, Sonny Roberts, Lord Sam, Heriberto Ricardo, Pablo Menendez, Winston Leach, Polly Richards, Charles Deledesma, Michèle François-Eugène, Malavoi, Elio and Odelquis Revé, Marina Rodriguez Lopez, 'Francisco', Tomek, John Child, David Barton, Dave Buttle, Hector Laguillow, Gilberto Gil, Jeremy Marre, Hector Daza, Raul de Freitas, Sue Steward, John Armstrong, Dave Hucker, Verna Gillis, Celsio Calmez, Mo Fini, Edgar Villarroel, Sandra Heelan, Tony Ferré, Edna Crepaldi, Diana Scrafton, Amparo Rodriguez, Fernando and Zoraya Chavarria, Cecilia Veraza, David Adams, Berta Thayer, Carlos Espinoza,

Discos Fuentes, Porfi Jiminez, Myriam Giraldo, Hector Fabio Garcia, Fiona McAlister.

Finally, I should like to thank Verdine Bradshaw for her efficiency and willingness to put up with disruption, and Guy Lloyd for his patience and good humour.

INTRODUCTION

In the summer of 1987, a series of meetings took place in an upstairs room of a North London pub, the Empress of Russia. Present were about 25 representatives of independent record companies, concert promoters, broadcasters and other individuals active in the propagation in Britain of music from around the world. The objective was to discuss details of a modest promotional campaign for the autumn, and to boost sales of the increasing numbers of records being issued, as the boom in interest in African music continued and extended to other parts of the world. One of the obstacles to persuading record shops to stock much of the new international product was reported to be the lack of an identifying category to describe it, record shop managers didn't know whether to call it 'ethnic', 'folk', 'international', or some other equivalent, and were inclined in the absence of an appropriate niche in their racks simply to reject it. It was decided, as part of a month-long promotion that October, to create such a tag and attempt to spread its use via one or two music press adverts, a cassette compilation of music on the various labels involved in the campaign, and the distribution to record shops of 'browser cards' bearing the new appellation, to be placed in the sections it was hoped they would now create in their racks. After a good deal of discussion the term chosen was 'World Music', other contenders such as 'Tropical Music' being judged too narrow of scope. I remember thinking, in view of the modest funding of the campaign and fairly laid-back nature of its participants, that nothing would come of it all, which shows how good my commercial judgement is. Within months the term was cropping up in the British press, within a year it had crossed the Channel and was rivalling the existing French phrase 'sono mondiale', coined three years earlier by the fashionable Paris glossy *Actuel* and its broadcasting subsidiary Radio Nova, and within three years it was in regular mainstream music industry use in Britain, the United States and northern Europe. This may be regrettable for those people, including myself, who dislike the term for its combination of a meaninglessly wide literal field of reference, with a capricious and subjective actual application, but it is also understandable. No better short phrase has yet been proposed, and thus the term World Music has taken on a quite sturdy life of its own, which is one of the reasons it forms the title of this book. The clinching reason is its nearest rival. The Virgin Directory of World Popular & Roots Music From Outside The Anglo-American Mainstream is somewhat lacking in *élan*. It is also still lacking in precision. The fact is that the music described in these pages is only approximately categorisable, and numerous deviations and extensions have occurred in the drawing of a boundary line. Broadly speaking, I have focused on music which is popular in the sense that it is not art or classical music, is in regular use by ordinary people to dance to, is listened to via radio or cassette, is perhaps performed, and is not artificially preserved folklore. (Already the definition is problematic: some genres, for example the Arab 'central domain' music, as it has been called by Professor Ali Jihad Racey, of the great Egyptian stars such as Oum Kalthoum and Mohamed Abdel Wahab, simply do not fall neatly to one side of a line between 'art' and 'popular' music.) My geographical/genre exclusion zone is also to a degree arbitrary: I have attempted to remove the great body of music belonging to the Anglo-American dominated pop and rock mainstream, and the music of those local artistes worldwide who simply re-create this style, and to describe what is left. But of course the boundary is again unclear: most local pop/rock artistes blend mainstream and indigenous styles to some extent, and the definition of what is mainstream in any event shifts continuously. I have taken note of the music becoming implicitly part of the 'World Music' domain by virtue of festival programming, public and media interest, etc., to the extent of including certain artistes, such as the Bulgarian traditional choirs so acclaimed lately, which do not strictly fit my criteria. The other area often associated with 'World Music', that of consciously experimental hybrid musics created by Western jazz and rock musicians with African or oriental counterparts, is not the subject of this book. My final, and most severe, limitation has been imposed by space. A truly comprehensive account of the world's popular and roots musics would require several million words. In deciding which nations, genres and artistes to include, I have taken as criteria not only the general importance and distinctiveness of the music in question, but also the interests of a hypothetical northern European or American reader. Thus, for example, North American, Scandinavian or British roots musics are afforded relatively less space, because to have done otherwise would have meant skimping on coverage elsewhere, and the probable readers of this book have much greater access to information on these areas than they do, for example, to information on the music of the Arab world. In the case of North America, I have not included accounts of undeniably 'roots' genres such as country and blues, on similar grounds: they are abundantly covered already. The principle of treating the subject matter geographically, which is also of course arbitrary (national borders do not necessarily represent musical borders), works very well in my opinion, though frequent recourse to the index to cross reference styles co-existing in different areas, etc., is to be recommended.

Philip Sweeney

AFRICA

The North and West

INTRODUCTION

Around 1976/77, a number of things began to build up my interest in African music. Some were pure chance – about that time, for instance, BBC Radio 4, which was my regular morning diet, moved frequency and one day while I was trying in a zombielike state to find it on the dial, I ended up on a Dutch station which was playing some fascinating music. It was from the soundtrack of a Stanley Baker film – it wasn't a particularly great piece of music but it had some really nice elements. There was a traditional African choral piece called 'Sho Sholoza' – a beautiful song, sung straight from the heart. It took me about a month to track it down at the specialist movie soundtrack shop in Soho. That started me listening to other things.

At around the same time, my interest in drumming, which had never been far from the surface, really took off. The main impetus was the invention of the programmable drum machine. This was an incredibly liberating tool, because for the first time when writing music you could take your hands off the keyboard, rest a moment and then come back with another idea . . . Also, you could experiment with focusing on different rhythms without the necessity of the cooperation of a drummer.

The first music that really enthused me was South African. I still think the black South African national anthem, 'Nkosi Sikeleli Afrika', is probably the best of any national anthem I know. It was the choir that I was drawn to initially – by Ladysmith Black Mambazo and others with their close kinship to gospel and their blend of sensuality and spirituality at the same time. Later, when I visited Zimbabwe on the Amnesty International tour, I saw another side of Southern African music – political, dance oriented, more social. I liked Zimbabwe enormously; it's so positive and optimistic, and rich in excellent music, from **Thomas Mapfumo** to the dozens of less famous bands who put out so many good singles. But for me the spirituality of South African music appealed especially. Even more than in South Africa I find this quality in West African music, and in West Africa the country I know best is Senegal.

Senegal was the first African country I visited in the early 1980s. I went there with George Acogny, the jazz guitarist and record producer, to visit his sister Germaine, who at that time was running a school of dance in Dakar. Germaine Acogny had set up the school, the Mudra d'Afrique, with the Belgian choreographer Maurice Béjart, with the aim of collecting and preserving traditional African dance and interpreting it with modern dance. I had met Germaine in Paris, she had introduced me to George, and he had told me I had to come to Senegal with him. It turned out to be a wonderful introduction to the country, one of my best travel experiences. The people were so alive and friendly and there were those tall, beautiful women with their remarkable, elegant posture.

Germaine Acogny is a remarkable woman, with a character of great power. At that time she was working with the Senegalese master drummer Doudou N'Diaye Rose and she was one of the few people who have ever told Doudou what to do. Doudou is quite a character himself – a real showman, a man of the world, much-travelled, but Germaine Acogny had a wonderful no-nonsense relationship with him. She was boss.

We had taken some recording equipment and Doudou was one of the people we wanted to record – he has an important place in Senegalese music as a collector of traditional rhythms. It turned out to be quite a saga, getting the equipment into Dakar. We had an eight-track machine and an F1, an early piece of digital equipment, and I remember nearly losing them at Customs at Dakar airport. As soon as the gear had been checked hands started reaching through the wire separating the Customs area off, all trying to earn a little money carrying our stuff, and the cases were getting pulled off the tables and crashing to the floor . . . When the equipment was eventually set up we had problems with the heat affecting the amplifiers.

Locating Doudou wasn't that easy either. For one thing, he might or might not turn up to an appointment he'd made. Also, as a Muslim he has his full complement of wives and if you visit one house asking for him, the wife in question might be a little sensitive about admitting he wasn't there but at another house. Eventually we did some recording at the open-air music school in Dakar.

One of the most striking things about West African percussion is the fluidity of the rhythms. This is partly due to the actual equipment used. The little drumsticks that Senegalese drummers like Doudou N'Diaye Rose use are often freshly cut from the tree, so they're much more flexible than Western drumsticks. They're also much shorter. The result is a more liquid tone, somewhere between a hand and a Western drumstick in sound. You hear this very clearly in the wonderful tama (talking drum) playing of remarkable musicians like Youssou N'Dour's or Baba Maal's tama players — Baba Maal in particular does a duet with his tama player, who follows and copies his voice.

The other outstanding characteristic of Senegalese and West African Islamic music, of course, is the singing, that extraordinarily powerful sound that many people outside Africa are now familiar with, thanks to Youssou N'Dour. I first saw Youssou play at his nightclub on my first visit to Dakar and I danced myself crazy.

The reason why Senegalese music is so powerful has a lot to do with the way the singing, which has for me an intensely spiritual feeling, is combined with the rhythms. I think that singing is more able to release the spirit and rhythm the body — that's not to say there's a total separation: both singing and rhythm act to a certain extent on both spirit and body, but you might say they are king and queen of their respective provinces. Incidentally, I believe there's a great deal for me to learn in terms of the psychological and physiological responses to sound and rhythm, and African music is in many ways closer to an understanding of some of these responses than other more 'sophisticated' regions.

Although Senegalese music is lyrically very rich — the griots' role in transmitting history and so on — it doesn't matter to me that I don't understand all the words of a song. The voice is such a powerful means of communication, and it's so direct, it can transmit a feeling without having recourse to words.

PETER GABRIEL

LIBYA

Libya's influence on Arab popular music was quite substantial from the eighties onwards, though most of this influence took effect outside the country.

Like all of North Africa, Libya has a variety of folk musics of mixed Berber, Arab and black Southern stock. Main instruments are flutes, assorted percussion and lutes.

In addition, Libya in the 1950s and 1960s had its share of singers in the pan-Arab style — main names were **Sayed Abou-Madian**, **Ali Al Sha'alia**, **Mohamed Sidiki** and **Salam Kadri**. Another classic singer, **Ibrahim Fahmi**, continues to be an important composer.

Two successive wavelets of Libyan musical creativity attracted the attention of a wider audience. The first was that of the two 'godfathers of Arab new-wave music', as some commentators refer to them, **Ahmed Fakroun** and **Nasser Al Mizdawi**.

Nasser Al Mizdawi was born in 1950 in Mizda, near Tripoli, and began singing and playing guitar as a student in the early 1970s. His first cassette (called 'Songs of Exile' although he was not yet in exile at that time) achieved considerable sales. His second, 'Libyan Melodies Around the World', sold even more. His guitar-playing prowess was much admired by young Libyans (**Hameed Al Shaary** – see below – named his first band **Al Mizdawia** after Al Mizdawi and his style). By the mid-1980s he was in more-or-less permanent exile and spent several years without recording in Jordan, before making a comeback record, again called 'Exile', in the USA in 1990.

Ahmed Fakroun, slightly younger than Al Mizdawi, was born in Benghazi, an Eastern city with a tradition both of artistic creativity and rebellion (the great anticolonialist leader Omar El Muktar came from Benghazi). The city's university population is regarded with great suspicion by Qadafy, whose regime publicly hanged three students there in 1977, at the beginning of a ten-year period of extreme harshness. The same year Fakroun, who had been playing electric guitar in rock groups in Benghazi hotel lounges, left for Italy, where he made a couple of Euroballad-style singles. Passing through London, he made his first rock record, 'Wadni' ('Promise Me'). In 1981 he arrived in Paris, and became part of a vague movement of musicians and alternative artistes beginning to incorporate North African Arab feeling into an assortment of fringe rock records and design projects. (**Jean-Paul Goude** was shortly to join this tendency.) The video clip for his 1984 record, 'Soleil Soleil', was directed by **Jean-Baptiste Mondino**, who went on to achieve major success, and designed by the **Musulmans Fumants** ('Smoking Muslims') group. A prime ingredient of Fakroun's music was (and is) the mirzkawi rhythm, a black style from the area south of Benghazi, and therefore an equivalent to the equally influential Moroccan gnaoui rhythm. From 1988 onwards, Fakroun's performance declined somewhat.

The second 'wavelet' of Libyan pop creativity took place in Egypt, and was again due to an action of the Qadafy regime. In 1985, it was decided to eliminate ex-colonialist influence from the country's music, and a symbolic bonfire of guitars and pianos was made in Tripoli's Green Square to launch an anti-Western music campaign. Another young Benghazi resident, Hameed Al Shaary, who had already travelled to England to train as a pilot, and to Cairo to study music, was at this time building a considerable reputation as a composer and performer, like Fakroun incorporating the hot black rhythms from the southern region around Mirzik. Al Shaary settled in Cairo, where he was joined by his brothers, Magdy and Mohsen. Within a short time he had almost single-handedly launched a new pop style which rapidly dominated the listening of Cairo's youth under the name 'New Wave', and later 'Al Jeel' music. See **Egypt** section for further details.

Inside Libya, Qadafy's late 1980s authoritarian thaw has slightly alleviated conditions for the youth. A young reggae-influenced singer currently rising fast in Tripoli is **Mohsen Beit Al Mal**.

A curious footnote to the Qadafy regime's effect on pop music is its creation, through the use of Western groups, of a genre of hilarious revolutionary pop songs, combining lyrics in praise of the Green Book or the lack of poverty in the country with a variety of hack Anglo-American rock melodies.

TUNISIA

The traditional musics of Tunisia overlap to the east with that of the Fezzan and Tripolitania regions of Libya and to the west with that of Algeria.

Earlier this century, Tunisian malouf music was of considerable influence on its neighbours. Malouf, which is also found in Algeria in the region surrounding the city of Constantine and the border with Tunisia, is a compound of the semi-classical Andalous style found in variations across the Maghreb and local folk styles. The father of modern Tunisian malouf was **Khmeyes Tarnan**, who died in 1964 after a long career as composer and director of the Tunis Radio Orchestra.

In addition to the noubas of the refined malouf style, peasant musics such as fondo and the all-conquering Egyptian light classical style of **Oum Kalthoum** contribute to Tunisian popular music. The outstanding singers of the 1940s and 1950s were **Hedi Jouini, Mohamed Jamoussi** and **Ali Riahi**. Riahi in particular achieved major fame throughout the Maghreb with his polished blend of Egyptian and Bedouin styles and the then fashionable tangos and rumbas.

Tunisian popular music, per se, has not produced anything in the 1980s to compare with the youth styles of Morocco or Algeria. The singer **Hedi Hebbouba** became very popular throughout the first half of the decade with an updated folkloric style using the flutes and percussion of the traditional rural mezwed music in combination with song texts adapted to a new urban youth audience. Now and again, a singer appears on the scene (one example is **Mohsen Rais**) who adds Arabic words to what is essentially Western pop.

Outside the country, the glamorous Tunis-born singer **Latifa Arfaoui** has achieved considerable fame in Cairo, where she studied at the Institute of Music, as did Oulaya, another Tunisian chanteuse to make a career in Egypt in the 1970s. Yet another glamorous Tunisienne to embark on a musical career outside her country is the Paris-based singer **Amina Annabi** whose 1990 debut album 'Yalil', produced by her friend, the pioneer Euro-Worldbeat practitioner **Martin Meissonnier**, mixed a standard Worldbeat-programmed synthetic backing with part-Arabic vocals and oriental instrument adornments including accordion, ney (flute) and qanun (zither). Amina was born to a musical family in Carthage, Tunisia; her grandmother was a classical singer and lutenist, her mother organised musical festivals and also wrote a number of the songs on Amina's debut LP. Amina came to Paris at the age of thirteen to study classical singing and dance and became part of the young Arab popular arts scene then experimenting with Arab rap and other ideas. Her first single, 'Sheherazade', was a minor hit in Japan. Amina's exotic good looks also secured her a small role in Bernardo Bertolucci's 1990 film of the Paul Bowles novel *The Sheltering Sky*.

Meanwhile, in Vienna, the younger singer **Walid Rouissi** has created a modern hybrid style based on his classically-trained lute playing and the input of a multinational group of musicians, including his Austrian pianist wife.

If Tunisian popular artistes are conspicuous by their absence in general, now and again a Tunisian song achieves sudden success outside the country. The big hit 'Ma Baker' by the group Boney M. was based on one, 'Sidi Mansouria'. Another, 'Jari Ya Hamaida', has been taken up by Joan Baez.

Tunisia: Discography

Various Tunisie Chants et Rythmes (Club du Disque Arabe AAA 001)
Hedi Hebbouba Untitled (Horizon ESP 7201)
Amina Yalil (Phonogram 838 609)
Walid Rouissi El Omr Hikaya (INT AMLP 1002)

ALGERIA

In the 1970s and 1980s, two Algerian popular genres achieved a certain breakthrough outside their own country. The later, chronologically, was the famous raï youth music of the western region around Oran, the product, more or less, of the Arab strand of the country's musical tradition. Much less fêted internationally, but equally important among Algerian immigrant communities in France in the 1970s, was the modernised form of Berber music originating in Kabylia, the most important of the five Berber regions of Algeria.

Historically, several Berber musical figures stand out in the twentieth century. A Berber singer-composer, **Aïssa Djarmoussi**, was the first Maghrebin artiste to give a major public concert in Europe when he played the Olympia in Paris in 1917. The Berber facility for the intellectual pursuits – commerce, politics, conversation – extends into music and poetry, and Kabyle songwriting flourished after World War II, in spite of periodic persecution by the Algerian government.

One of the first to suffer from unofficial but effective censorship after independence was the singer-poet **Slimane Azem** who, ironically, had already attracted the attention of the French police earlier with his 1956 song 'The Locusts' which metaphorically describes the colonialists as locusts ravaging the country, represented by a lovingly tended garden, and who continued to sing of the injustices perpetrated by the new authoritarian regime.

In the 1970s a new wave of Kabyle singer-songwriters appeared, and to the extent that they identified themselves with a movement to reassert Kabyle identity, they too suffered government persecution. **Aït-Menguellet**, the most popular artiste of this movement, who has spent a period of eight months in prison, is sometimes referred to as the Kabyle Dylan and his songs owe much in inspiration to the acoustic folk-protest movement of which Bob Dylan was figurehead.

Other prominent members of the 1970s Kabyle modern song movement are the male singers **Idir**, **Brahim Izri**, the male group **Imazighen** and the all-female group **Djurdjura**.

In the 1980s, a number of younger Kabyle artistes have maintained the impetus. Two of these have had French-released albums licensed to the Anglophone markets by the British record label Globestyle. **Ahcene Adjroud**, a poet-singer in his thirties, scored a considerable success in 1981 with his first album 'Ammis Boumjahed', a collection of songs on personal and political themes. The female singer **Ouardia** writes about the problems of women rather than about national politics, and thus has greater access to Algerian radio. Finally, the young male singer **Tak Farounass** sprang to popularity with a slightly harder-edged sound and a strong line in enigmatic lyrics. The instrumental accompaniment to modern Kabyle music has tended to be mainly acoustic: lutes, mandolins, percussion, including the derbouka, occasionally guitars. The vocal lines are melodically simple, minor keys often imparting a melancholy tone, less dramatic and less long-drawn-out and ornamental than Arab song.

Another Berber people to have maintained a musical profile are the Chaoui. In addition to the male song tradition of which Aïssa Djarmoussi, mentioned above, was an exponent, Chaoui musicmakers included a sorority of 'free women', the 'azriate', who entertained at marriages and were permitted much greater licence in terms of references to love than ordinary women would have been. One modern interpreter of the tradition now operates out of Paris, where she works as a teacher of sociology, and tours internationally. **Houria Aïchi** learnt the kernel of her repertoire of Chaoui songs as a child in Algeria and now performs these shrill, ancient-sounding airs accompanied by the sinuous rosewood flute (gasba) playing of **Saïd Nissia**.

The Arabic musical background of Algeria includes a number of basic strands. Played primarily on lutes, mandolins, violins and assorted percussion (mainly derbouka), and lyrically concerned either with religious or secular subjects, the quasi-classical Andalous music created stars of major stature, and overlapped into the cafés and cabarets of the pre-war years. Thus performers such as **Dahmane Ben Achour**, who died in 1977, provided a direct link between the medieval Arab court of Córdoba and the late twentieth-century recording studio.

An important Jewish body of musicians shared responsibility for the strength of Andalous music, particularly in Algeria and Tunisia; one prime exponent continued to perform through to the 1980s, when a new young European audience discovered her during the boom in interest in Arab music. **Reinette l'Oranaise** was born Sultana Daoud in Tiaret, Algeria, in the early 1920s. Blind from the age of two, she was sent by her mother to study music with the Jewish master **Saoud Medioni**, 'Saoud l'Oranais', in whose Oran café in the Derb Jewish quarter she started performing. From 1961, Reinette worked mainly in France, where she was well known among the large Jewish-Maghrebin population but not outside it. Until, that is, her deep, still powerful, voice, guttural lute playing and eye-catching presence – pink, sequined gown, vases of gladioli on stage – caught the imagination of numbers of young Parisians. Reinette l'Oranaise gave major concerts at the Albert Hall in London in 1989 and at the Paris Olympia the following year. Her recent work has been much aided by the unusual and elegant piano accompaniment, Satie-like in feel, of the Algiers master **Mustapha Skandrani**.

Combined with regional folk styles, Andalous music in Algeria also transmuted into a series of derivatives – malouf, as in Tunisia, in the Eastern region around Constantine; chaabi in the central Algiers region – which produced twentieth-century performers of great popularity. **El Hadj Mohamed El Anka**, who died in 1978, was perhaps the greatest star to emerge from this background.

In addition there was the chi'r el melhoun, a Bedouin tradition of lyric poetry, dealing with a vocabulary, rapidly becoming outmoded and irrelevant by the 1930s, of deserts, stars and stallions. This poetry was chanted to the accompaniment of gasba flutes by the chioukh (the plural of cheikh), learned and usually venerable Islamic masters.

While the chioukh were male, sedate, virtuous and formal, the female entertainers known as cheikhate were exactly the opposite. Rough and bawdy, these women, of whom the most famous, **Cheikha Rimitti El Ghilizania**, is still performing today, animated not only private parties but also the cafés, hashish dens and cabarets that began to proliferate in cities such as Oran and Algiers. Although the cheikhate started to make records at an early stage, in the 1930s, their discs were frequently confiscated and certainly would never have been played in a family home. The cheikhate were, in effect, the earliest raï singers, with their libertine lyrics and lifestyles, and their tradition is very much alive today. The aged but sprightly Cheikha Rimitti El Ghilizania (her name is composed of a corruption of the French 'remettez', meaning 'fill them up' or 'the same again' – she acquired the tag performing in a bar) is experiencing an upsurge in demand in the Algerian cafés of Paris and Lyon, and her songs are continually covered by the new young raï singers. Rimitti's traditional subject matter – the quest for love and pleasure in a strait-laced society, the escape afforded by alcohol, the joys and sorrows of ordinary people – is thoroughly appropriate to modern raï: thirty years before the new young pop-raï artistes were struggling free of the Islamic moral straitjacket, Rimitti was singing on the subject of the all-important female virginity, 'Rip it, tear it, Rimitti will mend it!' Another younger cheikha, **Djenia**, has actually taken on the pop-raï world at its own game, recording duets in 1988 with a number of the new young Oran singers. **Cheb Abdelhak** was the first, with the 1987 cassette hit 'Rah Igaber' ('He's Looking For a Woman') in which the young singer's strong male voice was easily matched by the coarse masculine tones of Cheikha Djenia. Djenia, by occupying the same stages as the new young chebs in nightclubs like the famous Biarritz of Oran, and by alternating freely between traditional flute and percussion, acts as a bridge between the worlds of old raï of the cheikhate and new raï of the young chebs.

The term 'raï' probably dates to the same period as the original cheikhate. The Bedouin male singers, and later the cheikhate, began to pepper their verses with the phrase 'Ha-er raï' or 'Ya raï', meaning something like 'it's my opinion' or 'that's what I think', which soon assumed the function of an all-purpose filler and adornment, rather like 'Oh yeah' in Anglo-Saxon pop.

It was in the western city of Oran that raï grew up, nurtured by the particular conditions of the port and its hinterland. By the 1940s a number of influences, including jazz, pop, flamenco and the black North African rhythmic gnaoui music, were combining to form the style known as 'Oran modern'. Gasba and ghaïta flutes, guellal and derbouka drums and karkabou iron castanets were augmented or supplanted by trumpets, saxophones, accordions and violins. Stars of this period included **Blaoui El Houari** and **Ahmed Saber**; the latter in particular forming an important link with modern raï. Saber worked through into the sixties, during which time rock and roll, the twist craze and all the other European pop phenomena made their mark on the Oran music scene. Saber's lyrics retained the sardonic, bawdy spirit of the cheikhate, and his outspokenness concerning his country's new ruling establishment ensured him several spells in jail. By the time Saber died in 1967, the cabarets and new discothèques of the Oran seafront were hosting a crop of Algerian pop and rock groups with names such as the **Red Stars**, **The Drifters**, **The Vultures** and **The Students**. Oran's traditional role as a port, a pleasure beach and a centre for general laissez faire and recreation blossomed until the early 1970s, when President Boumedienne's puritanical anti-immorality campaign 'Operation Anti-Dragueur' began to suppress the nightclubs and the musicians.

Two further artistes must be mentioned as links to the eventual 1970s and 1980s explosion of modern pop-raï. The young singer **Bouteldja Belkacem**'s string of hits through the 1960s and early 1970s leaned lyrically much more towards the popular street feeling of the cheikhate than any attempt at a cosmopolitan, Euro-rock veneer. Songs such as 'Zizya' and 'Serbi li Baoui' ('Give Me a BAO' − a brand of bottled beer) also featured traditional instruments such as the ghaïta flute beloved of the cheikhate. In 1975, **Belkacem** recorded a song called 'Ya Rayi'; the bandleader he worked with then was **Messaoud Bellemou**, frequently described later as the 'father of raï'. Bellemou was born in 1947 in the town of Ain Temouchent and began his professional career in the municipal brass band. He rapidly began to put together an instrumental line-up of considerable force, combining traditional instruments (derbouka, guellal, karkabou and the big bass drum t'bar) with new ones − electric guitar and bass and, above all, the silvery quarter-tone trumpet that became his trademark. Bellemou's singers, notably **Boutaïba Seghir**, managed to get away with a certain degree of mild suggestiveness in the strait-laced 1970s and his tutelage was a major factor in the later success of several of the new, young raï singers.

Among them was a young actress and singer, **Fadela Zalmat**, who had achieved notoriety in the 1976 television film *Djalti*, in which she appeared as a smoking, drinking, miniskirted delinquent. Fadela's 1979 smash hit 'Ana Ma H'lali Ennoum' ('I Don't Care About Sleep Any More') with its passionate wailing vocal line, and modern bass and synthesizer arrangement, opened the floodgates to the new wave of what was often called 'pop-raï' to distinguish it from earlier, traditional raï.

The new young raï singers were, for the most part, male, from modest to poor non-intellectual backgrounds − ideal rock and roll material in fact − and they rapidly began to prefix their names with the word 'cheb', meaning 'young' or 'kid'. Thus the 'Cheb' in 'Cheb Khaled' (the feminine version is chaba) is in pointed contrast to the use of 'cheikh', meaning 'old and respected', in the appellation of puritanical old singers such as **Cheikh Hamada** and **Cheikh Madani** who were still performing.

It is important to note that raï music has never been politically rebellious; very rarely has any raï singer included verses demanding political change or criticising the government.

Raï lyrics, however, are an interesting mirror of Algerian society. Alcohol figures largely − beer, or the more exotic anis, or whisky ('el birra 'arbia wa el whisky gaouri' − 'beer is Arab but whisky is European' was an early pop-raï refrain). It is used either as an aid to making non-Islamic whoopee or, frequently, as a self-destructive means of forgetting one's misery, for example after having been abandoned by a paramour, perhaps a divorcee, following a night of passion. Cars and the beach, echoing Oran's seafront libertine image, frequently add a faintly Californian nuance to the songs. Running through most lyrics is the common Arab theme of waiting, longing, enduring an endless stretch of time without the object of one's lament.

It remains to be seen to what extent the libertine content of raï will endure, at least publicly. For one thing, raï singers themselves showed signs of a willingness to tone down their music if doing so would make it more saleable. Furthermore, the great advance towards power of the Islamic fundamentalist party in the 1989 elections brought with it an ominous pressure for return to the days of puritanism, with raï music very much on the list of things not to be encouraged in society.

Only four years earlier, however, the Algerian climate had appeared to be favouring the acceptance of raï. In 1985, in Algiers, an officially sponsored Raï Festival took place from which the top star **Cheb Khaled** emerged as winner. Raï was now moving out of its traditional habitat − private parties and nightclubs − and starting to be performed in large rock-style stadia. The wide marble forecourt and mall of the Ryad-el-Feth cultural centre in Algiers began to be the scene of massive concerts. In 1986, a raï festival, attended by all the top stars, took place in the Paris suburb of Bobigny, and raï music took a major step into the French spotlight. Parisian trendsetters on the one hand − advertising director Jean-Paul Goude of Grace Jones fame, the magazine *Actuel* and its off-shoot radio station Radio Nova − and young French in daily contact with 'beurs' (French slang for second-generation Algerian immigrants) communities on the other began to spread the raï news. In 1988, Earthworks put out a raï compilation album, 'Raï Rebels', in London and two years later **Cheb Mami** was recording his latest album in Los Angeles with top producer Hilton Rosenthal.

Less than a dozen names dominate the pop-raï scene. If not of personal rock-star status, Messaoud Bellemou continues to be a substantial figure. His late eighties group **Gana** with a first-class new singer, **Cheb Ourrad Houari**, made a powerful exciting sound, rootsier and more trumpet-dominated than some of the synthesizer and drum line-ups.

Chaba Fadela more than fulfilled the promise of her huge 1979 success. After retiring briefly to marry another top singer, **Mohamed Sahraoui**, she returned triumphantly to perform as a duo with her new husband. Sahraoui, unusually for a raï singer a conservatoire-trained musician, had been in at the very start of the new raï movement, recording as early as 1976. His partnership with Fadela, as a sort of North African Sonny and Cher, was highly successful, attracting both male and female fans, and their 1983 recording 'N'Sel Fik' ('You Are Mine') became one of the greatest hits of the 1980s.

Universally recognised as the 'King of Raï' was Cheb Khaled, whose great hit 'Hada Raykoum' was the first raï record to be released on the Anglophone market by the London independent label Triple Earth. Khaled was born in 1960 in Sidi El Houari, near Oran, and made his first record, a 45 called 'Trigel lycée' ('The Road To School') while still at school. Throughout the early raï days, he built a quintessentially raï reputation as a devil-may-care, café-loving, irresponsible individual, completely insouciant about his career and life in general.

Based more in France, particularly Marseilles, than in Algeria, Khaled performed regularly in the 1980s, often with a group led by his old friend **Cheb Kada** on synthesizer. (Kada, when not accompanying Khaled, meanwhile became a mainstay of the Paris-based group **Noudjoum el raï** − 'the stars of raï'.) In 1988 Khaled became the first raï star to benefit from major record company investment, when he made the album 'Kutché' with the top world music producer Martin Meissonnier and the well-connected Algerian jazz/rock musician **Safy Boutella**. Its £80,000 production costs were underwritten, it was said, by substantial Algerian government investment. 'Kutché' did not live up to its promise, however, being judged at the Oran street level as too European and sophisticated.

The following year saw Khaled release a very different album, of traditionally orchestrated duets with another of the top half-dozen raï artistes, the mysterious Moroccan-born **Chaba Zahouania** of the rough, bluesy voice. Zahouania's mystery lay chiefly in her appearance, which was unknown to the many fans who bought her cassettes, as Zahouania insisted, to please her family it was said, on the old cheikhate device of printing a model's photograph rather than her own on her cassette covers.

Khaled's chief rival for the leadership of the raï market was **Cheb Mami**, dubbed therefore the 'Prince of Raï'. Mami was born Mohamed Khelifati in 1966 in the town of Saïda. Endowed with a high, agile, expressive voice, he came to prominence singing typical modern risqué raï lyrics at parties, weddings and circumcisions, but soon after sealing his growing reputation with an important television appearance in 1982, he began to tone down the language of his songs, in some cases returning to the use of the old, veiled, classical Arabic texts. A second astute career move was the acquisition of a French manager, **Michel Levy**, who began to channel the interest aroused by Mami's French LP 'Le Prince Du Raï'. Within a year of the Bobigny concert, Mami was playing dates in Germany, Japan and the USA and consolidating an apparent lead over Khaled, who remained resolutely blasé. This lead was reversed when Mami's career was suspended in 1987 by a two-year spell of military service: a relatively easy one, since Mami was found a privileged position in army entertainment. (The opportunity to shoot an Algerian version of *G.I. Blues* with Mami as an Oran Elvis was missed.) On completion of his army service, Mami resumed activities and became the second raï star to enter the big-time recording industry with his expensive, semicrossover album 'Let Me Raï', produced by Hilton Rosenthal in Los Angeles and featuring mainly American session musicians. Partly due to Mami's choice of traditional songs, this album did not suffer the same rejection as Khaled's 'Kutché' and sold well both in Algeria and in France.

During Mami's national service, his French manager began to develop a new young singer, Moroccan born but Paris resident, named **Cheb Kader**. Kader, who had made his first record while a delivery boy at a Paris Arab record distribution company, was very much in the mould of Mami – clean-cut, ambitious, diligent – and he succeeded in capturing a lot of the burgeoning non-Arab interest in the newly fashionable raï. Kader thus became the first genuine raï star (top ten hits in Germany and Holland; tours of Europe, Japan; a starring role in the first raï TV film) to achieve success while remaining totally unknown in Algeria.

Secondary raï artistes include: **Cheb Abdelhak**, whose most famous works were his two collaborations with female singers Chaba Zahouania and Cheikha Djenia el Kebira; **Cheb Hamid**, identified with a strong flamenco influence; **Cheb Houari Benchenet**, a talented composer and strong singer; **Cheb Tati**, a Paris-based singer whose excellent LP 'El Hammam' was well received in 1989; **Cheb Tahar**, a Moroccan-born singer noted for his energetic stage presence which involves much outrageous, even camp, dancing; **Cheb Sid Ahmed**, an openly homosexual singer who, for this reason, occupied the highly unusual position of member of a troupe of medahate female wedding musicians; **Cheb Moumen**, a former pop singer gone over to raï and **Raina Raï**, one of the earliest raï groups to function as a group, now based in Paris.

Finally, one should mention the brothers **Rashid** and **Fethi Baba Ahmed**, who, along with their younger rival **Mohamed Maghni**, are the leading raï arrangers and producers. By 1988, their Rallye studio in Tlemcen, equipped with 24-track recording equipment, was dominating the raï market.

Algeria: Discography

Ahcene Adjroud Adounith (Globestyle ORB 031)
Ouardia Assirem (Globestyle ORB 030)
Djurdjura Groupe de femmes algériennes (CBS CB 271)
Reinette l'Oranaise Tresors de la Musique Arabo-Andalouse (Horizon HM 012)
Cheikha Rimitti Ghir El Baroud (Sonodisc MLP 306)
Messaoud Bellemou Le Pere du Raï (World Circuit WLB 011)
Various Le Disque D'Or du Raï (Musidisc MU 221)
Cheb Kader Best of Cheb Kader (WEA WE 331)
Various Raï Rebels (Virgin/Earthworks EWV 15)
Various Pop-Raï and Rachid Style (Earthworks EWV 7)
Cheb Khaled Khaled (Barclay 511815-2)
Cheb Khaled and Zahouania Les Monstres Sacrés du Raï (Sonodisc MLP 305)
Cheb Mami Le Prince du Raï (Horizon HM 014)
Cheb Mami Let Me Raï (EMI PM 520)
Cheb Tati El Hammam (Blue Moon BM 125)

MOROCCO

Morocco remains a major guardian of the classical Andalous style of music formed across the Mediterranean during the Arab occupation of Spain. The Ministry of Culture in 1989 and 1991 undertook a major recording programme to preserve a record of the eleven great Andalous 'nouba' surviving out of a one-time total of 24, using the four most eminent Andalous orchestras in the country, those of Fez, Tetouan, Rabat and Tangiers. Interestingly, two of these orchestras, the **Orchestra of Tangiers** with **Juan Peña 'El Lebrijano'**, and the **Orchestra of Tetouan** with **José Heredia Maya**, have undertaken collaborations with flamenco singers in recent years.

On a popular level, the basic ingredients which in varying degrees shape most modern Moroccan musics are: chaabi or bidaoui − very roughly, country musics varying from region to region; the pan-Arab Egyptian style; in certain regions, Berber folk music; various European (Spanish and French) and American musics. In addition, the religious-spiritualist chanting and drumming of various Islamic sects and brotherhoods are of great influence. In particular, the music of the gnaoui, black descendants of slaves introduced into Morocco from Sudan and Guinea, brings a strong black African feel to certain styles. Gnaoui music, performed regularly by itinerant troupes in Marrakesh's famous J'ma El F'na square, features rough, wild percussion including iron castanets.

The most influential and famous Moroccan popular singer of the immediate post-war period was **Hocine Slaoui**, who created a blend of traditional bidaoui with touches of jazz and international pop, and whose sardonic lyrics ranged through the louche 1940s Casablanca world of wine, kif, visiting American warships and their effect on Moroccan women. His great street and café hits included the immortal 'OK OK C'mon Baby'.

Major stars of the 1960s were **Abdelhadi Belkhayat** and **Abdelwahab Doukali**, whose major influence was the all-pervasive Egyptian Oum Kalthoum style with its swathes of 'oriental' violins and melodramatically poetic love lyrics. Doukali's status continued undiminished into the eighties – in 1985 he won the Maghreb Song Contest with his composition 'Montparnasse'.

The 1970s saw a new style emerge, which rapidly dominated the imaginations of youthful listeners and soon spread outside the country. Its progenitors were a Casablanca group, **Nass El Ghiwane**, whose inspiration was a mixture of then prevalent radical politics and rock-and-roll ideas and a return to roots, both musically and in respect of lyrics. A further principal creative influence was the new lively demotic theatre style developed in Marrakesh in the late 1960s, which had tremendous influence on youth culture.

Nass El Ghiwane sang not about rarefied and abstract poetic notions of love, but about everyday domestic and political problems, in songs like 'Senia', while their instrumentation featured basic percussion (the small clay derbouka, the flat tambourine-shaped bendir and a variety of hide drums) and bouzouki, with bass guitar and, occasionally, keyboards.

Nass El Ghiwane were soon followed by the equally popular **Jil Jalala**, named after a Sufi leader, who also used traditional Moroccan instruments, including the bass guitar-like hajuj, but whose lyrics were less political than Nass El Ghiwane's. Their best-known song 'Chaamar' ('The Candle'), centred on a late-night reverie on life, death and marriage, sold hundreds of thousands of cassettes and travelled through the Arabic-speaking world.

The third member of the ruling 1970s triumvirate was **Lem Shaheb**, whose approach was similar to the other two, and who captured the Moroccan public with songs such as 'Palestine', as well as achieving a minor penetration of European rock circles via their collaborations with the German group **Dissidenten**, who added a hard drum and synthesizer backing to their rough, guttural, Moroccan folk style.

Though Nass El Ghiwane and Jil Jalala are still performing, Lem Shaheb split up, their driving force and mandolin player **Cherif Lamrani** going on to form a series of groups in Tunisia. Also dissolved is another secondarily important group from this period, the Berbers **Ozman**, whose leader **Larbi Larbi** is now making a career as a singer of Bob Dylan songs in Arabic.

In the 1980s, Moroccan popular music diversified considerably, one general feature being a move away from politics as subject matter.

The back-to-roots style of Nass El Ghiwane et al was taken up by a new generation and given added black gnaoui feel by two new groups, **Nass El Hall** and **Muluk El Hwa**. Again, Marrakesh and the kaleidoscopic traditional entertainment bustle of its J'ma El F'na was at the root of the new development. Nass El Hall's music tends more towards European fusion, with jazz and rock elements (the group plays either in an electric guitar and drums line-up or with traditional instruments), while Muluk El Hwa, formed around the hereditary musician brothers **Elaadili** and **Ben Bich Abderrahim**, plays strictly traditional instruments.

In the northeast of the country, Algerian raï music gained ground through the eighties, the epicentre of Moroccan raï being Oujda, the nearest sizeable city to Oran, the raï birthplace across the border. Certain Algerian-based raï stars – Chaba Zahouania, Cheb Tahar – already had Moroccan parentage and one of the raï stars most popular with the new European raï audience in France, Holland and Germany, the Paris-based Cheb Kader, is Moroccan-born. After living near Oran and, briefly, in Oujda, he joined his father, a butcher and traditional gasba (flute) player in Mulhouse, northern France, where he began to play Nass El Ghiwane-style in local groups before turning to raï in 1986, finding an astute French manager and making a series of records and television appearances which rapidly took him in into competition with the top Algerian raï artistes for the world market. Having in effect sidestepped the domestic market, Kader's appeal remained centred on European and Japanese world-music fans rather than on the Moroccan or Algerian youth market. Home-grown raï and raï-style performers around the Oujda area are the **Bouchenek Brothers**, sometimes referred to as the 'Chevaliers du raï', and an assortment of singers including **Cheb Mimoun, Cheb Samir, Cheb Bassami** and **Rachid Nadori**. The latter is interesting in that he is one of the few raï performers to sing in Berber rather than in Arabic. In addition, the Rif mountains and the Mediterranean seaboard near Melilla have seen a good number of raï-influenced rock groups such as **El Khawil**.

Both Casablanca and Fez have seen the arrival of new brands of bidaoui-based modern music. In Casablanca, the Liverpool of Morocco, **Mohamed Saïf** has modernised the shrill primitive sound of the traditional women entertainers known as cheikhates (see also **Algeria**). In 1986 his song 'Moul el Kutché' became a huge hit; it was taken up two years later and made internationally prominent by the Algerian raï star Cheb Khaled. In Fez, the singers **Fayssal** and **Hamid Imazighen** both purvey an extremely popular electrified updating of chaabi folk style, sometimes referred to as Atlas-style.

In additiion, a number of individual Moroccan artistes must be mentioned. The female Berber singer **Najat Atabou** was hugely popular throughout Morocco in the mid-1980s, performing songs with a vaguely (for Morocco) feminist approach to a piercing traditional arrangement.

The glamorous young Rabat-born **Samira Bensaid** has become a major star throughout the Arab world by basing herself in Cairo and performing a modern version of the mainstream Oum Koulsoum Egyptian style.

In France, several Moroccan artistes operate, in addition to Cheb Kader. **Tyoussi**, a young semiprofessional singer, has issued three increasingly well-received cassettes mixing chaabi, raï, gnaoui, folk and rock influences. The chic-bohemian-intellectual writer and singer **Sapho** is of Moroccan-Jewish origin, although her music owes more to European rock than to the Maghreb.

Finally, two interesting performers have based themselves to a large extent in London. **Hassan Erraji**, a blind multi-instrumentalist (lute, violin, percussion), has lived also in Belgium and has played throughout Europe in a variety of jazz/modern/classical Arabic fusion groups including **Arabesque**. **Sidi Seddiki**, a young singer-songwriter who moved to London's Notting Hill from Rabat in the late 1970s, has created an interesting pop style of his own, blending Western rock with Arab lyrics and a catchy Euro-Maghreb musical feel.

Morocco: Discography

Lem Chaheb and Dissidenten Sahara Elektrik (Globestyle ORB 008)
Lem Chaheb Untitled (Hassania 3392)
Nass El Ghiwane Taghounja/Lebtana (Disque Esperance SD14)
José Heredia Maya and Orquesta Andalusa de Tetuan Macama Jonda
  (Ariola 1-205400)
Juan Reña 'Lebrijano' and **Orquesta Andalusi de Tanger** Encuentros
  (Globestyle ORB 024)
Tyoussi Maroc 'N Rythme (Esperance SD50)
Sidi Seddiki Shouf (Globestyle ORB 063)
Hassan Erraji In Dounia (Riverboat TUG 002)

MAURITANIA

A large but sparsely populated (between two and three million inhabitants) desert republic straddling the border between the Arab/Berber North of the continent and 'Black Africa', Mauritania came into existence in 1960. Its traditional music is dominated by the iggawin, hereditary musicians who are the equivalent of the Mandinka griots of West Africa. Traditional instruments include the tambourine, the tbal and the ardin, a fourteen-string relative of the mandinka kora, which is played by women. Men play a basic guitarlike instrument called the tidinit, an equivalent of the West African xalam. Songs are poetry, usually in classical Arabic, set to music by the performer.

Some iggawin have taken up electric guitars and synthesizers to augment traditional instruments in groups. These include a group of musicians from the capital, Nouakchott, centred on the duo of **Khalifa Ould Eide**, guitarist and tidinit player, and **Dimi Mint Abba**, singer. Dimi Mint Abba, in particular, has built a considerable reputation during tours of Algeria, Morocco, Tunisia, Egypt and Saudi Arabia and has also visited Europe, where she and Kalif Ould Eide recorded a well-produced CD in 1990. Another prominent musician to have recorded on vinyl is the traditional guitarist **Saidou Bai**.

Two Mauritanian artistes operate outside the country. The singer **Yacine** has based himself variously in Saudi Arabia, France and the USA. He performs a mixture of traditional Moorish music, light classical Egyptian standards and pop, backed with guitars, synthesizers, etc.

Paris-based **Tahra** is a sometime model and serious singer who, in 1989, made a techno-pop LP with a mainly French backing group, which features Arabic, French and English lyrics and a faintly Moorish, Salif Keita-influenced international sound.

Mauritania: Discography

Yacine Dane Wa Dane (Boussiphone K7)
Khalifa Ould Eide and Dimi Mint Abba Moorish Music (World Circuit WCB 019)
Tahra Yamen Yamen (EMI France 7909141)

SENEGAL

Senegal was for most of the twentieth century the cultural leader of French West Africa. Its capital, Dakar, was the French West African capital; its first President, Leopold Sedar Senghor, was a poet and politician of great international prestige. The 1966 Dakar Festival of Negro Arts (precursor of 1977's even more influential Lagos Festival) was immensely significant in promoting indigenous African music.

Like most of the region, Senegalese pop through the 1950s and 1960s was heavily influenced by Latin-American, particularly Cuban, music. Traditional styles included the distinctive kora (harp-lute) music of the Manding people who live throughout the region of Mali, Senegambia and Guinea. An Africanisation movement grew up in the late 1970s, involving the substitution for French or Spanish lyrics of local languages, mainly the majority Wolof tongue, and the introduction of traditional instruments to the line-up of guitars, drumkit and brass. These included the drums known as tama (a small 'talking' drum with variable pitch, held under the left arm) and sabar (a big standing conga-like drum).

The most influential early group was the **Star Band de Dakar**, which formed the house band of a popular nightclub, the Miami, owned by a prominent entrepreneur and talent-spotter, **Ibra Kassé**. The Star band, which was originally created to play at Senegal's independence celebrations in 1960, provided a launch platform for most of the current crop of Senegalese groups. **Orchestre Baobab**, whose 1982 recording of 'Utru Horas' has become a much-loved African classic, was one of the first bands to follow.

The first Senegalese group to achieve European success was **Xalam**, named after a traditional guitarlike instrument of the region. The eight-piece Xalam created a jazzy fusion style which they took to Berlin in 1979 and the United States two years later. Xalam went on to record with the Rolling Stones in their 1984 album 'Undercover' and have carved a solid international career playing at festivals, particularly in Europe.

The second of the duo of Senegalese groups which spread their country's music to Europe was **Touré Kunda**, led by the four brothers **Ismael, Ousmane, Sixu** and **Amadou Kunda**, from the southern region of Casamance. Emigrating to Paris in the late 1970s, the brothers gradually built a following with a mixture of reggae and the relaxed Guinean-influenced melodies of their homeland. In 1983 Amadou died after being taken ill on stage at the chapelle des Lombards in Paris, but the group recovered and, helped by ace American jazz and rock arranger Bill Laswell's production of their album 'Natalia', began to achieve substantial international success in 1984.

The musician who dominated Senegalese music through the late eighties was the dynamic young singer **Youssou N'Dour**. N'Dour's association with Peter Gabriel, guesting on Gabriel's 1987 'So' LP, and his participation in the 1988 Human Rights Now World Tour with Sting, Gabriel and Bruce Springsteen brought him to world attention, though his 1989 high-tech European LP 'The Lion' received a mixed reception at home in Africa.

Youssou N'Dour was born in 1959 to a musician-caste mother (a gawlo, or griot) of Tukulor ethnicity and a Wolof mechanic father. His first musical experience was drumming in kassaks, or circumcision ceremonies. In 1976 he joined the Star Band of Dakar, which he left to found **Etoile de Dakar**, upgraded in 1979 to **Super Etoile de Dakar**.

Youssou's high wailing voice and prodigious output of attractive new songs brought him instant popularity. The musical mix his ten-piece band supplied was in the mould pioneered by the Star Band, moving away from a Latin American pachanga background towards a modernised indigenous sound. The name of the Wolof rhythm mbalax became a tag for first Youssou's music and subsequently the whole new generation of electric Wolof pop.

Traditional rhythm was a key element of Youssou's success. He had the guitars and keyboards pick up traditional ceremonial rhythms; and above all, he used the drums the sabar and tama, the latter played by his Star Band associate, the brilliant **Assane Thiam**. Although Youssou's earliest music echoed the post circumcision bawdy 'rascal dancing' of young men's ceremonies, Youssou later acquired a reputation as a women's star. This was partly because the dances his drummers recalled were often connected with female social and ceremonial activities. The most popular of the early 1980s dance crazes associated with Youssou's women fans was the sexy 'ventilateur' which involved bending over and rotating the bottom suggestively. The ventilateur and its various derivations are still seen on stage and off throughout Africa, though sadly it seems to be increasingly overshadowed by more sophisticated dances.

Youssou reached his Dakar public via a residence in the Thiosane nightclub, and the rest of the country via cassettes released every six to nine months (the famous 'Volumes 1–13') and regular concerts in stadia around the country. In 1982 he visited Paris for the first time and in 1984 played London's Venue. His 1985 album 'Immigrés' was the first release to attract European attention. With 'The Lion', his 1989 Virgin album, he abandoned Super Etoile's horn section and introduced a new, somewhat Europeanised sound. This tendency was reversed the following year by the European release of the album 'Set', which featured more or less 'as live' versions of a number of his best recent songs.

Throughout the late 1980s the Super Etoile de Dakar were rivalled, but never really threatened, by the group **Super Diamono de Dakar**, led by **Bob Sene** and **Omar Pene**, and featuring for a time the charismatic young Gambian vocalist **Moussa N'Gom**. Where Youssou N'Dour's mbalax was seen as traditionalist, unintellectual, 'ladies' music', Super Diamono's rather bluesier, jazz-rock-tinged sound was regarded as tougher, more street credible, more modern, in some quarters. Super Diamono were particularly keen to reject any association with praise-singing, a tradition still present to some extent in a good deal of West African popular music.

Not only approved of by intellectuals but an intellectual himself (he studied at art college in Dakar and later at the Ecole des Beaux Arts in Paris), **Baaba Maal** took on some of the traditional 'deep Wolof' image of Super Etoile as Youssou N'Dour turned increasingly to Europe. A Tukulor singing in the northern Peular language, Maal performed both traditional acoustic-based music, such as his famour 'Djam Leelii' recording with the guitarist **Mansour Seck**, and modern brass, tama, and electric rock material, often using the reggae-like Tukulor rhythm 'yella', with his group **Dande Lenol**. His music benefited from his research into a wide variety of traditional song forms, while his lyrics include paeans to great religious leaders such as Cheikh Amadou Bamba, semimystical meditations on culture and duty, and modern political issues such as the treatment of his fellow Peuls at the hands of the repressive Moorish-dominated government of neighbouring Mauritania.

Other prominent Senegalese musicians include **Ismael Lo**, a former Super Diamono singer sometimes referred to as the Senegalese Bob Dylan; **Thione Seck**, a former Orchestre Baobab singer renowned for the soulfulness of his voice, and the percussionist and singer **Idrissa Diop**.

Senegal: Discography

Orchestre Baobab Pirate's Choice (World Circuit ECB 014)
Touré Kunda Natalia (Celluloid CEL 6113)
Xalam Gorée (Celluloid CEL 6656)
Etoile de Dakar Absa Gueye (PAM 02)
Youssou N'Dour Immigrés (Earthworks EWV 10)
Youssou N'Dour Set (Virgin V 23634)
Youssou N'Dour Inedits 84−88 (Celluloid CEL 6809)
Super Diamono de Dakar Mam (Melodie 8011)
Baaba Maal and Dande Lenol Wango (Syllart SYL 8348)
Baaba Maal and Dande Lenol Baayo (Mango 162 539 907)
Ismael Lo Natt (Syllart SYL 8335)
Thione Seck Le Pouvoir d'un Coeur Pur (Sterns 1023)
Idrissa Diop Misaal (Celluloid CEL 6765)

MALI

The traditional musics which have had most influence on the popular music of this large Sahelian country are the griot-transmitted styles of the Manding peoples and of the related but distinct Bambara, the latter forming the country's largest ethnic group.

A key epoch in Manding history, and a continuing theme of Manding jalis' (griots') songs today, is the great empire which took the tribe's name and which reached its apogee in the thirteenth century, when Emperor Sunjata Keita was the most powerful leader in the region. The social and caste system codified under Sunjata still underlies Malian society today and the modern Kouyaté clan, composed exclusively of jalis, believe themselves to be descended directly from Bala Fasigi Kouyaté, the court musician and griot of Sunjata Keita.

Mali shares with the adjoining state of Guinea a postindependence political development which had a powerful effect on the country's popular music. Both Mali's first president, Modibo Keita, and his successor, Moussa Traoré, pursued a policy of state socialism with wholesale nationalisation coupled culturally with an effort to fight off European influence and reassert African values. State support for music meant the establishment of a number of bands whose members were salaried employees either of regional administrative bodies or of state enterprises. The most famous example of the latter is **The Rail Band of Bamako** (see below).

Mali's stance in the 1960s distanced it culturally from the West. As the Euro-American pop-rock influence waned, moreover, it was replaced by another influence from Cuba which only strengthened the already substantial Latin American feel common to all Central and West African musics since the 1940s. Indeed, numbers of musicians went to Cuba to study; a prime example was the band **Las Maravillas de Mali**, who returned from Havana expertly versed in every nuance of son and Latin jazz.

In Bamako today, the semi-professional group **Kolly et ses Acolytes**, led by a saxophone-playing magistrate, **Cheikh Samaké**, still deploys a repertoire containing a wide variety of Cuban songs. A fine example is their rendition of the old favourite 'El Manicero' ('The Peanut Vendor'), which can be heard on the record compilation of soundtrack music from the BBC TV series *Under African Skies*. With its lovely light blend of Latin and African, this style of music is still widespread in Mali: the Acolytes purvey it most evenings at cocktail time in the main bar of Bamako's biggest hotel, The Amitié.

The jali-griot tradition of Mali is very much alive, with kora, balafon and ngoni-backed singers performing regularly both in an acoustic and a modernised electric manner. Griots still attend all major family ceremonies, and animate many public events. A good example of the latter is the weekly Sunday horse-race meeting at Bamako's shabby but popular racetrack, where the races are interspersed with commentary and songs from a quintet of young griots, known collectively as the **Jumeaux de Lafiabougou**, playing electric guitars and drums, as well as by famous griottes such as **Awa Drame**. Nowadays, griots of course pursue a double career, combining praise-singing with the recording of commercial cassettes which can sell in large quantities.

The greatest griot of post-independence Mali, **Bazoumba Sissako**, sometimes known as the 'Old Lion', died in 1988, but dozens of successors carry on his work. One of the most influential jali clans is the Diabaté (often spelt Jobarteh in Anglophone areas such as the Gambia) and the village of Keyla near Bamako is a major family base, being almost entirely populated by Diabatés. Perhaps the best-known traditional kora players in Mali today are **Sidiki Diabaté** and his son **Toumani**. Toumani, in particular, achieved a substantial reputation in Europe during the late 1980s world music boom by regular touring but also by high-profile fusionist experiments with a succession of musicians of different nationalities. The earliest combinations were with classical Indian players. They were followed by a duet with the Dutch harp player **Ernestine Stoop**, and finally Toumani's most successful venture, a collaboration, under the group name **Songhai**, with the four members of the Spanish flamenco-rock group Ketama and the jazz bassist Danny Thompson.

Other Diabatés have moved further into the realms of modern pop-rock. **Keletuigui Diabaté**, a virtuoso balafon player in his fifties, combines a traditional instrument with a thorough 1960s Cuban-jazz-pop training to stunning effect and his career spans the early **Orchestre National 'A'**, one of Mali's first post-independence 'modern' groups, and session work for **Salif Keita**'s band in 1990. At home, he leads his group **Africa Ya** every Saturday night in a Bamako pizzeria, Les Pyramides. The guitarist **Zani Diabaté** combines a career as percussionist and arranger with the National Ballet of Mali with the leadership of the popular **Super Djata Band** (see below).

Lafia Diabaté is the principal singer with the Rail Band, while **Kasse Mady Diabaté** combined a career as a traditional jali with membership of the electric **Orchestre National Badema**, before following in Salif Keita's footsteps as a high-tech, would-be solo star.

In Mali especially, the vocal prowess of female griottes (or jalimusa) is greatly appreciated, and a number of hereditary women singers have become hugely successful, both as praise-singers and entertainers. Three jalimusa have dominated the last decade. **Fanta Damba**'s career stretches back to the early 1960s, when she released a series of singles which established her as Mali's leading woman recording artiste. Almost a decade later, **Tata Bambo**, a member of the great jali clan of the Kouyaté, became her chief rival with the launch of an international career at the 1969 Algiers Pan-African Music Festival. Tata Bambo's work with the arranger **Boncana Maiga** in the relatively sophisticated studios of Abidjan, capital of the adjacent Ivory Coast, was an outstandingly successful updating of pure Manding music, in which a spare, heavy bass guitar and minimal touches of synthesizer added a contemporary feel to the raw simple melodies and traditional ngoni and balafon accompaniment.

The third and youngest of the supergriottes is **Ami Koita**, who was born in

1952 in Djoliba, Salif Keita's home village, and learned her craft from her parents, who were both eminent musicians. She recorded her first cassette in 1978 and soon became famous for songs such as 'Djarabi' and 'Simba', which replaced praise-lyrics with texts denouncing the ills of society and calling for their remedy. She rapidly adopted the Boncana Maiga-Abidjan modernised recording sound, and with great success; her 1989 cassette 'Tata Sira' was one of the biggest hits of the year.

As the jali have gradually moved into the field of professional entertainment, so non-hereditary musicians have moved into the styles of music formerly the exclusive province of the jali. A number of Malian women singers now perform in this category. **Nahawa Doumbia** rose to prominence firstly in the 'solo singer' category of musical competitions held at school and regional administration level for amateur traditional performers. Within a short time she too was pursuing the well-trodden path to the arranger Boncana Maiga and 'Didadi', her album of traditional music augmented by top Ivorian session players on electric guitars, brass and backing vocals, went on to be released in Paris and the UK. In 1990, a new female recording star's career took off with a cassette album 'Moussolou', which became a smash hit throughout West Africa, reaching sales that year of around 250,000 legitimate copies, a remarkable feat in an impoverished market where most cassettes in circulation are pirated and/or recorded from the radio. **Oumou Sangaré**, the creator of 'Moussolou', was born in 1968 in Bamako, but her family was from Wassoulou, to the southwest of the capital. The style of music she took up was not Manding but a Bambara tradition, normally the preserve of men, associated with hunting rituals. Increasingly rivalling the Manding sound in recent years, the Bambara music of the Wassoulou region features a metallic scraper beat which slices across loping ngoni or guitar riffs and, in some groups, a fluttering birdlike flute calling to mind the southwest's forest areas. Oumou Sangaré combined this music with lyrics concerning the problems of modern life for a young woman – such as the conflict between obedience to one's family and one's husband, the pressures of the city – and her success was the most striking single example of a growing movement of Malian women singers taking over musical styles formerly associated with men. Oumou Sangaré was talent-spotted in 1988 by a scout of **Ibrahim Sylla**, the top West African record label proprietor, after several years performing with **Djoliba**, a group of traditional dancers and musicians. 'Moussolou' was recorded in Abidjan in early 1989 and on its release Oumou Sangaré embarked on a continuous succession of performances, radio shows and interviews throughout West Africa which rapidly achieved results.

The male electric groups of Mali continued to perform strongly and evolve. A number of the state-funded 'orchestres' are still playing, largely in the beautiful amalgam of Manding or Bambara traditional music, Latin American and Western rock which evolved in the 1960s and early 1970s. A prime example is the Rail Band, a.k.a. **Super Rail Band** or **Rail Band International**, which plays every Saturday night in The Buffet de la Gare in Bamako. The venue is the café-bar of the dilapidated 1895 railway station, and the musicians are salaried employees of the Société Malienne des Chemins de Fer, reporting for duty every morning at 7.30 for rehearsals. Founded in 1970, and former employer of Salif Keita as well as numerous other well-known Malian artistes, the band is currently led by saxophonist **Kabiné Keita** and star guitarist **Djelimady Tounkara**. Their Saturday-night performances start around 11 p.m. on a small, open-air stage. Two tall palms, a string of coloured light bulbs and a cloud of mosquitoes frame the ten members of the band, as they work their way professionally through a repertoire including both classic 1970s Malian numbers and covers of current Zairean hits or whatever happens to be popular. The Rail Band's relatively small recorded output was boosted in 1988 by a new Abidjan-recorded album, which was not released in Europe.

The second modern band to achieve major fame in the 1970s was **Les Ambassadeurs**, also known as **Les Ambassadeurs du Motel**, as their particular residency was the outside dance floor of a motel on the Koulikouro road in Bamako. Led by an inspired Guinean-born guitarist, **Kante Manfila** (see Guinea section), the Ambassadeurs reached their peak during the mid to late 1970s when Salif Keita joined as singer from the Rail Band. A number of great hit songs – 'Primprin' and 'Mandjou' in particular – date from this period. Listening to Ambassadeurs' recordings of this period, one is struck by the ease, simplicity and grace of the ensemble's playing, particularly Manfila's delicate, spare, almost acoustic guitarwork. By the early 1980s, the Ambassadeurs were making increasing numbers of international trips to concerts and to record, at first in Abidjan but later in Los Angeles, but tension between Keita and Manfila, plus Keita's growing personal fame, led Keita to embark on a solo career and the group drifted into semi-dissolution as its various members pursued individual projects.

Mali contains around half a dozen state-supported bands, all close variants on the old guitar, bass, percussion and brass line-ups. They may be attached to a particular institution, as in the case of the Rail Band and the SMCF, or to a regional administration. Important examples of the latter include the **Orchestre Kanaga** of the northern river town of Mopti, and the **Koule Star** of Koutiaba, led by the griot **Aldoulaye Diabaté**, which did much to popularise Bambara hunters' rhythms, including the 'didadi' later taken up by Nahawa Doumbia (see above). Supported by the Ministry of Tourism, the **Super Biton Band** is based in the Niger River city of Ségou, where it plays weekly in the GTM Hotel garden. Super Biton takes its name from Biton Coulibaly, the founder of the Bambara Empire which was based in Ségou, and its music contains much Bambara influence, with faster, funkier rhythms than the gentle Manding style.

Another group supported by the Ministry of Tourism is the **Orchestre National Badema**, which was founded in the early 1970s and contains a number of former members of the Maravillas de Mali, ensuring a continued strong Latin tinge to its music. As is the case with most groups, its song lyrics mix moral commentary, references to the great figures of Mali's past and present, and, sometimes, narratives of important events: an example of the latter is Badema's famous 1983 song 'Nama', which tells the story of a motor pirogue accident on the River Niger in 1971 in which fourteen people died on their way to take part in the country's eleventh anniversary of independence celebrations. Badema's long-time star singer was **Kasse Mady Diabaté**, who in 1988 launched his solo career with an album 'Fode' under the auspices of Ibrahim Sylla's record label and the arranger Boncana Maiga. 'Fode' (named after the last of the Manding kings) was firmly in the mould of Salif Keita's hugely successful 'Soro' sound of the previous year, and marked the consolidation of this sound, slicker, harder, more complex and self-consciously dramatic, as an objective for many Malian musicians, replacing the relaxed Latin-Manding rock fusion of the 1970s. Many of the French, Ivorian and Antillean, as well as Malian, session musicians who had worked on 'Soro' did so on 'Fode'.

One other long-standing Malian group continues to survive without direct government funding. The **Super Djata Band** (the name refers yet again to the Manding Emperor Sunjata), consisting of up to sixteen musicians, is led by **Zani Diabaté** (see above), whose exciting Jimi Hendrix-influenced guitar work is a major feature of the band's music. Another characteristic is its use of the fast Bambara rhythms, including the hunters' style, and the general hypnotic intensity of its rock music.

In terms of fame, one solo artiste, of course, dominates eighties Malian music: **Salif Keita**. Quite apart from his strikingly tortured high-pitched vocal style, Keita is distinctive for two major reasons. Firstly, not only is he of non-griot caste, but he is actually noble, tracing his lineage back to the great Emperor Sunjata Keita. His traditional status, therefore, is as a patron of griots, and it was highly controversial of him to choose the lowly occupation of a singer. Secondly, he is albino, a condition regarded traditionally with superstitious awe.

He originally left his home village of Djoliba, thirty miles from Bamako, to study as a teacher in the capital. He took to playing guitar and singing the songs he was beginning to compose in a small bar, the Café des Sports, and sleeping rough in the central market. In 1970, he graduated to The Rail Band of the Buffet de la Gare (see above) where he met his future collaborator, the Guinean guitarist Kante Manfila. Three years later, they both left to join the Ambassadeurs du Motel, where Salif produced some of his most famous songs, including 'Primprin', an anti-drug song, and 'Mandjou', in praise of the hero-tyrant President of Guinea, Sekou Touré, and his illustrious ancestors.

From 1984 onwards, Salif based himself in Paris and began to work towards a solo career. In 1987, he recorded his first album for three years, for the ubiquitous Ibrahim Sylla, using a multinational cast under the direction of the French producer François Breant, at the 48-track Harryson Studio. The musicians were almost entirely non-Malian, consisting of Paris Cameroonians such as guitarist **Yves N'Jock** and many members of the Paris Antillean zouk scene – **Michel Alibo** on bass, **Alain Hatot** on saxophone – as well as **Breant** and **Jean-Philippe Rykiel** (son of the top couturière Sonia) on keyboards. The sound was hard, dramatic, flashy and strident, and the record was a huge success. 'Soro' (the word means a fetish object used to protect a house from evil spirits) set an entirely new standard, and sound, for Malian pop music and spawned a succession of imitators such as Kasse Mady's 'Fode' (see above). 'Soro' was followed up in 1989 by 'Ko-Yan', on the Island/Mango label, an expensive and lengthy production using much the same instrumental line-up and producers. Salif Keita continues to base himself in Montreuil, where he lives an African-oriented life (meals from the communal dish, rice taken with the hands) and works obsessively at his recording projects.

Salif Keita is not the only Malian artiste of noble birth to have achieved fame. **Ali Farka Touré**, the descendant of an illustrious family of warriors originating in Morocco, also carved an unorthodox and highly individual musical career until his dignified decision to retire from music in 1990 at the age of 50. From an early age, Ali Farka Touré has lived in Niafunké, a Niger river village not far from Timbuktoo. As befitted their high caste, his family supported griots who warned his mother to suppress her young son's interest in learning the gurkel, a single-string traditional guitar. He persisted, however, and eventually graduated to a Western guitar on which he began to compose songs. After Malian independence, he found himself working as an ambulance boatman on the river and at the same time running the Government-supported Niafunké district cultural troupe. During the 1960s he listened a great deal to black African music, above all to Ray Charles and Otis Redding, but also blues stars, notably John Lee Hooker, who had a profound influence on Ali Farka's playing. However, he maintains that the blues guitarist was himself reworking much older, African-based melodies, and insists that the itinerant Tamashek tribe of black Tuaregs who live around Timbuktoo are the real originators of his musical style. Whatever the full explanation, this remarkable combination results in an extraordinarily haunting and atmospheric sound, the guitar (electric or acoustic) and bleak vocals backed usually by no more than a staccato stick percussion played on a dried, empty half gourd. Touré pursued a mixed career throughout the 1970s and early 1980s, occasionally touring abroad, to Bulgaria and France, where he made a number of records including an LP on Sonodisc with his well-known song 'La Drogue'. In 1987 he was contacted in Niafunké, via a message broadcast over national radio, by a British concert promoter. A series of highly successful tours of Britain and Europe followed, during the course of which he made two excellent new albums, 'Ali Farka Touré' and 'The River', the latter featuring subtle and effective guest appearances by, among others, members of the Irish group the Chieftains.

Mali: Discography

Songhai Songhai (Hannibal HNBL 1323)
Tata Bambo Kouyate Djely Mousso (Sterns SYL 8360)
Various Mali Music (Sterns 3001)
Nahawa Doumbia Didadi (Sterns SYL 8337)
Oumou Sangaré Moussoulou (World Circuit WCB 021)
Super Rail Band New Dimensions In Rail Culture (Globestyle ORB 001)

Kasse Mady Fode (Sterns 1025)
Super Biton Mali Stars (Syllart SYL 8389)
Zani Diabaté and Super Djata Band Super Djata Band (Island 162 539 814)
Salif Keita, Ambassadeur International Mandjou (Celluloid CEL 6721)
Salif Keita Soro (Mango)
Salif Keita Amen (Mango)
Ali Farka Touré The River (Mango)

GUINEA

The Republic of Guinea has much in common with its neighbour Mali, and the musics of the two countries are very similar. Ethnically both countries are part of the territory of the Manding peoples, with their powerful, distinctive musical tradition.

Politically, Guinea was strongly committed to the process of Africanisation and abandonment of colonial values adopted by countries such as mali, Ghana, and later Zaire and others. Indeed, Guinea's first president, Sekou Touré, was the leader and initiator of this movement and achieved hero status for his famous 'No' to de Gaulle's offer of membership of a French West African Community. The French response was to sever all connections, and newly independent Guinea embarked on two decades of hermetic existence, with a minimal relationship with the West and only limited contact with the Eastern bloc. By the end of this period the hero Sekou Touré had become a bloody and paranoid tyrant and his cultural whims, along with all other policies, were imposed ruthlessly. Musically this isolation, coupled with a simultaneous policy of encouraging the creation of modernised indigenous music, had highly felicitous results, however, with the creation of a very beautiful new sound by bands such as the great **Bembeya Jazz** (see below).

The third common factor with Mali was the influence of Latin-American music, general in West Africa since the 1940s but rendered doubly potent by a series of visits of Guinean musicians to study in Havana, and by a natural compatibility with Manding music.

Traditional Manding music flourishes. It is played on kora, balafon and traditional guitar, and features lyrics praising the great men of the manding Empire, or more modern patrons, frequently including the PDG, the ruling political party. Out of many practitioners, two must be mentioned. **Sory Kandia Kouyaté** began his career with the **Ballets Africains**, an influential traditional dance group founded by the choreographer **Keita Fodeba** in 1952, which, on independence six years later, became the country's national troupe. He has worked with a traditional trio and as a member of the large electric group **Les Balladins,** and his large repertoire of songs is now starting to be updated by a new generation of younger griots, including his sons. **Jali Musa Diawara** is a younger traditional kora player who plays generally in Abidjan, Côte d'Ivoire, and made a sizeable impression in Europe with the release of an eponymous album in 1983. He subsequently developed a sort of kora-hero stage act, standing at the microphone instead of sitting and wielding the instrument like a rock guitar.

The impetus for the creation of Guinea's new brand of electric group music came immediately and decisively from the government on independence. Conakry's pre-independence complement of French-style jazz-pop bands – **La Douce Parisette, Les Joviales Symphonies** etc. – were abruptly requested to change to African music, and a plethora of new groups was created by regional administrations and local branches of the PDG, who distributed sets of instruments to dozens of young musicians. Among the first was the group **Bembeya Jazz**, named after a river in their home province, whose governor recruited the fifteen or so musicians and supplied their guitars, drums and brass section. Bembeya's music blended Manding and Cuban influences along with Ghanaian highlife and other local rhythms such as the temtemba, which was a speciality of the group's charismatic singer, leader and star, **Aboucar Demba Camara**. Bembeya's early songs praised Sekou Touré, the Party and the Manding empire grandees. In 1966, Bembeya were appointed Guinea's national band. In 1969, at the Algiers Pan-African Festival, their reputation began its continent-wide spread, and in 1977 at the Lagos FESTAC Black Arts Festival they won prizes for best orchestration and best guitarist. Their star guitarist, **Sekou Diabaté**, who acquired his honorific 'Diamond Fingers' at the Lagos FESTAC, took over leadership of the band in 1973, after the death in a car crash of Camara, an event which shattered the group and caused them to go into semiretirement for three years. Bembeya Jazz's recorded work has never quite matched their magnificently rich live performance, but mid-1970s LPs on the Guinean Syliphone label give an idea of their sound. By the 1980s, the group were obliged to record in Paris as bankrupt Guinea's recording facilities virtually collapsed. Sekou Diabaté's 1987 solo album, 'Digné', is a somewhat inadequate showcase of the guitarist's genius.

Other Guinean bands playing in the same style include **Balla et ses Balladins, Keletigui et ses Tambourins,** and **Camayenne Sofa,** while a new crop of similar regional bands created a decade after the Bembeya wave include the **Tropical Djoli Band,** the **Orchestre Nimba Jazz, Tele-Jazz de Télìmélé,** and, especially, **Kaloum Star.** The latter, formed in 1969, supported Miriam Makeba when the South African star was resident in Guinea with her then husband, the American black power leader Stokely Carmichael, in the 1970s.

One of the most interesting of Guinea's Manding-tradition electric bands is the **Amazones de Guinée**, a fifteen-strong all-woman band formerly known as the **Orchestre Feminin de la Gendarmerie** and composed, as the name implies, of policewomen. The Amazones were formed in 1961, originally using traditional acoustic instruments, and changed to an electric guitar and brass line-up in 1965. A number of the members are from Manding griot families, among whom women are not normally permitted to play instruments other than bell-percussion, so their role in a modern popular group is doubly unusual. The Amazones have frequently toured abroad but recorded little; their sole album is the live French-recorded 'Au Coeur de Paris'. The Amazones' rhythm guitarist, **Sona Diabaté**, is the sister of Bembeya Jazz's star Sekou Diabaté; the two have performed as a duo. Sona Diabaté has also toured Europe playing traditional music with the Amazones' singer **M'Mah Sylla**.

A younger female singer currently trying her luck at the European market via Paris is the griotte Djanka Diabaté, a cousin and backing vocalist of **Mory Kanté**. After a residence in Côte d'Ivoire, she moved to Paris in 1984 and six years later issued a solo album, 'Djanka', using assorted Salif Keita/Soro backing musicians under the direction of the ubiquitous Malian arranger Boncana Maiga.

The Guinean artiste to have made the biggest breakthrough outside Africa is, of course, Mory Kanté, whose modern disco-ised version of the old Manding song 'Yeké Yeké', also prominently featured by Bembeya Jazz, made the pop charts in Europe in 1988. Kanté was born in 1950 into a prominent family of griots from whom he learned traditional music and lore. As a teenager he moved to Bamako in Mali to join the famous Rail Band of the Buffet de la Gare. After several successful years he left to move to France, where he began to develop a network of international musical contacts and a new hybrid Manding rock style he once described as 'kora funk'. Kanté's showmanlike use of his instrument, playing it standing up rock guitar-style, was innovative, and his use of American, European and Antillean session musicians to create a pleasant pop sound, Guinea-tinged but not too much, so that it appealed easily to a European audience, was highly successful. His 1986 album 'Ten Kola Nuts' was a significant success, paving the way for 1988's smash 'Akwaba Beach' containing the hit single 'Yeké, Yeké', about a sexy young girl, rather than a tyrant President or a Manding emperor. The follow-up, 'Touma', was recorded in Brussels and Los Angeles, using mainly American session musicians to encase Kanté's lead voice and Djanka Diabaté's chorus, along with token flashes of kora, in a pure disco-funk setting.

Having made their early reputations along with Salif Keita in the seminal Malian band Les Ambassadeurs du Motel, two other members of prominent Guinean griot families continued to work internationally in the late 1980s. **Kante Manfila**, the master guitarist whose delicate, inspired playing had made the 1970s Ambassadeurs sound so delightful, made his way on to the Paris-Abidjan circuit and by the late 1980s was aiming at the European world music market with the by now standard post-Soro mix of French and Antillean session musicians, mechanical-sounding drums and touches of 'synthé-kora' and 'synthé-balafon' for colour.

The path of the guitarist **Ousmane Kouyaté** was roughly similar. While Kante Manfila, a mercurial and difficult man, separated definitively from Salif Keita after their work in the Ambassadeurs, Kouyaté followed the star vocalist and continued to work with him in Europe. Kouyaté's two solo albums, 'Kefimba' and the later 'Domba', while featuring certain members of the Euro-African Paris clique such as Jean-Philippe Rykiel on keyboards, retains a stronger West African feel than some of the new wave Mory Kanté/Salif Keita-influenced productions.

Guinea: Discography

Kouyaté Sory Kandia L'Epopee du Mandingue (Syliphone DK 016)
Bembeya Jazz La Continuité (Syliphone SLP 61)
Bembeya Jazz Sabu (Sonodisc ESP 8442)
Les Amazones de Guinée Au Coeur de Paris (Syliphone SLP 76)
Mory Kanté Touma (Barclay BA 281)
Kante Manfila Diniya (Sonodisc CD 8467)
Ousmane Kouyaté Domba (Sterns 1030)

GUINEA-BISSAU

This small state shares as musical influences the gentle melodic musics of the Manding and Diola ethnicities of its neighbouring states Guinea and Senegal, and the music of its Portuguese former colonisers. It was formerly a composite state with the Cape Verde islands and its music has a similar Brazilian feel.

Two of its leading artistes have made excellent records in Eruope, in both cases arriving in Paris via a preliminary period in Lisbon. **Kaba Mane** was brought up by his farming family to play a variety of traditional stringed instruments, and, having begun to mix with the African musical fraternity once in Paris as a student, decided to try to update his ancestral folklore, in particular the koussoundé rhythm used for ceremonial dancing at funerals, circumcisions, etc. His first record, 'Chefo Mae Mae' demonstrated an extremely impressive, novel sound, subtly different from Zairean rumba, but with all its joie de vivre.

Ramiro Naka also acquired his early foundation in music from the song and dance associated with circumcision ceremonies. As a child he sang on national radio and, having been sent to Lisbon to study to be a nurse, decided instead to turn to music. Moving to Paris he made a series of records strongly featuring the traditional goumbe rhythm and culminating in 'Salvador'.

Guinea-Bissau: Discography

Kaba Mane Chefo Mae Mae (Import cassette only, not catalogued)
Ramiro Naka Salvador (Cobalt WM 332)

CAPE VERDE

This small country, a group of nine islands in the Atlantic off the coast of Senegal, was formerly a Portuguese colony and subsequently a joint nation with the mainland state of Guinea-Bissau, before gaining independence in 1982. Its music is heavily Portuguese in origin and therefore has a good deal of the feel of Brazil. Cape Verde has several distinctive genres of its own, however, which have transmuted into some of the most vital popular musics of West Africa. Cape Verde musicians looking to the sophisticated technology of Europe head for Lisbon, where there is a substantial expatriate community, as well as Paris. Portuguese instruments, notably the guitar, violin, cavaquinho (small Portuguese guitar) and accordion feature strongly in traditional Cape Verdean music and an exciting, hypnotic accordion sound, often supplied now by a synthesizer, remains a feature of the latest records.

The most important style of Cape Verde is the morna, a lilting and soulful lament clearly based on the Portuguese fado and lyrically often concerned with the emigrant's nostalgia for a lost homeland (more Cape Verdeans live abroad than remain in the islands). The best practitioner of the morna is the sixty-year-old female singer **Cesaria Evora,** who performs in The Piano Bar of Mindelo on the island of Sao Vicente, and who has acquired the sobriquet the 'Barefoot Diva of Cape Verde'. The name is connected with her one visit to Paris where she apparently refused to wear shoes, although it is not known whether she was given the nickname as a result of this or whether she eschewed footwear in Paris so as to live up to her name. Evora, like most Cape Verdeans, sings either in Portuguese or, more often, in the local creole.

Two more dance-oriented genres are the coladera, a measured rhythm originally played on violins but latterly on saxophones, and the funana, a faster, more African-peasant dance associated with accordions. Both musics are used as accompaniment for erotic dance movements rather like those of more languid, reggae-like lambada. Two top groups share the home market for dance music. **Os Tubaroes** – 'The Sharks' – have been together for twenty years and play at the Di Nos Club in the Cape Verdean capital, Praia. As the more established group, they have an older audience than the newer, younger group **Finacon** (named after a song form). Finacon was founded in 1985 by the singing brothers **Zeze** and **Zeca di Nha Reinalda** and rapidly conquered both the home market and youthful Cape Verdeans abroad. In 1989 Finacon recorded an album in Lisbon which was partially rerecorded by the Zairean-Parisian producer Ray Lema in Paris in 1990 and issued as 'Funana'.

Certain other Cape Verdean artistes live outside the country. The singer **Cabral** operated in Senegal for a number of years before moving to Paris and starting the group **Cabo Verde Show,** with Cape Verdeans **Manu Lima** and the **Mendes Brothers. Manu Lima** went on to arrange and produce a number of records by expatriate Cape Verdean artistes including **Norberto Tavares, Nando Da Cruz** and the saxophonist **Luis Moreia,** while **Boy G. Mendes,** resident by now in Nice, was taken up by EMI in the hope of repeating a lambada coup and issued the record 'Grito de bo Fidje' in 1990.

Cape Verde: Discography

Cesaria Evora Musique du Cap Vert (Buda 82484-2)
Finacon Funana (CBS CB 811)

Cabral and Cabo Verde Show Beijo Cu Jeti (Melodie 387782)
Boy G. Mendes Grito de bo Fidje (EMI 22381-02)

SIERRA LEONE

Sierra Leone, with Ghana, was the cradle of highlife music in the 1920s, but, even more than Ghana's, the country's music industry has declined in the 1970s and 80s. In the 1960s the highlife boom subsided under the influence of imported pop and rock. The first home-grown pop group was the **Heartbeats,** led by one Gerald Pine, who changed his name to Geraldo Pino on taking up Latin music in the mid-1960s, a move which brought him considerable West African success.

In addition to highlife, Sierra Leone was home to palm wine music and a local rhythm, similar to the Dominican merengue, called the maringa, whose greatest exponent was the guitarist and saxophonist **Ebenezer Calender**. Calender released a string of hits – 'Jollof Rice', 'Baby Lay Your Powder On', 'Double Decker Bus' – in the 1950s and in 1960 became Director of Traditional Music for the Sierra Leone Broadcasting Service.

Curiously, it is an elderly palm-wine guitarist, **S.E. Rogie**, who most visibly represented Sierra Leone in Europe in the late 1980s. Sooliman Rogie combined singing with tailoring until a series of hits in the 1960s made him a national star. His most famous song 'My Lovely Elizabeth' was covered throughout West Africa. Rogie formed a band, the **Morningstars**, in 1965 and toured outside the country, including America where he settled in 1973. In 1988, he began to acquire a new young British audience via a series of concerts in pubs and small halls.

Britain was also the main area of operation of two more Afro-rock-oriented performers. In 1981, the singer **Bunny Mack** scored a big international hit with the single 'Funny Lady' and a subsequent album, 'Let Me Love You', produced by the Sierra Leonan **Aki Dean** in London. In the late 1980s, the singer and guitarist **Abdul Tee-Jay**'s band **Rokoto** began to purvey a tight expert mixture of highlife with a variety of other African and tropical sounds including more than a touch of soukous. Tee-Jay (real name Abdul Tejam-Jallah) wrote all of the songs on the group's debut LP 'Kankakura' in a variety of Sierra Leonan dialects.

Sierra Leone: Discography

S.E. Rogie Workers Playtime (Cooking Vinyl)
S.E. Rogie The Palm Wine Sounds of (Sterns 1050)
Abdul Tee-Jay's Rokoto Kankakura (Rogue FMSL 2018)

CÔTE D'IVOIRE

The popular music of Côte D'Ivoire has never been of a richness commensurate with the country's post-independence economic success or its influence within the continent; the only current Ivorian artiste of world stature is **Alpha Blondy**, who performs reggae. The high point of the country's creativity is generally felt to be the late 1970s and early 1980s, when **Manu Dibango** directed the orchestra of Ivorian national television, and the singer **Ernesto Djé Djé** was at his peak. The musical infrastructure of the big capital Abidjan is good, however, with three major recording studios, led by the popular JBZ Studio, attracting artistes from the whole of West Africa to work there.

Côte D'Ivoire's earliest pop star was **Amedée Pierre**, 'the Dopé' – the Nightingale – who retired in 1991 after 35 years of singing a mixed local and international repertoire in his first language, Bété, and in French. He was followed by **François Louga**, who rose to fame in the late 1960s after returning from France and embarking on an Africanisation of his music. Louga has retained his popularity with a wide range of the Ivorian public.

The most innovative and distinctively Ivorian artiste to date was Ernesto Djé Djé, who rose to fame as the populariser of the ziglibithy, a dance originating with the Bété peoples which Djé Djé transformed into a shoulder-twitching, crab-stepping disco craze. Djé Djé performed more European pop for a number of years in Paris, before returning to Abidjan and entering the Africanisation fray. His late-seventies LPs 'Ziglibithy' and 'Zibote' launched the new dance craze and made him a star, but his lifestyle – he had a rock-and-roller's appetite for women and whisky – sapped his health. A host of rumours – to do with magic, etc. – surrounded his premature death, reportedly from a stomach ailment, in 1983. A number of young singers – **Luckson Padaud, Blissi Tebil, Johnny Lafleur** and others – attempted to take on the mantle of the King of Ziglibithy, but none remotely approached Djé Djé's stature.

Two other male singers, **Bailly Spinto** and **Sery Simplice**, had considerable success in the late 1970s, with a variety of attempts to create blends of traditional rhythms and modern sound. But by far the most successful was **Daouda**, a former TV technician who was overheard practising in a studio and offered a TV slot and a recording deal. His 1978 hit 'Mon Coeur Balance' was recorded in Paris and issued in London on the new Sterns record label, but his career stagnated somewhat in the late 1980s.

Around 1984, a new dance craze, the gnama gnama, surfaced in Abidjan. Meaning approximately 'rubbish' in the Dioula language, it was a sort of cross between remnants of the ziglibithy and breakdance, with strong martial arts overtones. Originally practised by the 'nouchi' street kids of the Treichville poor quarter of Abidjan, it was eventually taken up by the singer **Kéké Kassiry**, whose 1984 'N'Ne Menika' had the good fortune to be adopted by the early gnama gnama club dancers at exactly the time the dance was attracting media attention. Kassiry had started singing in the clubs of Abidjan and worked for a number of seasons in Club Mediterranées in Africa and Europe before attracting the attention of the Paris couturier Paco Rabanne, an enthusiast for black culture and budding record producer. Backed by Rabanne, Kassiry proceeded to promote the gnama gnama via a series of videos and records in what he described as the Afro-funk style, but the craze died away rapidly and Kassiry's international aspirations failed to be realised.

The 1970s and 1980s have seen a number of major woman performers in Abidjan. The doyenne is **Reine Pelagie**, whose powerful voice and skilled adaptation of traditional songs have kept her popular for two decades. **Aysha Koné** is a trained singer who has also appeared in two films. **Nyanka Bell** is a glamorous young woman who has recorded successful zouk-influenced music in Paris, at first with members of **Kassav**. **Monique Seka**, like **Ade Liz** and the improbably named **Dan Log**, is a leading young, glamorous choral singer.

By far the most successful Ivorian artiste is in fact the reggae singer Alpha Blondy, whose first record, 'Jah Glory' registered the most rapid and largest sales of 1983. Born Seydou Koné (his adopted name Blondy is a deformation of the Douala for 'bandit', in acknowledgement of his poor record at school), Blondy studied briefly at Columbia University and experimented with rock and reggae music in New York before suffering a form of nervous breakdown and returning to Côte D'Ivoire, where his family had him incarcerated in a mental institution for two years. After his discovery working as a translator in Ivorian television, Blondy's soulful, high voice and feel for catchy melody and interesting lyrics – he blends Douala, French and snatches of English in the space of a couple of lines – rapidly made him a star throughout the continent, with a succession of well-produced hit albums – 'Cocody Rock' (1985), 'Apartheid Is Nazism' (1986), 'Jerusalem', recorded in Jamaica with former members of **The Wailers** (1986), and 'The Prophets' (1989). Blondy is a devout Rasta and a religious-political idealist who speaks regularly of reconciling Islam and Judaism; he is also an avowed supporter of the country's octogenarian president Houphouët-Boigny, despite his early antiauthority position in songs against police corruption such as 'Brigadier Sabari'. He is also mercurial of temperament: in 1988 he abruptly left Abidjan for Paris, having been grilled on television about his alleged delinquent lifestyle (a lifestyle he indignantly denies).

The late 1980s have seen a number of new younger artistes step into the limelight, though none are of more than passing interest. The **Keita Brothers** play in a style much influenced by the Manding music from the north, while **Woya** is a guitar-led quartet performing lightweight Afro-funk-rock, a similar genre to the singer **Meiway**'s field. Finally, the end of the decade saw a new dance craze emerge. The polihet was based on a traditional village dance 'discovered' by the singer **Gnaoré Djimmy**, who proceeded to develop it into an act which sold out clubs and dance halls throughout Abidjan in 1990 in much the same way that the gnama gnama and ziglibithy had at five-year intervals before it.

Côte D'Ivoire: Discography

Ernesto Djé Djé Tizere (Star SHA 032)
Daouda Le Sentimental (Sterns 1008)
Kassiry N'Ne Menika (Paco Rabanne PRD 45002)
Alpha Blondy Cocody Rock (Pathé PM 252)
Alpha Blondy Apartheid Is Nazism (Sterns 1017)
Alpha Blondy with the Wailers Jerusalem (Sterns 1019)
Woya Kacou Ananzé (Sonodisc 425004)

GHANA

The Ghanaian highlife sound made the country a musical leader from the 1920s to 1950s, but the economic depression caused by the oil crisis and the fall of cocoa prices reduced the level of activity dramatically in the 1970s and 1980s. Modern Ghanaian music retains a high indigenous content, however, partly due to the efforts of successive governments. First President Kwame Nkrumah was a strong advocate of Africanisation and later revolutionary leaders, notably Jerry Rawlings, have taken a strong interest in music. The present Provisional National Defence Council, in effect the Cabinet, has formed a pop group, **The PNDC Band**, and most institutions, such as the police force, support groups.

Highlife was one of two distinctive genres to flourish in Ghana; in its original dance band form it was a blend of European jazz-band instrumentation with local Akan and Ga rhythms, given added spice by an assortment of influences from Latin to calypso. Its name came from the smart dress (black ties and ball gowns were quite common) adopted by the relatively prosperous urban audiences highlife dances attracted.

The second genre was palm-wine music, a relaxed mixture of lilting vocal and simple accompaniment of acoustic guitar and perhaps a clinked bottle for percussion. Palm-wine music was so called because it was played and listened to during the afternoon relaxation period in villages when the men would sit under a big tree drinking palm wine, the fermented sap of the palm tree. Every village would have at least one singer to entertain the gathering in these informal bars.

Palm-wine music has a prominent modern exponent in the form of **Koo Nimo**, whose repertoire still includes songs made famous by the great twenties singer-guitarist **Sam**. Nimo's own songs, like most traditional Ghanaian lyrics, are rich in advice, commentary and parable. Nimo, whose numerous non-musical activities include work as a laboratory technician, lecturing on guitar techniques and presidency of the Ghanaian Musicians' Union, is connected by marriage to the Ashanti royal family and tours regularly with his group **Adadam Agofoma**.

The 1950s saw a boom in the guitar highlife bands which superseded the earlier brass band highlife in the towns. In addition to playing alone, highlife bands were for a long time associated with touring 'concert parties' which would consist of a troupe of entertainers – the most famous was the **Jaguar Jokers** – incorporating music in their act.

The greatest early highlife star was **E.T. Mensah**, whose career started in the late 1930s in the **Accra Rhythmic Orchestra** and who was still playing retirement concerts in 1988, having made a comeback at the beginning of that decade. When Mensah took over the **Tempos**, the twelve-piece group was Ghana's only professional dance band and the young trumpeter and bandleader rapidly spread their reputation throughout West Africa with a series of hits such as 'Donkey Calypso', 'Tea Samba', 'Sunday Mirror' and 'School Girl'. The late 1960s saw a decline of highlife as imported pop and rock records took over the market. Mensah was obliged to work as a pharmacist, but a highlife revival in the 1970s saw him back in demand, releasing albums such as the 1977 'King of Highlife'.

The first great stars of the new guitar highlife style were **The African Brothers International Band**, led by **Nana Ampadu**, whose first big hit was 'Ebi Tie Ye' in 1967. The African Brothers' appeal lay in their tight multiple guitar front line and the lyrics of Ampadu, which often featured lengthy, moral-laden folk tales of the animal kingdom. The band was receptive to the rock and reggae sounds of the 1970s and toured abroad as far as the USA and UK.

The 1970s saw another band, the **Sweet Talks**, carry the guitar highlife banner internationally. Their leader and founder was **A.B. Crentsil**, who started his career in a group sponsored by the Aboso Glass Factory and formed The Sweet Talks in response to being given a residency at a club named The Talk of the Town. Their first LP, 'Adam & Eve', led to an American tour in 1975, but the Sweet Talks broke up shortly afterwards. A.B. Crentsil briefly formed a successor, the **Super Sweet Talks**, but was obliged to abandon the name in favour of the **Ahento Band**. Crentsil's controversial song 'Moses' immediately became a grat hit for the new formation.

Other substantial highlife stars of the 1970s included **C.K. Mann, Pat Thomas** and **Jewel Ackah**. Mann, a former seaman, persisted through the lean disco-dominated seventies partly by updating a traditional rhythm, the osode, and was still playing in the late 1980s. Thomas started his career as singer with a number of bands, including the **Sweet Beans**, the official group of the Cocoa Marketing Board, before becoming a top solo artiste in the 1980s.

The 1970s saw two Ghanaian expatriate offshoot movements in England and Germany respectively. London had always contained a community of Ghanaian musicians – notably **Ambrose Campbell** in the 1940s and 1950s – and in 1969 the group **Osibisa** was formed by singer and saxophonist **Teddy Osei** with a mixed Ghanaian-Nigerian-West Indian line-up. Their blend of Afro-rock became very successful, leading to top ten UK hits with songs such as 'Sunshine Day' and 'Coffee Song', and opening the way for other London Afro bands such as **Hi-Life International.**

In Hamburg and Berlin, meanwhile, so-called burgher highlife, a slightly Eurodisco-modified variant of the music, was created principally by **George**

Darko, whose 1983 album 'Friends' featured a major hit song 'Akoo Te Brofo', rerecorded in English as 'Highlife Time'. Darko's singer **Lee Doudou** subsequently formed the second burgher highlife band, **Kantata.**

The end of the 1980s saw three major trends in Ghana. Traditional guitar highlife was represented by the very popular **Alex Konadu and his International Band.** Konadu rose to the top by dint of twenty years' continuous work playing villages and towns throughout the country, during which time he honed his fast, rough and vital style. His nickname, One Man Thousand, or One Man Army, was acquired after a concert in Accra in 1977, shortly after his huge hit 'Asaase Asu' caused a huge traffic jam in the streets of the capital.

A more polished modern form of highlife, meanwhile, in the mould of George Darko, is purveyed by a variety of young performers, some based partially in Europe. **Ben Brako,** a London-based singer, scored a bit hit in 1987 with his 'Baya' album, a smooth production which retained enough highlife feeling to sell well at home, while other singers such as **Nana Budjei** and **Kumbi Saleh** added pinches of zouk or reggae to the blend.

At the same time, a number of rough-voiced traditional street entertainers attained greater popularity than ever before. The chief example is **Onipa Nua,** a blind, gravel-voiced old man who has played the same 'kalimba' thumb-piano, home made from a pilchard can, for forty years. At first he played in markets and lorry parks, but in 1978 he was taken up by the producer and entrepreneur Feisal Helwani, who started putting him on at major venues, including Accra Sports Stadium, with extraordinary success. In 1989, Onipa Nua (the pseudonym means 'the people's brother') made his first record with a highlife band and the following year performed at Rennes Festival in France.

Ghana: Discography

E.T. Mensah All For You (Retro Afric RETRO 1)
Koo Nimo Osabarima (Adasa ADR 102)
Various The Roots of HiLife (Sterns ACFH 100)
A.B. Crentsil Tantie Alaba (Earthworks ERT 1004)
Alex Konadu Live in London (World Circuit WCB 009)
Ben Brako Baya (Musica MCL 870801)

TOGO and BENIN

The two small countries are sandwiched between Ghana and Nigeria; both are therefore influenced heavily by highlife as well as by the Congolese sound, reggae and 'Western' pop styles. Three individual artistes have gained a certain reputation outside the country; two of them are women. The Togolese singer **Bella Bellow** worked with Manu Dibango in the late 1960s and was beginning to acquire a substantial reputation in Europe when her career ended in a fatal car crash in 1973.

In 1979 **Angelique Kidjo**, a young singer from Ouidah in Benin, began to attract national attention with her interpretation of a Miriam Makeba song, followed rapidly by two hit songs – 'Pretty' and 'Ninive' – of her own. Moving to Paris, she began to work with a mixed Afro-Antillean group of musicians to produce a sound composed of 50% standard pan-global funk, 25% vaguely Salif Keita-ish synthesized ornamentation and 25% traditional-crossed-with-jazz vocal lines. An Island LP resulted in 1991.

Finally, Benin has also produced one of the most prolific composer-arranger-producers working in the Paris/New York Afro-rock-jazz sphere. **Wally Badarou** has worked with a wide range of international artistes including Fela Kuti, Grace Jones, Level 42, Herbie Hancock and Robert Palmer, and had a long association as arranger and synthesizer player with the Island label, while also finding time to make occasional records of his own, as a singer in an appropriately multi-influenced style.

Togo and Benin: Discography

Bella Bellow Album Souvenir (Safari Ambience SAF 61001)
Angelique Kidjo Parakou (Island PY 900)
Wally Badarou Echoes (Island 422 842 503)

NIGERIA

A huge nation with a population of over 90 million, Nigeria is divided racially into three main ethnic groups, the western Yoruba, the eastern Ibo and the northern Hausa-Fulani. It is Yoruba-derived music which dominates the popular scene today. Nigerian popular music, with its big drum ensembles, is notably independent of Western influence. With its quizzical-sounding melodies and harmonies and unusual features such as the talking drums, known as dundun, and pedal steel guitars cutting through a mass of traditional percussion, it offers one of the most distinctive sounds in the continent. In almost all genres, songs tend to be long, up to half an hour each, and performances by juju and fuji groups frequently go on all night. Nigeria possesses a substantial recording industry, acting for the Anglophone multinational majors much as Côte d'Ivoire does for the Francophone. Though the wealth generated by the country's oil revenues dissipated in the crisis-ridden late 1980s, large numbers of records as well as cassettes are manufactured and sold in Lagos. The big 1977 FESTAC Festival of Black Arts, held at great expense in Lagos when oil money was still flowing, was a major morale booster and showcase for African music.

Although it is not the most important of the country's genres, and is not indigenous, having been imported from Ghana in the 1950s by E.T. Mensah's band The Tempos, Nigeria nevertheless has a strong highlife tradition. Since Nigeria also has a palm wine tradition (see **Ghana**), highlife caught on quickly. Early stars were **Victor Olaiya, Bobby Benson, Ambrose Campbell** and **Rex Lawson**, all of whom worked with London bands to round their arranging skills and returned to lead big bands with full brass sections, guitars and percussion. The decline of highlife was greatly accelerated by the civil war of 1967–69 which not only disrupted civilian life throughout the country but forced many non-Yoruba easterners to retreat to the Eastern region (the short-lived secessionist state of Biafra) or further, to exile in adjacent Cameroon. After the war, the Yoruba west, containing the capital Lagos, adopted the new juju music (see below), while the highlife tradition blended with Cameroonian, Zairean, soul and rock influences and lived on in the Ibo-populated Eastern region. Its main practitioners had a penchant for new hybrid names for their sounds. Thus **Prince Nico M'Barga** started with a blend of highlife and makossa named panko, before changing to Rockafil Jazz (also the name of his group) at the time of his great pan-African hit 'Sweet Mother' in 1976, the peak of his career. **Oliver de Coque** named his highlife derivative the Ogene Sound and released a string of hit albums throughout the 1970s and 80s. Both of these bands featured a predominantly guitar-based sound, unlike the old brass-led highlife, as did the **Orientals**, a third, immensely popular Ibo band of the 1970s. The Orientals later split, one offshoot becoming the delightfully named **Dr Sir Warrior and the Original Oriental Brothers**, who visited London in 1985.

The most important modern musician to work in a highlife-derived style, however, is undoubtedly **Fela Anikolapu Kuti**, the bandleader, saxophonist, keyboard player, composer, showman and irritant to the Nigerian political establishment. Kuti was born in 1938 to a well-connected family (his brother became a Government minister) and played at an early age in Victor Olaiya's highlife band the **Cool Cats**, before resuming his studies in music at London's Trinity College of Music. He formed his band, the **Koola Lobitos**, in London; returning to Lagos he was much impressed by the visiting Sierra Leonean Latin-soul singer Geraldo Pino. Kuti visited the USA in 1969 and absorbed the flourishing rock and Black Power movements there. Back in Lagos, he opened a club called the Shrine, founded his twenty-piece band **Africa '70**, established himself and numerous 'wives' in a sort of commune-compound he entitled the Kalakuta Republic, and announced the invention of his new sound, 'Afro-beat'. A series of vituperative recorded attacks on what he considered the corrupt and incompetent governments ('Expensive Shit'; 'Kalakuta Show'; 'V.I.P. – Vagrants In Power'; 'I.T.T. – International Thief Thief') led to an army raid on his compound which amounted to a military assault, leaving the place burnt out. In the 1980s he was as provocative as ever. In 1984 he was jailed on what he claimed were trumped-up currency smuggling charges, but was released after a year and a half. By the end of the 1980s his powerful percussion-heavy music, with its chanted choruses, brass ornamentation and Fela's own lazy baritone singing and jazzy sax and keyboard improvisation, was popular throughout Europe and the USA. His son **Femi** both stars in Fela's band and runs a virtually identical outfit of his own, playing music which is a sort of junior copy of his father's.

While highlife was an import to Nigeria, the style which succeeded it in popularity in Lagos, juju, was an indigenous genre. Based in the Yoruba west, it consisted of simple percussion, especially the talking drum, until modernised in stages by musicians such as **Tunde Nightingale** in the 1940s and **I.K. Dairo**, the 'Father of Juju', in the 1950s. Dairo, a preacher in the Christian Aladura Church, added accordion and guitar to his basic drum juju and released several dozen albums through the 1960s to 1980s, during which time his status was rewarded in Britain with an MBE.

The next great moderniser of juju was **'Chief' Ebenezer Obey**, who established his first band, **The International Brothers**, in 1964 and first created the slower modern juju style in which numerous interrelating congas, big goumbeh drums, talking drums, multiple guitars and bass guitars spin out a lazy complex web of sound behind the vocals praising local figures such as one-time President Murtala Muhammed or making moral and social comments. Obey renamed his band **The Inter Reformers** in 1970 and started calling his music the Miliki System, after his Lagos nightclub. In 1983, he signed with Virgin Records in London, the second juju star to do such a deal, and released the album 'Je Ka Jo'.

The first juju star to sign with a British label was **King Sunny Adé** in 1982; three LPs, 'JuJu Music', 'Synchro System' and 'Aura' resulted, but Adé was dropped by the label in 1984. He was not particularly bothered, as he was accustomed to selling twenty times his best UK sale (10,000 copies of 'Synchro System') in his home market. Adé was the son of a Methodist minister who had started in the Lagos highlife band **Moses Olaiya and his Rhythm Dandies** before turning to juju and forming his own group, **The Green Spots**, with whom he had a hit single, 'Challenge Cup', in 1967. Sunny Adé was responsible for adding a number of new instruments to the juju line-up, notably pedal steel guitar. By the time he signed with Island he had changed his group's name to **The Afrobeats**; the band split after a stressful Japanese tour and the loss of the Island contract in 1984. Adé formed a new group, **Golden Mercury**, which continued to play in Adé's Lagos Ariya Club and to make successful records. Rumours of a serious illness attended Sunny Adé's disappearance from the scene in late 1990.

By this time, the top spot in juju music had been taken over by **Segun Adewale**, a younger guitarist and singer from a Yoruba royal family, who learned music from I.K. Dairo and played with **Chief S.L. Atolagbe and his Holy Rainbow** before forming a band named **Shina Adewale and the Superstars International,** jointly led by himself and his friend **'Sir' Shina Peters**. In 1980 Peters went his own way and Adewale proceeded to forge a new, fast, compressed style he called Yo-pop; hit albums including 'Ope Ya Baba' and 'Play For Me' (on the London Sterns label) followed. In 1985 Adewale played at the Edinburgh Festival. By the end of the decade, he had launched a new slogan and dance, Peperempe, which kept him hugely popular in spite of the advance of the new fuji style threatening juju's dominance.

By this time Adewale's main juju rival was his former collaborator Sir Shina Peters, who had led his twenty-piece band into the creation of what he claimed to be a derivation, Afro-juju; its chief difference seemed to be its allegedly more positive, moralistic lyrics. A fifth juju star, **Dele Abiodun**, also continued to be popular.

As juju music gradually became more Westernised and international in outlook in the 1980s, it was overtaken by a more traditional style, fuji. Fuji was in fact based on a synthesis of two (or more) Yoruba forms strongly associated with Islam. These were sakara, based on the dundun drums, and apala, a mixture of talking drums and vocals which was used originally to awaken people for their pre-dawn meal during Ramadan and which proceeded, in the hands of its great popularisers **Haruna Ishola** and **Ayinte Omowura**, to transmute into recreational music.

The two most popular fuji bands are those led by **Sikiru Ayinde**, generally known as **Barrister**, and **Ayinla Kollington**, known simply as **Kollington**.

Barrister – this nickname comes from an early ambition to study law – is generally regarded as the inventor of fuji, which in effect strips down the instrumentation to a large number of drums, cowbells and other percussion, led by the talking drum, and possibly a pedal steel guitar and a synthesizer for occasional embellishments. Performances last many hours, with prominent citizens coming to the stage to 'spray' the band with banknotes, whereupon Barrister may interject a sentence or two of praise for the illustrious donor into his vocals. After leaving the Nigerian army, he gradually built his new style of music with his band, **The Supreme Fuji Commanders**. Hits include 'Ise Logun Ise', 'Ijo Olomo', 'Fuji Vibration' and his live, London-recorded LP 'New Fuji Garbage' 1990. A second, younger 'Barrister', **Alhaji Chief Wasui Barrister and his Talazo Fuji Commanders** should not be confused with the original.

Barrister's chief rival, Kollington, leapt to prominence with his new band **Fuji 78**, featuring a faster rhythm with a slightly different range of drums and lyrics, Fela Kuti-style, attacking the corruption and inefficiency of politicians and, at one point, welcoming the return of a military government.

In addition to these indigenous styles, reggae has flourished in Nigeria. The first artiste to espouse reggae seriously was **Sonny Okosun**, a singer and guitarist who worked in the theatre and covering Western pop before turning to more Nigerian forms of music. In 1972 he formed his group **Ozzidi**, called after the similarly entitled brand of music, a mixture of rock, reggae and sundry Nigerian elements, which he claimed to have created. His 1978 album, 'Fire In Soweto', was an international hit and in 1984 his increasing American success was crowned by the Shanachie label album 'Liberation'.

In the late 1980s, the singer **Majek Fashek** took over as top reggae artiste. Majekodunmi Fasheke, as he was christened, was influenced as a child by the African drums and gospel singing of the Aladuro Church. On obtaining his first guitar from an American-domiciled uncle, he forced his way into show business via a spot on the talent-spotting *Music Panorama* TV show arranged with the help of his brother, a television comedian. By 1981 he had a Rasta-influenced band, **Jahstix**, and in 1988 his first album, 'Prisoner of Conscience', became a massive national hit and was licensed for Europe by Island Records.

A whole crop of young singers followed Fashek's footsteps in 1990 and 91, many of them also professing Rastafarianism; most popular is the charmingly named **Ras Kimono**.

An outstanding Nigerian musician who works outside the country is **Gaspar Lawal**, the London-based master percussionist who arrived in the UK in the early 1970s and made an international reputation as a session musician working with Ginger Baker's Airforce, the Rolling Stones, Robert Palmer, Hugh Masakela and Joan Armatrading, amongst many others. Lawal's solo work includes the 1991 CD 'Kadara'.

Nigeria: Discography

I.K. Dairo Juju Music of .. (Decca West Africa WAL 1206)
Fela Kuti Army Arrangement (Celluloid CEL 6109)
Fela Kuti Beasts of No Nation (Eurobond 360 153)
Ebenezer Obey Je Ka Jo (Virgin V2283)
King Sunny Adé Juju Music (Island 162 539 712)
Segun Adewale Ojo Je (Rounder 5019)
Sir Shina Peters Ace (CBS Nigeria CBS-N 1002)
Barrister New Fuji Garbage (Globestyle ORB 067)
Sonny Okosun Liberation (Shanachie 43019)
Majek Fashek Prisoner of Conscience (Mango 162 539 870)
Gaspar Lawal Kadara (Globestyle ORB 071)

AFRICA

Central Africa, The South and East

INTRODUCTION

It's true that I'm very well qualified to talk about music-making in Africa, having been involved in most aspects of it and having seen it from most angles over the last thirty years. I've been a professional musician, playing in cabarets, bars, at weddings. I was a member of one of the first and greatest modern Congolese bands run by Le Grand Kallé in the 1960s. I've toured my own bands all over the continent, and the world. I've run my own nightclubs – the Tam Tam in Kinshasa, then later Soir Au Village in my home town Douala, in Cameroon. I started a magazine – *Afro-music* – and ran it for a year and a half, but it was ahead of its time and didn't make money. I've seen the politics of music, too. For four years I directed the house orchestra of the national television station of the Ivory Coast. You gradually eliminate the things you don't want to do from your life, however, and that's a job I wouldn't repeat. There were artistic triumphs and satisfactions, but the political jealousies, the jockeying for position, the manipulation behind one's back – by the end of my period in the job I was quite seriously watching to see my drinks were opened in front of me to make sure there were no opportunities for someone to slip poison into them. That happens in Africa, they're more skilful at it than medieval Florentines . . .

On a purely musical level, my career reflects all the same elements which make up modern African music. I was born in a country – Cameroon – which was still a French colony, though it had earlier been German. The Germans had brought Protestantism, which was still strong. My family were civil servants, reasonably privileged. My mother directed the church choir and I still remember the church as a spiritual place, and the impression of the voices and the harmony . . . My uncle was a hunter, and in his spare time he played the traditional African guitar. (The guitar first came to Cameroon with the Portuguese in the fifteenth century, by the way, so there's another colonial input.) My uncle played in the style called assiko, which is found from Cameroon up to Ghana. So there I had church music on one side, on another village music. Plus of course the music of the sailors. Douala is a big port, and sailors brought western discs. Any musicians who played in the port's bars had to adapt to these new styles, because the sailors had the money, so you had to play what they wanted. So the musicians got hold of what western instruments they could and tried to adapt what they heard on the records . . .

One of the most important imports was Latin music, especially Cuban. This arrived by record and on the radio, which became widespread in Central Africa in the 1940s. Right throughout the equatorial region, Latin-American music played a major part in the formation of African pop. I remember particularly the trios at first, like the Trio Maravilloso, singer, guitar and a bit of percussion. Later they added one or two trumpets. Cuban music was especially popular in Zaire, but in Cameroon too. A bit later, in the 1960s, merengue became very popular in Cameroon. It's a rhythm which corresponds to that of one of the central and southern ethnic groups and it was very much taken up and adapted. Partly it was adopted in its original Caribbean instrumentation, even to the accordion, but the African version also had a way of making itself a little different. There was a way of using the guitar and a particular amplifier with a vibrato effect on a certain frequency, so that the guitar would get the swing of the merengue. The same sort of thing happened with the African version of the cha-cha-cha – the beat was adapted for guitar, because they didn't have pianos.

Of course, a major part of Latin American music, especially Cuban, came from Africa in the first place, and you can hear this very clearly in the older roots music of Cuba, the son, the guaguanco. This is very different from the modern, smooth New York-Puerto Rican sound. In the deep Cuban culture there's still this African side, very spiritual, very connected with voodoo, initiation rites, which are a part of African music. Though of course Africa too had changed and developed; its music has modernised.

Many of the styles of music I have been involved with share a common 'foyer'. I mean in Europe and the United States, the jazz world, the Latin world and also other musics like soul have overlapped a lot. Back in the 1950s when I used to play jazz in Brussels and Paris I used to meet Tito Puente, Machito, Mongo Santamaria, and then later, after the success of my record 'Soul Makossa' in the USA, I was in demand from many sectors. The American Black

Pride movement valued the association with an African musician, but the Latinos were keen to claim their bond of Africanicité, too.

Later on I played a lot with reggae musicians – Sly Dunbar and Robbie Shakespeare – and made records in Jamaica, and here too this reflects an African musical trend because reggae has been very big in Africa, at first Anglophone countries like Nigeria, later Francophone via people like Alpha Blondy. The spiritual aspect of Bob Marley, as well as the music, was a very important factor.

So African music is a constant process of fusion in a way, and my musical career has been also. I was making fusion music, actually, long before the term came into use; this has been my life, à cheval between two cultures – straddling two cultures.

Manu Dibango

CAMEROON

Cameroon is musically one of the half dozen most significant nations on the continent, in international terms. The country possesses a dual (French and British) colonial background, and an exceptionally large number of ethnicities, including numerous pygmy groups in its forest areas. Its religions include, in addition to traditional animism, Islam, in the north, and large and active Catholic and Protestant churches. Both religion and tribal custom were prime influences in Cameroonian popular music. Church and school choirs, with indigenous drum, rattle and xylophone accompaniment, introduced many of the country's musicians to their future profession. Ethnically, two rhythms – the makossa and, to a lesser extent, the bikutsi – have assumed national and international prominence.

The modern makossa developed primarily on the coast, around the great seething port of Douala, in the 1950s. Its antecedents included earlier traditional dance musics, including the percussion-based assiko and the guitar-based, highlife-influenced ambasse bey. The great bandleader **Manu Dibango** (see below) supplied the boost which made the makossa the country's favourite style with his 1973 hit 'Soul Makossa'.

Among early Cameroonian popular entertainers were **Oncle Medjo**, a singer and guitarist who adapted the traditional assiko style in the 1940s and made early recordings in the 1960s; **Mama Ohandja**, an early moderniser of the **bikutsi** rhythm whose career started in the early 1960s and who achieved national prominence leading bands such as **Mandoline Jazz** and **Confiance Jazz**; and **Ann-Marie Nzie**, sometimes referred to as the 'Queen Mother of Cameroonian song', another early bikutsi moderniser, whose recording career started in the 1950s.

Both of Cameroon's first major continental and international musical stars transcended specific ethnic styles. The first was **Francis Bebey**, an intellectual whose adaptations of a variety of African folk styles complement his other main activity as a poet and novelist. Much influenced by European classical guitar, he specialises in the arrangement of mixtures of traditional African (for example, pygmy flutes) and Western acoustic instruments (guitar, bass) into a light, sophisticated, personal style of music. His importance as a role model and inspiration for African musicians wishing to enter the world of modern art music far outweighs his current popularity with an international audience. Bebey's book *African Music: A People's Art* was an important contribution to African popular musicology.

In terms of the international market, no African musician is of greater importance than **Manu Dibango**. Emmanuel, as he was christened, was born in Douala in 1933 to Protestant parents. His mother was a prominent member of the church choir, and choral music is still a significant element of the rich palette of sound deployed by Dibango today (listen to the track 'Les Negriers' on his 1990 album 'Polysonik'). Sent to Paris to study as a teacher, Dibango first took up classical piano, then saxophone, and rapidly developed a passion for jazz.

Moving to Brussels, he played with many prominent French and Belgian jazz musicians in clubs such as the Anges Noirs and the Rose Noire. In 1960 he joined the **African Jazz** orchestra of **Joseph Kabasele**, known as Kallé, one of the great progenitors of modern Zairean music. The following five years were spent with Kallé, both in the Zairean capital Kinshasa where Dibango opened his own nightclub, the Tam Tam, and touring Africa. In 1965 he returned to Paris, where he continued to work with Congolese and Zairean bands, including Kallé's, as well as gaining experience of the French pop world, as keyboard player and arranger for the TV show of the entertainer Nino Ferrer. In 1971, on a visit back to Cameroon, Dibango wrote and recorded an instrumental which he called 'Soul Makossa'. Two years later, the record was picked up by a New York radio station and rapidly became a huge American hit, with numerous cover versions. The American and then European success of 'Soul Makossa' not only boosted the status of the makossa at home in Cameroon to that of national dance rhythm, but launched Dibango's international career.

The rest of the 1970s saw Dibango continuing to broaden and deepen his experience of all aspects of music production. In the USA he played with leading jazz artistes – Tony Williams, Billy Cobham, and others – and with top salsa band the Fania All Stars, as well as headlining at world-famous black venues such as the Apollo. For two years he worked as musical director of the orchestra of the national television station of the Ivory Coast, a period widely regarded as constituting the zenith of recent Ivorian music, but one in which Dibango felt himself to be excessively constrained by national political objectives rather than purely musical ones. The end of the decade saw him recording two notable reggae-influenced albums for the British Island label in Jamaica with the top Kingston rhythm team of Sly Dunbar and Robbie Shakespeare.

In the 1980s, Dibango continued to evolve his modern, eclectic, jazz-influenced, pan-African but makossa-tinted sound, continually incorporating new ideas into his music. A range of producers, including the Frenchman Martin Meissonier and the American Bill Laswell, both leaders in the field of updating African recording ideas, helped him to produce a series of prominent fusion albums, with guest work from musicians of the stature of Herbie Hancock.

The beginning of the 1990s saw Dibango's creativity as prolific, and as catholic, as ever, with a new album, 'Polysonik', produced by the young London jazz-dance guitarist Simon Booth. The line-up of his band now featured long-standing musicians such as his Cameroonian guitarist and bassist, as well as a top-notch new choral section including Cameroonian singing star **Charlotte M'Bango** (see below). 'Polysonik's line-up also featured a South London rapper, MC Mello, singing in English, while Dibango sang in French and Douala and played his usual cool, understated saxophone, as well as Hammond organ, an early love he had first heard in the hands of Jimmy Smith and Booker T. The rhythms included makossa and bikutsi, the lyrical themes covered slavery, a jazz-rap view of the problems of Africa, and brief sound impressions of African scenes – pygmy flutes, a free-ranging 'village' conversation between **Jean-Marie Ahanda** of **Les Têtes Brulées** (see below) and a Cameroonian journalist.

Three other Cameroonian artistes achieved a degree of international attention in the 1970s. The first of these, **André Marie Tala**, was actively assisted by Manu Dibango, who helped the young blind guitarist to travel to France to record. Tala's speciality was a rhythm he christened the tchamassi, which was the basis of his two big 1970s hits 'Sikati' and 'Potaksima'. A fellow member of Tala's group the **Tigres Noires** was **Sam Fan Thomas**, another guitarist who parted company with Tala in 1976 and went on to record the song 'Afric Typic Collection', which subsequently became a dance-floor hit all over West Africa and in Europe. 'Afric Typic Collection', a roll call of West and Central African dance styles, featured a strongly Zairean feel as well as more than a hint of the then-influential Antillean zouk style, while other recordings by Sam Fan Thomas featured the rhythm most closely associated with his name, the makassi.

The third artiste from this generation was **Bebe Manga**, a composer, pianist and singer who played nightclubs in Douala and in Gabon for a number of years before recording in Paris in the early 1980s where she made the pop hit 'Amie' which sold over a million copies internationally.

By the mid-1980s, a new, harder style of pop makossa was booming regionally and throughout the continent. Produced equally in Paris and Douala, its sound was much influenced by the all-conquering Martinique-Guadeloupe zouk style of the hugely popular Antillean supergroup **Kassav**. Indeed, makossa and zouk became more and more alike, with a thumping bass beat surrounded by keyboards, relatively clipped guitars and pared-down touches of brass.

Certain session musicians and producers were central to the mid-1980s makossa boom. **Toto Guillaume**, a Douala guitarist who had come to national prominence with the **Black Styles**, played on dozens of records, including several of his own. Bassist, arranger and producer **Aladji Touré** became similarly omnipresent on many of the top Paris/Cameroon albums, and built his companies, Touré Jim's and AT Records, into leading record labels of the new hard makossa. As the worlds of zouk and makossa came closer together in the Paris studios where both were recorded, prominent Antillean musicians such as **Michel Alibo, Jean-Claude Naimro** and **Hamid Belhocine** were increasingly to be heard playing on makossa recordings.

Among individual artistes, **Moni Bile** dominated the late-1980s makossa scene with a series of catchy, well-arranged recordings and a polished stage show. Another Douala artiste, Bile recorded in the Ivory Coast and Paris, where his most famous songs, 'Bijoux Sucrés' and 'O Si Tapa Lambo Lam', were produced by Aladji Touré.

Cameroon, particularly the coastal region around Douala, continues to supply an inexhaustible stream of makossa singers whose hits succeed each other in filling nightclub floors at home and in Paris. **Guy Lobé** has six albums to his own name, while his songs are much in demand among other artistes. Charlotte M'Bango's album 'Nostalgie' (1990) consolidated her position as the leading female makossa star. The twin brothers **Epée** and **Koum** (surname, not used professionally, M'Bengue) scored a major hit in 1989 with their first record 'Bouger Bouger', guided by Aladji Touré. **Ben Decca** achieved substantial fame in the mid-1980s, retired, and passed on the baton to his sister **Grace**, whose record 'Besoin d'Amour' was a hit in 1989. **Pierre de Moussy, Pierre Didy Tchakounté, Gilly Doumbé, Johnny Tezano, Ekambi Brilliant, Hoïgen Ekwalla;** all were names which featured strongly in the makossa stakes. Finally, an interesting variation on the familiar theme was **Lapiro de M'Banga**, sometimes known as 'Ndinga Man' ('guitar man'), whose album 'No Make Erreur', featuring guests Jean-Claude Naimro and Jimmy Cliff, was a major hit in 1986. Lapiro de M'Banga's speciality singing in the pidgin English used by the slum kids of Douala, and dealing lyrically with topics – the problems of daily life for the slum dwellers – other than the run-of-the-mill love themes favoured by blander songwriters. While de M'Banga's lyrics had a rough, rap-influenced humour, his music, particularly in the multiple guitar parts, was a refreshing blend of makossa and Zairean elements.

If the makossa rhythm of Douala and the coast dominated Cameroonian music in the 1970s and 1980s, bikutsi, the rhythm and dance of the Beti people of the forest area around the capital Yaoundé, maintained its presence in the popular music arena. **Les Vétérans**, a ten-piece band who came to prominence in the early 1980s, specialised in the rhythm, leavening its fast, lumpy, galloping pace with a touch of soukous smoothness and accentuating the hypnotic quality with an insistent accordion.

Until the late 1980s the bikutsi rhythm, although used intermittently by musicians such as Manu Dibango, failed to make any great impression outside its home region, with the exception of the neighbouring state of Gabon where members of the Beti ethnicity also live. In 1988, however, this situation began to change. One factor was said to be the influence of Cameroon's president,

Paul Biya, of Beti origin, who was felt to favour the music. Another was the rise to prominence of Les Têtes Brulées, a group which succeeded brilliantly in capturing the attention of the world's press.

Les Têtes Brulées (the literal English translation is 'Burnt Heads', but 'Blown Minds' is in fact nearer, with the connotation of self-destructive, visionary madness) were the creation of a French-trained Yaoundé-born journalist and former fine art student, Jean-Marie Ahanda, who formed the five-man group in order to play modernised, rock-oriented bikutsi. His masterstroke was the look he created for the group – beautifully applied white striped and dotted body paint, ripped T-shirts, huge trainers, day-glo knapsacks worn on stage and hair shaven into tufts and bands. This look proved controversial as well as simply being eye-catching: there is considerable antipathy in Africa to the idea of mutilating one's hair, as the Têtes appeared to be doing. The Têtes Brulées' major boost in terms of European publicity was the lucky result of a meeting with the French film director Claire Denis, then shooting her first feature film *Chocolat* in Cameroon. She made a documentary film, *Man No Run*, of Têtes Brulées on their first visit to Europe which, coupled with the Têtes' look – they were the first African band to adopt a punk/destroy visual scheme – generated French media coverage vastly in excess of that normally accorded a relatively minor African group. The Têtes received a temporary setback in 1989 when their guitarist **Théodore Epème**, generally known as **Zanzibar**, died of an overdose of alcohol and barbiturates – the death was officially recorded as suicide, although rumours of sorcery or poisoning circulated in Yaoundé. The following year, having added a keyboard player to their line-up, the Têtes recorded their first European LP and embarked on a second European tour.

The Têtes Brulées' European fame in fact rapidly surpassed their Cameroonian reputation. Despite its spate of national publicity, the bikutsi remains a relatively minor regional dance craze, restricted to the bars of Yaoundé where the Chacal Bar, in the European absence of its house band the Têtes Brulées, was rapidly superseded in popularity by the Las Vegas, home to new bikutsi star **Mbarga Soukouss**. Mbarga Soukouss's music is of a more traditional, rough and percussive style than the Têtes Brulées' – he has commented that the Beti people don't like modernism – and his success seems therefore to be limited strongly to the regional cultural associations of the music.

Cameroon: Discography

Francis Bebey Super Bebey (Ozileka OZIL 3314)
Manu Dibango Ah Freak Sans Fric (Sonodisc 362018)
Manu Dibango Rasta Souvenir (Esperance ESP 7512)
Manu Dibango Abele Dance (Celluloid CA 616)
Manu Dibango Polysonik (Bird 850 120)
Sam Fan Thomas on Afric Typic Collection compilation (Earthworks EWV 12)
Toto Guillaume Makossa Digital (Disques Esperance ESP 8404)

Moni Bile Chagrin D'Amour (Touré Jim's AT 0064)
Guy Lobé Union Libre (Sonodisc TG 3304)
Pierre de Moussy Reviens Moi Fatimatou (Gefraco MOV 015)
Epee and Koum Makossa Collection Non Stop (Sonodisc AT 083)
Charlotte M'Bango Nostalgie (Touré Jim's AT 072)
Lapiro de M'Bango Ndinga Man (Sonodisc NE 5003)
Les Têtes Brulées Les Têtes Brulées (Sterns 9001)
Les Veterans Les Veterans (Sonodisc TC 001)

ZAIRE

The dance music of Zaire dominates Black Africa like that of no other nation, featuring in discotheques across the continent. Its principal ingredients are a skipping snare drum beat, tight, sweet harmony choruses behind a light, mellifluous lead voice and, above all, the famous multiple intermeshed guitar lines. Latterly, an important adjunct has been the plethora of dance crazes invented by the 'animateurs' of the groups, who shout out the catch phrases and perform the steps front-stage.

A good deal of Zairean pop's success lies in the ease with which traditional likembe (thumb-piano) lines have adapted to the guitar. The incorporation of traditional elements into the musical mix was encouraged by President Mobutu's 'authenticité' campaign, which attempted to eradicate European manners and dress and reassert African identity.

As in West Africa, Latin American, particularly Cuban-based, music was an important influence in the 1940s and 1950s, supplementing the earlier brass band, choir and waltz and mazurka input of the Belgian colonialists. The term rumba is still used to describe Congolese-Zairean pop, although it was supplemented to a certain extent in the 1970s by soukous (from the French verb secouer, to shake), and later by a host of new dance names such as cavacha and kwassa-kwassa.

The most important stylistic feature of the modern soukous sound was the development of the two-stage song: a slow, melodic opening section which breaks suddenly with a burst of conga drumming into the 'seben', a fast, galloping section marked by hypnotic guitar work and the call-and-response of the 'animateurs' spurring on the dancers. By the 1980s, a new generation of bands, particularly those based in Paris, were dispensing with the opening section and launching straight into the seben.

Zairean communities in Europe are centred on Brussels and Paris and the French capital is the second home of a number of the major stars and the natural destination for recording purposes of ambitious musicians, as Zaire's capital Kinshasa contains only a handful of relatively unsophisticated studios. In effect, a division has come into existence between the handful of stars – **Kanda Bongo Man, Papa Wemba** and others – who have opted for an international, Paris-based career and those who have stayed home, catering to the tastes of the Zairean street. The Paris school now tends to feature a faster, harder sound, with fewer musicians to a group and a tendency to adopt influences ranging from Antillean zouk to rock effects. The Kinshasa contingent remains faithful to the bigger line-ups with multiple guitars and slower, more long-drawn-out numbers.

Though Zaire, a nation the size of Europe, contains at least 240 tribal groups and many languages, it is Lingala, the river region's multiethnic language used by traders everywhere, which dominated the song lyrics once French was gradually dropped in favour of authenticité.

The great river port of Kinshasa remains a huge market for music in spite of the increasingly dire poverty of many of its inhabitants. The popular quarter Matongé pulsates after dark to the music of a thousand sound systems in bars and on street stalls, and in the small hours nightclubs are filled with young people drinking the beers whose sponsorship is much prized by the many struggling groups.

The precursors of the modern Congo guitar style were early guitarists such as **Antoine Wendo** and **Jean Bosco Mwenda**, but the first great name in Zairean pop music was **Joseph Kabaselle**, le Grand Kallé, who died in 1983, thirty years after founding the band African Jazz, which launched the modern Latin-influenced Zairean rumba sound. Kallé's band accompanied **Patrice Lumumba** to Brussels to negotiate the then Belgian Congo's independence, celebrated by his famous 'Independence Cha Cha'. African Jazz and Kallé's associated record label between them nurtured all of the subsequent wave of Zairean stars — **Franco**, the great guitarist **Dr Nico** whose premature death occurred in 1985, and **Tabu Ley**, as well as the Cameroonian star, Manu Dibango.

Kallé's successor as top star of Zaire, and soon of the whole of Africa, was the guitarist, singer and bandleader **Luambo Francis Makiadi**, generally known as Franco. Franco founded his band **O K Jazz** in 1956 — the initials stood both for Orchestre Kinois (from Kinshasa) and for Omar Kashama, an early bar-proprietor sponsor. Later the name expanded to **T P O K Jazz**, 'tout-puissant' (all-powerful) having been added. While retaining the Latin rumba base, Franco's music was soon at the forefront of the authenticité campaign, as he incorporated traditional rhythms and feeling into his sound. Franco's sound came to represent the rootsier, more African branch of a dichotomy among Zairean bands, the other half of which was the smoother, more international style of Tabu Ley Rochereau (see below).

Lyrically, Franco's huge output of songs describing and commenting on all aspects of the country's life earned him the sobriquet the 'African Balzac'. His early love songs gave way in the 1960s and 1970s to political statements, including numbers supporting President Mobutu, but daily life and manners provided his richest source of material. His great 1985 hit, 'Mario', in which he takes to task a fictitious young gigolo for sponging off a wealthy widow and crashing her Mercedes, was followed two years later by the wonderful 'Réponse de Mario', in which the young ne'er-do-well, impersonated tremendously by T P O K Jazz star vocalist **Simaro 'Le Poète'**, presents his defence, only to be roundly tongue-lashed by the dark brown tones of Franco in a stream of Lingala laced with French ('Ah, vraiment! . . . mmmm-MMH!'). In 1988, Franco addressed the subject of AIDS, a particular scourge of the music milieu in Zaire, with a riveting and utterly bizarre recording, 'Attention Na Sida', a twenty-minute Churchillian rallying call to the different sectors of the populace backed by a sombre hopping bass and bittersweet chanted chorus. By the 1980s, Franco was a huge (literally) figure in African music, with a recording empire based between Brussels and Kinshasa, at least two twenty-member bands and a vast recorded output.

Although he denied it, AIDS (in addition to sorcery) was rumoured to be the main cause of the illness that caused his death in 1990, an event marked by four days of national mourning in Zaire. His band T P O K Jazz continued in a certain amount of confusion, with star singer **Madilu 'System'** and Le Poète Simaro chief contenders for leadership, but retained its great popularity. Their first self-named cassette after Franco's death, released in 1990, sold 50,000 copies within a matter of weeks and their live performances continue to be among the top-drawing acts in Kinshasa.

A number of 'tribute' albums, some featuring members of T P O K Jazz, followed le Grand Mâitre's death, one of the better examples being **Dieudos's** 'L'Immortal Luambo Makiadi Franco'.

While Franco represented Africanicité in his work, his rival Tabu Ley 'Rochereau' was known for urbanity and an international approach. Tabu Ley's 1970 concert at the prestigious Paris Olympia hall made him a hero at home and inspired him to rename his band **Afrisa International**, which it still is. Tabu Ley (his nickname Rochereau, acquired at school, refers to a Napoleonic general) started his career in the ranks of le Grand Kallé's African Jazz, which he left in 1963 to form his first band, **African Fiesta**. Tabu Ley's voice is more polished and sophisticated than was Franco's and he has deliberately incorporated a wide variety of influences into his act, from European-style 'slows' (such as his 1970 Olympia song 'Pitié') to the latest Kinshasa madiabas and kwassa-kwassas. His band was one of the first in Africa to develop and polish an organised, choreographed stage show; other innovations were the 'soum' guitar style of the 1970s and, according to Tabu Ley, soukous itself. While Franco's bands always featured male front line singers, Tabu Ley's became known for their female vocalists, the most prominent of whom was Tabu Ley's one-time companion **M'Bilia Bel**, who co-starred with Tabu Ley from 1982 until her departure for a solo career in 1988. (She was replaced by two newcomers, also budding stars, **Faya Tess** and **Bayou Ciel**.) M'Bilia Bel's tenure of the Afrisa International microphone coincided with a period during which a series of Franco songs (such as 'Mamou') attacking the misdeeds of women was answered by Tabu Ley and Bel pro-woman numbers such as 'Esuri Yo Wapi'. By the late 1980s, Tabu Ley, with 2,000 songs and 150 records behind him, was still popular but somewhat eclipsed by younger bands.

Between them Franco's and Tabu Ley's bands nurtured many of Zaire's second rank of musicians. One who was, unusually, a member of both is the singer **Sam Mangwana**, who started his career as an arranger and vocalist with Tabu Ley in 1969 and moved three years later to Franco's band. In 1976 he formed his own group **African All Stars**, touring widely in Africa, Europe and the Caribbean and scoring a major hit with his 1982 recording 'Maria Tebbo'. In 1982 ('Cooperation') and again in 1989 ('For Ever'), Mangwana recorded successful albums with Franco, confirming his major star status. Mangwana's linguistic facility − he learned a large Latin American repertoire in Spanish with Tabu Ley − and his Angolan family connections and periods of residence in Mozambique (and consequent fluency in Portuguese) lend a distinctive Latin aspect to some of his songs, notably his 1984 'Canta Mocambique' and 1989 'Aladji' albums. His music, with its cocktail of influences from Angola, Zimbabwe, the Caribbean and elsewhere, is less purely Zairean in feel than that of many of his compatriots, but is immensely popular throughout the continent, especially in the south.

The most important musical event to follow the creation of Franco's and Tabu Ley's big bands was the arrival on the Kinshasa nightclub scene, around 1969–70, of the new group **Zaiko Langa Langa**. Formed by relatively well-to-do students, Zaiko Langa Langa's stylistic advance was to abandon the brass section and bring up-front firstly the three guitarists and secondly the snare drum; both innovations are standard practice today. Zaiko's personnel and young audience had travelled in Belgium and France and encountered the new rock music of Europe and America. The excitement caused by Zaiko's arrival led them to be compared to The Rolling Stones; their music was also occasionally referred to as 'new wave'. A further Zaiko innovation to be universally adopted was the continual introduction of new dance crazes, demonstrated by their animateurs during the long frenetic guitar-led sebens. One of Zaiko's earliest dances, with accompanying rhythmic variations indiscernible to the average listener, was the cavacha. Zaiko's vocals were, and are, handled by a team of four star singers in addition to the two animateur shouters, bringing the group, with dancers, percussionists, bass and synthesizer, to around twenty members in total.

By the 1980s, Zaiko Langa Langa were touring Africa, Europe and even Japan (1988, live album 'Nippon Banzai') and a host of imitators and spin-off groups had been created by former members. In 1988, a major split occurred, since when two Zaiko Langa Langas have existed. The first, **Zaiko Langa Langa Familia Dei**, generally regarded as the 'rebels', were sponsored by a Gabonese politician, proprietor of the N'Goss Club in Kinshasa where they became resident band. Subsequent activities included the invention of the dance Tukumata na BMW ('Pushing the BMW') and the production of two LPs 'Eh N'Goss' (1987) and 'L'Oiseau Rare' (1990). The 'legitimate' Zaiko, sub-titled **Nkola M'Boka**, continued to be led by founder vocalist **Nyoka Longo**. Acquiring a former T P O K Jazz singer, **Malage de Lugendo**, they resumed residency at the Kimpwanza Club and proceeded to go from strength to strength; their 1990 album 'Jetez l'Éponge' was a huge hit, and they are still one of Kinshasa's top attractions.

Zaiko Langa Langa's spin-off groups are far too numerous to list exhaustively. Some, like **Grand Zaiko Wa Wa**, lasted only briefly. Others, such as the **Langa Langa Stars**, acted more as ephemeral vehicles for well-known individual artistes (in this case **Evoloko Jocker**, who was still performing in Paris in 1990). Three, however, merit description.

The group **Victoria Eleison**, founded in 1982 by **Emeneya Mubiala**, a.k.a. **Kester**, a.k.a. **Dr Emeneya**, reached its peak in 1985 with a hit song 'Kimpiatu' and accompanying dance, the injection pump, and is still popular.

The singer **Bozi Boziana** was a member of several other post-Zaiko groups before founding the **Choc Stars** in 1984 and, after achieving substantial success with their dance the roboti-robota, creating **Anti-Choc** in 1986. This group, whose name derives convolutedly from yet another Zaiko Langa Langa tag, 'tout choc, anti-choc', is unusual for the genre in its use of female vocalists, notably its star singer **Déesse Mukangi**, and as of 1990 it was one of the top half dozen live draws in Kinshasa.

The third, and earliest, Zaiko Langa Langa breakaway group was **Viva La Musica**, and its founder, **Papa Wemba**, is still a substantial figure, though latterly more so in the Paris/international sphere than at home. Wemba (real name Shungu Wembadia) first became noted for the incorporation of 'authentic' Zairean percussion, including the lokolé log-drum, into his music and for his catchy slang language, mixing English catch phrases with Lingala. Wemba's mother, a professional chanter at funerals, was an influence on Wemba's sense of melody, injecting a plaintive, almost liturgical feel to songs such as 'M'Fono Yami'. In 1986 Wemba moved to Paris with his family and two years later recorded an expensive and slick LP 'Papa Wemba', under the direction of world music producer Martin Meissonnier, which attracted considerable European attention although Wemba's absence from Kinshasa eroded his support at home. In 1988 he starred in the Paris African feature film *La Vie Est Belle*.

A major part of Papa Wemba's considerable capacity to generate gossip and headlines was his leading role in the 1980s movement of young male fashion fanatics known as the SAPE, standing for Société d'Ambianceurs et Personnes Elegantes. Sapeurs would parade their flashy new clothes ostentatiously at nightclubs and in the street. Italian and French (and for top sapeurs such as Wemba, Japanese) brands of prêt à porter were highly prized, and their labels flaunted, sometimes being resewn on the outside of the garment. Weston, and later steel-tipped Doc Marten, shoes were de rigueur. Valentino, Gaultier or Yamamoto suits were supplemented by extravagant Afro creations by Parisian boutique-owners such as Wilfried, who designed linen, gabardine and leather items adorned with flaps, buttons and multiple lapels. A number of Zairean record sleeves, up to and including Franco's, feature credits to, or even pictures of, Wilfried Street, Wilfried's shop on the Boulevard de Strasbourg.

In addition to Papa Wemba, the most solidly established Paris-Zairean artistes are **Kanda Bongo Man, Ray Lema**, and an assortment of star session players who form and disband groups continually.

Kanda Bongo Man moved to Paris in 1979 after a decade in groups in

Kinshasa, and supported himself with work in a glass factory before his 1981 recording 'Iyole' began to attract serious attention. He continued to perfect a sharp, professional act, playing high-speed, stripped-down dance music with a small group which for several years featured the ace session guitarists **Lokassa, Ringo** (a.k.a. **Rigo) Star**, and above all **Diblo Dibala**, whose hypnotic lead riffs were a central feature of songs such as 'Sai', 'Lisa' and 'Malinga'. A performance at the 1983 WOMAD Festival was the beginning of a number of successful British appearances, where the reliability and professionalism of his act put him at a considerable advantage in relation to equally gifted but less diligent compatriots. By 1988 he had adopted the new kwassa-kwassa dance and became in effect its European distributor.

Ray Lema is very much the odd man out of modern Zairean music. An intellectual and trained musician — he was a Rockefeller Foundation-aided music student in the United States, after leaving a seminary in Kinshasa — he directed the Zairean National Ballet before moving to Paris and embarking on a multifaceted career as composer, session musician, arranger and collaborator with the range of international artistes including the Police's Stewart Copeland. His 1990 album 'Gaia' shows his many influences, from Jimi Hendrix to soul and jazz.

The miscellaneous star Paris-Zaireans number at least a dozen. One of the earliest arrivals was **Souzy Kasseya**, whose 1984 song 'Le Téléphone Sonne' was a substantial mainstream success. Four top session musicians, **Bopol, Nyboma, Wuta May** and **Syran**, operated successfully if intermittently from 1983 onwards as **Les Quatre Étoiles** until Syran M'Benza formed his new group, **Kass Kass**. The guitarist **Diblo Dibala** acquired a formidable reputation for his high-speed work with Kanda Bongo Man among others, and in 1989 formed the group **Loketo** with the singer **Aarlus Mabele** (see **Congo**), before leaving a year later to found another band, **Matchatcha**.

Two substantial performers retain a foot in both Paris and Kinshasa camps. The first of these is the group **Empire Bakuba**, featuring the somewhat grotesque double attraction of the hugely obese singer **Pepe Kalle**, the 'Elephant of Zaire', and the dwarf animateur **Emauro**, not to mention an ace three-man guitar section glorying in the names **Boeing 737, Doris**, and **Elvis**. Empire Bakuba, named in the days of 'authenticité' after a Congolese tribe, was founded in 1972 and its high-powered dance music scored a series of hits over the following decade and a half, culminating in the 1989 smash 'Pon Moun Paka Bouger'.

Empire Bakuba's records continue to be popular in Kinshasa, though the group's live performances no longer rival the big six, a condition which also applies to the romantic star singer **Koffi Olomide**, whose career peaked in 1987 and 1988 with songs such as 'Henriquet' and 'Rue D'Amour'. Olomide, a former member of Zaiko Langa Langa and Viva La Musica, went solo in 1984 and his sapeur proclivities and whitening-creamed complexion became as much a part of his image as the slower pace of his music, which he christened 'rumba love'. The semi-nonsense phrase, 'Generation Tcha Tcho' he coined to describe both his music and his audience, also enhanced his publicity value.

Two of the major star bands of Kinshasa at the end of 1990 had not exported their music at all. The first was **Wenge Musique**, a large classic soukous band very much in the mould of Victoria Eleison. The second group, **Swede Swede**, represented something entirely new. Using mainly traditional percussion, including lokolé log-drums, and harmonica but no guitars, Swede Swede play a rough traditionally-based music updated with suggestive lyrics and catch phrases, and, naturally, a new dance, the sunduma, whose bottom-waving steps rapidly entered the repertoire of all the top live groups.

Finally, three important Zairean women singers must be mentioned. **Abeti** started her career in the early 1970s, and her highly professional and entertaining act, which includes a backing band, **Les Redoubtables**, and a troupe of male dancers, **Les Tigres**, continues to be successful. **Tshala Muana**, daughter of a family of traditional musicians, rose to prominence via her adaptation of the traditional mutuashi dance into a sexy and exciting stage show and, working with a succession of top Paris-Zairean session players, notably Souzy Kasseya, forged a highly successful recording career. **M'Pongo Love** surmounted the obstacle of childhood polio to achieve equal success, only to die in 1989 after a long illness.

Zaire: Discography

Franco Originalité (1956 recordings) (RetroAfric 02)
Franco Editions Populaire − Mabele (Sonodisc 360 056)
Franco La Réponse de Mario (African Sun CHOC 010)
Franco Attention Na Sida (African Sun ASM 001)
Franco and Sam Mangwana Cooperation (Edipop POP 17)
Tabu Ley Rochereau With M'Bilia Bel (Shanachie SHAN 43017)
Tabu Ley Rochereau Tabu Ley (Shanachie SHAN 43017)
Sam Mangwana Georgette Eckins (Celluloid CEL 6729)
Sam Mangwana Aladji (Sterns 8336)
Zaiko Langa Langa Ici Ca Va − Fungola Motema (Prozal PZL 82-84)
Zaiko Langa Langa Jamais Sans Nous (Tamaris TMS 91003)
Anti-Choc Anti Choc (Sterns 1022)
Papa Wemba Le Voyageur (Virgin Real World CDRW 20)
Kanda Bongo Man Amour Fou (Hannibal HN 1337)
Kanda Bongo Man Kwassa Kwassa (Hannibal HN 1343)
Loketo Mondo Ry (Jimmy's JP 014)
Pepe Kalle Gigant-afrique (Globestyle ORB 062)
Koffi Olomide Tcha-tcho (Sonodisc KL 031)
Swede Swede Toleki Bango (Crammed Discs CRAW 1 CD)
Tshala Muana Biduaya (Celluloid 66873)

CONGO

The popular music of the Congo is virtually identical to that of its big neighbour Zaire. Its capital, Brazzaville, lies a ferry ride across the river from Kinshasa and musicians come and go freely between the two cities.

Historically, the Congo's most important band was **Les Bantous de la Capitale**, founded in 1959, who have played classic Congo-Zaire rumba and soukous for thirty years. During this time they have contributed one major dance craze, the boucher, a good number of hits, notably 'Mibale' and 'Marie Jeanne', and acted as launching pad for several solo careers. These stars include **Pamelo Mounka**, who joined the Bantous from Tabu Ley Rochereau's group and by the early 1980s was making a series of successful recordings of which the best was 'En Plein Maturité'. Another ex-Bantou, **Tchico**, moved to Paris where he founded the **Les Officiers de la Musique Africaine** with a mixed Congo-Zaire personnel.

The guitarist and singer **Aarlus Mabele** built a reputation as one of the best Paris-Zairean session musicians and in 1988 became a founding member of the group **Loketo**, taking over leadership on the departure of star guitarist **Diblo Dibala**.

One of the top Congolese artistes of the late 1980s has been the comic singer **Zao**, a former teacher whose humorous impersonations of a variety of characters, notably the 'Ancien Combattant' – old soldier – of his biggest hit record, have been hugely successful. Other interesting new Congolese artistes include **N'Zongo Soul** and **Djo Cassidy et les Zombi de Brazzaville**.

Congo: Discography

Les Bantous de la Capitale Marie Jeanne (Sonafric SAF 50022)
Tchico Full Steam Ahead (Globestyle ORB 007)
Zao Ancien Combattant (Melodisc CD46002-2)
Aarlus Mabele Aarlus Mabele (Disc Inter F 142)
Djo Cassidy et les Zombi de Brazzaville Jeune Deroute (Sonodisc LB 236)

GABON

The popular music consumption of Gabon is dominated by the sounds of its big neighbours. The Congo and Zaire to its south and east provide soukous, from the north Cameroon provides makossa, and bikutsi comes from the border region. The Gabonese capital, Libreville, possesses good facilities for broadcasting and recording, however. The powerful radio transmitter of the

Africa No. 1 station is among the best on the continent, and several 24-track studios rival Abidjan for recording purposes.

Much the best-known Gabonese artiste internationally is the blind singer, guitarist, poet and dramatist **Pierre Akendengue**, an intellectual in the mould of Cameroon's Francis Bebey. Educated in France at the universities of Caen and the Sorbonne, Akendengue lived in exile in Paris between 1972 and 1977 after criticising the government, but was pardoned and invited home as his songwriting began to attract international praise. Since 1985 his earlier, more international style has gradually transmuted into a rootsier dance music and his lyrics have shifted from French to his native Myéné language. His 1991 album, 'Silence', featured a multinational and multi-influenced pan-African line-up.

Les Diablotins, a fifteen-piece soukous band, formed at the beginning of the 1980s, offer high-class Zaire-style pop, but work mainly within the country, as do the equally talented **Orchestre Massako**. One gabonese singer to have achieved some success elsewhere on the continent is **Hilarion N'Guema**, whose 1987 hit 'SIDA' was one of the earliest songs to tackle the subject of AIDS.

Gabon: Discography

Pierre Akendengue Espoir à Soweto (Mélodie ENC 141)
Pierre Akendengue Silence (Mélodie DK 016)
Hilarion N'Guema SIDA (Safari Ambiance SA 103)

ANGOLA

The development of modern Angolan music has been hindered by two major factors. Firstly, the Portuguese colonial regime was outstandingly harsh in the suppression of indigenous culture, leaving the country devoid of any Africanising dance groups on independence in 1975. Secondly, the vicious civil war with UNITA since independence has economically shattered the country. Nonetheless, the capital Luanda possesses a well-equipped sixteen-track National Radio station studio and a number of groups with good modern equipment.

Angolan music has similarities with that of Zaire to the north, including a basis of likembe thumb-piano melodies. It also has much in common with Brazilian music; Angolan slaves may have introduced their semba rhythm to Brazil, thus creating the samba, while Brazilian troops imported by the Portuguese to suppress Angolan uprisings last century may have returned the influence.

In the past, Angolan musicians have often had links with Lisbon. The singer **Bonga** started his career as a sportsman there − firstly as a 400-metre running champion, secondly as a player with Benfica football club − before taking up music and making his first album in 1972. Subsequent albums developed his music, a mixture of soukous and a softer Brazilian-influenced sound, in songs dealing with political and social issues. Bonga has performed in Europe and the USA and is now based again in Luanda. Another younger singer, **Waldemar Bastos**, has recently begun to perform in a similar style in Lisbon. In Paris, the singer **Tete Lando** has recorded excellent semba-based dance music.

Several large Zairean-style groups are operating in Angola, where they perform on radio or at weekend dances in work cooperatives or social centre halls; the most important are the ten-piece **Orquestra Caravelo**, the **Bobongo Stars**, led by a singer named **Diana** who worked in Zaire during the 1960s, the fifteen-piece **Sensacional Maringa de Angola**, and the twelve-piece **Dimba Dya Ngola**.

The rumba style is also favoured by the **Trio Aka**, one of a pair of groups to have had albums released in London in 1989. The second, the **Kafala Brothers**, perform in a much more Portuguese-influenced ballad style. The Kafala Brothers, **Moises** and **José**, sing their own compositions in Portuguese as well as in the local languages Kimbundu and Umbundu; they also perform songs based on the poetry of the country's president, Agostinho Neto. Although their preferred mode is a soft, yearning, acoustic guitar-backed European sound, they also sing pieces in the local dance rhythms of kilapango and nhatcho.

Angola: Discography

Bonga Marika (Sunset-France SF 202)
Trio Aka Mama Cristina (AA Enterprises AAER 002)
Kafala Brothers NGola (AA Enterprises AAER 001)

ZAMBIA

Zambia contains a large number of ethnic groups and languages, of which the principal ones are Bemba, Mambwe and Tonga; it is also rich in a wide variety of musical styles and instruments. Its modern music has been dominated by the Zairean rumba sound, which has given rise to an offshoot known as Zamrumba. One locally based style which competes strongly is the kalindula rhythm of the northern 'Copperbelt' bands such as **Shalawambe**. The main record company, Teal, a subsidiary of the South African Gallo company, produces singles and the occasional LP when vinyl importation is not too problematic.

One of the biggest recent stars of Zambian music was the singer and songwriter **Emmanuel Mulemena**, who died in 1982, leaving his former group, the **Sound Inspectors**, to struggle on operating as the **Mulemena Boys**.

Two principal groups, **Julizya** and **Amayenge**, are now based in the capital Lusaka; others work in N'Dola, the centre of the Copperbelt, or further north. Julizya are a recently-formed (1987) seven-piece group, while Amayenge, fifteen-piece combining singers, acrobats and dancers with a guitar and drum line-up, take their name from a local dance. Amayenge's songs, in a variety of Zambian languages, describe elements of the traditional life of the country or, like 'Lelo Bleisa', praise football teams or relate episodes from the band's experience, in the case of 'Moscow 1985', their first Russian visit. In 1986, Amayenge were voted Zambian Band of the Year.

Of the Copperbelt groups, the most famous is **Shalawambe** (the name comes from a Bemba word meaning to linger and gossip), a five-piece band led by the three **Kabwe** brothers, who continue to farm when not performing, and who visited Britain in 1988 and again in 1990.

Shalawambe are followed by the **Masasu Band**, another five-piece who specialise in a variety of northern rhythm known as the mantyantya and have achieved considerable popularity in their five-year career. In 1990 they visited Britain backing the blind singer **P.K. Chisala**, a performer in the kalindula tradition noted for his striking and controversial songs. Chisala's 1985 number 'Pastor', in which he criticised priests for misquoting the Bible and managed to outrage a sector of the public with a line implying that Jesus consorted with women, made his name and subsequent songs such as 'Moving Coffin', written after his father died in a car crash, consolidated it.

Other well-known Zambian groups include **Kalambo Hit Parade**, a prominent kalindula moderniser led by the brothers **James** and **Noah Siame**; the **Fikashala Band**, featuring another blind singer, **Labani Kalunga**, the **Olya Band**; and **Serenji Kalindula**.

Zambia: Discography

The Mulemena Boys A Tribute (ZMP ZMLP 70)
Various Zambiance! (Globestyle ORB 037)
Various Shani! The Sound of Zambia (WOMAD 009)

MOZAMBIQUE

Mozambique shares the same characteristics which have impeded the development of modern music in other former Portuguese colonies, namely relatively late independence (1975) preceded by severe repression of indigenous culture and social organisation. The rejection of African culture by a strongly 'assimilated' urban class who regarded only European values as worthwhile was also particularly pronounced in Mozambique. A ten-year war of attrition with the brutal Renamo insurgents has wrought havoc with the country's infrastructure; groups have spoken of having to take the light bulbs from their homes to light their performances. Radio Mozambique posseses a sixteen-track recording studio in the capital Maputo, however, and with the liberalisation of the formerly Marxist-Leninist economy, there are signs of increased initiatives to encourage the organisation of music-making.

From a wide range of ethnic groups, the mbila (wood-block xylophone) music of the Chopi people is probably the most characteristic traditional music of the country. Recorded by the noted musicologist Hugh Tracy in the 1940s, orchestras of timbila (plural of mbila) are still prevalent, usually attached to village or provincial administrations or local political party officials. In 1989, Ben Mandelson and Roger Armstrong of London's Globestyle Records recorded the orchestra led by **National Company of Dance and Song** member **Eduardo Durâo**, mixing timbila, rattles and traditional percussion with electric bass guitar on a set of modern Chopi songs mixing traditional themes with contemporary social commentary.

In terms of modern dance music, the marrabenta style is most representative of Mozambique. Born out of the old rural majika music, marrabenta was first played on home-made oil-can guitars in bars and dance halls which were often closed down by the Portuguese on suspicion of harbouring freedom fighters. The marrabenta phenomenon also covers dance and fashion, both of which have transmuted with changing external circumstances: in the 1950s marrabenta 'popas' (something like 'punks') affected American hairstyles while their girls wore starched, flounced skirts. The most successful exponent of modern marrabenta is the **Orchestra Marrabenta Star**, who have scored major national hits with songs such as 'Nhimba Ya Dota' and 'Sapateiro' (shoemaker). Marrabenta Star features a dozen or more musicians (guitar, drums and brass) and dancers.

Since 1980, the smaller group **Eyuphuro** have worked in the more melodic, quieter style of their home region of Nampula in the north of the country. Based around the female singer-songwriter Zena Bakar and singer-guitarist Gimo Abdul Remane, Eyuphuro plays gentle, Portuguese-influenced music supported by bass and traditional percussion. After having recorded three albums at Radio Mozambique, the group toured Europe in 1989 and again in 1990 with the WOMAD organisation, recording an album on the Real World label during the second tour.

Mozambique: Discography

Eduardo Durâo and Orquestra Durâo Timbala
(Globestyle ORBD 065)
Orchestra Marrabenta Independence (Piranha pir 12)
Eyuphuro Mama Mosambiki (Real World RW 10)

ZIMBABWE

Along with Zairean rumba and soukous, the popular music of Zimbabwe has, since independence in 1980, been the most influential in the southern half of the continent, dominating the listening of adjacent countries such as

Mozambique. Prior to the explosion of Zimbabwean pop following this date, the country's indigenous music built gradually.

In the 1940s and 1950s, imported South African styles dominated the Zimbabwean townships; first the jazz and jive bands, later the Kwela pennywhistle sound of artistes such as **Lemmy Mabaso**. In the 1960s Zairean rumba flooded into the record stores, and soon a number of Zimbabwean bands, sometimes composed partly of Zaireans like the **Real Sounds of Africa** (see below), began to play rumba. The likembe, or thumb-piano, the traditional instrument whose transposition to electric guitar was at the root of the Africanised rumba of Zaire, had its equivalent in the Zimbabwean region, however, where its name in the majority Shona language is the m'bira. Just as in Zaire, traditional m'bira melodies began to be played on electric guitars, with the same success, and the lumpier, rougher Shona rhythms blended with the m'bira/guitar sound and plaintive vocal lines produced Zimbabwe's own distinctive dance style, variously known as chimurenga, jit or an assortment of other names. As chimurenga, pioneered and typified by **Thomas Mapfumo** (see below), the new Zimbabwean roots rock music was closely connected with the anticolonial struggle and with the armed opposition to the white minority breakaway regime of Ian Smith in the 1960s and 1970s; for this reason a good deal of revolutionary spirit still attaches to it.

Though tightly constrained by lack of funds, Harare's recording scene is healthy by regional standards (excluding rich South Africa). The major record company Gramma presses albums and singles and the leading recording studio, Shed, operates effectively. Live music flourishes too; the old rural tradition of weekend-long village dances, accompanied by copious amounts of home-brewed beer, persists in the many township beer gardens where groups will play from mid-morning on Saturday through to the small hours of Sunday.

The m'bira consists of a tuned set of iron prongs fixed in a half-gourd resonator (or nowadays sometimes a glass-fibre replica gourd) and plucked downwards by the thumbs. It is traditionally accompanied by the hosho rattle, and played by males only. A considerable aura of mysticism still attaches to m'bira music, as it was long regarded as a way of communicating with spirits. For this reason, colonial missionaries were as keen to discourage it as was the government on political and cultural grounds.

Township private parties with m'bira music persisted as an alternative to beer-hall dance music, and a number of major traditional m'bira groups are extremely popular today. Interestingly, the two most important both feature women, a departure from traditional Shona practice.

The **Rwizis**, an ensemble of three m'biras, singer, hosho, drums and dancer, is led by a reputed medium, **Hakurotwi Mude**, and includes the charismatic woman percussionist and dancer **Mai Muchena**. The m'bira player and singer **Stella Chiweshe** learned from her uncle and rapidly gained acceptance by sheer expertise, persistence and the force of her powerful personality, building a career at first based on local weddings, funerals, political gatherings and gradually, in the cities, concerts before branching into theatre with the National Dance

Company of Zimbabwe. Her recorded work has included over twenty hit singles, including the major seller 'Kasahwa', and several albums. Her most successful LP, 'Ambuya', features her new formation, the Earthquake Band, with its unusual and highly effective combination of three marimbas (wood-block xylophones), hoshos, two m'biras, and bass guitar and drum kit.

The m'bira sound is a principal feature of the style which came to be known as chimurenga (meaning 'struggle') music. The originator of chimurenga, and Zimbabwe's biggest star, is the singer Thomas Mapfumo. Mapfumo started his career covering Elvis Presley and Otis Redding songs in a group called the **Springfields**, and gradually started experimenting with Shona language lyrics in the 1970s. In 1973, he joined the **Hallelujah Chicken Run Band** and began to incorporate m'bira melodies in the music, working closely with the guitarist **Jonah Sithole**, who developed a damped rhythmic style capturing perfectly the sound of the m'bira. Mapfumo was by now writing songs in Shona, mixing local lore, proverbs, anecdotes and a considerable and outspoken element of support for the armed struggle against the Smith regime. In 1977 Mapfumo moved to a new group, the **Acid Band**, and released an album 'Hokoyo!' ('watch out!') which attracted major national attention, including that of the authorities, who pressurised Mapfumo's record company, Teal, and the radio stations into suppressing the album. This pattern continued until independence in 1980, with a variety of ploys being used to diminish Mapfumo's by now major role in encouraging the black population in their support of the two pro-independence parties ZANU and ZAPU. These included, in 1978, helicopter broadcasts over the bush of Mapfumo's music with an accompanying claim that Mapfumo was backing Bishop Muzorewa's call to abandon the armed struggle. After independence, Mapfumo, with his new group **Blacks Unlimited**, became a musical figurehead for the government of Robert Mugabe, playing at major political rallies in the national stadium and releasing successful albums including 'Mabasa', 'Congress' and 'Mr Music'. In 1983, a collection of Mapfumo's chimurenga singles was released by the British Earthworks label, and the following year the dreadlocked singer began a series of European appearances, reducing a reggae element which had been increasingly coming to dominate his repertoire in favour of his older chimurenga sound. Mapfumo's 1990 Island LP 'Corruption' saw the singer, plus an enhanced Blacks Unlimited, railing against the continued inability of the poor masses of Africa to better their lot, even though nominally independent.

Mapfumo's innovatory lead was rapidly followed by another of the country's most popular singers. **Oliver Mutuzudzi** left his former group the **Wagon Wheels** in 1978, formed a new group similar to Mapfumo's which he named the **Black Spirits**, and released an album 'Ndipeyiozano' shortly after Mapfumo's 'Hokoyo!' which repeated the latter's success. Mutuzudzi's gruff, 'coughing' voice continues to make him popular in Zimbabwe, but as yet he has not made his mark outside the country.

In 1987, Thomas Mapfumo, though still a much greater star at home, was overtaken in terms of European fame by a younger, relatively minor Harare group, the **Bhundu Boys**. Their success was achieved essentially by common sense, good timing and hard work; the Bhundus accepted the invitation of a Scottish graphic designer to come to Britain to tour and, rapidly disillusioned of their images of limousines and big concert halls, embarked on a rapid forty-date tour playing pubs and small halls. Pausing for the release of an album, 'Shabini', they immediately continued for another fifty similar dates, by the end of which they had built a substantial reputation for their energetic and charming performance and joyful dance music at a time when the major eighties vogue for African music was building fast.

The Bhundus were formed in 1980 from members of an older cover-version band called the **Wild Dragons**. They associated themselves, like all young Zimbabweans, with the struggle for independence − their name means 'bush boys', with its connotation of guerrilla fighters − but they were not a part of the chimurenga movement, and their music had none of the m'bira, spiritual, political intensity of Mapfumo's. The Bhundus based their sound on what they called jit, or jit-jive, a fast guitar-and-snare-drum dance beat, quite like rock and roll in some ways, of great appeal to a younger generation. Prior to their international success they were moderately successful at home, scoring several hits including the number one single 'Hatisitose', but it was the prestige resulting from their overseas stardom which boosted them to true star status in Zimbabwe. In 1987 they became one of the earliest African bands to sign to a multinational record company, WEA, but the relationship was not a happy one. Three increasingly watered-down and inauthentic albums failed to sell as hoped and the band returned in 1990 to their original small UK label, Disc Afrique. By this time, the Bhundu's singer **Biggie Tembo** had left the group; the remaining four Bhundus released a live album, cheekily entitled 'Absolute Jit', and got back to touring.

A good many other professional guitar-based groups work in Harare, playing beer halls and nightclubs, and making records. The **Four Brothers** were formed in 1978 by the singer and drummer **Marshall Munhumumwe** and in 1980 scored two huge hits with the singles 'Mokorokota' and 'Vimbay'. Since then they have alternated residencies at Harare's Saratoga Bar with tours abroad, including Moscow in 1985 and the UK in 1988, following the success of which they released a British LP entitled 'Bros' in playful reference to the hyper-Aryan English teenybopper stars of the same name.

If the Four Brothers' smoother m'bira-based sound appeals to a slightly older audience, township youth favourite in the late 1980s was **John Chibadura**, with his group the **Tembo Brothers**. Chibadura formed the band in 1985 and his charismatic antistar approach, wild soulful voice and dramatic heartfelt lyrics describing the pleasures and, above all, the grief, of everyday life, rocketed him to widespread popularity, above all with an army of teenage girl fans. Chibadura's best-known songs include '5000 Dollars', about an excessive bride price demanded by a greedy father for his daughter, and 'Nhamo Yatakawona' ('The Suffering We Saw') with its beautiful and hypnotic m'bira guitar solo.

Other exponents of 1980s Zimbabwean m'bira-rock include **Lovemore**

Majaiwana, a singer-guitarist from the second city, Bulawayo, whose sound is a variant of that of the Harare bands; the **Sungura Boys** and the **Ocean City Band**, both of whom feature strong m'bira influence, and the **Marxist Brothers**.

In its Zimbabwean-modified form, the Zairean rumba style continues to be popular in Harare; two bands in particular purvey the sound with considerable success. The **Real Sounds of Africa** is composed mainly of Zairean émigrés who arrived in Harare in the 1970s via a successful stay in Zambia. The eleven-piece band has a polished act with a contortionist dancer, for certain performances 'tribal' stage dress of mock tiger-skin skirts and bare torsos, and a simulated on-stage football match to accompany their hit song 'Dynamos v. Caps'. At home resident in Harare's Seven Miles Hotel, the Real Sounds have toured the UK twice, most recently in an ensemble comprising also the British club mixer Norman Cook and an assortment of rappers, UK dancers and graffiti artists.

More popular than the Real Sounds at home are **Jonah Moyo and Devera NGwena**, a five-piece rumba band sponsored by the Mashaba Asbestos Mining Company where most of the band members still work, in spite of their many hit singles and great success in the beer halls.

Finally, the gospel tradition provides an alternative input to Zimbabwean popular music, both via pure South African-style gospel choirs and gospel-influenced guitar music. A prime example of the latter is **Machanic Manyeruke**, who with his group, the Puritans, produces a lovely, simple, yearning blend of plangent electric guitar, organ and vocals. Manyeruke took up music in the gospel choir of his local Salvation Army Brigade and works as a waiter in the executive restaurant of a large Harare multinational company when not playing with his group, which sometimes includes his wife **Helen** and his sister **Success**. His music, including songs such as 'Cain and Abel' and 'Resurrection of Lazarus', is well showcased on an eponymous 1986 UK album.

Choral music is also represented by acts such as **Black Umfolosi**, an a cappella group somewhat in the mould of the South African Ladysmith Black Mambazo, who sing in the minority NDebele language and dance spectacularly with shields and spears.

Zimbabwe: Discography

Stella Chiweshe Chisi (Piranha pir 27)
Thomas Mapfumo Chimurenga Singles (Earthworks ELP 2004)
Thomas Mapfumo Corruption (Mango 162 539 848)
Thomas Mapfumo Shumba (Earthworks EMV 22)
The Bhundu Boys Shabini (Disc Afrique AFRI 02)
The Bhundu Boys Absolute Jit (Disc Afrique AFRI 09)
The Four Brothers Makorokoto (Cooking Vinyl COOK 014)
John Chibadura The Essential (CSA CSLP 5002)
Jonah Moyo & Devera NGwena Taxi Driver (K-KO 1)

Machanic Manyeruke M. M. (Flying Fish 025)
Various Zimbabwe Frontline (Earthworks EWV 9)
Various Spirit of the Eagle (Earthworks EWV 18)
Various Jit, the Movie (Earthworks EWV 23)

SOUTH AFRICA

The South African music industry is one of the strongest in the continent, with a sophisticated infrastructure and a broad range of popular styles. Record companies have been established in the country since the early years of the twentieth century, when Eric Gallo founded his business making recordings which by the 1930s included the music of the various Bantu tribal groups. With a much more urbanised and industrialised black population than most African countries, and a relatively rich and cosmopolitan white ruling élite, possession of radios and record players was soon widespread, encouraging the recording industry to flourish.

Whereas in other nations European or Latin American musics were prominent external sources of influence, black South Africans have always looked very much to the United States for inspiration. This seems to be partly because of the similarity of experience between North American and South African black people, living for the most part in ghetto areas of large cities. Whatever the reason, American music and fashion have always been rapidly followed in the townships of South Africa. Jazz rapidly became the music par excellence of the 1930s and in the 1950s zoot suits were all the rage in the streets of the black cultural capital Sophiatown (subsequently demolished to make way for a white residential area).

Indigenous musics of the main South African black ethnic groups — principally Zulu, Xhosa, Sotho — made their own input into popular music styles, of course. One of the earliest and most substantial styles was marabi, which developed from the 1920s on, mixing Dixieland jazz with local musics. Marabi was the sound of the black workers, performed at shebeens — illegal drinking dens — and as such looked down upon by blacks aspiring to higher social position, who preferred purer jazz bands such as the Merry Blackbirds, with their Louis Armstrong-replica trumpeter.

In the 1940s, kwela, a mixture of penny whistles, acoustic guitars and tea-chest basses, arrived, played by township kids on street corners. The skifflelike kwela became a veritable craze, and record companies such as Gallo rapidly moved in, recording dozens of street musicians for the price of a three-hour session, resulting in a huge output of highly profitable singles. A number of notable musicians emerged from this process, notably Spokes Mashiyane, Lemmy 'Special' Mabaso, and Elias Lerole and his Zigzag Flutes, whose 'Tom Hark' actually made the European charts in 1956. Kwela was paralleled by the hard, jumping sax, accordion, bass and drum sound, sometimes known as sax jive, which continues today. This recording boom was to be repeated in the late sixties as mbaqanga music boomed as kwela had earlier.

Mbaqanga was a tough, rough, bass-heavy rocking sound typified by its pioneer and greatest star **Mahlathini** (see below), and dominating the townships until superseded in the 1980s by the fusion and pop sounds of artistes such as **Johnny Clegg, Brenda Fassie** and **Mango Groove** (see below).

Two circumstances boosted South African music's international visibility and influence. One was the exodus of South African musicians to London, New York and other cities as refugees from apartheid and cultural suffocation. Travelling musicals such as *King Kong*, which played London in the 1950s, often left members of their casts behind as they toured. A later boost was the hugely popular Paul Simon LP 'Graceland', which featured mainly South African musicians: **Ray Phiri, Stimela**, the **Boyoyo Boys, General M.D. Shirinda**, the **Gaza Sisters** and **Ladysmith Black Mambazo**.

The doyenne of South African popular music is singer **Miriam Makeba**, who came to international prominence in the 1960s with songs such as 'The Click Song' and 'M'bube' which blended jazz, folk, Western pop and Xhosa or Zulu elements. Makeba was born in 1932 in Johannesburg and first sang professionally with the **Jazz Dazzlers**, the backing band of top vocal combo the **Manhattan Brothers**. She diversified into musical theatre – in *King Kong*, the tale of a black boxing hero – and cinema – the outstanding 1957 antiapartheid film *Come Back Africa* – and in the 1960s settled in the USA, where Harry Belafonte befriended her and produced her records. First married to the trumpeter **Hugh Masakela** (see below) she remarried the American Black Power activist Stokely Carmichael and moved with him to Guinea in 1969, since when she has worked in Africa with a Guinean backing group. Regarded as something of an elder statesman of African culture, she is much in demand for symbolic concerts such as Paul Simon's 1987 'Graceland' tour.

Makeba's male counterpart is the trumpeter and bandleader Hugh Masakela, whose career equals fellow international fusionist Manu Dibango in range and variety. The second instrument he possessed was a gift from Louis Armstrong, arranged by his school chaplain Father – now Bishop – Trevor Huddleston. After playing in a series of local jazz bands, Masakela joined the orchestra of *King Kong* in 1959, and immediately afterwards, deciding to flee apartheid, moved first to London and then to New York, where a series of jazz-pop instrumental records included the number one hit 'Grazin' In The Grass' in 1968. Masakela travelled in Africa in the 1970s, working variously with the group **Xalam** in Senegal, **Fela Kuti** in Nigeria and the Ghanaian group **Hedzollah Soundz**, with whom he visited America. The mid to late 1980s saw him continue to travel and record prolifically, with, among other collaborators, **Herb Alpert**, the **Soul Brothers**, and **Gaspar Lawal**. By now his style, well showcased in the 1987 WEA album 'Tomorrow', encompassed elements of jazz, mbaqanga, lyrical ballads, Afrobeat and funk.

Masakela's emigrant lead was followed in the mid-1960s by the jazz pianist **Dollar Brand**, who later changed his name to **Abdullah Ibrahim**. After early work with the **Jazz Epistles**, with whom he recorded the first South African jazz 33⅓ rpm LP, Brand moved to Europe, was spotted by Duke Ellington, and went to major success in American and European festivals before returning to South Africa to a hero's welcome and recording his seminal 1974 LP 'Mannenberg'. A number of Brand's former accompanists went on to individual success, notably Basil Coetzee whose saxophone playing has made him a star of modern Cape jazz.

The third major South African jazz musician to achieve international success was the saxophonist **Dudu Pukwana**, who arrived in Britain in the 1960s and played with Chris MacGregor's Blue Notes, subsequently the Brotherhood of Breath, and finally Zila.

Less known outside South Africa but more and more popular at home is the guitarist **Philip Tabane**, who rose through the kwela scene, via talent competitions and weddings, to the jazz world, but whose music defies categorisation. By the late 1980s his group **Malomba** was a unique mixture of traditional drums, blues-rock-jazz guitar and lyrical flute.

Mbaqanga burst onto the South African musical scene in the mid-1960s, a mixture of a hardened, electrified progression of the kwela-marabi sound, new influences from the blues-rock groups coming up in the West – the Beatles, the Rolling Stones – and an element of choral singing from the m'bube style of choirs like **Ladysmith Black Mambazo** (see below). Its first stars were **Mahlathini and the Mahotella Queens** and, not to be overlooked, their backing group the **Makgona Tsohle Band**. The three elements were put together by the eminent producer and talent scout Rupert Bopape, who was already familiar with the prolific and excellent session work of saxophonist **West Nkosi** and guitarist **Marks Mankwane** and who saw that the three Queens' tight harmony chorus singing and close formation Zulu dance steps were perfect complements to the music. The lead singer, Mahlathini, born Simon Mkabinde, rapidly became famous as a 'groaner'; he had developed his fearsome baritone 'goat's voice' singing traditional 'ingoma ebusuku' choral music. He recorded under a variety of names, including **Boston Tar Baby**, before rocketing to fame with the Queens. The single 'Orlando Train' first took the group into the charts and the term mbaqanga, meaning 'dough' and bearing all the English word's simultaneous connotations of mixture, heaviness and money, was coined in a radio interview shortly afterwards. By the 1980s, the mbaqanga craze was well past its peak and other, more Western, pop-oriental styles were taking over, but it returned to fashion a decade later, mainly as a result of Mahlathini and the Queens' success in Europe and America. A succession of electrifying concerts and the release of classic albums such as 'Thokozile', 'Paris-Soweto', and the Earthworks series 'The Indestructible Beat of Soweto' brought the group considerable success abroad, and by the 1990s they were topping bills at major stadium concerts at home.

The **Soul Brothers**, Mahlathini's only rival for leadership of the mbaqanga stakes, are also riding high at home, their 1989 'Impimpi' album having been a massive hit. The Soul Brothers were formed in 1975 and acted at first as backing group for a Johannesburg female trio, the **Mthembu Queens**. A key move was their acquisition of the Hammond organist **Moses Mgwenya**, whose distinctive sound, along with their rich kwela-inspired brass section, is a Soul Brothers hallmark. The group's second single, 'Mshoza', became one of the biggest selling singles in South African history; their work also became familiar in Europe in the 1980s via Earthworks compilations.

A component of the Mahlathini-Queen mix and a genre well promoted in Europe is the choral, a cappella style sometimes known as m'bube or 'bombing', a description it acquired in the 1940s as its zooming vocal effects were thought to resemble the sound of an aeroplane passing low and fast overhead. The name of the group which has become the chief proponent of m'bube explains its past: 'mambazo', meaning 'axe', because they vanquished their competition in choir competitions; Ladysmith is the area of origin of their leader **Joseph Shabala**, and also of **Solomon Linda**, the composer of the first hit single in the genre in the 1950s. Ladysmith Black Mambazo's participation on Paul Simon's 'Graceland' was partly responsible for their European fame which resulted in the best-selling WEA LP 'Shaka Zulu'. By the 1990s, they were still popular and increasing the religious content of their music.

By the 1980s, a new breed of singer was dominating the South African pop market. Mixing soul, funk and disco and miscellaneous US pop sounds with a greater or lesser degree of African feeling, the genre was known by a variety of catch-all names including 'township pop', 'township disco' and mpantsula. Several of these artistes achieved success outside the country.

The white Lancashire-born academic **Johnny Clegg** and his multiracial groups, firstly **Juluka** and subsequently **Savuka**, became extremely popular in France with their Zulu dancing and easy-listening mbaqanga/rock mix. At the same time, their political impact as a mixture of races sharing the stage, at a time when apartheid still ruled in music, was considerable. Their progressive image, incorporating a modern rock feel, appealed to a public tired of the old-style mbaqanga.

The singer **Sipho Mabuse** started his career in the **Beaters**, a band purveying Beatles and Rolling Stones-style rock in the late 1960s. The first Africanisation of the group's music took place after a visit to Zimbabwe, when the Beaters became **Harari**, and began to play first rumba-influenced, and subsequently mbaqanga-influenced, rock. In 1984 the band split up and Sipho Mabuse pursued a solo career, with a huge single 'Rise' and an album, 'Burn Out' which was released in America by CBS. In 1987 Mabuse signed with Virgin in the UK; two albums, 'Afrodizzia' and 'Chant of the Marching', resulted.

The singer and guitarist **Ray Phiri** was introduced to music by his Malawian swimming-pool cleaner and guitarist father 'Just Now' Phiri, and enjoyed a decade of success as groaner with the mbaqanga/soul group the **Cannibals**. On the death of **Jacob Radebe**, the band's star singer, Phiri formed his current group, **Stimela**, and began to produce highly successful records such as 'Highland Drift', combining outspoken social and political messages with a catchy jazz, mbaqanga and jive musical mix. Phiri's work with Paul Simon on the 'Graceland' record and tour brought him to wider international attention.

By the late 1980s, probably the biggest-selling recording artiste in South Africa was the glamorous and dynamic disco queen **Brenda Fassie**, whose albums, 'Weekend Special' in 1986 and 'Too Late For Mama' in 1989, were the biggest hits of their respective years. Fassie's famous song 'Black President' optimistically refers to her uncle, Nelson Mandela. Her predecessor, **Yvonne Chaka Chaka**, continues to have success in a similar vein.

Among many dozens of other, more or less township pop artistes, the following should be mentioned: **Condry Ziqubu**, a guitarist who has incorporated West African rhythms as well as mbaqanga into his sound; **Chicco**, a singer-songwriter-producer whose album 'Soldier' was released in Europe; **Tananas**, a group combining Cape Town jazz with pop and other styles to considerable effect as a club star; **Mango Groove**, a multiracial eleven-piece group enjoying huge concert success; **Tau Ea Matsekha**, leading practitioner of the Sotho language music currently so popular; and **Steve Kekana**, a blind Soweto singer who has scored hits both at home and in Scandinavia.

Reggae has made major inroads in South Africa. Its leading practitioner is **Lucky Dube**, whose first album 'Think About the Children', released when he left the Skyways, was a hit. It was followed by the much greater 'Slave' and 'Together as One'. Other notable reggae artistes are **O'Yaba, Jose Carlos, Sister Phumi** and **Carlos Djedje**.

Finally, the poet-performer-activist **Mzwakhe Mbuli** sprang to great popularity in the late 1980s with his recordings 'Change Is Pain' (1986) and 'Unbroken Spirit' (1988). Mbuli was born to a Xhosa mother and a Zulu father, and spent many years working with the Cultural Desk of the ANC. When that organisation was unbanned, he began, with great success, to record his simple, strongly political poems with the backing of the **Equais**, a group he founded. In 1991, obtaining a passport after many refusals, he visited London and was commissioned by BBC television to write a poem on the theme of the history of the struggle against apartheid.

South Africa: Discography

Hugh Masakela Tomorrow (WEA K 254 5734)
Dudu Pukwana In The Townships (Earthworks EWV 5)
Mahlathini and the Mahotella Queens Paris-Soweto (Celluloid DK023)
Mahlathini and the Mahotella Queens Thokozile (Earthworks EWV 6)
Jo'burg City Stars Grooving Jive No. 1 (Globestyle NST 123)
Various The Indestructible Beat of Soweto (Earthworks EWV 14)
Various Thunder Before Dawn (Earthworks EWV 1)
Various Freedom Fire (Earthworks EWV 17)
Various Kings and Queens of Township Jazz (Earthworks EWV 20)
Ladysmith Black Mambazo Shaka Zulu (WEA 25582)
Ladysmith Black Mambazo Two Worlds, One Heart (WEA 7599261251)

Juluka Musa Ukungilandela (Totem 760 440)
Sipho Mabuse Chant of the Marching (Virgin V2582)
Mango Groove Mango Groove (Totem 760 227)
Various Urban Africa (Polydor 841470-1)
Mzwakhe Mbuli Unbroken Spirit (Shifty 2SIF 34)

MADAGASCAR

This large island, stretching a thousand miles North to South off the coast of Mozambique, bears cultural traces of the Southeast Asians who first populated it as well as of Arabs, East Africans, Portuguese, and its eventual colonisers, the French. Modern musical and recording links are with Paris, and its 15,000-strong Malagasy population.

Traditional Malagasy instruments include the little guitarlike kabosy, the marovany (box zither), valiha (tubular zither) and sodina (flute). Masters of these include the late valiha player **Rakotozafy**, who expanded the range of the instrument and whose legendary life (and death in the late 1960s) is well documented on the Globestyle album of his music, and the still highly respected sodina player **Rakotofra**.

The development of modern popular music has been much affected by the island's post-independence (1960) political history. The early 1970s saw a wave of strikes and popular protests, eventually leading to the military coup which ushered in the hardline socialist regime of President Ratsiraka. The wave of nationalism, re-exploration of cultural roots, and rejection of Western influence which accompanied the new government resulted in a rash of new groups, but by the 1980s the economic stagnation and isolation which the new government had created severely limited development of a popular music infrastructure. By 1990, the once booming local record market of the 1970s had all but disappeared.

The modernising groups of the 1970s had recourse to a variety of national dance rhythms including the basese, the salegy and its variant, the sigaoma, the watsa-watsa, influenced by Congolese and Mozambique rhythms, and the sega of neighbouring islands Mauritius and Reunion.

The first group of the new movement, and still Madagascar's most popular, is **Mahaleo**, an eight-piece band originally formed by college students from Antsirabé, the country's second city, who two decades later are doctors (three), sociologists (three) and administrators (two), when not playing. They are followed by **Rossy**, another eight-piece called after the nickname of their leader **Paul Bert Rahasimana**, who play fast, happy dance music based on the mixture of popular sayings and oral poetry known as hain-teny and, like a number of modern groups, using electric valiha; **Tarika Sammy**, who have a similar sound to Rossy, dominated by the plaintive multipart harmony vocals common in Malagasy music; **Jean Emilien**, a singer who plays amplified kabosy and Dylan-style harmonica on a neck-frame; **Jaojoby Eusebe,** an older specialist of the salegy dance rhythm; **Ny Sakelidalana,** an older group of excellent harmony vocalists; and **Les Smockers,** who play in one of the capital Antananarivo's few surviving nightclubs.

Madagascar: Discography

Various Madagascar Vols. 1–4 (Globestyle ORB 012, 013, 027, 028)
Rossy Madagascar (Celluloid 66856)

MAURITIUS AND REUNION

These two large islands, situated in the Indian Ocean east of Madagascar, were colonised in the eighteenth century by the French, who imported slaves from East Africa to work on the sugar plantations. Under the subsequent British occupation of Mauritius, many Indian immigrants arrived in the country. Mauritius became independent in 1968, while Reunion is an overseas département of France, if an increasingly restive one – major riots broke out in 1991 as a result of the closure by the metropolitan authorities of the island's only independent radio station.

The two islands share a similar musical culture, with two distinctive national rhythms and dances. The first is the sega, originally a percussion-based style similar to the Cuban rumba widespread among the slave population and accompanying an erotic dance, which partly accounts for its suppression during the nineteenth century. The traditional sega was accompanied by the shallow, hand-held drum called a ravanne and by the maravanne, a sort of rattle. In the 1950s and 1960s, ensembles began to update their instrumentation with electric guitars and bass and the sega assumed the status of a national dance, with the concomitant danger of the proliferation of saccharine tourist versions. A good number of popular sega singers keep the form alive with a continuing flow of new songs in French Creole, featuring down-to-earth punning or suggestive lyrics and the characteristic fast, lumpy beat. Top names are **Max Lauret, Michel Admette, Roger and Marie-Josée Clency, Pierre Roselli, Jean-Claude Gaspard** and **Compil' Créole.**

The second rhythm/dance is the maloya, a similarly choppy beat. Like the sega, the maloya also involves down-to-earth lyrics, often improvised, and the music is played on home-made or improvised percussion (household utensils, etc.) at popular kabars or community parties. Modern maloya groups such as **Ti-fock** or **Ziskakan** appeared intermittently in Paris during the 1980s, but by the end of the decade the genre's most prominent artistes were the group **Baster,** named after the poor district Basse-Terre from which they come. Originally members of the **Mouvman Kiltiral Basse-Terre** (Creole for Mouvement Culturelle), the group is led by the dreadlocked **Thierry Gauliris** and has made three popular cassettes, featuring songs such as 'Rasine Momon Papa', but no records.

Mauritius and Reunion: Discography

Michel Admette Le Prince du Sega (Piras P5131)
Max Lauret A L'Ombre Des Palmiers (Krissémax MC 086)
Grat Fils Planète Creole (Playa Sound PS 65064)

TANZANIA and ZANZIBAR

More than any other country in East Africa, Tanzania is a meeting-point of cultures. The Indian Ocean coast, with its big cosmopolitan port capital Dar es Salaam, is strongly influenced by the Arab and Indian traders and seamen who have visited it for centuries. The interior of the country borders to the west with Zaire, whose music has been a prime component of modern Tanzanian pop. The politics of the modern state, as outlined in President Nyere's 1967 Arusha Declaration, have had a significant effect on music development. The ujaama antiurbanisation drive has kept rural life strong and thus preserved traditions which might have perished in a rush to the cities. The promotion of the coastal language Swahili as a national language has helped foster nationally acceptable music, as has the active promotion of indigenous arts by trade unions, police and army units, major companies and the government, which in 1973 went so far as temporarily to ban imported music from the radio.

Traditional music survives both at village level and in formally preserved forms. A stronghold of the latter is the country's Bagomoyo College of Arts, where a group of musicians, led by the chirimbo (thumb-piano) player **Hukwe Zawose**, researches and performs the country's musical heritage. Zawose's seven-strong group visited Britain in 1965 to perform and record the album 'Tanzania Yetu'.

In spite of Tanzania's national authenticity policies, the country's popular music has been heavily influenced from outside. In the 1950s, Latin American music had its effect on groups such as the late **Salim Abdullah**'s **Cuban Marimba** and **Morogoro Jazz**. In the 1960s and 1970s, it was Zairean rumba which swept Tanzania. This was partly due to an influx of actual Zairean musicians escaping from unrest and financial hardship at home. Two prime examples are the **Orchestre Makassy** and **Remmy Ongala**'s **Orchestre Matimila**.

Makassy was founded by **MZee Makassy** and included at one point **Mose Se Fan Fan**, who founded the London-based soukous group **Somo Somo**, and who composed the song 'Misese', a favourite in Tanzania. Orchestre Makassy were signed to Virgin Records in Europe in 1983.

The Zairean singer-guitarist **Remmy Ongala** originally moved to Tanzania to join Orchestre Makassy. Soon after arrival he composed his famous song

'Sika Ya Kufa' (The Day I Die), a vividly simple evocation of the African experience of death, written to commemorate a deceased musician friend. The song was a hit for Makassy but Remmy received no royalties, so he joined another band, the Orchestre Matimila, of which he inherited the joint leadership on the death of the businessman-manager who owned the group's instruments and therefore, in effect, the group. Remmy's charismatic presence, distinctly redolent of magic to an African audience, and his powerful 'deep' songs such as 'Sika Ya Kufa', combined with an effective Franco-crossed-with-Tanzanian rhythmic guitar band sound, have made the Orchestre Matimila one of Tanzania's top bands. Following extremely successful tours with the WOMAD organisation in Europe in 1988 and 1989, the band has also built itself a considerable international profile.

Other popular guitar bands include **Milimani Park, Vijana Jazz, Safari Sounds, Juweta Jazz Band**, the **Orchestre Marquise** and the **Orchestre Afriso**.

Tanzania and the big off-shore island of Zanzibar are also the principal centres of the Swahili Arab/African Muslim music, known as taraab, which is also found in Kenya, Mozambique and a number of adjoining states. The name 'taraab', based on the Arabic word 'enchantment' denoting an area of classical Arab music, describes the concert as well as the music, which is strongly associated with weddings. The origins of taraab, which is hugely popular in Zanzibar, are very diverse, but it has as its roots an approximately Egyptian orchestration of violins, 'ouds, tambourines, derbouka-style hand drums, and sometimes the qanun Arabic zither. More recently, electric guitar, bass, keyboards and accordion have been added. Influences earlier this century have included Turkish bandsmen imported by the Sultan of Zanzibar and professional musicians from Goa who were popular entertainers in the 1950s. One of the earliest recording stars of the genre was the female singer **Sitti bit Saidi**, who died in 1950 having achieved great fame for her powerful voice and mildly scandalous behaviour.

Until the Zanzibar revolution in 1964, taraab was performed in all-male social clubs, where the instruments and written stock of songs and music were kept. After the revolution, a period of anti-Arab and anti-élitist feeling led to the suppression of some clubs and the Africanisation of names and texts, which were henceforth entirely in Swahili. Although anti-Arab feeling has since abated, the opening up of the clubs has persisted and many women's organisations now also exist.

A flourishing market for 45 rpm discs and cassettes exists, and in 1988 a recording expedition by the London company Globestyle resulted in a batch of high-quality LPs of some of the most prominent taraab artistes. These include the **Black Star and Lucky Star Musical Clubs** from Tanga, on the Tanzanian coast, which feature a wide range of both more poetic, 'listening' music and the ngoma dance style, performed by a ten-piece group and the star female vocalists **Shakila** and **Sharmila**; **Seif Salim Saleh**, a lutenist and violinist who is also Director of Arts and Culture of Zanzibar and a member of the **National Taraab Orchestra**; **Abdullah Mussa Ahmed**, a renowned qanun player who has performed taraab in, of all places, North Korea; the Orchestra of the **Ikhwani Safaa Musical Club**, Zanzibar's oldest club, which has just reverted to its original Arabic name after being obliged after the revolution to change to the **Malinda Musical Club**. The National Taraab Orchestra visited London in 1985 to perform while the grande dame of taraab, the elderly singer **Bi Kidudé**, performed in France in 1990.

Tanzania and Zanzibar: Discography

Hukwe Zawose Tanzania Yetu (Triple Earth Terra 101)
Orchestre Makassy Agwaya (Virgin V2236)
Remmy Ongala and Orchestre Super Matimila Songs For The Poor Man (Real World 91315-2)
Black Star and Lucky Star Musical Clubs Nyota (Globestyle ORB 044)
Various The Music of Zanzibar, Vols. 1 & 2 (Globestyle ORB 032 & 033)
~~Various~~ Tanzania Dance Bands Vol. 2 (Line MSCD 9011170)

KENYA

As the title of the 1990 Virgin/Earthworks compilation 'Guitar Paradise of East Africa' indicates, Kenyan pop revolves around guitar styles. There are other important elements: the Christian church's strength means there is a strong gospel choir tradition; Muslim Arab-influenced taraab music (see **Tanzania and Zanzibar**) has a considerable Kenyan base in Mombasa, where it has been influenced by Indian film music; former colonial military brass bands have been important.

The 'dry' (acoustic) guitar began to flourish in the 1950s, when Kenyan troops returning from World War II Europe brought with them money, guitars and gramophones. One of the earliest styles was a finger-picked guitar with tapped soft-drink bottle accompaniment, much influenced by the great Zairean Jean-Bosco Mwenda. This style was adopted with particular success by the Luo and Luhya peoples, whose traditional instruments included lyres and harps; it persists today in the light, pretty omutibo music of artistes such as **Shem Tube**.

In the 1960s, two external influences invaded Kenya. The first was the ubiquitous Zairean rumba/soukous, brought by emigrating Zairean musicians and by Kenyans returning from abroad. The second was the heavier South African kwela sound which merged with the simultaneous Western craze of the twist, leading to a spate of Kenyan twist hit singles by **John Mwale** and his **AGS Boys Band**; 'Angelica Twist', 'Amina Twist', and so on. Like virtually all Kenyan pop of the period, Mwale's music was performed in Swahili.

In the mid-1970s a new, more indigenous style, benga, developed and soon became popular throughout the region. Originating among the Luo people, benga incorporated elements of the traditional lyre music, nyatiti, which still sometimes accompanies benga concerts, and a hard, agile bass guitar sound, with a generally Zairean base.

A key figure in the transformation of early acoustic benga into the 1970s and 1980s electric guitar and drum style was **Daniel Owino Misiani**, whose group **Shirati Jazz** (named after their home region) is still doing good business as house band at the River Yala Club outside Nairobi, though their peak days of selling 20,000 singles a month in the 1970s are gone, due to the slump in the record industry. Shirati Jazz's vivid lyrics, in Luo and, occasionally, Swahili, tend to praise, encourage or tell anecdotes about a wide and fascinating range of individuals, a continuation of the Luo praise-singing tradition. Shirati Jazz have several LPs on the European market, including one, 'Benga Beat', recorded live in London in 1987.

Another group to have worked to an extent in Europe is the **Orchestre Virunga**, led by the Zairean singer **Samba Mapangala**, whose early 1980s hit album, 'Malako' was released by Virgin/Earthworks in London in 1984. Remastered and augmented, it was rereleased in 1990, again by Virgin, under the new title 'Virunga Volcano'. Samba Mapangala, who sings in Lingala, Swahili and French, spent much of the late 1980s in Europe, where he mixed with the Paris-African musical milieu and made the four-track mini-album 'Vunja Mifupa' in 1989 with session musicians such as ace Zaireans **Bopol**, **Syran Mbenza**, **Wuta May** and **Passi-Jo**.

Two more major Zairean-majority groups shared the Nairobi limelight in the 1980s. **Les Mangalepa** achieved major success with a tight mixture of virtuoso guitar and brass work, well represented by their track 'Odesia' on 'Guitar Paradise' (see discography), but were decimated by a 1985 Kenyan government clampdown on foreign nationals working in the country. **Orchestra Super Mazembe** ('Earth-movers') scored one of the biggest hits of the eighties with 'Shauri Yako', also on the album 'Guitar Paradise'.

Of the non-Zairean groups, the Swahili language **Les Wanyika** continue to be immensely popular, having created a number of spin-off groups – **Super Wanyika Stars**, **Simba Wanyika** and others – in the manner of Zaire's great Zaiko Langa Langa. Other top Kenyan artistes include **Sukuma Bin Ongaro**, **Daniel Kamau**, the **Famous Nyahururu Boys**, the **Kilimambogo Brothers**, the **Orchestra Vundumuna** and **Orchestra Ibeba System**. The latter two groups acquired Japanese recording contracts in 1989.

Kenya: Discography

Zein Musical Party Mtindo Mombasa (Globestyle ORBD 066)
Shem Tube Abana Ba Nasery (Globestyle ORB 052)
Shirati Jazz Piny Ose Mer (Globestyle ORB 046)
Samba Mapangala and Orchestre Virunga Virunga Volcano (Earthworks EWV 16)
Various Guitar Paradise of East Africa (Earthworks EWV 21)

UGANDA

Ugandan music is primarily influenced by Zairean rumba and by the Kenyan Luo benga sound, both guitar led. The country is economically in dire straits, and AIDS has accounted for the death of a number of musicians, but music does survive. In its more traditional form, it is played by ensembles such as the **Kayaya Players**, the **Ndele Group** and **Aida**, the group led by Willy Mukabya-Aida, featuring flutes, drums, guitars and the local violin known as ndingidi.

Of the more modern guitar and drum groups, **Jimmy Katumba and the Ebonies** are the ensemble most often seen outside the country. Katumba describes his music as 'Imbalu jive'; his deep melodious voice is a central feature of the group's appeal, and tends to steer their repertoire towards ballads. The group's first UK visit in 1982 also featured students of Kampala's Makerere University who transformed their performance into a musical travelogue of Uganda.

Other popular groups in Kampala are the **Philly Lutaya Band**, who, having worked in Sweden for some years, continue in the absence of their deceased leader, the **Afrigo Jazz Band**, whose 'Batunso' ('They've Arrived') was a huge cassette hit in 1990, the **City Dwellers**, the **Mascotts** and **Mutebi and the Thames**.

The Ugandan singer **Geoffrey Oryema** has been based in France since fleeing his country in the boot of a car following the death of his father, a prominent government minister, in a car 'accident' during the Amin dictatorship. Oryema, an intellectual educated partly in Europe and influenced by the likes of Bob Dylan and John Lennon, performs atmospheric, brooding ballads backed by acoustic guitar and thumb-piano; in 1990 he was taken up by the WOMAD organisation and released an LP, recorded in Peter Gabriel's Real World Studios, which also featured Gabriel and Brian Eno.

Uganda: Discography

Geoffrey Oryema Exile (Real World 14)

BURUNDI

The small landlocked state of Burundi is relatively undeveloped and lacks the modern popular industry of bigger, more modernised states. Its traditional drum troupe, however, has made such an impact abroad that it deserves brief description. **Drummers of Burundi**'s music has been sampled by artistes from Joni Mitchell ('The Hissing of Summer Lawns') to Malcolm Maclaren, who used their rhythm for Adam Ant and Bow Wow Wow productions. The drummers, between twelve and twenty in number, are employed by the Burundi Ministry of Culture, although their profession is passed from father to son and, when not playing, they survive as subsistence farmers. The troupe was originally in the service of the king, whom they would accompany through all the ceremonial aspects of his life; now they perform at public ceremonies. Burundi drum culture is ancient and complex, the drums being traditionally stored in sacred lairs, anointed with libations and guarded by a priestess whose role included symbolic sexual union with the king at an annual ceremony. The modern drummers' performance remains an awe-inspiring spectacle, with the gleaming red and white draped drummers maintaining a thunderous beat, using their heavy drumsticks alternately to hit the hide drumskins and to beat against the sides of the great log drums. Meanwhile, two or three drummers leap and twirl athletically around the inkiranya lead drum in the centre of the circle.

Burundi: Discography

Drummers of Burundi Musique de Burundi (Ocora OCK 40)

ETHIOPIA

Modern Ethiopian music is highly distinctive, with its plaintive, quavering pentatonic vocals, funky Amharic soul backing groups and accompanying shoulder-shaking eskeuta dance. Recordings are rare outside the country, however, partly because the music scene within the capital Addis Ababa is impeded by civil war and curfews, and partly because the repressive and suspicious Marxist government of Mengistu Haile Mariam imposed strict censorship and draconian restrictions on the export of tape recordings. Similar restrictions on foreign travel by Ethiopians have prevented a number of performers appearing abroad and have driven others into exile, notably in London and Washington.

Apart from its annexed territory of Eritrea, Ethiopia has never been colonised, and what foreign musical influences exist were deliberately imported. The bands of the Imperial Guard and the police, for example, under Haile Selassie and his predecessors, were responsible for introducing the brass sections which are so strong today. In the 1970s, Ethiopians returning from study abroad brought home new rock and soul ideas; an example is the producer-arranger **Mulatu Astatke**, who worked in London and returned to introduce 'soul-swing' and co-founded the seminal **Wallias Band**, still one of the three top popular groups in Addis. For two decades these groups have been the mainstays of Ethiopian pop. Originally they backed foreign singers appearing at big Addis hotels such as the Hilton, where they were house bands; nowadays they back the top Ethiopian solo artistes, each band featuring three or four top singers. The

Wallias Band, led by **Johannes Tokola**, still plays in the Hilton and backs the older Elvis-equivalent **Alemayu Eshete** as well as younger stars such as **Netsanet Melessa**. The **Roha Band**, with their wonderful Alabama soul sound, also backs older stars **(Mahmoud Ahmed)** and younger **(Neway Debebe)**, while a new young group, the **Ethio-Stars**, have lately arrived on the scene. Traditional Ethiopian music varies according to its province of origin (Tigre, Oromo and Gragué regions all offer distinctive variants) but frequently feature the masenko fiddle and the kraar lyre, which, when amplified, sounds remarkably like a Keith Richard-played Stratocaster. The lyrics of the majority language Amharic song texts are complex and poetic and often employ a double level of meaning, referred to as 'gold versus wax', whereby the same phrase, according to interpretation, may be taken to have a lofty, spiritual 'gold' meaning or an earthier or more idiosyncratic 'wax' meaning. The songs of the deep-voiced traditional poet **Mary Armede** are good modern examples.

The following are the most popular artistes representing modern Ethiopian music today.

Alemayu Eshete, much influenced by James Brown and Elvis Presley, to whom he is often compared, remains reasonably popular after a thirty-year career which started in the 1960s with the introduction of guitars and accordions into the country.

Of a similar vintage is **Tilahun Gessesse**, who started his career in the Army band before launching into the recording of a long succession of hit 45-rpm singles, one of which, 'Yetintu Tizaleng' ('Remember the Old Times'), was covered internationally by Miriam Makeba. A two-year disappearance created rumours of marital problems, nervous exhaustion and conversion to Islam, but in the 1980s Gessesse returned triumphantly to form.

The most popular of the older singers, however, is **Mahmoud Ahmed**, who combines an astute business career running an Addis TV and music shop with a considerable recording and performing career. Trusted by the regime in a way the less canny, more artistic Gessesse is not, Mahmoud Ahmed travels relatively freely and in 1986, when his great hit 'Ere Mela Mela' was released in Belgium, became the first Ethiopian artiste successfully to negotiate the myriad problems of licensing his recordings for external production.

Of the younger male singers **Neway Debebe**, the current star of the Roha Band, is the most important. Debebe, a trained musician with a theatrical background, is a protégé of Ali Tango, a businessman, promoter and proprietor of Addis's Tango Music Shop, and also one of the most influential entrepreneurs of the post-1970s cassette market.

A number of strong female singers are very popular. Chief among them is **Netsanet Melessa,** an outgoing and sociable sometime star of the Wallias Band, with a string of hit cassettes and famous songs to her name. Most famous of all is 'Fawa Fawa Yelal Dodgu', in which she compares the smooth ride of a Dodge car in which she is passenger to the anything but smooth progress of her relationship with its driver. Her main musical rivals in Ethiopia are **Amalmal Abete**, a mellifluous vocalist with the Roha Band who specializes in

Oromo songs as well as Amharic, and **Bezawork Asfew**, whose beautiful rendition of the sad T'Zeta blueslike style was a high point of the BBC-TV documentary on Ethiopia which formed part of the series *Under African Skies*. Several important Ethiopian artistes work outside the country. Best-known of these is the young female star **Aster Aweke**, based since the early 1980s in Washington, DC, where she performs in restaurants and at parties for the substantial Ethiopian community. After a series of successful cassettes – 'Agaré', 'Gomlalé' and 'Wolela' are some of her best-known songs – Aweke recorded an LP in Washington for the London label Triple Earth. The album features mixed Ethiopian, American and British musicians and a light, jazzy soul-rock sound, and Aweke later did several well-received crossover concerts at venues such as Ronnie Scott's.

A collaborator on Aweke's LP, the London-based kraar and keyboards player Kassa Admassu, was the front man for a London Ethiopian band, **Kokeb**. In 1990 Kokeb became the **Niles**, and built a new repertoire combining Ethiopian and Sudanese music with pan-African elements supplied by a Ghanaian drummer.

In the Sudan, meanwhile, the exiled Ethiopian singer **Menelik** became a major star.

Finally, the Rasta connection (the late Haile Selassie being regarded as their spiritual leader by Jamaican Rastas), though generally of little musical or other relevance to Ethiopia, has resulted in Ziggy Marley's backing group, **The Melody Makers**, which includes the excellent Ethiopian musicians **Mulu Gessesse** (guitar), **Zeleke Gessesse** (bass) and **Dereje Mekonnen** (keyboards).

Ethiopia: Discography

Mahmoud Ahmed Ere Mela Mela (Rounder 1354)
Aster Aweke Aster Aweke (Triple Earth Terra 107)
Tukul Band and Ethio Stars Amharic Hits (Piranha PIR 44-2)

SUDAN

Modern Sudanese music, in its delicacy of arrangement, its melodiousness and the poetry of its lyrics, is among the most beautiful in the continent. Although it is becoming increasingly popular in the Arab world and in certain parts of Africa – Nigeria, for example – it is little known in the developed world. The devastation wrought by drought, the civil war in the south and the increasing cultural and political repression following the imposition in 1983 of the harsh Islamic shari'a law have made conditions extremely difficult for musicians, as for everyone else, but the profession is still in good shape. Cassette sales are high, and the demand for groups to play at weddings is strong. The classic test of which singer is most popular is still to visit the Union of Musicians Club in Omdurman, the cultural capital, and wait to see who is most in demand when the heads of families call to ask for a singer for a wedding.

Sudanese traditional music, or haqeeba, is performed by singers and players of the riqq tambourine. Hadeesa, or modern, city music, is accompanied by the 'oud (Arab lute), violin, accordion – introduced from Cairo in the 1920s – and latterly augmented by electronic keyboards, electric guitar and bass, and sometimes brass sections introduced by army and police bands. Songs are in classical or local Sudanese Arabic. In recent decades a gradual Arabisation of Sudanese music has taken place, with quarter tones and septatonic scales joining the traditional Sudanese pentatonic melodies.

The doyen of Sudanese music, **Mohamed Wardi**, sought exile in Cairo in 1990 after his nephew was among a group of army officers executed on suspicion of political opposition to the government. Wardi, then chairman of the Musicians' Union, is a former teacher who took up music in 1957 and has since produced over 300 songs, often, like 'Banadeeha' ('I Call Her') or 'Ors al Sudan' ('Wedding of Sudan'), symbolising his country as a beloved woman. Wardi's lyrics, like those of all the top Sudanese singers, are highly poetic and allusive and are analysed keenly by the public for veiled comment on the state of the nation.

Mohamed Al Amin, one of the best 'oud players in the country, is nicknamed 'the senior clerk' for his writing skills. He too has suffered for his independence of thought, expressed between the lines of songs such as 'Wahayat Ibtissamtak' ('I Swear by your Smile'), having been imprisoned in 1971.

Abdel Karim El Kabli, another of the greats of postwar modern music, started his career as an official in the judiciary, taking up music in 1961 and becoming fully professional only in the early 1980s, when great hits like 'Sukar' ('Sugar') and 'Laou ta Sadiq' ('If You Believe') made him a household name.

Salah Ibn al Badia, on the other hand, is from a rural background, and since 1958 has specialised in simple songs, often based on the traditional dobeit style of poetry, rendered dramatic by his famous high-pitched voice.

Sayed Khalifa, of the same generation, has achieved particular fame outside Sudan by touring the Middle East, Africa and, to a certain extent, Europe. Born in Khartoum, Khalifa is noted for his short, light, pretty songs, of which the most famous is 'Izzeyakum' ('How Do You Do?') which offers greetings in a whole succession of languages.

Two younger artistes, **Abdel Gadir Salim** and **Abdel Aziz El Mubarak**, have combined great popularity at home with a high profile among new European aficionados of African music. Both studied at Khartoum's Institute of Music and Drama. Abdel Gadir Salim, an accomplished 'oud player, combines a successful recording career with teaching; in the late 1980s he was headmaster of the Sudanese school in Njamena, capital of neighbouring Chad. A native of the Western desert province, his songs often eulogise the beauty of the stark hills and gazelles of his home. A fine example is the beautiful 'Maqtool Hawaki Ya Kordofan' ('Your Love Has Killed Me, O Kordofan'), well captured on a 1989 World Circuit album.

Abdel Aziz El Mubarak comes from a family of musicians and a town — Medani, east of Khartoum — famous for its musical culture. Noted from his school days as a fine singer, El Mubarak soon began to perform on Radio Omdurman, for whom he works today, and in 1975 an early song 'Laih Ya Galbi Laih' ('Why, My Heart, Why?') was a national hit. His music is very adaptable; he plays 'oud and performs both with a modern electric group and with more traditional line-ups and uses a range of modern dance rhythms and styles. In 1987 he visited London with an ensemble including the top saxophonist **Hamid Osman Abdalla**, an instructor in the Music Corps of the Sudanese army, a four-man violin section, guitar and bass guitar, accordion, tabla and bongos.

Other new young Sudanese musicians include **Khojali Osman**, a major star whose top songs 'Haba Haba' ('Easy, Easy') and 'Asman Amara' ('Listen Just Once') tend to be written by professional composers and feature a more electric hybrid sound, with reggae among the more traditional rhythms; **Mahmoud Tawer**, performer of the substantial hits 'Al 'ira' ('Jealousy') and 'Bansaqa' ('I'll Forget You'); and **Abou Araqi**.

Sudan: Discography

Mohamed Wardi Untitled (EMI Greece TC SDS 50)
Abdel Karim El Kabli Live (EMI Greece TC SDS 201)
Abdel Gadir Salim and Abdel Aziz El Mubarak Sounds of Sudan (World Circuit 018)
Abdel Aziz El Mubarak Straight From the Heart (World Circuit 010)

EUROPE

INTRODUCTION

Since I was a young child I've been surrounded by both Irish traditional music and more American-based pop music. In fact they go together very well, and Irish music may well be an important root of country music, for example. My early pop music listening was courtesy of my father, who had a showband called Slieve Foy. He played accordion and sax, my mother played piano, and the band used to do Glenn Miller, Nat King Cole, Elvis, the Everleys – everything that was popular in the 1950s and 60s. They used to get sheet music sent from a shop in Derry, which was the nearest city to where we lived in Donegal. Often, in the middle of a dance, when the modern music stopped, they'd play Irish music, and there'd be a bit of a ceilidh. The dances were in public halls, usually, with no licensing – there'd be a minerals bar at the back. I remember going to Glasgow with my father's band for a St Patrick's Day dance, wearing an Irish traditional costume – there are a lot of Donegal emigrants in Scotland – and singing 'My Boy Lollipop' on stage. In 1968 my father bought himself a pub so he could stop touring but still have somewhere to play and that's where Clannad was born. The pub is still going – very much so – and then as now visitors would get up on the stage and perform; people would bring instruments along with them. My brothers and sisters and I would play when we got home from school and gradually the band was formed. I was learning the harp at the time. When we started we played a lot of songs that were internationally popular then – Dylan, the Mamas and Papas, Joni Mitchell – but we also got very interested in collecting the traditional songs of Donegal. We used to go out on expeditions with a tape recorder and a half pack of Guinness and go round talking to the old folks. They'd never just give you the song straight off, they'd have to give you the story of how they came by the song, and then the words, but as a poem, and lastly they'd give you the melody. We collected hundreds of old Gaelic songs in this way, songs which had been preserved by the rich pattern of social events which persisted much later than in most European countries. In Ireland, for example, there were still crossroads dances into this century, where people from different villages would join together and songs and stories were a means of communication. Irish Gaelic songs have a wonderful, very poetic way of putting over the content in pictures, and cryptic images, such as Ireland being described as a woman – just think of 'Nanci mhile grá' ('Nancy of a thousand loves'), or 'Roisín Dubh' ('My Dark Rosaleen').

When we started touring, our music wasn't at all fashionable – there was none of the present pride in people's own culture. We used to avoid England when we toured – we were popular earlier in Germany – and when I first moved to Dublin I was almost afraid of speaking Gaelic in a pub in case people thought I was a redneck – a 'culchie' as you'd be called. Now there's a tremendous interest in Gaelic culture and language. Young people are learning Gaelic again – some other musicians envy us having grown up speaking the Gaelic language. Ireland is also becoming a place of pilgrimage for a new rock generation in the way it has been for years for folk musicians and music lovers. Donegal was always at the centre of it – also people would go down the West Coast to find the great traditional players. Now you can find these sessions in Dublin too – in places like Slattery's, Donnaghue's and Hughs'.

There are, of course, similar traditions elsewhere in Europe – we used to do a lot of European folk festivals, both on and off the Celtic circuit. This is where you would meet up with all the different traditions of folk and could end up singing with a Bulgarian group or playing dance music with Scandinavian fiddle players backstage. One of the great strengths of the Irish is that we've always mingled, got on well with others. That must be part of the reason why you find echoes of Irish music so widely spread.

Máire Ní Bhraonáin

The North

IRELAND

Dublin in 1990 was prominently on the international popular music map, with top non-Irish bands going to the city to make use of the many excellent session musicians and a booming live music scene, with rock musicians playing alongside traditional instrumentalists in pubs and clubs such as Slattery's or The Point. Part of the strength of Irish music is the lack of exclusivity of its audience; traditional and modern musics also mix freely in the record charts. Irish music's high international profile is not new: for centuries the Irish have travelled in search of work, and Irish song has been a crucial ingredient of many hybrid styles abroad. Plausible musicological links have been traced in such arcane directions as North African Berber music, which bears a striking resemblance to the Sean-Nós – old style, unaccompanied song, but one of the clearest family connections is with the United States, where folk and country musics have been strongly infused with Irish melody. It is no coincidence that country and western is immensely popular with the Irish, and home-grown C&W stars include **Big Tom**, a farm labourer's son from the Republic, whose front gates bear Graceland-style wrought iron guitars; **Daniel O'Donnell**, a suave young Donegal star; and **Susan McCann**, the Newry Dolly Parton, who has sung in Nashville's Grand Ole Opry.

If country and western is staple fare in Irish country pubs, it has by no means driven out traditional music, which is still a regular feature of rural bars, particularly on the West Coast. The renowned Irish fiddle playing, dominated in the 1930s and 1940s by the Sligo style of **Michael Coleman**, and in the 1960s by Kerry musicians such as **Dennis Murphy**, is currently, most notably represented by Donegal players, championed by the late **Johnny Doherty**, and starring new young virtuosi such as **Mairead Ní Mhoanaigh** of the group **Altan**, who learnt to play from her father Francie, a well-known local fiddler. Though an internationally travelled recording artiste, she is still from a background in which local stylistic variations were preserved by the difficulty of the twenty-mile journey to another town on an unpaved road.

Discounting purely local traditional musicians, the modern Irish popular music field can be divided into two broad lines, one more traditional, the other rock-based, which nonetheless meet at numerous points.

Seminal to both tendencies were the **Clancy Brothers** who, with **Tommy Makem**, worked variously in traditional groups and 1940s and 1950s dance bands, before becoming an early 1960s feature of New York's Greenwich Village, where they had an immense influence on Bob Dylan and his entire generation of folk artistes. The traditional line descends via the **Dubliners** to the **Chieftains** whose first record in 1964, with its vituoso blend of fiddle, harp, tin whistle, uillean pipes and bodhrán (a shallow hand drum), inspired a new generation of bands such as **De Danaan**, the **Bothy Band** and **Planxty**. Formed in the early 1970s, Planxty were another key group, introducing Balkan instruments such as the bouzouki and counting as members important solo artistes such as **Christy Moore**, subsequently a highly successful singer and sought-after songwriter; **Andy Irvine**, who moved on to develop the Celtic bouzouki sound in the group **Patrick Street**; **Paul Brady**, a cult performer and writer of songs taken up by Dire Straits, Bob Dylan, Tina Turner and many more; and **Davy Spillane**, a brilliant uillean piper who went on to become, with Christy Moore, a founder member of the successful group **Moving Hearts**.

Formed shorty after Planxty, **Clannad**, whose lead singer Máire Ní Bhraonáin was born in the same village in Donegal as Altan's Mairead Ní Mhoanaigh, also straddle the worlds of pop and traditional music as well as being much in demand as composers of dreamily Celtic-tinged film music (their theme music for the TV series *Harry's Game* launched their British chart career in 1985).

The rock strand of Irish music is less distinctively Irish, consisting essentially of rock, blues or whatever precise blend is in question rendered with a certain melodic flair which is indefinably Celtic – the much discussed 'Celtic soul' feel. Its modern doyen is **Van Morrison**, whose 1967 'Astral Weeks' album is still one of its finest expressions. Morrison's collaboration with the Chieftains is also a strong link in the interconnections between traditional and rock, as is that of The Pogues with the Dubliners (on their joint hit single 'Irish Rover') in 1987. With their studiedly rough post-punk renditions of traditional songs, The Pogues were one of the key bands of the 1980s, along with U2, who capitalised on the Celtic affinity with a powerfully melodic electric lead guitar sound. Among numerous other Celtic rock practitioners are **Simple Minds, Hothouse Flowers, Sinéad O'Connor, Energy Orchard, Enya, Fatima Mansions,** the **Waterboys**, the **Men They Couldn't Hang, Brendan Croker and the Five O'Clock Shadows,** and the singer **Ron Kavana,** who performs both solo traditional songs and electric material with his band **Alias Ron Kavana.**

GREAT BRITAIN

Attempting to identify areas of British popular music distinct from the mainstream of Anglo-American/international pop may seem a futile exercise given the crucial position of Irish and British music in forming that mainstream. Nonetheless, there are non-folk artistes deliberately maximising the traditional content of their music and updating folksong. All Irish-tradition bands, even those domiciled in England or Northern Ireland, are listed here under **Ireland**.

ENGLAND

Folk song has been a source of material for popular entertainers since the days of nineteenth-century London music hall, when comedy singers such as **George Leybourne (Champagne Charlie)** and **Harry Clifton** would add their own lyrics – 'Polly Perkins of Paddington Green' – to folk melodies such as 'To Hear The Nightingale'. Mild interest on the part of some folk enthusiasts, and a minor cult around the figure of the Wigan-born 30s to 50s comedy singing star **George Formby**, son of a great music-hall artiste, are the limits of any revival of Music Hall equivalent to that of early French chanson. Pure folk music is for the most part firmly outside the popular music domain, although several major vocal groups – the **Watersons** of Yorkshire and the **Copper Family** of Sussex – perform and record successfully. In the 1980s a number of young musicians began to take up moribund instruments; a fine example is the young Northumbrian bagpipe player **Kathryn Tickell**, much in demand as a session player, and an inspiration to dozens of new, young, would-be pipers.

English-inspired folk-rock bands were led in the 1960s by the **Pentangle**, a 'folk supergroup' featuring bassist **Danny Thompson** and guitarists **John Renbourn** and **Bert Jansch**, and **Fairport Convention**, whose members included **Richard Thompson, Ian Matthews** and the bass guitarist **Ashley Hutchings**. Hutchings, a key figure, left to form first **Steeleye Span** (with singer **Maddy Prior**) and then **The Albion Band**, which worked a great deal with productions in the National Theatre's Cottesloe Hall, and which transmuted into **The Home Service** when Hutchings left, taking the name Albion Band with him. Other important bands were **Blowzabella**, formed in 1978 and featuring hurdy-gurdy (played by **Nigel Eaton**), bagpipes (**Paul James**), drums and assorted wind instruments, and the **Oyster Band**, who mix fiddle and melodeon with electric guitars and drums to play pub-rock versions of Cornish six-hand reels and much else.

A key figure of the new wave of English country music, as the movement including such bands is sometimes called, is the melodeon player **Rod Stradling**. Stradling was much influenced by archive recordings of old English village musicians such as **Scan Tester** in Sussex and **Walter Bulwer** and **Billy Cooper** in Norfolk, a taste later shared by the Leeds punk group the **Mekons**, who joined the tendency. Stradling was a founder member of the groups **Oak**, the **Old Swan Band**, the **English Country Blues Band** and **Tiger Moth**. He also founded the group **Edward the Second** and **the Red Hot Polkas**, who include 'black English music', by which they appear to mean reggae, in their repertoire. A number of these bands suffered from an inability to resist adding blues-guitar parts (1970s English school) to the mix, thereby destroying the distinctive melodic base of the music. Other substantial names in English modern folk music include the veteran guitar and fiddle duo **Martin Carthy and Dave Swarbrick**, the singer **June Tabor, Red Shift, Gas Mark Five**, the **Ran Tan Band**, the **Barely Works** and **Ancient Beatbox**.

SCOTLAND

The pibroch (bagpipe) is not the only instrument at which the Scottish traditionally excel; the Scots harp was revived in the 1970s by players such as **Alison Kinnaird,** and the fiddle has been a speciality of the country since the famous eighteenth-century player **Neil Gow** studied violin in Italy – the major present-day virtuoso is the Shetland player **Aly Bain.**

Contemporary singer-songwriters include **Rab Noakes** and **Dick Gaughan,** a graduate of the 1960s and 70s Celtic folk groups **Boys of the Lough** and **Five Hand Reel. The Battlefield Band** is an interesting four-man group combining the young virtuoso bagpipe player **Iain McDonald,** from a famous family of pipers, with fiddle, guitar and electronic keyboards, while the duo of **Hamish Moore and Dick Lee** have intriguingly blended pipes with jazz saxophone and clarinet.

GERMANY and AUSTRIA

Former West Germany has long been an efficient producer of more or less muzak-level international pop, such as the **James Last Orchestra** in the 1960s, **Milli Vanilli** in the 80s, while former East Germany shared the Soviet bloc's legacy of fascination with American rock on the part of young people and mixed incomprehension and persecution on the part of the authorities. The result is a unified Germany with well-developed heavy metal and Euro-pop/dance scenes, but also two interesting areas of music making.

The first is popular song in the tradition of **Kurt Weill,** the spirit of which is very much alive in the new interest in cabaret, displayed both in the rash of small Berlin cabarets and major productions by impresarios such as Andre Heller. Weill was a key commposer in 1930s and 1940s European song, not only collaborating with Bertolt Brecht in Berlin on popular works such as *Mahagonny* and *The Threepenny Opera,* but also contributing to Parisian chanson (songs for Florelle and Lys Gauty) and New York musicals with Ira Gershwin. Half a dozen years after the death, aged 93 in 1981 of Weill's most famous interpreter, his wife, the deep-voiced Austrian singer and actress Lotte Lenya, a new young artiste began to claim the position of foremost Weill specialist. **Ute Lemper,** daughter of a Münster banker, first attracted international attention in Paris, playing Sally Bowles in a Jerome Savary production of *Cabaret.* Her Dietrich looks went on to conquer firstly the demanding Kurt Weill Foundation, who sponsored her series of recordings of the composer's stage works, and later the general public.

A further link with the Brecht-Weill legacy is the work of **Wolf Bierman,** the Hamburg-born satirical balladeer who moved to the newly created East

Berlin in 1952 as a socialist sympathiser. He became a brilliantly caustic thorn in the flesh of the East German government, while simultaneously becoming a cult hero in the West, to which he was expelled in 1976 after singing his anti-Secret Police song 'Stasi-Lied' in Cologne.

Among modern German rock/ballad singers, **Herbert Grönemeyer** and **Udo Lindenberg** stand out as distinctively German by virtue of lyrical preoccupations, but not especially music, while certain groups use strongly regional dialects in an otherwise standard rock setting − an example is **BAP**, who sing in the Kölsch dialect of Cologne.

The second interesting trend is the revival or modernisation of regional folk musics, which is undertaken by equivalents of the Oyster Band (see UK), such as the East Berlin group **Jams**. It is particularly strong in the Alpine regions, where the diversity of musical forms, which once varied from valley to valley, have been almost replaced by a uniform, commercial Alpine folk style, and of course by modern pop. In Bavaria, scores of young amateur 'Stubenmusik' ensembles now follow the lead of the pioneering **Sepp Eibl** group in recreating mid-nineteenth century folk styles, while other professional groups are involved in creative updating. Among the best are **Biermosl Blosn**, a trio featuring trumpet and accordion who graft provocative new lyrics on to traditional music; **Rudi Zapf**, a hammer dulcimer player who includes traditional songs in a repertoire also featuring jazz and classics; **Georg Glasl**, a similarly inventive young zither soloist; and **Die Interpreten**, a trio from a jazz/avant garde theatre background, who use tenor and baritone saxophones and drums to produce a lively, somewhat parodic, but successful music, described very aptly in one German press article as sounding 'as if Albert Ayler got lost and ended up in a Bavarian beer tent.'

Over the border in Austria, similar endeavours include **Roland Neuwirth**'s updating of the old Viennese 'schrammel musik', and the duo of **Markus Binder** and **Hans-Peter Falkner**, from the cider country around Linz, playing either as **Attwenger** or **Die Goass** (The Goat), who bring a raucous, minimal and thoroughly appropriate post-punk sensibility to bear on the Öberösterreich dances − polkas, landler and schleininger, which they bash out lustily in local inns on drums, tuba and Styrian accordion, the latter played with wah-wah pedal.

SCANDINAVIA

The northern countries of Norway and Sweden have a folk heritage very similar to that of northern Soctland − a Shetland musician would feel entirely at home in either country − and an extremely strong and living fiddle tradition. Village musicians (spelman in Swedish, spellemann in Norwegian), playing either standard violin or the Norwegian variant, the Hardanger fiddle, used to provide music for all social occasions from weddings to Saturday night parties, and a number still perform a village role, obviously reduced in scope but not entirely artificial. The Swedish master musicians **Laggar Anders** and **Rojas Jonas Andersson**, who toured and taught young urban musicians, also continued to play at dances in their home village of Boda into the 1970s. In addition, numerous young urban folk and folk-rock groups modernise the tradition: prominent Swedish examples are **Filarfolket, Norrlatar, J.P. Nyströms, Burträskarna** and **Gunfjauns Kapell**.

In the Northern region of Lapland (known in its native language as Sámiland), which is divided between Norway, Finland, Sweden and the USSR, a number of young Sámi artistes began in the 1980s to incorporate features of traditional music, including the joik song style with its circular breathing techniques and its similarities to Inuit (Eskimo) song, into a modern musical setting. Chief among these is **Mari Boine Persen**, whose Virgin/Real World album 'Gula Gula', with its multinational ragout of instruments and dramatic vocals, provided her with an entrée to European world music circles in 1990. The Sámi group **Pohjanhtahti** offer a more traditional sound.

Of the highly derivative Scandinavian rock groups, many of whom have English names, Finland's have latterly displayed most originality, in the shape of bands such as the **Sugarcubes** and **22 Pisterpirkko**. Top 1970s Swedish favourites **Abba** look set to join Liberace and Queen in the all-time pantheon of kitsch, with an Australian quartet in satin flares and pageboy haircuts doing excellent business impersonating them.

Northern Europe: Discography

Altan The Red Crow (Green Linnet GL 1109)
Patrick Street Irish Times (Special Delivery SPD 1033)
Clannad Anam (RCA PD 74762)
Ron Kavana Home Fire (Special Delivery SPD 1043)
Various Tap Roots – A History of the New Wave of English Country Dance Music (Folk Roots FROOT 002)
Battlefield Band Home Ground (Temple Records TP034)
Laggar Anders and others Authentic Swedish Fiddle Music (Sonet SNIF 740)
Mari Boine Persen Gula Gula (Real World RW 13)
Filarfolket 1980–1990 (Amaltha AM76)
Ute Lemper Ute Lemper Sings Kurt Weill (Decca 425204)
Die Interpreten Nicht Ganz Sauber! (Trikont US 00172)
Attwenger Most (Trikont US 0174)

The South

FRANCE

Heavily influenced by successive waves of American styles – jazz, pop, rock – French popular music nevertheless retains a good deal of national character. As elsewhere in Europe, the eighties have witnessed a variety of young French groups looking back to earlier periods for inspiration.

France is particularly rich in regional folk styles, of which a number of groups are creating modernised versions. This movement began in the early 1970s; the Breton harp player **Alain Stivell** was a pioneer, as was the group **Malicorne**, led by former Stivell collaborators **Gabriel** and **Marie Yacoub**, which mixed electric guitars and drums with traditional and ancient instruments such as crumhorns, rebecs, bagpipes and hurdy-gurdies. Malicorne made a number of big-selling records, including 'L'Extraordinaire Tour de France d'Adelard Rousseau' and 'Le Bestiaire', before breaking up in 1987, leaving leadership of the strong Breton folk-rock field to **Tri Yann**, whose act features giant marionettes and extravagant costumes.

Another flourishing regional genre is that of Corsican polyphonic singing, for centuries an art of shepherds or priests, which had faded into the custodianship of the male members of a few families – **Rocchi, Guelfucci** – before attracting a new generation of singers, male and female, often from the University of Bastia, in the 1970s. The landmark group **Canta U Populu Corsu** was followed by others such as **I Muvrini** and **Nouvelles Polyphonies Corses**: the latter's 1991 recording 'Giramondu' featured traditional songs with synthesizer and other electronic additions by John Cale, Ryuichi Sakamoto and Manu Dibango.

Prominent among the traditional instruments of the regions of France – the hurdy-gurdy of Savoie, the oboe of Languedoc, the various Basque drums – is the musette bagpipe known in the Auvergne as a 'cabrette'. It is this instrument which gave its name to the popular nineteenth- and early twentieth-century Parisian bal musette dance halls, whose traditions are claimed as influences by a new crop of young groups such as **Les Negresses Vertes**. Instrumentally, the accordion superseded the musette as the distinctive element of the bal musette band around 1910. The originator of this development was **Charles Peguri**, son of an Italian accordion maker, who took over from the Auvergnat cabrette player and proprietor of the early Bal Bouscat, starting a trend followed by famous musette accordionists such as **Emile Vacher**, the Belgians **Marceau** and **Deprince** and later virtuosi such as **Marcel Azzola (Jacques Brel**'s accompanist), **Richard Galiono (Barbara**'s), **Yvette Horner** and, of the latest generation, **Corinne Rousselet**. The accordion is taken seriously in France, as in Russia: its best practitioners play not only dance music at bals populaires all over France, but also a classical repertoire by **Saint-Saëns, Gounod** and others. One of the accordion's most colourful stars is **Yvette Horner**, whose legendary 1950s tours launched a thousand press photos of her standing up in the back of her open car and sold hundreds of thousands of records. The advent of rock relegated the accordion to pariah status among the chic young, but Yvette Horner's 1990 Paris revue featured her in parodic costumes by the madly chic (and more than a little kitsch) couturier Jean-Paul Gaultier, while the music included an accordion version of Michael Jackson's 'Bad' and a rap piece choreographed for breakdancers. None of the new young rock-musette accordionists, it must be said, can hold a candle to the aforementioned artistes in terms of technique.

The distinctively French chanson, which term bears much greater depth of meaning than merely 'song', is a central element of French popular music. It is experiencing a return to fashion in both its romantic and realist forms as well as in modern equivalents of its various hybridisations, for example with jazz in the 1950s. Chanson's character lies in the poetry and feeling of the lyrics and, like Italian song, in their phrasing, the way the words occupy and shape the melody.

The chanson realiste, an important strand of the genre, dates back to the songs of Parisian low life half shouted, half sung by **Aristide Bruant** in belle époque cabarets such as Le Chat Noir (and still prized many decades later in renditions such as **Veronique Sanson**'s 1970s recording of Bruant's 'St Lazaire', about the prostitutes' prison of that name).

Bruant was succeeded in the 1920s by now-legendary female singers such as **Mistinguett**, who created at the Moulin Rouge the famous Apache (ruffian) dance, **Fréhel**, noted for her degenerate youth and the litre of red wine she kept on the piano as she sang, and **Yvette Guilbert**, a vastly popular 'diseuse' whose sardonic, drawled delivery made songs such as 'La Soularde' and 'Madame Arthur' internationally famous.

The early 1920s saw the singer **Gaby Deslys** return from New York to introduce a jazz shading to chanson; this was notably developed by the duo **Charles et Johnny**. The latter became the famous swing singer **Johnny Hess**, beloved of the 'zazou' wide boys and the former the even more famous singer-songwriter-poet **Charles Trenet** ('La Mer'), whose 1989 comeback concerts at the age of 76 attracted a new, fashionable young Parisian audience. In the 1930s **Jean Sablon**, the 'French Bing Crosby', was the first artiste to introduce a new, soft, microphone-oriented singing style to chanson, leading to the abandonment of the old, mannered, operatic delivery, with its exaggeratedly rolled 'r's', of singers like **Edith Piaf**.

The 1950s and 60s saw a new crop of chansonniers: the earthy and satirical **Georges Brassens**; the bleak and intense Belgian-born cult figure **Jacques Brel**; the Chaplinesque singer-songwriter (for Piaf and Chevalier, at first) **Charles Aznavour**; the people's actor and left-wing champion **Yves Montand**; the Left

Bank intellectual-Bohemian **Juliette Greco** and the soulful, romantic **Barbara**. Two more key names bridged the gap between chanson and the wave of Anglo-American pop that became known in France as 'yé yé'. **Leo Ferré** became a respected father figure to the new young musicians – in 1968 he recorded an album of his songs ('La Solitude', 'Le Chien') with a pop group named **Les Zoos** – and, above all, **Serge Gainsbourg**, who opted to embrace new forms rejected by other stars of chanson. Gainsbourg (born Lucien Ginsburg), a Beaux-Arts educated intellectual and archetypal Rive Gauche figure, started his career in the 1950s much influenced by the High Bohemian dandy-surrealist-musician-novelist **Boris Vian**. He became controversially famous for his droll, libertine persona and his lyrics, cynical, worldly and sexually suggestive. A prolific and much sought-after writer, Gainsbourg benefited from the publicity-attracting interpretations of his songs by a number of young chanteuses: **France Gall**'s demure, straight-faced 1965 version of 'Annie Aime Les Sucettes' (sucette – from sucer, to suck – meaning lollipop) and his steamy 1969 duet with **Jane Birkin** on 'Je T'Aime, Moi Non Plus'. While Gainsbourg, whose death in 1991 was met by national mourning, embraced many other styles (including his equally controversial 1979 reggae reworking of the French national anthem), the girl singers he wrote for constituted what was almost a subgenre of chanson, characterised by its breathy juvenile sex appeal. Other noted practitioners of this style were **Françoise Hardy** in the 1960s and **Vanessa Paradis** (also a singer of Gainsbourg compositions) in the late 1980s.

In the 1970s and 80s, the spirit of the chanson française had to compete with the internationalising impetus of American rock. Nevertheless, it remained present, and in somed cases dominant, in the work of top male artistes such as **Jacques Higelin**, **Patrick Bruel**, **Julien Clerc**, **Michel Sardou**, the evergreen **Johnny Hallyday**, whose early cover versions (such as 'C'est Le Mashed Potatoes') gave way to a substantial style of his own, and **Francis Cabrel**, whose romantic southern chanson has resonances of the ancient 'romances' singers of the Pays d'Oc. On the female side, the romantic line of Piaf, Barbara and Sanson has descended to new rock artistes such as **Patricia Kaas**, 1990's biggest-selling French artiste abroad, whose hits include chansons such as 'Les Hommes Qui Passent' by the ubiquitous new composer **Didier Barbelivien**. Young 'retro' specialists include **Juliette**, who performs Barbara songs, **Marie-France**, a Parisian singer-actress who reprises old chansons as well as 60s yé yé, and **Liane Foly**, whose genre is 1940s and 50s chanson-jazz.

A further, if somewhat tenuous area of chanson heritage is found among the collection of post-punk/independent rock groups of the eighties who adopted certain features of musette and chanson – chiefly accordion and vulgar street lyrics, either realist or surrealist – as part of a mix often also including Latin or North African touches. The most successful of these is **Les Negresses Vertes**, an eight-piece formed in 1987 of part-southern, part-Parisian, squatter-alternative circus-performance artiste stock, whose 'Zobi La Mouche', a saucy tale of a wandering zazou fly, gained them international attention. Other members roughly within this tendency include the two pioneering groups of singer-songwriter **François Hadji-Lazaro**, the **Garcons Bouchers** and **Pigalle**; the ska-musette practitioner **Blanchard**; retro stylists **Haine et ses Amours**; **Les Têtes Raides**; the comic jazz-chanson group **VRP**; and the talented original music-hall revivalists **Les Endimanchés**. **Mano Negra**, a group composed of friends and fellow travellers of Les Negresses Vertes, have followed the latter's mainstream success with a blend containing fewer chanson and more Latin elements.

Latin music, especially Spanish flamenco, is one of four significant minor strands of French popular music. The south of France has a substantial population of Spanish, often gypsy, origin whose music periodically infiltrates the national pop domain, often via the summer parties of the geographically close Côte D'Azur beau monde. The 1960s flamenco guitarist **Manitas de Plata**, a favourite of St Tropez-dwellers such as Brigitte Bardot, was a case in point, and the **Gipsy Kings**, from the Reyes and Baliardo families whose members also include Manitas de Plata's singer **José Reyes**, are the 1980s most striking example. The six Gipsy Kings had been together for fifteen years, playing a light flamenco-rumba in the style of Spanish pop-flamenco artistes such as **Peret** and **Los Chunguitos**, when the general vogue for things Spanish (Barcelona, bullfighting, etc.) and the support of the trendsetting Paris station Radio Nova in 1987 boosted their records 'Djobi Djoba' and 'Bamboleo' (see **Venezuela**), to first national and later international hit status. A substantial number of similar artistes includes **Roé**; **Malou**; the Gipsy Kings protégés **Alma de Noche**; and rock acts such as Corazon Rebelde, Los Carrayos and Ricky Amigos which include token flamenco touches in their sound.

The second external source of influence is Italy. The smoother, Italian accordion sound has entered the French tradition, as have the vocal styles of chanson artistes of Italian origin, from **Tino Rossi** through **Serge Reggiani** to **Enrico Macias**. The third influence is North African. Though all of the distinctively Algerian (such as raï) and Moroccan musics recorded in Paris are described here under **Algeria** and **Morocco**, a number of decidedly French artistes have Maghrebin blood or musical traits. These include Edith Piaf, brought up and tutored until age eighteen by her Kabyle dancer grandmother, the 1950s cabaret artiste and Boris Vian interpreter **Mouloud Dji**, modern 'beur' (second-generation Algerian immigrant) rock groups such as the Lyonnais **Carte de Séjour**, and artistes such as the Moroccan Jewish writer and singer **Sapho**.

Finally, the French Caribbean islands, notably Martinique and Guadeloupe, though described here separately, are constitutionally part of France and their musics have been a part of 'metropolitain' entertainment from the creole biguine orchestras of **Alexandre Stellio** in the 20s to the pop-zouk of French Eurovision representative **Joelle Ursull** in 1990.

France: Discography

Malicorne Legende (Hannibal HN 1360)
Nouvelles Polyphonies Corses Giramondu (Phonogram 848 515-1)

Various Top de l'Accordeon (EMI 791 3764)
Fréhel Tel qu'il Est (EMI C178 15410)
Charles Trenet Integrale 1937–63 (EMI 1555692)
Charles Aznavour Les Grandes Chansons (Trema 710311)
Juliette Greco Les Feuilles Mortes (EMI 7903822)
Francis Cabrel Sarbacane (CBS 463462)
Patricia Kaas Scene De Vie (CBS 466746)
Liane Foly Reve Orange (Virgin 30778)
Les Negresses Verts M'lah (Rhythm King LEFT LP11)
The Gipsy Kings Gipsy Kings (PEM 15501)

SPAIN

The music of the southern region of Andalucia, particularly flamenco, is often regarded as synonymous with Spanish music in general. This is a fallacy, although one that the Spanish authorities encouraged for many years. Southern music is, however, highly distinctive and is the style which has best adapted to modern times and influences. For these reasons it dominates an account of the country's indigenous popular music.

Flamenco itself was, and is, a genuinely popular music. Product of a tangle of gypsy, Indian, Judaeo-Arab, early European and Moorish roots, it grew up among the gypsy butchers, cane weavers and blacksmiths of the Seville-Jerez-Granada triangle and after a disreputable start infiltrated polite entertainment in the classic blues-tango manner. At its best an impromptu, communal form – until the 1950s it was common in the bars of gypsy districts, such as Cadiz's La Viña barrio, for people to drop in and hire a couple of singers for a 'juerga' – party – at home. In the mid-nineteenth century flamenco moved into the new 'café cantates' of the cities and the first professional star performers – **El Planeta, El Fillo, El Loco Mateo** – appeared on the scene. From this period dates the cuadro flamenco – the troupe of between four and a dozen singers, guitarists and dancers, taking turns at solos, still found in the staged flamenco tablao shows which are probably the least interesting of the current manifestations of the art.

Between the 1920s and 1960s flamenco was at an artistic low point, with a proliferation of shallow, glossy stage shows, although private gypsy gatherings and a number of great performing artistes, first **Manuel Torre**, then later **Tomás Pavón** and **La Niña de los Peines** and lastly **Antonio Mairena** and **Manolo Caracol** carried the torch. The Franco years were damaging to flamenco in that the dictator promoted a sanitised, saccharined image of Andalucian music, politically uncontentious, colourful and attractive to tourists, thereby damning the music in the eyes of progressive youth.

A revival of fashionable interest in flamenco, and allied Southern cultural manifestations such as bullfighting, began in the 1960s, gathered pace in the

1970s and boomed in the 1980s. This phenomenon was partly linked to the death of Franco in 1975, the first years of democracy and the election of a Southern-dominated socialist government in 1984, all of which removed the last trace of Franquist stigma from the music. Its focus was provided by the rise of two new star performers, the guitarist **Paco de Lucia** and the singer **El Camaron de la Isla**.

Paco de Lucia, a gacho (non-gypsy) from Algeciras, studied guitar obsessively from the age of twelve and at fourteen won his first prize at the Jerez Catedra de Flamencologia (in his precociousness as well as his playing style he was a trendsetter: the ten-year-old **Jerónimo Maya** began the 1990s as the latest of a line of guitar prodigies). De Lucia started out accompanying classic cantaores (singers) such as **Fosforito** and **La Niña de la Puebla**, and mastered a large repertoire of substyles – the seguiriyas and soléas of the cante jondo (deep song) – as well as lighter forms such as fandangos and bulerías (his speciality). His breakthrough to major fame, however, was achieved with his 1974 recording 'Entre Dos Aguas' and came as a result of his mingling these forms with newer flamenco cantes chicos (little songs), particularly the rumbas, colombianas and milongas (musica de revuelta – returned music) which had re-entered the flamenco canon after transmutation in the Latin American colonies, and with jazz and rock. (Chick Corea, John McLaughlin and Al di Meola are noted collaborators of de Lucia, as is Placido Domingo on the tenor's 1989 venture into the popular market.)

José Monge Cruz, better known as El Camaron de la Isla (the Isla de Leon is near his Cadiz birthplace and 'camaron', meaning 'shrimp', refers to his skinny frame) has made this eclectic modernised sound (arguably) an acceptable feature of flamenco puro, with his use of musicians such as **Paco de Lucia** and the ground-breaking Catalonian bass guitarist **Carles Benavent**. Camaron, from a gypsy blacksmith family, is a mercurial, charismatic individual, capable of attracting huge audiences of mixed gypsy families and leather-clad youths, the personification of the new drug-consuming convergence of gypsies and rock fans. At his best, backed only by a guitarist such as his main 1980s accompanist **José Fernandez 'Tomatito'**, Camaron is a magnificently soulful, purist's cante jondo singer, but his recordings continue to be both adventurous and hugely popular; the 1989 best-seller 'Soy Gitano' featured the Royal Philharmonic Orchestra.

Modern flamenco is performed in four principal settings; private, mainly gypsy, weddings and other fiestas; tablaos varying from the purely tourist to the serious, such as Madrid's Casa Pata; organised concert-hall art flamenco such as the government-sponsored **Cumbre Flamenca** troupe which tours internationally; the dozens of government-subsidised festivals and competitions such as the prestigious Festival del Cante de las Minas in Murcia which take place throughout the south every summer. Current top performers from the older generation are cantaores **Pepe de la Matrona, Fernanda and Bernada de Utrera, Chocolate, Fosforito, Chano Lobato** and **Juana la del Revuelo** and tocaores (guitarists) **Niño Ricardo, Melchor de Marchena** and **Diego del Gastor** (the great **Sabicas** having died in 1990). Top names from the younger generation are singers **Enrique Morente, El Lebrijano, El Cabrero, Vicente Soto, Antonio Carbonel, Maite Matín, Aurora Vargas, Chiquetete**, and **El Turronero** and guitarists **Manolo Sanlúcar, Paco del Gastor, Gerardo Nuñez, Antonio Carbonel, Vicente Amigo**, and the various members of the **Habichuela** family.

An interesting, if minor, recent development has been the series of collaborations between flamenco artistes and Arab musicians, especially Moroccan Andalus orchestras whose musical tradition dates from the Arab occupation of Andalucia. The first such experiment was by the singer **Lole Montoya**, who recorded the classic Egyptian song 'Anta Omri', by Mohamed Abdel Wahab, in 1977. This was followed by **José Herredia Maya**'s 'Macama Jonda' with the **Orchestra Andaluza of Tetuan** in 1983, and El Lebrijano's 'Encuentros' with the **Orchestra Andaluza of Tangiers** two years later. Apart from flamenco fusions, the Valencian neo-medievalist group **Al Tall** has recorded with the Moroccan black gnaoui enesemble **Muluk El Houa**.

In addition to the development of flamenco puro, the new sound of flamenco rock created a lot of interest in the 1980s. This hybrid was a continuation of the fast, light pop rumba, first popularised in the sixties by the Catalan gypsy singer **Peret** and the Madrid singer-guitarist **Tijeritas** and followed by the seminal groups **Smash** and **Triana**, who grafted flamenco guitar onto a seventies rock base. The early seventies saw a new crop of groups composed of young gypsies from the run-down peripheral barrios of Madrid playing rough, vital semi-flamenco rumba backed with guitars and drums. The leaders of the movement, which was christened the Caño Roto sound after their district of origin, were **Los Chorbos**, who were followed by the female group **Las Grecas** and the two most popular bands **Los Chichos** and **Los Chunguitos**. A variant was provided by the Galician gypsy singer **El Luis**, whose 'Gitano Soul' LP attempted a sort of amalgam of James Brown and El Camaron.

Los Chichos and Los Chunguitos continue to be extremely popular; by the mid-1980s they had discarded their original rough ghetto image for a tuxedo look and were scoring regular gold discs. These included live double albums, boasting a mixture of flamenco and guest rock artistes, such as Los Chunguitos' 'Vive A Tu Manera' with the rock singer **Alaska** and the semi-flamenco artistes **Ana Reverte, Tijeritas** and **Azucar Morena**, and Los Chichos' 'Y Esto Es Lo Que Hay' with the ballad singers **Carlos Cano** and **Joaquin Sabina** and the guitarist Gerardo Nuñez. Both groups have younger family members continuing in the flamenco-rock vein. The **Salazar** brothers of Los Chunguitos saw their glamorous sisters, **Encarna** and **Toñi**, who operate as **Azucar Moreno** (Brown Sugar), achieve major success in the Spanish-speaking world with their 1990 album 'Bandido'. 'Bandido' benefited cannily from the wave of Spanish interest in salsa at the time, featuring as it did covers of the 1988 erotic salsa smash 'Ven Devorame Otra Vez' and the old Tito Puente/Santana number 'Oye Como Va'. At the same time **Aurora**, the daughter of Los Chorbos' founder member **Amador Losada**, released an LP entitled 'Besos de Caramelo', featuring top flamenco-fusionist artistes such as the ubiquitous Carles Benavent on bass and various members of **Ketama** (see below).

A key role in the intermingling of the worlds of flamenco and rock was played by the singer-songwriter **Kiko Veneno**. The son of a military family, he grew up in Seville in the 1960s and 70s attuned, like most hip urban youngsters, to the unfolding, and at first forbidden, Anglo-American rock scene. His first serious look at flamenco was a result of a visit to San Francisco, where an American flamenco fan questioned him about the legendary flamenco town of Morón de la Frontera, near Seville, which he had never visited. On his return to Spain, Veneno began to listen to his native music; in 1977 his punk-based album 'Veneno' featured flamenco guitars played by the brothers **Rafael** and **Raimundo Amador**, young Sevilleans from a renowned gypsy flamenco family. 'Veneno' was an immensely influential album, and its author continued his intermittent and irreverent updating of Andalucian culture with other artistes such as **Martirio** (see below) whose first record he produced.

Two important new groups dominated flamenco-rock in the eighties. Raimundo and Rafael Amador founded **Pata Negra** (Black Leg, a reference to the choicest cut of Andalucian ham), whose recording career was launched with a successful mini-LP 'Guitarras Callejeras', followed up by 'Blues de la Frontera'. Pata Negra's somewhat uneasy mix of acoustic flamenco and electric rhythm and blues guitars attracted a lot of attention, but differences between the brothers made for an unreliable career, with the group periodically dissolving and re-forming minus one brother (usually Rafael). A less blues-rock and more rumba and Latin and even Brazilian-based style was adoped by the Jerez group **Ketama**, composed of young members of two more eminent gypsy flamenco families, the **Sotos** and the **Carmonas**. Ketama, named after a Moroccan village whose hashish is very popular with young Spaniards, achieved considerable success with their albums 'Ketama' and 'Y Es Ke Me Han Kambiao Los Tiempos' as well as their collaboration in the group **Songhai** with the Malian kora player Toumani Diabaté and the English bassist Danny Thompson.

Another genre which returned to fashion in the 1980s, having elements of flamenco but entirely distinct from it, was the composite variously referred to as the tonadilla or cancion española. Analogous in some ways with the French chanson, the tonadilla developed in the 1920s and 30s in the hands, notably, of the great Sevillean composer **Manuel Quiroga** who, with his lyricists **Antonio Quintero** and **Rafael de Léon**, wrote dozens of songs – 'Tatuaje', 'Ojos Verdes', 'Francisco Alegre' – which have become standards. Throughout the 1940s and 1950s the voices of top female tonadilleras such as **Juanita Reina**, **Marifé de Triana**, **Rosita Ferrer**, **Imperio Argentina** and the queen of the genre, **Conchita Piquer**, animated the radios of ordinary families across the country. They were succeeded by a later generation of glossy showbiz equivalents, notably **Lola Flores** and **Rocio Jurado**, who is still a major star today. In its melody and frequent use of guitars or castanets, the tonadilla was very much a part of the Andalucian-dominated image of Spanish popular culture and it suffered the same Franquist association and consequent intellectual rejection in the 1950s and 60s. Young Andalucian artistes were mainly responsible for its return to fashion in the 1980s. As with music-hall styles elsewhere (see for example Yvette Horner, **France**) a certain ironic, kitsch or camp sensibility characterised part of the young avant-garde's attraction to the tonadilla. The star director Pedro Almodovar, for instance, much attracted to the gaudy, melodramatic Catholic south, featured snatches of old tonadillas in his films, and one of the first new artistes to dabble in the genre was the singer Martirio, a member of the Sevillean movida famous for her semi-kitsch, semi-surreal neo-Andalucian costume of lace mantilla, giant sculptural hair combs and RayBans. Martirio (real name Isabel Quinones Gutierrez) also incorporated elements of flamenco and rock into records such as 'Estoy Mala' produced by Kiko Veneno, an Andalucian Jean-Paul Goude to her Grace Jones. In addition to Martirio's part tongue-in-cheek, part serious contributions, a number of other young singers began to make the revived tonadilla as much a feature of Madrid's live music bars as blues had been in the seventies. Chief names are **Tona Olmedo, Maria Vidal, Trinidad Iglesias, Candela** and **Luisa San Leandro**. On a national recording level, the cancion española features in the repertoire of the Sevillean balladeer **Carlos Cano**, the Catalans **Ana Reverte** and **Maria del Monte**, the southern duo **Paco Ortega** and **Isabel Montero** and the young **Maria Maria**, among others. A further slight overlap links the repertoire of 1950s cancion española with that of the modern balladeers, themselves descended from the Spanish, Cuban and Mexican bolero singers of the 1950s. **Julio Iglesias** is a huge star across the Spanish-speaking world, although his style is now internationalised Las Vegas rather than distinctively Spanish.

The 1980s vogue for Andalucian culture had one more major musical aspect in the nationwide craze for the Sevillanas dance and its accompanying songs. The dance 'por Sevillanas' originated in medieval Castile and was assimilated into Seville as one of the flamenco cantes chicos. It took two forms, each linked to a different setting. The first was the Sevillana corralera, performed with guitar and palmas (hand-claps) in the courtyards of country houses. Its greatest modern exponent was **Francisco Palacios**, **'El Pali'**, an archetypal cigar-smoking, sherry-loving pure Sevillean whose twenty LPs sold hundreds of thousands of copies and who died in 1988, shortly after the release of his final record, 'El Trovador de Sevilla'. Other prominent performers of this style include **El Mani** and **Tato Ramirez**. The second form of Sevillana is the rociera, associated with the annual spring pilgrimage in honour of the Virgin of El Rocio, a village in the Guadalquivir estuary. The Rocio, as the pilgrimage is known, boomed in popularity in the 1980s, with attendances of over a million. Prominent in the rociera culture of polka-dot dresses, decorated horse carriages and all-night sherry-fuelled revelry are the Sevillanas rocieras, with their stirring if syrupy multiple-Olé choruses. Every spring, dozens of new albums of rociera songs appear, the top contenders selling huge quantities. Among the many specialist groups are **Los Cantaores de Hispalis; Los Amigos de Gines; Los Marismeños; Los Romeros de la Puebla** and **Los Hermanos Reyes**.

The rock and pop music scene which has exploded in Spain in the 1970s and

80s models itself on the American-International mainstream, though certain regional characteristics creep in. The Basque punk-folk-rock movement, for example, included groups such as the now defunct **Kortatu**, who used gaitas (bagpipes) in their Clash-based sound, and **Oskorri**, who mix Basque folk, reggae and electronic instruments with considerable success. Catalan groups such as the very famous **El Ultimo de la Fila** and the less known **Sopa de Cabra** venture into Catalan lyrics.

Spain: Discography

Various (inc. many top singers) Antologia del Cante Flamenco (3 disc box + booklet) (Hispavox 40 30113)

Paco de Lucia Siroco (Phonogram 830 913)

El Camaron de la Isla Flamenco Vivo (Philips 832 783)

El Camaron de la Isla Soy Gitano (Philips 842 0502)

Juan Pena Lebrijano con la Orquesta Andalusi de Tanger Encuentros (Globestyle ORB 024)

Al Tall and Mulak El-Hwa Xara Al Andalus (Erde 002)

Los Chichos Y Esto Es Lo Que Hay (Philips 838 726)

Los Chunguitos En Directo (EMI 158 790 580)

Various Los Jovenes Flamencos (Nuevos Medios 15553)

Azucar Moreno Bandido (Epic 466 7722)

Pata Negra Blues De La Frontera (Hannibal HNBL 1309)

Ketama Y Es Ke Me Han Kambiao Los Tiempos (Philips 846 2442)

Martirio Estoy Mala (Nuevos Medios 13211)

Various (inc. Concha Piquer, Juanita Reina) Antologia De La Cancion Espanola (20-plus vols.) (Hispavox 056122178-191 and 056790028-34)

Various (inc. El Pali, Los Marismenos) Sevillanas De Oro (a continuing series of top songs) (Hispavox various, released annually)

PORTUGAL

The fado song style is to Portugal very much as flamenco is to Spain. It is a regional genre from around Lisbon which has come to be associated with the country as a whole. After two decades' promotion by the Salazar dictatorship as a colourful, sanitised national music, it returned to progressive favour since the 1974 democratic revolution. Finally it is, at least in part, a low-class, disreputable music later adopted by the upper classes, although the precise modulation of this last point is in dispute. The Lisbon fado flourished at the turn of the century in the bars and brothels of the Alfama and Mourania districts, but there is a distinct tradition of aristocratic fado singers who may, it is sometimes argued, have taken the song slumming, as it were. There is also a second subdivision of fado, named after the university town of Coimbra, which was traditionally an intellectual pursuit, sung by black-cloaked students. The fado is nowadays played in the bars of Lisbon's Barrio Alto, some tourist oriented but others authentic and genuinely popular and, in the case of stars such as **Amalia Rodrigues**, it is performed in concert halls. Fado means 'fate' and the songs are usually melancholy, minor key and suffused with the poignant quality known as 'saudade', which is a compound of emotions connected with longing, yearning, unrequited love and a sense of indefinable loss. Saudade is often connected with the loneliness and restlessness of seafarers, and its musical manifestations are a mark of many styles connected with the great age of Portuguese colonial trade and navigation, for example the Cap Verdean morna (see **Africa**), the Brazilian modinha (see **South America**) and the Indonesian knoncong (see **Far East**). The fado singer is traditionally accompanied by viola (regular Spanish guitar) and guitarra (pear-shaped, twelve-string Portuguese guitar). Fado is not a strictly defined form, and songs of non-fado origin may be treated in fado style so that fado merges at times with other styles such as ballad or regional folk.

Fado's greatest star is Amalia Rodrigues, the daughter of a poor Lisbon amateur musician, who started singing in old clubs such as the Café Luso, and rose to fame in the 1950s and 60s with songs such as 'Um Casa Portuguesa' and 'Barca Negro'. She entered the 1990s as a remarkably well-preserved 70-year-old, forgiven by the new generation for a whiff of compliance with the Salazar dictatorship, and the nationally loved grande dame of Portuguese song. Less well known but still great old-school fadistas include **Alfredo Marceneiro**, who died in the late 1980s, and **Maria Teresa do Noronha**.

Instrumental in liberating fado from its fascist image in the 1970s was the chanson/fado singer (he also covered Jacques Brel songs, etc.) **Carlos da Carmo**, once a Communist militant, whose musical innovation was a freer, more conversational singing style, with lines broken up into shorter phrases.

In the 1980s, two new popular singers, both semiprofessionals from upper-class backgrounds with careers outside singing, developed a successful, smoother, modern semifado sound, with overtones of pop and crooning. **Antonio Pinto Basto** and **Nuno Da Camara Pereira**, sometimes referred to as 'charm singers', made their fados regular features of the Portuguese charts. A further step in the modernisation of the fado, somewhat equivalent to that of the chic young rediscoverers of the tonadillera in Spain and the chanson in France, is represented by the work of two young women, **Anabela Duarte** and **Misia**. The former, an anthropology student and former member of the avant-garde rock group **Mler Ise Dada**, reinvestigated old traditional fado for her late 1980s album 'Lisbunah'. Misia's performance of traditional fado is more innovative in its presentation − the singer has a sexy dress sense − than in its music.

A further, highly successful modern blend of fado attributes is the work of the group **Madre Deus**, whose two albums 'Os Dias de Madre Deus' (1987) and 'Existir' (1990), combine the simple, beautiful songs of **Pedro Ayres Magalhaes** and **Rodrigo Leão** with the equally lovely voice of young fadista

Maria Teresa Salgueiro and a haunting accompaniment of accordion, guitars bass and cello. Magalhaes was guitarist of the 1980s experimental rock group **Herois do Mar**, controversial for their use of vaguely fascist imagery and costumes, while Leão is still keyboard player for a second very interesting group, **Setima Legião**, noted for their melancholy, troubled atmosphere and use of Portuguese bagpipes and other Celtic touches. Salgueiro was discovered by Leão singing the round-form 'fado vadio' – tramp fado – in a Lisbon bar.

Portuguese rock has existed only since 1980, before which English-language cover versions were the standard repertoire. Few groups have developed a strongly national sound; in addition to the two above,the semi-jazz saxophonist **Rão Kyao** has recorded up-tempo dance fados, while the group **Ritual Tagus** has a Portuguese feel to its music.

Two other very popular and interconnected national styles do exist in Portugal: the ballad form which developed into New Song, and commercial, recreated folk music. The New Song movement was led by **José Afonso**, like most of its practitioners a protest singer and one-time exile under the dictatorship, whose songs became highly political after 1974 and who died in 1987. Other top singer-songwriters are **Sergio Godinho**, noted for strong, humorous, intelligent lyrics, **Luís Cilia**, who combines a French chanson influence with both traditional instruments and synthesizers, and **José Mario Branco**, a one-time Maoist activist now, like the Portuguese cultural climate in general, mellowed. Branco has produced records for groups such as the very important **Grupo De Accão Cultural (GAC)**, whose series of albums 'Pois Cante', 'E Vira Bon' and 'Ronda Da Alegria' have included traditional instruments and styles such as the northern female choral song contributed to the records by the sixteen-piece choir **Cramol**.

The booming Portuguese commercial folk scene has been much stimulated by political-traditional initiatives such as GAC, which was the model upon which the Communist Party based its own creation, the group **Trovante**, in 1975. Eventually freed of their political associations, Trovante went on to become extremely popular. Other top artistes include **Vai de Roda**, led by an Oporto architect **Manuel Tentugal**, **Romancas**, **Rosa dos Ventos** and semiclassical Portuguese guitarists such as **Carlos Paredes** and **Pedro Caldeira Cabral**.

Portugal: Discography

Various Portuguese String Music 1908–1931 (Interstate HT 323)
Amalia Rodrigues Um Melhior De Amalia Vols. I and II (EMI Portugal 2606921, 2608761)
Nuno Da Camara Pereira Guitarra (EMI Portugal 7934291)
Setima Legião De Um Tempo Ausente (EMI 7935641)
Madre Deus Os Dias De Madre Deus (EMI 7487761)
Romancas Romancas (Discos Sete LP 558)

ITALY

Historically the Italian bel canto-derived singing style has been immensely influential on the world's popular music, including the very American-bred pop and rock forms which have tended to overwhelm Italian popular music in recent decades.

Italian music is highly regional, with local stars using their own dialects and commanding loyal followings in their home regions. Curiously, imported forms have also been adopted in a regional pattern so that Venice, for example, has a strong blues tradition while Padua is a heavy metal centre.

Italy experienced a muted version of the 1970s European folk revival, led by Naples groups such as **La Nuova Compagnia di Canto Popolare, Musica Nova** and the politically committed **Operaio é Zezi**. In the 1980s a somewhat less political, more musicological and, to a limited extent, popularising and updating approach has been taken by northern groups such as **Ritmia, La Ciapa Rusa, Calicanto, Barbaran** and **I Tre Martelli**.

Record sales and concert attendances of Italian popular artistes boomed in the late 1980s, with top stars such as **Eros Ramazotti** easily outpacing internationals Prince or Madonna. Although many Italian stars adopt the international rock idiom, the Italian emphasis on voice and intelligent lyrics, echoing the similar preoccupations of French chanson, give home artistes the edge. A number of Italian singers have retained a strong indigenous feel to their music.

One of the main centres of distinctive popular music has always been Naples, home of the late nineteenth-century Neapolitan songs, somewhat like operatic arias without operas, created by composer-lyricist combinations such as **Tosti** and **Di Giacomo** and **Capurro** and **Di Capua**. The latter's 'O Sole Mio' is one of the world's best-known popular songs, though its composer sold it, like all his work, for a small one-off fee, and died in poverty. 'O Sole Mio', 'Santa Lucia' and others of the genre formed an important part of the concert repertoire of opera stars such as **Enrico Caruso**, one of the world's earliest recording artistes, and **Beniamino Gigli**, whose status was that of a pop star. The Neapolitan song is still flourishing today: Tosti and Di Giacomo's classic 'Marechiare' was among the operatic arias on **Luciano Pavarotti**'s crossover hit 'Essential Pavarotti' albums in 1990 and 91.

Postwar Naples, with its large American military presence, was the home of one of the two fathers of Italian pop music, **Renato Carasone**. Carasone, a singer-songwriter-pianist and bandleader with a penchant for comedy, melded a Neapolitan melodic sensibility to a band format strongly influenced by then current US and Latin-American music and also deployed a range of silly effects such as Donald Duck voices on irresistible hits such as 'Caravan Petrol', 'Torero' and 'Pigliate 'Na Pastiglia'. Carasone's rival in the 1950s was the raffish Turin singer **Fred Buscaglione**, nicknamed 'L'Uomo Del Whisky Facile' for his nightclubbing and underworld connections. Buscaglione's songs mirrored the louche, Chicago gangland image he cultivated and hits such as 'Guarda Che Luna' and 'Che Bambola' kept him highly popular until his premature and appropriate death in 1960 in a car accident after a night on the tiles.

From the late 50s onwards, Italian popular music has been faithfully reflected in the annual San Remo Song Festival, and the earliest San Remos were dominated by the Sinatra-style swing ballads of artistes such as **Domenico Modugno** who first sang the hugely famous song 'Volare', **Peppino di Capri** and **Mina**, the still popular 'Tigress of Cremona'. The 1960s saw the Dylan/Baez folk-rock-protest idiom widely adopted, and in some cases combined with regional Italian dialect lyrics and other indigenous elements. Top artistes from this period are **Fabrizio de André**, the master of Genovese song; **Gabriella Ferri**, noted for her interpretations of earthy Roman ballads; **Francesco de Gregori**; **Francesco Guccini**; **Pier Angelo Bertoli**, whose later work incorporated Sardinian choral and other effects; and the immensely popular jazz-influenced artiste **Lucio Dalla**.

The 1970s, the 'years of lead', overshadowed by extremist politics and terrorism, saw the rise of heavy metal and the nascent Italian 'dark' music, whose followers wore black and purple and later idolised the British group the Cure. Distinctively Italian musicians to come forward included a number of Neapolitan artistes: the blues-jazz guitarist and singer **Pino Daniele**; the singers **Massimo Ranieri**, **Tullio de Piscopo** and **Eduardo and Eugenio Bennato**, all of whom used local linguistic and musical features in their work; and the group **Matia Bazar**, who revived 1920s Neapolitan songs as well as recording new pastiches such as 'Cavallo Bianco'. The 80s added a new crop of singer-songwriters: **Paolo Conte**, much influenced by French chanson and jazz; **Renzo Arbore**, showman, TV host and heir to the Neapolitan-American tradition of the 1950s; **Enrico Ruggieri**, Milanese former punk and later poetic song-writer; the playful and ironic musical bricoleur **Francesco Baccini**; and talented female artistes **Fiorella Mannoia** and **Fior da Lisa**, the latter an ex-singer with a liscio popular dance band, a genre similar to the local accordion-led general-purpose dance groups of French provincial weekend bals populaires. Liscio bands, and the waltzes and mazurkas traditionally danced to them in town squares in the summer, were something of a vogue in the late 1980s, with academies opening to teach a new young generation the dances, and bands like those of **Vittorio Borghese**, **Enrico Musiano** and **Casa Dei** experienced renewed popularity.

The other Italian dance music to boom in the late 1980s was the heavy, international, electronic disco sound of artistes such as **Black Box** and **Spagna**, who scored international hits. Milan DJ-producers such as **Daniele Davoli** and **Piero Fidelfalti** were behind the polished combination of Italian melody and American rhythm which sold this music. Finally, it is worth noting that Italian female artistes, notably **Sabrina**, are at the forefront of the Euro-genre, also worked by the British Samantha Fox, in which the size of the singer's breasts, displayed regularly in the popular press, is the chief selling point.

Italy: Discography

Enrico Caruso Caruso in Song (Nimbus NI 7809)
Renato Carasone Il Meglio Di . . . (Duck Record DKCD 121)
Fred Buscaglione Il Meglio Di . . . (Duck Record DKCD 120)
Fabrizio de André La Nuvole (Ricordi TLP 260)
Pino Daniele Un Uomo In Blues (CGD 9031 73310)
Paolo Conte Parole d'Amore Scritte a Macchina (CGD 9031 72778)
Francesco Baccini Il Pianoforte Non e Il Mio Forte (CGD 9031 72180)
Enrico Musiano Un Cuore Un Amore Un Eta (Duck Record DKCD 122)

YUGOSLAVIA

Yugoslavia's confederated republics, six including the breakaway Slovenia, contain an extraordinary wealth and variety of folk musics, ranging from the Alpine Austro-Bavarian-linked styles of northern Slovenia through the wild lute and flute backed, Transylvanian-influenced dances of Serbia to the Turkish songs of the formerly Ottoman states of Bosnia and Montenegro. Although much of this tradition is still alive original folk music, referred to as 'narodna muzika' – national music – has been superseded at a mass-media level by modernised, stylised versions known as 'novokomponovana' – newly composed – narodna, or 'pop' narodna muzika, which is similar in status to American country and western.

Pop narodna features electric guitars and drums as well as the accordion, which took a strong hold on village music-making in the twentieth century, and its top stars are hugely popular, particularly with a lower-class, unsophisticated audience. The number one singer is **Lepa Brena**; other, older stars include **Vesna Zmijanac, Miroslav Ilic** and **Tozoval**, while top younger singers are **Halid Muslimovic** and **Rifat Tepic**.

As elsewhere in the Balkans, gypsy musicians are an important presence in Yugoslavia, which has the largest gypsy community, over a million strong, in the region. Yugoslav gypsy music contains the usual dichotomy between the primarily non-gypsy styles played with flamboyant 'gypsy' ornamentation by professional entertainers – the violin-dominated restaurant ensembles, but also genres such as pop narodna, of which the gypsy singer **Saban Bajramovic** is a big star – and the gypsies' own traditional styles. Yugoslavian gypsies retain a strong attachment to the culture of India from which certain, and possibly all, tribes originated, and Hindi film music is extremely popular in areas of major gypsy concentration such as Skopje, capital of Macedonia. Many Yugoslav gypsies are settled, rather than travellers, and these people often dominate the brass bands which are an important element of rural musical life. The brass bands, which originated in the 1930s, feature up to a dozen trumpets, saxophones and cornets, underpinned by tuba and bubanj bass drum, and play for weddings and other celebrations as well as competing in festivals. Certain top bands occasionally play outside Yugoslavia. The Macedonian gypsy band **Kadriovi**, composed, like many of the brass bands, of members of the same family, has toured Europe, while its leader **Kurtis Jasarev** provided soundtrack music for the 1989 Cannes prize-winning film *Le Temps des Gitans*. The same year, the Serbian-based **Duvacki Orkestar** of **Jova Stojiljkovic**, another family band, released an excellent British album on Globestyle Records.

Yugoslav pop and rock consists for the most part of light Westernised ballads with a faintly Franco-Russian chanson shading, typified by older artistes such as **Arsen Dedic** and **Djordja Balasevic**, or a range of derivative rock bands such as the hugely popular **Bjelo Dugme** and **Riblja Corba**. The most distinctive rock scene developed in the Slovenian capital Ljubljana, where punk rock, represented by **Pankrti** ('The Bastards') caught on strongly, and two later groups, **Laibach** and **Borghesia**, attracted local controversy and a degree of international attention. Laibach, formed in 1984, is the German name for Ljubljana, and the group's stage costumes of field-grey uniforms, their artwork (often echoing Nazi-era poster design) and adherence to a neofascist-sounding, and possibly semi-ironic, aesthetic movement they describe, again in German, as 'Neue Slowenische Kunst' ('New Slovenian Art'), have raised eyebrows, not to mention hackles. Laibach's music is in keeping with this image – ponderous, Wagnerian arrangements, often of Western songs, such as the Rolling Stones' 'Sympathy For The Devil', which they recorded in six different versions for a 1987 LP, or the Beatles' 'Let It Be'. Borghesia are more into homosexual sadomasochism, which forms the leitmotiv of the ditty 'Beat And Scream' from their LP 'Escorts and Models'; their other lyrics are politically antiestablishment.

Yugoslavia: Discography

Jova Stojiljkovic and Orkestar Blow, Besir, Blow! (Globestyle ORB 038)
Laibach Opus Dei (Mute STUMM 44)
Laibach Let It Be (Mute STUMM 58)

GREECE

Greece has an extremely rich, diverse and vital range of traditional musics, played on instruments such as the Cretan lyra (three-stringed fiddle) and the violin. Reflecting the country's four centuries of Ottoman Turkish rule, a number of instruments of Turkish and Arab origin are played, including the dulcimer-like santouri, the Arab lute-equivalent outi, and the bouzouki, related to the Turkish saz and Arab bouzouk. It is the small, tear-drop shaped, long-necked bouzouki, inlaid with mother-of-pearl and ideally made by Zozef, the modern Stradivarius of Athens, which has come to be regarded as quintessentially Greek; it was promoted to this position by the 1920s and 30s urban music known as rembetika (or rebetika).

In the classic blues-tango manner, rembetika came into existence in the poor immigrant districts. Some of the immigrants in question were job-seekers from the countryside, but a considerable number were former members of the large Greek populations of the Turkish cities of Constantinople (Istanbul) and Smyrna (Izmir); over a million Greeks expelled from Turkey in 1922 and 1923 formed the most dramatic single wave of immigration. From among this sector of the population sprang the manges, or rebetes, a subculture of small-time crooks and delinquents who frequented a world of bars, tekés (hashish dens) and brothels, wore the distinctive black fedora and jacket with the left arm only in its sleeve, ready to be whipped into a padded shield in case of a knife fight. The manges were the first performers, and subjects, of rembetika songs. Rembetika consisted in fact of two schools; the Smyrna style, very oriental in melody, was sung frequently by women such as the great **Roza Eskenazi**, who died in 1981, and **Rita Abadzi**, who died in 1969, accompanied by more Turkish instrumentation (violin, santouri, kanun, outi), and included the sad songs known as amané because of their characteristic refrain, 'Aman, Aman . . .' ('Have pity, have pity . . .'), which is also found today in modern Algerian raï music. While the Smyrna musicians were often from the relatively sophisticated background of their former Ottoman homes, those of the Piraeus school were hard-core manges underworld, their voices typically simple, rough and unadorned. Their instruments were the bouzouki, then of three double strings, and the miniature baglamas, much prized for its ease of concealment in prison, where much of early rebetes was developed. Piraeus rembetika was essentially dance music, and its most distinctive steps were the zebekiko, with its characteristically Greek, complex and emphatic time signature, often performed as a spontaneous and brooding male solo, and the well-known hasapiko butchers' dance, performed by several men side by side with arms on each others' shoulders. The greatest of the 1930s rembetika singer-composers was the bouzouki virtuoso **Markos Vamvakaris**, composer of probably the best known rembetiko song ever, 'Franco-syriani', who also formed one of the earliest recording groups, the **Piraeus Quartet**. His chief rival was **Iannis Papaiounou**, composer of 'Ase Me, Ase Me' ('Leave Me Alone'). Although Vamvakaris and Papaiounou died in the 1970s, several old artistes from this period still occasionally play. Chief among them is **Iorgos Mouflouzelis**, a magnificent, gruff-voiced baglamas player and singer, often accompanied by his son **Lefteris** on guitar, and the equally charismatic Stalin-moustached **Michaelis Genitsaris**.

In the 1940s, two artistes, **Manolis Hiotis** and **Vassilis Tsitsanis**, were leaders in modernisation of rembetika. Hiotis added an extra double string to the bouzouki, which rapidly became universal practice, and retuned it to facilitate a more prominent solo role; he also added strings and brass to the accompaniment. Tsitsanis, not a rebete but a former law student, substituted romantic lyrics for the hashish and prison references and recorded with star female singers such as **Sotiria Bellou** and **Markia Ninou**.

Old-style rembetika died away during the 1940s and 1950s, and its successor evolved into a related music known as laika, featuring electric guitars, drums, early electric keyboards and prominent paired bouzoukis, which flourished in restaurants and cabarets of late 1960s and 1970s Athens. It was here that the habit of plate-smashing developed as a spontaneous sign of approval and joy, and later became a tourist cliché. Laika was, and is, primarily a non-intellectual, working-class taste, though, like all Greek popular genres, it transcends precise social typifying. By far its greatest star is **Stellios Gazanzilis**, who started performing in 1952 and created and recorded dozens of famous songs such as 'Dhio Portes Ehi e Zoi' ('Life Has Two Doors'), expanded his repertoire to include demotiki (folk), protest songs, Turkish songs (controversially and successfully crossing over to a Turkish audience), and after a nine-year silence, released three albums to tremendous excitement in the mid to late 1980s. Other top early laika artistes included the hard-drinking, smoking and gambling gypsy singer **Manolis Angelopoulos**, who rivalled Gazanzilis in Athens nightclubs such as the Oniro before succumbing to throat cancer (a traditional rebetes' disease) in 1989, whereupon videos of his huge funeral became as sought after as his records among Greek gypsies; **Stratos Dionysiou** and **Panis Gavalás**, both also deceased, in Gavalás' case of throat cancer; and **Rita Sekelariou**, a lively, middle-aged lady with a headline-catching appetite for young male escorts and cosmetic surgery.

Two other important strands of Greek popular music, which certain major laika stars such as Gazanzilis also performed, were developed in the 1960s. Néo kima (new wave), performed by artistes such as **Giannis Spanos**, combined folk musics including, to a certain extent, rembetika, with influences from Brel-era French chanson and Dylan folk-protest, and Communist-inspired lyrics. More importantly, the serious but popular composer-performers **Theodorakis**, **Hadjidakis** and **Xarhakos** began to create an eclectic body of protest songs, sophisticated, European-style ballads, film music, symphonies and choral works, all with their individual creative imprints but with a clear Greek feeling, which came to be regarded as the standard-bearer of mainstream Greek music. Mikis Theodorakis, a graduate in composition of Athens Conservatory, studied with Messiaen in Paris in the 1950s and devoted decades of energy to left-wing politics, during which he was banished and his music banned throughout the dictatorship of the Colonels' Junta (1967–74), only to return as a Communist MP in the 1980s and government minister in 1990. World-famous for his theme music for the film *Zorba the Greek*, his work also includes settings of poems by the great Yannis Ritsos and Nobel-winning George Seferis. Manos Hadjidakis, known internationally for his film music for *Never On A Sunday*, is a similarly prolific and wide-ranging composer noted also for his refinement of rembetika.

A resurgence of interest in rembetika by a new young generation in the mid to late seventies was due in part to the fact that the Colonels' regime had frowned on public airing of the old antisocial songs. A blues-style cult developed, with reissues of early recordings and a series of groups recreating the original acoustic style emerged. Chief among them were the **Athinaiki Kompania, Ta Pedia Tis Patras** and **To Palio Mas Spiti**. The latter is still resident band in the Athens taverna of the same name. In addition, a number of popular artistes took to playing rembetika, including the young female singer **Eleftheria Arvanitaki** and above all the star **George Dalaras**, whose 1975 double album 'Fifty Years of Rembetika' featured strong, original but non-pastiche versions of songs by great artistes such as Vamvakaris, Tsitsanis and his own father, **Lukas Daralas**, a second-rank singer-composer.

The rembetika revival petered out in the 1980s and laika singers began to diversify into other areas, principally rock-pop ballads with or without a token Greek feel. Two major contemporary artistes to remain faithful to 'pure' laika are the solid, working-class idol **Dimitris Mitropanos**, whose deep emotional voice sells all the records he can make, and the young Salonika-resident **Nikos Papazoglu**, who is much influenced by old acoustic rembetika. Many other artistes feature one or two pure laika tracks on an otherwise rock-pop album, or play the hybrid style known as 'elaphrolaika' – light laika. Much the most important Greek artiste remains George Dalaras, a creative and innovative writer, guitarist, bouzouki player and singer, who retains his deep laika roots but transcends any single category, working in numerous genres and collaborating with musicians from Mikis Theodorakis to Al di Meola, who starred on Dalaras's successful double album, 'Latin', of Greek adaptations of Latin-American songs. Dalaras's female equivalent is the pop-laika-demotika singer **Haris Alexiou**. Other contemporary artistes to retain a significant degree of 'Greekness' in their music include the still-effective **Marinella**, former wife of Stellios Gazanzilis; **Grigoris Bithikotsis**, with Theodorakis a fellow musical fighter against the dictatorship; **Tolios Voskopoulos, Yannis Poulopoulos** and Greece's biggest-selling recording artiste, **Iannis Parios**, each of whom could roughly be described as a Greek Julio Iglesias.

Greece: Discography

Various Greek Oriental-Smyrnaic-Rebetic Songs and Dances (Folklyric 9033)
Various (inc. Vamvakaris, etc.) Rembetika Vols. 1–5 (Music Box Int. MB 110406)
Michaelis Genitsaris Rebetiko Live! (Trikont US 016809)
Various (inc. Gazanzilis, Angelopoulos, etc.) Laika Monopatia Vols. 1–10 (Music Box Int. 10351-10361)
Mikis Theodorakis Sings Theodorakis (Intuition INT 30592)
George Dalaras Fifty Top Rembetikas (Minos Matsos MSM 248-249) (RCA 70096)
George Dalaras Live Recordings (Minos Matsos MSM 832)
Haris Alexiou Haris Alexiou (Minos Matsos 852)
Dimitris Mitropanos 15 Years of Mitropanos (Philips 824525)
Nikos Papazoglu Synerga (Lyra 4559)

The East

The popular musics of what used to be called the Eastern bloc countries share broadly similar characteristics, varying with the styles of their individual musics and with their differing recent economic and political histories (relatively prosperous and liberal in the case of Hungary, deeply impoverished and repressed in the cases of Romania and Bulgaria.

All of the countries in the region are avid consumers of Euro-American mainstream pop-rock, and also have groups creating their own versions of it. The Gorbachev-inspired collapse of the hardline regimes in the late 1980s put an end to decades of hopeless government attempts to stem the tide of decadent Western music, from Stalin's ban on jazz in the 1940s and 50s Soviet Union through the Romanian militia's brutal beating of fans who dared to dance to Blood Sweat and Tears in the 1970s to the Bulgarian despot Zhyvkov's last-ditch crackdown on discothèques in 1984.

The beginning of the nineties has seen repeated across the region the phenomenon of newly freed entrepreneurs signing up local rock acts, competing with the ponderous, inefficient former state monopoly record companies, wrestling with the problems of lack of hard currency to buy new equipment or promote concerts by visiting Western groups and in many cases going into partnership with Western businessmen to facilitate matters. For the most part the local acts are modelled on either middle-of-the-road US rock or heavy metal, though a number of interesting experimental rock/performance groups exist. A substantial part of the official pop-rock scene, however, remains around fifteen years behind the West, with rock operas, for example, a popular phenomenon on the 1980s.

The traditional musics of the region vary greatly in their vitality. In some cases, state troupes and institutes have preserved a colourful but sterile 'national music' which has otherwise almost died out at village level; in others folk forms remain in daily popular use. One ethnic group which transcends national boundaries and has preserved a lively culture is that of the gypsies, whose traditional function as professional entertainers also persists.

The extent to which traditional musics have been updated by new young groups also varies, and is subject to two opposing tendencies. On the one hand, many young people came to regard everything Western as desirable and their national culture as something from which to escape. On the other hand, for persecuted ethnic minorities such as the Transylvanians of Romania, retention of traditional music represents a stand against cultural annihilation, while nationalism expressed through music could also be encouraged in countries under Soviet subjugation.

HUNGARY

One of the most interesting features of Hungarian popular music was the 'dance house' movement of the early 1970s, which flagged but revived in the late 1980s after Western interest, and which had large numbers of young people dancing in Budapest clubs to groups such as **Muzsikas, Vujicsics, Makvirag, Vasmalom** and **Kormorán**. These groups played traditional instruments such as zither, cymbalom, bagpipe, hurdy-gurdy, three-string double bass and various flutes and pipes, in certain cases (that of Kormorán, for example) combined with electric guitars and drums. Their repertoires were based on folk dances of the rural communities of Hungary which they often researched at first hand, following in the footsteps of the pioneering classical composers Bartok and Kodály. The music of Transylvania, a former Hungarian region given to Romania in 1918, whose rich musical heritage was threatened in the 1970s by the Romanian dictator Ceaucescu's attempt to modernise (by destroying) the villages, was a major source of material. In 1983 the rock opera *King Stephen*, set in united medieval Hungary and carrying an unmistakably nationalistic message, starred the dance-house singer **Marta Sebestyen**, whose clear, pure voice has been a feature of collaborations with the groups Vujicsics (named after another eminent composer-musicologist) and Muzsikas.

The dance house groups also played original gypsy music, which is quite different from the stylised 'gypsy' violin repertoire associated with Budapest tourist restaurants and thus Hungary as a whole. This latter style, played by both gypsies and non-gypsies, is based on Hungarian folk melodies adorned with flamboyant 'gypsy' ornamentation and taught to prospective restaurant-band performers in establishments such as the Ryko School of Music.

Hungary was to the forefront of the growth of East European rock, with relatively liberal policies allowing numerous groups, usually covering British or American pop, to spring up in Budapest cafés such as the Dalia Coffee House. Much the most famous group was **Illés**, led by the songwriting team of **Janos Brody** and **Levente Szorenyi** (later to go on to write rock musicals, including *King Stephen*, who modelled themselves on The Beatles to the extent of adopting Sergeant Pepper's Band uniforms and producing their own 'White Album'. Illés also encountered periodic official hostility which resulted in the censoring of their songs 'Europe Is Silent' and 'If I Were A Rose'.

More recent Hungarian groups include **Tatrai**, a blues-oriented formation featuring the star guitarist **Tibor Tatrai** and singer **Karoly Horvath**; **Bikini** and **Europa Kiado**.

CZECHOSLOVAKIA

Czechoslovakia was deeply affected by sixties counter-cultural ideas. Not least of these were Beatlemania, which inspired numerous Czech versions, notably top group **Olympic**, and the drug culture, which also inspired local adaptations, such as the use of the stimulant fenmetrazin in the absence of an adequate supply of Western narcotics. The poet Allen Ginsburg's visit in 1965 (he was deported after two months) sparked a wave of 'happenings'. This phenomenon continued euphorically through the reforms and liberalisations of the Prague Spring of 1968, until the Soviet-Warsaw Pact invasion of that year snuffed out political reforms and artistic licence. In the final months of open intellectual resistance after the invasion, protest songs by artistes such as **Karel Kryl** and **Marta Kubisova** of the group the **Golden Kids**, provided a focus. Kubisova's song 'Prayer For Marta' became a particular symbol of hope, for which she paid with banishment to a lowly office job for twenty years. The country's music stagnated during this time, with carefully monitored ballad-singing **(Karel Gott)**, traditional jazz **(Peter Lipa)**, Dylan-style folk (at the famous Porta Festival) and apolitical rock-pop **(Stromboli, Zentour, OK Band, Elan)** providing permissible entertainment. One of the most dramatic musical signs of the new reforms of 1989 and 1990 was Marta Kubisova's performance to a crowd of 200,000 in Prague's Wenceslas Square and the subsequent re-release of her 1969 album 'Songs And Ballads'.

POLAND

Polish rock has followed the traditional Eastern European pattern; the **Red Guitars** were leading Beatles-imitators in the 1960s, a decade which saw relative leniency on the part of the government in dealing with manifestations of Western youth culture. The Rolling Stones' 1967 concert in Warsaw was a landmark event throughout the entire region, and the following year a 'Beat Mass' was held and recorded in the church of Father Leon Kantorski, subsequently a leading Solidarnosc activist. During the repression of the late 1970s and early 1980s, a strong punk-rock movement developed, with groups such as **Lady Pank** attracting both official censure (for indecent exposure on stage in Lady Pank's case) and a degree of international attention. Along with Hungary, Poland led the way in permitting private business ventures, and Polish entrepreneurs are consequently particularly active, though little distinctively Polish popular music has yet emerged.

ROMANIA

The Ceaucescu regime of the 1960s and 1970s permitted the intrusion of a limited degree of modern music, largely in order to cater for the foreign tourists it was trying to attract, but youth culture was strictly regulated – the early officially permitted disc jockeys were submitted to periodic haircuts and a dress code, and few young people were bold enough to grow beards or sport denim. In the 1980s, sheer grinding poverty was an efficient suppressor of any music culture requiring more than a couple of light bulbs' worth of electricity. During this period, officially approved popular music consisted largely of artificial folklore ensembles, but various marginalised groups maintained a living folk tradition. Among them were surviving pockets of Transylvanian peasants (see **Hungary**) and certain similarly oppressed gypsy communities, whose 'tafar', informal bands of singers, accordionists, fiddlers and cymbalom players, passed on and developed a repertoire of narrative ballads, love songs and dance tunes. At the same time, a handful of urban intellectual singer-songwriters, at the risk of job and liberty, occasionally inserted veiled criticism into their performances: an example was **Alexandre Andries**, a lecturer in architecture and a singer whose 'Dracula Blues' had brought him to the point of arrest on the eve of the December 1989 revolution, which may in time permit a regrowth of modern and indigenous music.

BULGARIA

The folk music of this mountainous country, poised between Europe and Asia, and with a correspondingly Turkish-Oriental melodic feel, is extremely rich and, as embodied by the various choirs which have recorded and toured externally under the name **Le Mystère des Voix Bulgares**, has been remarkably visible in the West in recent years. The dramatic polyphonic choral music, with its characteristic 'open-throat' sound, is based on a mixture of popular village songs and Byzantine liturgy, and its modern development and propagation is due in large measure to two men. The first is the Bulgarian composer **Philip Koutev**, who was placed in charge of the newly formed national folklore ensemble in 1951 and whose meticulous scholarship and artistry raised a potentially sterile institution to a high level of excellence. The second is the Swiss amateur musicologist **Marcel Cellier**. His private 1950s recordings of rare Eastern European folk music included those released successfully on record, at first in the early 1970s to a small audience of cognoscenti, and later in the mid-1980s to sudden, massive international interest. The chief performers of this style are the twenty-eight-strong **Bulgarian Radio Choir**, who adopted the name 'Le Mystère des Voix Bulgares' after the success of the recordings under that title; the star singers **Yanka Rupkina**, **Eva Georgieva** and **Stoyanka Boneva** who perform together as the **Trio Bulgarka**; the **Koutev Ensemble**, as the National Folklore Ensemble is known; the **Bisserov Sisters**, who sing both alone and with The Koutev Ensemble; and the large **Trakia** choir. This music, which had never been popular within Bulgaria, has begun to attract a certain interest due to its Western success.

A second variety of traditionally based Bulgarian music, stambolovo, or Balkan wedding-band music, is immensely popular. Its leading performer, the clarinettist **Ivo Papasov**, who also plays with the Trakia Ensemble, brings a blend of wild gypsy jazz improvisation to the standard instrumentation of his band – drumkit, bass, electric guitar, saxophone and accordion – and the resultant fast, exciting jumpy dance music makes him nationally sought after for wedding bookings. The genre itself boomed in the late 1980s, with highly successful festivals in 1986 and 1988.

Bulgarian rock had its obligatory Beatles simulacrum – **Schturtzite** ('the Crickets'), whose early Fab Four covers gave way to faintly antigovernment songs such as 'Twentieth Century' during a late-1970s liberalisation led by President Zhivkov's daughter Lyudmila, who was head of the Committee of Culture from 1975 until her death in a car accident in 1981. The mid-1980s saw a crackdown – with the establishment of 'new model discothèques' with no smoking, alcohol or foreign music – before the reopening of of 1989. Schturtzite remain popular, as do **FSB**, the state monopoly record company's top band, and **Era**, **Kontrolle** and **Orion**.

THE SOVIET UNION

Soviet folk and traditional music consists of a huge variety of ethnic genres spread over a vast geographic area. Recent years have seen a reduction in the traditional content of the state cultural troupes charged with their rather artificial preservation (the **Red Army Choir**, until the early 1970s backed almost entirely by balalaikas, has subsequently gone over to mainly modern instruments). Demand for the ersatz popularised folk songs of popular tenors such as **Ivan Rebrov** has died away with their ageing audiences. At the same time, new ensembles are investigating and re-creating folk traditions; examples are the Leningrad-based **Terem Quartet** and Moscow's **Dimitri Pokrovsky Ensemble**. However, little of this activity overlaps the popular music domain.

Russia, in particular, has a strong solo singer-songwriter tradition, and this genre was an early subject for the 'magnizidat' unofficial tape recordings, equivalent to the samizdat underground publishing system. **Alexander Galich**, a contemporary of Solzhenitsyn and fellow critic of the Stalin gulag legacy, was followed by the first magnizidat star, **Bulat Okudzhava**, in the late 1950s and finally, in the late 1960s, by the great **Vladimir Vysotsky**, Russian-Jewish actor and singer whose direct, colloquial songs of the tribulations of the ordinary, even criminal, classes — soldiers in disciplinary units, alcoholics in vodka queues — and mocking parodies of officialdom made him hugely popular with the public at large and equally unpopular with the authorities, who ensured he was never properly recorded. Vyotsky, a heavy drinker, died in 1980 at the age of forty-two; his death was marked by widespread unofficial mourning and virtual silence from the State media, although, as glasnost gained ground, his work was officially recognised later in the decade.

Nascent Soviet pop and rock experienced a less turbulent development than that of countries such as Poland and Czechoslovakia which were nearer the source of Western contamination and therefore less subdued. Stifling red tape was the controlling tactic employed by the authorities, who were notably out of touch with modern developments, for a considerable time referring to The Beatles and the Rolling Stones as 'jazz groups'. While the early Beatles clones gave way to a large number of amateur garage bands, access to the media and recording was rigorously restricted by the Ministry of Culture, who licensed only those 'Vocal Instrumental Ensembles' whose hair length, clothing and song content conformed to detailed specifications. Thus groups such as **Pesniary** or the **Singing Guitars** publicly renounced the excesses of Western rock and in some cases began to include folk tunes in their repertoire to gain favour and access to an audience.

The advent of the liberalised late 1980s saw the Soviet pop-rock market divided among middle-of-the-road international showbiz figures such as the Streisand-equivalent star **Alla Pugachova**, whose high international profile was boosted by a 1988 appearance at New York's Carnegie Hall; a huge number of undistinguished and derivative heavy-metal bands, such as **Gorky Park**; and a number of more interesting experimental groups, often including strongly theatrical visual elements in their performances, such as the Leningrad groups **Aquarium**, **Kino**, **Alisa** and **Avia**. The latter, along with the fellow underground Moscow group **Zvuki Mu**, have on several occasions performed in the West, where their ironic 'physical culture group' of female dancers doing Stalinist sports-parade routines was well received.

Eastern Europe: Discography

Muzsikas with Marta Sebestyen Blues for Transylvania (Hannibal HN 1350)
Vujicsics Serbian Music From Southern Hungary (Hannibal HN 1310)
Various Porta (Czech Folk Festival) (Supraphon 1113 4230 H)
Stromboli Stromboli (Panton 810 698)
Le Mystère des Voix Bulgares A Cathedral Concert (Jaro 4138)
Ivo Papasov and his Orchestra Balkanology (Hannibal HN 1363)
The Dimitri Pokrovsky Ensemble The Wild Field (Real World RW 17)
Vladimir Vysotsky In Memory (Ness Music NS 886075)
Avia Avia (Hannibal HN 1358)

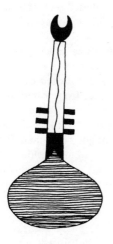

THE
MIDDLE EAST
AND INDIAN
SUBCONTINENT

INTRODUCTION

Asian music is found all over the world; wherever Asian people have emigrated, they have formed a new audience for their music. Indian film music, for example, is very widespread. You find it in Africa, Europe, the Arab World . . . But Asian music is also created outside the continent. My own career is an example of this. When I first went to Japan to perform, I remember someone saying, 'How come we're getting Indian music from Britain rather than India?' Of course, I'm not the only artiste to have been born in Britain who is now making Indian music – the bhangra rock style is an obvious example of this phenomenon.

Let me explain my musical development a little, and in doing so, mention a few of the many aspects of popular musics across this large region of the world. I was born in Chelmsford, Essex, where my family had arrived from India in the mid-1950s. My parents brought me up speaking English – for the first six or seven years of life I never learnt Urdu – and so my very first musical memories were English nursery rhymes. Like most Asians, whether abroad or not, the first Indian music I heard was film music. I was in a particularly good position to listen to Indian film music as my father had a business distributing Indian films and then, later, a printing business which did the film advertising. He knew everyone in film circles here, all the cinema owners, and wherever we went, up in Bradford in the north of England, down south, we'd get to see all the latest films. This partly taught me Urdu in fact.

By the time I first went to India and Pakistan at the age of seven or eight to visit cousins, grandparents and so on, I could understand quite a lot and that visit got me speaking as well. At that age I didn't have any ambition to sing professionally, although I used to sing to myself – I remember singing along with recordings of the great film singers, Lata Mangeshkar and Asha Bosle.

I first became seriously interested in the songs called ghazals, which eventually gave me my entry into performing, when I was a student in London. A friend of mine gave a birthday party, and she'd invited over a group of ghazal performers led by the singer Pervez Mehdi from Pakistan. This was how the singers would operate – they'd come over to do a short tour, performing in people's houses. You call this sort of get-together with music a 'mehfil', which means 'gathering'. There might be around fifty people present. It makes the atmosphere very nice and intimate, with close contact between the musicians and the audience. Actually, this particular party was very amusing, because we had to change the location in the middle of it. It was in a Hall of Residence – my friend was also studying for a degree – and there were complaints about the noise, so everybody had to get into a whole troupe of cars and follow each other to a new address, where the party carried on. It was snowing, I remember. So this was my first ghazal concert – in London in the cold.

Pervez Mehdi was a very good singer in fact – he'd studied with the great ghazal performer Mehdi Hassan – and I was really interested. I'd never even seen a harmonium or a tabla before, but the rapport between the tabla and the voice was quite hypnotic. Unfortunately, my Urdu was still not good enough for me to appreciate the lyrics, and this was a great pity because in ghazals the poetry of the lyrics is of great importance. The songs use a very high standard of Urdu, with many learned words not used in everyday conversation, and they have great depth.

The great classic ghazals of fifty or a hundred years ago were the preserve of the rich and educated patrons, who would pay the musicians to come to the great houses to perform. The musicians were very highly trained; often their profession had been in the family for many generations. Not only were the words complicated and metaphorical – they might describe in an improvisational way a flame, for example, or the eye – but the music was complex and very long. For this reason ghazals for decades were not accessible to common people, who preferred folk music, or film music.

This began to be changed by Mehdi Hassan, but the real popularisers of the ghazal, around the mid-1970s, were Jagjit and Chitra Singh. They simplified the poetry, so that anyone could understand it, and they shortened the songs and made the music simpler and more modern. They began to introduce Western instruments, for example. When I began to sing ghazals, I followed their lead in a way. I sometimes take lyrics from the great poets of the past, but I try to have them made understandable to a modern audience, not like the original Persian and Arabic texts which you have to study to understand.

Apart from ghazals and film music, another very common source of music for Asians is religion. If you're Sikh or Hindu, the temple ceremonies all feature music. In theory, Muslims don't use music in a religious setting, except perhaps occasionally certain drums. The main big exception, though, is qawwali music, which is still very popular in India and Pakistan. Qawwali music starts in a religious context but then takes on a general role. On occasions such as a wedding, or the birth of a baby, or a child's first starting to learn the Koran, it's customary for people to gather and listen to religious songs. Because of the rhythm and the tempo, the listeners get 'vibed' up and they give money to the singers – that's how qawwali singers earn their living.

Bhangra is also a social, ceremonial music, but it has been modernised more than most folk music from the subcontinent. Bhangra originally came from the Punjab. It was played at harvest time in the fields, backed by big drums, and the people would wear those colourful headbands and do a special dance. As Punjabi workers emigrated, their language and their music went with them. Punjabi is a very common language – you find Punjabi speakers all over the world, in Africa, Europe, and England, of course. At an Indian wedding in England, Punjabi would be perhaps the most common language, and there would always be a couple of people who could sing, one or two more who could play the tabla. The guests would want to celebrate, so they'd need musicians, and as more and more immigrants came over there'd be more and more demand, and amateur performers would gradually get reputations. What happened next was that certain musicians began to take it a step further by forming bands and then using Western instruments. This is how Alaap, the leading British bhangra group, started.

There are people who feel that by Westernising bhangra, the new groups have spoiled it, but there are also many Asians who think it is great. You must understand their point of view – they're used to the old traditional style, it's ordinary to them, but hearing it performed in this new and unusual way is extraordinary and exciting.

My music is a sort of crossover music, too. Although I sometimes sing very traditional styles, I experiment with new ideas, new arrangements. I'm now reaching whole new non-Asian audiences, for example, in France and Japan. And of course, I'm building up audiences in India and Pakistan, having started from my British base. I'm also getting more and more popular in the Arab world. There's always been a big market for Indian music in the Middle East, both from the large populations of Indian and Pakistani workers resident there and, increasingly, from the Arab audience too. I know my videos – often pirated – are common in the Emirates, for example – I've recorded a number of film spots for the BBC in Britain, and I did an Asian Live Aid charity show, and pirate tapes of all these regularly turn up. Somebody told me recently they'd seen me on an in-flight entertainment video on a flight to the Gulf.

All in all, the situation of music in the Indian subcontinent and the Arab world is very encouraging, in my opinion. The many different folk styles are still surviving, the learned semiclassical and classical traditions are very much

alive, and new modernised forms are arising and crossfertilising each other.
It's an interesting time to be performing.

NAJMA AKHTAR

EGYPT

For most of the twentieth century, Egyptian or Egyptian-style music has
dominated the Arab world, and Egyptians are still accustomed to considering
other Arab popular musics as, at most, a minor curiosity. The Algerian raï
youth music so celebrated in Europe is vitually unknown in the intellectual and
commercial capital of the Arab musical world, Cairo, while a dozen years after
her death, every Arab in the world would instantly recognise the voice of the
great Egyptian singer **Oum Kalthoum**. The Egyptian style, often referred to
as 'musiqqa sharqiyyah' or 'Oriental music', has its exponents throughout the
Arab world, so that artistes performing more or less in the manner of Oum
Kalthoum and her orchestra exist from Morocco to Iraq.

The classic Oriental sound basically consists of a male or female singer
performing long-drawn-out, melodramatic (to Western ears) ballads generally
referred to as 'aghani' or 'songs' (singular 'ughniyah'). The backing is a
substantial orchestra of upwards of a dozen musicians, combining Western
strings, perhaps electric guitar and bass, possibly saxophone, accordion and
percussion, with Arab instruments such as the 'oud (lute), nay (flute), qanun
(plucked zither) and riqq (tambourine). An instrumental introduction, which
can range from a few minutes to half an hour in length, opens the song,
building tension in the listener. The lyrics, which are extremely important,
are written by a professional lyricist (frequently famous in his own right)
and often concern love: typically the song is an obsessive mixture of joy,
sadness, longing and inability to attain the object of one's desire. The musical
mix can be complex, drawing on a range of other genres and traditions
to colour the work. This 'colour' (in Arabic, 'lawn') is explicitly recognised
and appreciated by the audience. Thus a song might be said to be rich in
'lawn tarab', referring to a traditional concept of a subdivision of Arab
music known as 'tarab' or enchantment; lawn tarab would refer to the use
of traditional Arabic maqam systems of modal improvisation and vocal
ornamentation. A song featuring musical references to a Western, 'serious'
composer might be said to have 'lawn gharbi' ('Western colour'). 'Lawn
chaabi', meaning 'people's' or 'common' colour, might refer to elements
based on simpler folk styles. The ughniyah form possesses the characteristics
of a more serious, light classical music, as well as of popular music. This
has been particularly noticeable in the last decade, now that more pop-
equivalent youth-oriented musics have sprung up. The Oriental song style
remains hugely popular, however: many young Egyptians, asked who the

country's most popular singer is, will still answer Oum Kalthoum, even though she died a dozen years ago.

The Egyptian recording industry established itself rapidly. By the 1930s, however, Egyptian radio had overtaken the gramophone in popularity, with huge audiences listening to the regular live broadcasts of all the top stars. As in India, film was a key vehicle for popular music throughout the period from the 1920s to the 1950s, and artistes such as **Farid Al-Atrash** and **Abdel-Halim Hafez** performed many of their most successful songs in this medium.

If the great Oum Kalthoum achieved fame as the foremost exponent of the modern Oriental song, her musical origins were religious. At the beginning of the century, popular-level musical performance was dominated by the sheikhs: learned, devout Muslim men who would perform religious songs, with a leavening of secular texts, at weddings, circumcisions, village celebrations and in places of public entertainment such as coffee houses. While lesser sheikhs would operate on a simple community level, more accomplished singers would be sought out to perform in the salons of the wealthy and influential. Certain musicians could even achieve the status of stars. The most famous example of the latter was **Sheikh Sayyid Darwish**, the composer of the present Egyptian national anthem, who developed his music into an art form greatly surpassing its narrow religious and ceremonial origins. Darwish's grandson, **Imam Badr Darwish**, still performs in Cairo today; it is possible to attend one of his concerts in the plush Marriot Hotel and hear performed, as well as Badr Darwish's own compositions, the original texts with which Sheikh Sayyid Darwish would have regaled enthralled audiences seventy years ago.

Darwish père was a principal influence upon, and teacher of, the two eminent musicians who were responsible for the young Oum Kalthoum's first step from provincial obscurity to metropolitan stardom around 1920. The musicians in question, the singer **Sheikh Aboul Ala Mohamed** and the lute player, and subsequently popular composer, **Zakariya Ahmed**, were guests during Ramadan at the house of a rich merchant, where Oum Kalthoum was singing religious texts with her Imam father. Aboul Ala Mohamed, impressed by her powerful and expressive voice, invited her to Cairo to perform and study poetry and music with him. Thus Oum Kalthoum continued further along the path, most unusual for a woman, of a musical profession. In Cairo, she studied intensively with the best teachers, including **Ahmed Rahmi** and **Mohamed El Kasabgi**, who became respectively her favoured lyricist and composer. In 1924 she made her first recording, and by 1934 was the most highly paid star of Egyptian radio. For the next forty years her radio performances continued to be an institution throughout the Arab world. By the 1960s, her domination of Egyptian radio was so complete she felt obliged to ask for her records to be played less often in order to preserve a degree of anticipation on the part of the public. Always a proud and private woman, Oum Kalthoum resisted any attempts by the press to inquire into her personal life, and employed her own private photographer to supply pictures to the newspapers. Although film was never as important to Oum Kalthoum as it was to many other singing stars, she made half a dozen movies, the first being *Wydad*, in 1935, in which she starred as a slave-girl singer, and the last *Fatima*, in 1948. Physical beauty was never a major feature of her appeal, and the image that dominated the decades of her major fame was that of the heavy-faced woman in diamanté-ornamented dark glasses, a severe hairstyle and elaborate pendant earrings, fronting her seated orchestra in a long dress, with the famous silk handkerchief in her left hand.

Oum Kalthoum supported the Egyptian Revolution which overthrew King Farouk in 1952 and became a devoted follower of President Gamal Abdul Nasser, who in turn was an admirer of Egypt's greatest artiste. Her songs were by no means restricted to love themes; one of her most famous musical interventions in public life occurred in 1957 when Nasser offered in public to resign after Egypt's crushing defeat by Israel in the Six Day War. Oum Kalthoum's song 'Love of the Nation', set to music by the great composer **Riad al Sunbati** ('Stay, you are the love of the nation . . . Comfort us after defeat . . . Let the heads of the people be raised again . . .'), perfectly interpreted the public mood and was instrumental in persuading Nasser to stay in power. Nasser in turn intervened in the diva Kalthoum's career; it was at Nasser's wish that Oum Kalthoum and **Mohamed Abdel-Wahab**, the most famous composer of the postwar period, agreed to the collaboration which so inflamed the imagination of the country. 'Anta Omri' ('You Are My Life'), the song Abdel-Wahab wrote and Oum Kalthoum sang, was one of the greatest successes of the 1960s. In 1957, Oum Kalthoum's first concert outside the Arab world took place in Paris, and was attended by President de Gaulle and many celebrities. She died in 1973, to national and international mourning on a huge scale, and almost twenty years later her position in the hearts of Arabs everywhere is still unassailable. Her private relationships – her childless marriage to a Cairo doctor, her lifelong friendship with her inseparable dresser and confidante Sayyeda – remained enigmatic to the end.

Quite apart from the continuing sales of Oum Kalthoum's own recordings, the songs she made famous are still covered by artistes across the Arab world. In the late 1980s, a young, blind boy singer, **Baha Mostafa**, shot to fame singing faithful renditions of Oum Kalthoum's repertoire, accompanied by an Oriental orchestra.

Though none quite equalled her status, a handful of stars shared Oum Kalthoum's level of fame. Following her death, the composer and singer Mohamed Abdel-Wahab was indisputably Egypt's greatest popular musician. The son of a muezzin (the public singer from the minaret of a mosque), his musical gifts manifested themselves before he was ten years old when he began to entertain theatre audiences in his childish soprano, dressed in dinner jacket and Arab chechia headgear, during the intervals in a Cairo theatre. He soon became a protégé of the poet and lyricist **Ahmed Shawky** and began to compose for some of the country's foremost lyricists, including Shawky and Sheikh Sayyid Darwish, whose operetta *Cleopatra* he completed after Darwish's death. Abdel-Wahab's fame rested on his innovatory blending of Western scales and themes with traditional Arabic styles, and his incorporation of violins, cellos, and later brass instruments and guitars into the Egyptian orchestra. In addition to the songs he wrote for Oum Kalthoum and his own, hugely popular renditions of his songs, he wrote many pieces for the younger male star **Abdel-Halim Hafez**. In the 1930s, he became a partner in the Lebanese-founded major Arab record company Baidaphon, and his activities also encompassed radio and film.

In the late 1980s Abdel-Wahab broke a ten-year silence by recording a song which he had written in the 1970s for Abdel-Halim Hafez, but shelved after the latter's death. 'Min Gher Ley' ('Without Why' is a rough translation) was a turbulent existential love song, and its sentiments were strong enough for it to be criticised in the Egyptian press. 'Min Gher Ley' was covered by a handful of new young singers including **Amr Dieb**, **Hani Shaker** and **Bahar Mostafa**, proving that at 80 years of age, Mohamed Abdel-Wahab was still a highly influential figure. He died in May 1991 in Cairo.

Abdel-Wahab's chief contemporary rival as male singer-composer was **Farid Al Atrash**, whose sister **Asmahan** also rivalled Oum Kalthoum until her premature death in a car crash in 1944. The Al Atrash family was Syrian, of aristocratic Druze origin; previous generations had been Emirs of the Druze mountain territory, and Farid and Asmahan's father had held high administrative office in the French-mandated Lebanon. On his death in 1924, the family was impoverished and moved to Cairo, where the mother began to use her musical talents to earn a living singing at private parties. Farid Al Atrash studied Arabic lute at the Institute of Arabic Music and embarked on a career as a singer and musical film actor. His dramatic voice, Levantine good looks and virtuoso 'oud playing rapidly propelled him to stardom, and his output of films and musics (he composed all his own material) was prodigious. He was responsible for a dramatic increase in popularity of the 'oud, and an 'oud solo is still a characteristic element of Farid Al Atrash's music. His songs were wildly emotional − his voice was famous for its sobbing quality − but did not all concern love themes. One of his most famous songs, 'Arabya', was a paean to the Arab nation and its performance was a feature of the Cairene Eastertime 'Spring Day' holiday for over twenty years. He died in 1974 and, as with Oum Kalthoum and Mohamed Abdel-Wahab, his records still sell in large quantities.

Asmahan's voice, more delicate and feminine that that of Oum Kalthoum, attracted many of the great diva's composers to offer her songs; on a number of occasions Asmahan also collaborated with her brother in both song and film.

One more major artiste shared the uppermost reaches of Egyptian, and therefore Arab, stardom through the 1950s and 1960s. **Abdel-Halim Hafez** was born, twenty years after Oum Kalthoum and Mohamed Abdel-Wahab, in the Nile Delta. He studied oboe at the Cairo Institute for Theatre Music and taught music in schools before joining the national radio orchestra. His dramatic tenor voice soon came to the fore, and he began to sing the works of major songwriters, among them **El Tawil** and Abdel-Wahab, with whom he became strongly identified. His first great success, 'Safini Mara' ('Love Me Once'), was a love song and other famous numbers such as 'Al Fingen' ('The Cup

Reader') confirmed his reputation as a romantic idol, but he was equally identified with the nationalist political cause. For many years, Hafez performed a new patriotic song at the annual National Day concert in Cairo; the most outstanding example was 'Sora' ('Picture'), which described the different elements of Egypt's people, suffused with joyous patriotic fervour as they went about various tasks, such as building the Aswan High Dam, under the leadership of their idealistic young president. Hafez was also much fêted outside Egypt. He regularly performed in countries such as Morocco, whose King Hassan was rumoured to be one of the donors of the succession of Ford Mustangs and Mercedes which contributed to his playboy image. When in his late fifties, Abdel-Halim Hafez eventually succumbed to liver failure in a London hospital, having suffered the debilitating effects of schistosomiasis since his youth.

Of the second rank of performers in the Oriental style, **Warda** continues to be notable, although many Egyptian young people would regard her as passé, something nobody, however hip and modern, would say about Oum Kalthoum.

Warda (her name means 'rose' in Arabic) is not Egyptian; her father was Algerian, as Warda's commonly used soubriquet 'El Djazairia' ('the Algerian') acknowledges. She was born around 1940 in the Latin quarter of Paris, where her father ran a restaurant and cabaret. She began to sing in her father's cabaret, and her early models and guides were the Tunisian singers such as **Mohamed Jamoussi** and **Ali Riahi** who visited the establishment. As the Algerian independence struggle intensified, Warda began to acquire a reputation for performing songs in its support and was invited to perform in Cairo by Egyptian radio. Warda married an Algerian colonel and retired to Algiers for ten years without performing. Her return to the stage was the result of a request by Algerian President Boumedienne to participate in the celebrations of the tenth anniversary of the country's independence. Warda's return to the stage marked a new phase in her life; she divorced and got remarried, to the Egyptian composer **Baligh Hamdi**, moved to Cairo and relaunched her career with considerable success. Her elegance, expressive voice and stage demeanour (she moved easily and gracefully, unlike the static Oum Kalthoum) propelled her to the front ranks of the Oriental singers, a status confirmed by her relationship with the great Mohamed Abdel-Wahab, who began to write songs for her and coach her. Warda continues to perform internationally, in London, Paris, Cairo and Algiers, and her style and repertoire (250 songs) make her something of an institution.

Stylistically, the 1970s saw the beginnings of a challenge to the Oriental popular song which had been dominant for so long. Generally known as shaaby (people's or common music), it was simpler, rougher, shorter and rooted in the teeming, working-class districts of Cairo. The first of the singers to shoot to popularity by breaking with tradition was **Ahmed Adeweya**, who came from a poor background and worked as a café waiter before becoming a full-time entertainer. He began to specialise in taking the form known as 'mawwal' — the slow improvised introductory lament sometimes used to open a song — and performing versions in a mixture of slang and imaginative and suggestive nonsense phrases. His songs often painted vivid pictures of Cairene street life; his first great hit 'Ayal Soghayer Tah' ('A Little Child Is Lost') echoed the street cry of a child-finder, an individual whose profession consists of locating lost children for their parents in the rabbit warren alleys of the poor areas. Working in the nightclubs of Cairo, and frequently also of Arab London, Adeweya rapidly transformed his rough, low-class image into at first cult and then full-scale stardom, gaining himself droves of imitators. By the late 1980s he was wealthy and famous, and maintained a lifestyle rich in scandal potential. In 1989, Adeweya was flown to hospital in Paris in a coma, having met with a mysterious accident. He had been found in the apartment of a rich and powerful but anonymous public figure, mutilated by knife wounds. Drugs were involved, claimed the Cairo papers, and the wife of the powerful individual was presumed to have instigated the attack. It was said that an attempt had been made to castrate the singer. It was generally felt that his career was finished. After lengthy recuperation, however, Adeweya was able to release a new cassette, 'Margariya', in 1990, of which the main track, 'Mawwal Zaman' ('The Mawwal of Time') became a big hit.

While Ahmed Adeweya was consolidating his unique new style, other young seventies artistes were developing modern musics. **Mohamed Mounir** was one of the first to succeed nationally, and he did so partly by using the funky black African rhythms of his native region of Nubia, the southernmost area of Egypt and the most northerly of Sudan. Mounir was born in the southern Nile city of Aswan and studied film and photography in Cairo. His mix of Nubian rhythm, a modern rock setting (electric guitars, saxophone, keyboards, along with traditional percussion) and quality poetic lyrics, sometimes romantic, sometimes social comment, has given him substantial appeal among intellectuals as well as young people. His collaboration with the German rock experimentalists Roman Bunka and Edgar Hofmann of the group Embryo have helped.

Other young shaaby-based pop singers include **Magdy Talaat, Magdy Shaabeeni** and **Shaaban Abdul Raheem**. The Nubian influence has also played an important role in the popularity of several other new singers, notably **Mohamed Fouad, Hassan el Asmar, Khedr, Hassan Djizouli** and, above all, **Ali Hamaidi**, whose hit song 'Lolaaky' ('Because of You'), recorded with top New Wave singer-arranger **Hameed Al Shaary** and his band (see below), is reputed to have sold over a million cassettes in 1988 and 1989.

Overlapping the new shaaby-rock sound, but distinct from it, is the music known for a number of years as New Wave, and more recently, courtesy of a London-based Egyptian music journalist, as 'al jeel', or 'generation' music. Whereas the quintessential shaaby audience is the young urban poor, that of al jeel is the university students. The new sound combines rock and disco feel and instrumentation with Egyptian percussion, local rhythms and mainly romantic lyrics which retain the old sense of tragedy and melodrama but keep it short and relatively bouncy. If the old Oriental song style was a banquet, exquisitely prepared and relished at length, the new pop sound is a hamburger.

The Egyptian establishment, however, is so far not amused, and the new music is not to be heard on the radio or television.

The main instigators of the Egyptian new wave were in fact Libyan. Chief among them, and Cairo's leading pop arranger, is **Hameed Al Shaary**. Al Shaary was born in the western Libyan city of Benghazi, and studied to be a pilot in England and was later at music school in Cairo, where he settled in the mid-1980s after Qadafy's symbolic burning of Western instruments put paid to any attempt to develop a rock career at home. Al Shaary was much influenced by the Libyan singer and guitarist Nasser Al Mizdawi, naming his first group **Al Mizdawia** after his compatriot. Like Mizdawi, his music mixes a variety of Libyan rhythms, including the hot black mirzkawi wedding rhythms of the south, and a sprightly version of the maalouf of Tripoli and Tunisia, with electric guitars, synthesizers, and Al Shaary's light tuneful voice, surprisingly girlish and in total contrast to the high-intensity melodrama of the old school. Al Shaary's first hit 'Soud Andara' ('His Eyes Are Black') was an adaptation of an old Libyan popular song; it was soon followed by the self-penned 'Shara' ('Sign') and a string of compositions and arrangements for other new singers, including his brother. **Magdy Al Shaary**, having been a member, with Hameed, of a band called **Children of Africa**, forms part of the Jeel circle of musicians; his 1990 recording of 'Heleiwa' ('Honey' or 'Darling') was the top hit at the end of that year. Hameed Al Shaary is very much an observer and adaptor; he follows the international pop scene from his home and mixes, practises and experiments with his synthesizers. He is also the first Egyptian artiste to move seriously into the production of videos to market his songs. His band also plays live, however, and is capable of attracting extremely large audiences at open-air concerts in the universities.

On the production side of the new music, two important figures stand alongside Al Shaary. **Tarik Khalil**, the 'Warrior of New Wave' and a former jazz musician, is the most creative producer, working with the new record companies SLAM and Al Sharq, and using the increasingly important and busy studios of M-Sound, Echo Sound and the big, new 32-track Americana. **Adil Omar**, meanwhile, a close associate of Hameed Al Shaary, writes many of the Al Jeel group songs. Omar is an intellectual, a painter who teaches at Cairo Art School, and an avid researcher into Arab folklore and music.

Of several dozen young singers who now fuel the cassette market, the most substantial are **Ihab Tawfik**, who possesses an outstanding voice and is also a serious student of the 'oud; **Omar Dieb**, whose clean-cut good looks and pleasant voice have been responsible for a string of hits; **Medhat Salih**, whose 1990 hit 'Kawkaptaany' ('I Want To Live On Another Planet') sold in enormous numbers across the Maghreb; and **Hanan**, an attractive female singer, classically trained, whose first big bit 'Beima' ('Smile'), written by the Libyan composer **Ibrahim Fahmi**, established her as a serious new talent.

Egypt: Discography

Oum Kalthoum Anthologie de la Musique Arabe Vols. 2–6 (1926–35) (Club du Disque Arabe CD 024–028)
Oum Kalthoum The Golden Voice of (EMI Greece 171)
Mohamed Abdel-Wahab Cleopatra (Soutelphan GSTPCD 501)
Mohamed Abdel-Wahab Immortal Melodies (EMI Greece 122)
Farid Al-Atrash The Best Of, Vol. 1 (Voice of Lebanon VLMX 23)
Farid Al-Atrash Soundtrack Recordings (Voice of Lebanon VLMX 17)
Asmahan Archives de la Musique Arabe (Club du Disque Arabe CD 004)
Abdel-Halim Hafez Les Succes (EMI Greece 203, 204)
Warda En Concert (Blue Silver DK008)
Ahmed Adeweya Ahom, Ahom, Ahom (EMI Greece 355)
Mohamed Mounir Untitled (Line MSLP 400695J)
Various Yalla, Hitlist Egypt (Island 162 539 873)
Hameed Al-Shaary Herada (SLAM K7)

LEBANON

Before Lebanon collapsed into violent anarchy in the 1970s, Beirut rivalled Cairo as a centre for Arab music. Several great artistes remain, including the Arab world's superstar since the death of Oum Kalthoum, **Fairouz**.

The area comprising the modern states of Syria, Lebanon, Jordan and the occupied territory of Palestine was for centuries a cultural unity known as Al Sham. Whether an artiste was Syrian or Lebanese by birth was of little importance, as both countries accepted the same music.

Pre-1970s Lebanon, the Switzerland of the Arab world, was rich, sophisticated and culturally very Eurocentric, so that a strong feature of Lebanese music was its assimilation of Western styles. Beirut had, in any event, a substantial population of French and other non-Arab residents. On the other hand, many of Beirut's Lebanese residents still had associations with the villages from which their families had quite recently arrived, so regional folk cultures were also an important musical influence.

The rise of Lebanese modern music in the 1950s and 60s was greatly helped by the annual Baalbeck Festival, which was founded in 1957, and acted as a launching pad for a number of the rather glitzy musical tableaux, often featuring updated folk dances, such as the boot-stamping mountain dabké dance, which were an important part of the appeal of artistes such as Fairouz.

The war in Lebanon drove most serious music-making either to Cairo, where stars such as Fairouz went to record and rehearse, or Paris, as in the case of **Wadih Al Safi**.

Fairouz, the Arab world's top female singer, was born Nouhad Haddad in 1934 to a modest Beirut family, showed singing talent at school and studied at the Conservatoire Nationale, where she was spotted by Halim El Roumi, director of Lebanese Radio. Her interpretations of two songs by **Farid** and **Asmahan Al Atrash** were an immediate success and she became a member of Radio Beirut chorus, and very rapidly a promising solo performer. It was El Roumi who gave her the stage name Fairouz, the Arabic for 'turquoise', and who introduced her to her future husband and musical Svengali **Assi El Rahbani**, whom she married in 1954. Assi El Rahbani and his brother **Mansour** were crucial as composers and arrangers in creating the sound which made Fairouz famous. They were cosmopolitan, intellectual and innovative and incorporated into Fairouz's music a whole range of Western styles and details of orchestration, resulting in fascinating hybrids such as a suite of Arab tangos and rumbas inspired by the Argentinian bandleader Eduardo Bianco, as well as cleverly modernised but evocative pastiches of folk melodies, such as her early hit 'Itab'. At the same time they gained the respect of traditionalists with more classical pieces such as 'Ila Raïa'. By the mid-1950s, Fairouz was also a star in Syria, with continual performances on Damascus Radio. She starred in the first Baalbeck Festival and thereafter used the event to present many of her new songs, tableaux and, ultimately, the string of musicals – *El Shakhs* ('The Person'), *Ya'Ich Ya'Ich* ('Hurrah, Hurrah') and many others – which the Rahbanis created for her throughout the 1960s. Although noted for her sympathy for the plight of the Palestinians – her song 'Sanarja 'ou' ('We Shall Return'), recorded after the 1967 Arab-Israeli war, is still powerfully emotive – Fairouz is an outstandingly apolitical and reconciliatory figure in terms of her own country, a Maronite Christian refusing to leave for safe exile and obstinately maintaining homes in both Christian West and Muslim East Beirut. Since the death of Assi Rahbani, her son **Ziad Rahbani** has been her musical director and composer and has continued to update her music, incorporating into it jazz and other elements. Fairouz is the only Arab star able to fill any concert hall in Europe. In 1986, a performance at London's Royal Albert Hall reputedly broke Frank Sinatra's record for box-office takings. Two years later, at Paris Bercy Hall, ten thousand Arabs from all over Europe wept, applauded and held candles at her first French concert for nine years.

The second of the triumvirate of great Lebanese popular singers is **Sabah**, extravagantly blonde older rival to the brunette Fairouz. After three decades of great success with hit songs such as 'Addaya' ('To The Village') and in a number of major musicals (*The First Lady, Honeymoon, Helwe Ktir*), Sabah's creativity waned in the mid-1980s after a major hit 'Iya Mil Loulou' ('The Days Of Pearl') at the beginning of the decade.

Like Sabah, the third great Lebanese artiste, the singer and lutenist **Wadih El Safi**, is still performing in his seventies. After five decades of work, El Safi's repertoire is huge. He is noted for his virtuoso interpretation of a wide range of styles – classic Egyptian-Arabic, Lebanese folk melodies, more Western material – and his reputation is one of the highest in the Arab world. El Safi's squat physique and homely looks denied him success in the Cairo film musical world which he tried to enter in the 1940s, but his fine voice brought him success in the 1950s as interpreter of Lebanese-style songs such as 'Al Oma Al Oma' and 'Leyla ya Leyla'. He became a mainstay of the Baalbeck Festival in the 1960s, and began to work in Paris, where he has lived since the end of the 1970s, since when his performances have taken place either in exclusive and expensive cabarets or at private parties, of several dozen people at most, for which he is able to command very high fees.

The descent into civil war during the 1970s ended the golden age of Lebanese music and ushered in a new generation of singers, only one of whom, **George Wassouf**, is of major stature. Some of the new artistes are overtly political; an example is **Marcel Khalifa**, whose lyrics concern both his own country's troubles and the Palestinian problems. Others are more lightweight entertainers: **Walid Tawfiq**'s speciality is the crossover Anglo-Arab or Franco-Arab mixture of Arabic and English or French lyrics in the same song, and his best-known recording is his version of 'Happy Birthday To You', half in Arabic. His name is gossip worthy for his marriage to a former Lebanese Miss World contestant.

Other younger entertainers include **Majda El Roumi**, a classically trained female singer of Palestinian origin, very much in the mainstream mould of the Syrian **Mayda El Hennawi**, and **Raghib Alama**, a male heart-throb to teenage girls, whose fast modern songs (notably 'Sahran Li Meen' — 'Who Are You Staying Awake For?') are immensely popular but whose voice lets him down when he attempts, as many young singers still do, to perform items of the great Oum Kalthoum repertoire.

The brightest new hope for Lebanese music, however, arrived in the early 1980s when **George Wassouf** began to play the cabarets of Beirut. Now in his early twenties, Wassouf was born in Syria but has Lebanese nationality. His rough country background has been rapidly overlaid with urban suaveness as his voice is more and more in demand for exclusive soirées, for which he is reputed to command tens of thousands of dollars, in Tunis, Cairo and Paris. His high, agile voice and clever mixing of folk melodies from throughout the region with the classic Egyptian style of Abdel-Halim Hafez, or a snatch of Andalous music from the Maghreb, are the source of his musical success, while his lyrics can be provocative, as in his celebrated mawal equating the Bible with the Koran.

Lebanon: Discography

Fairouz Dix Années De Succes (EMI Greece GVDL 16)
Fairouz Ya 'Esh Ya 'Esh (EMI Greece GVDL 45)
Sabah Greatest Hits (Voice of Lebanon VLMX 17)
Wadih Al Safi Vols. 1–3 (EMI Araby 1017-1022-1023)
George Wassouf El Hawa Soltan (Relax-in K7)

SYRIA

Though historically of the same cultural background as Lebanon, Syria has not produced as many top-ranking popular musicians. Beirut-based artistes such as Fairouz have always counted nearby Damascus as part of their audience.

The top Syrian singer is the female star **Mayda El Hennawi**, a serious performer in the mainstream Egyptian style whose relatively static performance at large concerts is very much in the manner of the great Oum Kalthoum. A good deal of Mayada's career since her debut in the early 1970s has been spent in Cairo. There she worked with top songwriters, notably **Baligh Hamdi**, who authored great hits such as 'Ahla Omri' ('Best of my Life'), 'Kanya Makam' ('Once Upon A Time') and 'Sidi Ana' ('My Master').

Also a serious musician, the 'oud player **Sabah Fakri** is famous throughout the Arab world for works such as 'Ya Biladi Al Sham' ('The Lands of the Syrian-Palestine Region').

Up-and-coming Syrian artistes include **Marouan Hussam Aldine**, **Samir Samra** and **Asala**, another mainstream singer with a very attractive voice.

JORDAN and PALESTINE

The Jordanian capital Amman is not noted for its popular music scene. Traditional singers playing ney (flute) and rabab (single-string violin) are not lacking: a notable example is **Abdo Moussa**. In addition, a number of groups combine Western rock music with Arabic lyrics. Prominent among these are the **Tigers** and **Mirage**, three men and a woman, whose song 'Tougoulahwak' ('You Say I Love You') was very popular.

Whether living in Jordan, Israel or the other areas of their diaspora, the Palestinians have obviously not been in a position to foster an established, modern music industry, although before 1948 Palestine was, along with Syria, Lebanon and Jordan, very much part of a culturally homogenous region. The now Israeli but formerly Palestinian towns of Jaffa and Haifa had concert halls which would host all the great Arab stars of the day, such as the young Oum Kalthoum.

Modern Palestinian musicians tend to be either locally based folk performers, working for a restricted local audience, or semi-itinerant. **Mustapha El Kurd**, a Jerusalem-born singer, recorded in the early 1970s before moving to Lebanon, where he continues a not particularly successful career.

Ahmed Kabour is a political singer-songwriter in the same style as the Lebanese Marcel Khalifa, whose Western-instrumented recordings, including 'Ana Dikoum' ('I'm Calling You') have been popular.

The Silver Stones had a major hit with their song 'I Love You' in the Arab world in 1983, and their former singer-songwriter **Bassam Bishara** has managed to keep up a successful career, mainly performing at parties inside Palestine, and has composed songs for, amongst others, the Libyan exile singer Nasser El Mizdawi.

Al Ashikeen ('The Lovers') are a group mixing Western instruments with traditional percussion. In the late 80s they were resident in Tunis, home of Yasser Arafat's PLO Command.

Sabreen, a Jerusalem-based group using traditional instruments to perform a mixture of folk music and modern protest songs, in 1991 produced a cassette 'Maut Al-Nabi' ('The Death of the Prophet') with the Galilee-based female singer **Kamila**, an exponent of the mountain music of that region.

Other Palestinian singers include **Atallah Shoufani, Samir El Hafez, Ibrahim Azam, Khalil Mohammad Shaheen** and **Muhiddine Al Baghdadi**. In 1989, the latter two produced and recorded in Berlin an album of protest songs, performed by a number of German-exiled Palestinians, entitled 'Music of the Intifada'.

Jordan/Palestine: Discography

Various Music of the Intifada (Virgin VE 29)

IRAQ

Baghdad has long been a centre of Arab classical and semiclassical music, and the country is rich in folk musics of a wide variety of styles, often featuring complex and lively percussion. Iraq is not, however, a leader in modern Arab popular music.

In the 'oud player **Mounir Bachir** Iraq possesses one of the top Arab lutenists. Bachir was born in 1925, in the northern city of Mossul to a poet and musician father, and studied cello and 'oud at Baghdad Institute of Music. His style is rigorous, academic and, in concert, Western oriented (he prefers a silent audience to the traditional Arab outburst of exclamations at high points of a recital). His repertoire consists of taqsim improvisations on a body of classical themes.

Substantial Iraqi government finance helped establish the Academy of Arab Music, founded in 1967 in Baghdad under the patronage of the Arab League, and the city also supports several full orchestras of 'ouds, qanums (zithers), santurs (dulcimers), nays (flutes) and percussion, of which the most recent is **The Orchestra Al-Barayariq**.

The greatest Iraqi light singer of the recent past was the late **Nazim Al Ghazali** and present-day singers include the female **Souad Abdallah** and the top male artiste **Saadoun Jaber**. The latter, before the Gulf War a frequent visitor to London where he was a student, is known for his modernised versions of Iraqi folk style, typified by his song 'Bint Al Dira' ('Village Girl').

SAUDI ARABIA

The popular music scene in conservative, strictly Muslim Saudi Arabia is somewhat limited. For anything more risqué than an all-male clap-along performance at a private party (there are no public concerts), Saudis go to the fleshpots of Cairo or London.

Nonetheless, there are two major, and a number of minor, Saudi artistes whose music is also enjoyed throughout the Gulf. The two leading performers, and fierce competitors, are **Talal Madah** and **Mohamed Abdo**. Talal Madah, who is generally reckoned to be number one inside the kingdom, is a more traditional performer who relies on 'oud and hand-clap percussion to back his songs, one of the most famous of which is 'Wa tirhal' ('And You've Gone'), written after the tragic accident in which he killed his son in a car crash.

Mohamed Abdo, born in Yemen but naturalised a Saudi, is the best known internationally of his country's singers, and has accumulated a considerable fortune through his performances and recordings on his own label, Sout Al Gazira ('Sound of the Island', referring to the old concept of the Saudi/Yemen landmass as Gazirat Al Arab – the Arab island).

Abdo, a retiring, private man, made his name with shorter, more modern versions of traditional songs, scored for a full Western band with brass: top titles are 'Lailat Khamis' ('Thursday Night') and 'Hala Bi Atayeb Al Ghali' ('Welcome, Dear People'). He was a prominent performer of the pro-Kuwaiti 'national songs' which circulated during the 1991 Iraq–Kuwait occupation and war.

Other Saudi artistes include **Abdul Majid Abdullah**, a traditional 'oud player famous throughout the Gulf, and **Itab**, the first Saudi female singer, who didn't last long inside the kingdom, leaving rapidly to marry the Egyptian writer of her best-known song, 'Jani Al Asmar' ('The Dark Man Has Come').

KUWAIT

Kuwait's wealth and relatively relaxed social climate made the country an important centre of Gulf music, and in **Nabil Sha'el** (see below) it possesses an artiste of major regional stature. Before the Iraqi invasion in 1990, Kuwait City possessed well-developed radio and TV stations much listened to in Iraq and other Gulf countries, while the private Al Natha'er recording studio, which was relocated to Qatar during the occupation, was the best in the Gulf. Major stars would perform at seafront cabarets, such as **Al Shaab** and **Bneid Al Gar,** or in the big hotels at feasts such as Eid El Adha, the Feast of the Sheep.

The writing of verse, the basis of Kuwaiti song, is virtually a national pastime, and radio programmes such as the popular *Bakai'a Leil* late-night show would feature light music on cassettes sent in by listeners. The Kuwaiti royal family contains noted poets and songwriters including the Emir himself, who writes under the nom de plume 'Son of the Desert', and, especially, the Emir's popular younger brother, the late Sheikh Fahd, who was killed defending the Royal Palace in the first hours of the invasion. Sheikh Fahd was responsible for the song 'Ana Kuwaiti' ('I Am A Kuwaiti'), originally written to celebrate the successful conclusion of the 1988 hijack of a Kuwait Airways plane and broadcast on Kuwait TV's *Gulf Night* show, and revived in 1990 as the first of a rash of patriotic 'national songs' which began to circulate within weeks of the invasion. Another of Sheikh Fahd's songs, 'Ana Khaleeji' ('I Am From The Gulf'), became the theme tune of the Gulf Cooperation Council, and the year before his death the royal tunesmith was the subject of a TV show *An Evening With Sheikh Fahd* during which his songs were interpreted by top stars including **Abdullah Al-Ruwaishid** and **Rabab** (see below).

Kuwaiti popular song consists of a mixure of varying proportions of local Gulf folk rhythms, classical Egyptian style and Western rock and pop. Instrumentation consists of a similarly varying mixture of electric instruments, chorus and string sections with 'oud soloists. At the more traditional end of the spectrum (though not pure folklore) are artistes such as **Shath El Khaleej** ('The Nightingale of the Gulf') who sings at the glitzy National Day concerts featuring extravagant musical tableaux with huge chorus, who have been known to be dressed by Yves St Laurent. Nabil Sha'el and Abdullah Al-Ruwaishid are examples of the younger, more progressive tendency.

The patriotic genre known as 'al-ani watanya' ('national songs'), an established feature of Kuwaiti music, was revitalised with great urgency by the Iraqi invasion. Immediately all of the main singers began to record, usually in Cairo, cassettes rallying the Kuwaiti people and affirming their belief that God would shortly deliver them from their trial. The cassettes were distributed rapidly to communities in London, Riyadh and New York, and played on the Kuwaiti radio shows rapidly set up, for example, by refugee broadcasters on London's Spectrum Radio.

The first post-invasion 'national song' hit was the revived Sheikh Fahd song 'Ana Kuwaiti', rapidly rerecorded by **Abdul-Karim Abdul Kader** and Abdullah Al-Ruwaishid. The Second was 'Allah U Akhbar Ya Kuwait' ('God is Great, O Kuwait') recorded in one 24-hour session in Cairo by Nabil Sha'el and Abdullah Al-Ruwaishid, who, on the night of the invasion, had been in London about to perform at the Royal Lancaster Hotel. These were followed by a rash of similar songs, all equally emotional and dramatic and adorned with stirring martial choruses. A number of these songs were by artistes from countries sympathetic to Kuwait: the top Saudi singer Mohamed Abdo contributed 'Hal Al Tawheit' ('So United') and 'O Kudu Al Nar' ('Start The Fire'), **Khaled Al Sheikh** and **Ali Abdul Karim** from Bahrain, and others.

In addition to Shath El Khaleej, the older generation of Kuwaiti popular song is best represented by the romantic star Abdul-Karim Abdul Kader, whose sentimental ballads 'Gharib' or 'Mahal El Kheir' are immensely popular within the country.

A brighter, more up-tempo style was introduced by Nabil Sha'el who rose to great popularity in the mid-1980s with a succession of songs notably 'Ya Shams' ('Oh Son'), by the lyricist **Rashid Al Khoder**. Sha'el, known as the Demis Roussos of the Gulf for his portliness and piercing tenor voice, sings mainly love songs and travels continually, giving concerts in concentrations of Gulf population throughout the world.

Latterly he has been rivalled by Abdullah Al-Ruwaishid, who began his career in 1980 after studying briefly at music school and performing as a member of the group **Ribahi Al Kuwait**. He rose to prominence with his hit song 'Rahal Te'i' ('You Are Gone'). Al-Ruwaishid's family is musical: his younger brother **Adel** is also a singer, while his older brother **Mohamed** composes for him. Abdullah Al-Ruwaishid extended his fame greatly in the Arab world during the Gulf crisis: his brother Mohamed's capture by the Iraqis was widely reported, as was an interview he gave with the magazine *Al Majellah*, regretting his performance at the birthday celebration for President Saddam Hussein in Baghdad earlier that year, and renouncing his friendship with the Iraqi dictator. At a concert in Cairo to mark the prophet Mohammed's birthday, he was given controversial top billing over the much greater Egyptian star Warda, it was said at the express wish of President Mubarak.

Other prominent Kuwaiti singers are **Faisal Al Saad**, **Mohamed Salmeen**, **Salim Al Abdullah** and the female artistes **Nawal** and **Rabab**.

Kuwait: Discography

Abdel Karim Abdel Kader An Evening With (Bouzaidphone BUZ 10)
Miscellaneous Stars of Kuwait (Bouzaidphone BUZ 503)
Rabab The Artist of the Gulf (EMI YHCD 501)

OTHER GULF STATES

With its relatively mild religious climate and a well-developed tourist industry (mainly attracting visitors from other Gulf states) **Bahrain** has a climate reasonably conducive to music-making. This has been helped by the state's rise as a financial centre, following the decline of Beirut. There are, broadly speaking, two sorts of music in Bahrain. Traditional singers follow in the line of 1920s master **Mohamed bin Farres** and his student **Mohamed Zuweid**, who died in 1980; their repertoire includes songs about the hardship of seafaring life, of the pearl divers, etc. One modern singer who retains a proportion of this traditional subject matter while also incorporating modern themes of love and patriotism is **Ahmed Al Jumery**. The star 'oud player and singer **Khalid Sheikh**, whose style is more Western, is well known throughout the Gulf. Bahrain also contains guitar and drumkit groups singing traditional melodies in a Western style: the best known are **Alajaras** and **Sultanise**.

Qatar and the **United Arab Emirates** are less well developed, although the successful Al Nathe'er studio of Kuwait relocated to Qatar during the Gulf War. Top Qatari artistes are **Johar Abadi** and **Ali Abdu Satar**. Emirates singers include **Khaled Hamed, Mehad Hamed, Jaber Jassem, Ali Baroka, Abdullah Hamed** and **Abdullah Belkaer**.

Oman, because of its long seaboard connecting the Gulf with East Africa, and its substantial population of African slave descent, is a rich source of hybrid traditional music, little of which is, as yet, modernised. Charismatic mass-healing ceremonies to the rhythm of a variety of drums and conch shells, 'maalid' religious poetry chanted on the occasion of feasts and weddings, 'sowt al khaleej' male song and dance entertainments with 'oud, drum and violin accompaniment; all of these offer continual opportunities for music-making on a community level. The best known Omani semiprofessional popular singer is **Salim Ali**, who makes numerous cassettes and performs at parties and celebrations, while retaining a job in Omani Radio.

ISRAEL

The popular music of Israel consists of a number of strands, reflecting the many different nationalities of origin of the country's Jewish population. For most of the state of Israel's short existence, its cultural life has been dominated by citizens of European origin, particularly the Ashkenazi Jews of Eastern Europe, and sentimental Yiddish songs by artistes such as **Ben Zimet** are still popular with older Israelis, though no rock-age updating has taken place. One old Eastern European form, the klezmer wedding dance band, is undergoing a small-scale revival after having almost died out. Klezmer, played by small traditional jazz bands featuring skirling, gypsylike clarinet, was particularly associated with the town of Odessa, the so-called New Orleans of Russia. But it is in the USA, especially New York, that the revival is taking place, led by new, younger bands such as the **Klezmer Conservatory Band** and the **Klezmorim**.

Various other regions and communities have their musical representation: the Ladino genre consists of Hebrew lyrics with vaguely Hispanic and LatinAmerican music, while artistes such as **Matti Caspi** use a Brazilian-tropical colouring. One of the oddest and most interesting mutants is the religious rock of the New York-based **Piamenta Brothers**, members of the strict Hassidic sect, who ornament the music they play for ecstatic ritual dance sessions with wild Hendrix phrases on electric guitar and flute.

By far the largest part of the Israeli record market, however, is occupied by rock or pop in the Western style with Hebrew lyrics, and a distinct predilection for Eurovision boom-bang-a-bangery is present – the infamous Song Contest is held in great esteem by the Israeli showbiz milieu.

Of the less saccharine rock acts, the older, country-tinged singers **Arik Einstein** and **Shalom Hanokh** are perennially popular, while a clutch of younger stars include the faintly punkish female singer **Si-Himan**, whose hit song 'Shooting And Crying', focusing on the moral dilemma of young Israelis faced with the Palestinian intifada, created great controversy. A different tendency – the Tel Aviv beach and fun – is reflected by the music of the group **Machina**, while a more modern Russian influence is perceptible in the sound of **Givatron**, composed of second-generation, Russian-origin Kibbutzim.

One interesting non-European-based modern popular form has emerged in Israel in recent years. Referred to as Oriental pop, or rock mizrahi, the style has drawn on Arab, Greek, and Turkish musics to create a sound which appeals to the country's large population (now a majority) of Jews of Moroccan, Yemenite, Syrian, Greek and Central Asian origin, long an economic and cultural underclass in a country whose élite has always been Ashkenazi. The Oriental music simmered quietly outside the country's media for a decade – cassettes were traditionally sold by vendors at the numerous coach stations but not in shops – before the singer **Zohar Argov** (see below) brought it to mainstream popularity in the early 1980s. Overlapping with the hasla local dance-party circuit of Israel's Arab population, Oriental music was, and still is, associated also with boisterous, down-market wedding feasts.

Oriental rock has two sources, Arabic and Greek music. The Greek side not only catered for Greek-origin Jews, but acted as a sort of compromise music for many Jews of Arab origin before Arabic-based music began to spread.

Arabic-based pop itself takes various forms, one being the simple translation of Arabic songs into Hebrew; prominent examples are the male singer **Ruby Chen**'s Hebrew version of the classic Egyptian Farid Al-Atrash song 'Leila'; and the numerous versions of the song 'Linda, Linda', which itself started life as a reworking by **Samir Shukri**, an Israeli Arab violin player and hasla circuit veteran, of a 1950s Lebanese tune, before becoming a major hit in Arabic for **Haim Moshe** (see below) and in Hebrew for **Jacki Makayten** (see below).

The second class of Arab-influenced Israeli rock is a hybrid music derived from the traditional musics of Jewish communities resident in the Arab world. The principal example of this has been Israel's large population of Yemenite Jews, who were airlifted en masse from Yemen shortly after the foundation of the Jewish state in 1948, and whose ancient and distinctive music formed the basis of a number of rock fusions in the 1980s.

The father of Yemenite Israeli pop is **Aharon Amram**, a traditional singer born in Sana'a, South Yemen, who started performing and recording in 1955, shortly after his arrival in Israel. Amram had studied Yemenite Jewish religious music as well as the songs of the Diwan, a collection of festive devotional lyrics composed mainly by the great seventeenth-century messianic rabbi **Shalom Shabazi**, and his innovation was to set this body of music to electric guitar, drum and organ backing.

The first star of modern oriental rock was Zohar Argov, whose surname was Hebraised from its original Yemeni Orkabi, and who was a classic rock-and-roll delinquent. Born in the wine town of Rishon Le Zeon to an impoverished alcoholic father and housemaid mother, he started singing in Tel Aviv nightclubs in the mid-1970s and rapidly scored a cassette hit with his song 'Elinor', which blended rock guitar, organ and percussion with a dash of bouzouki ornamentation from the Greek wedding-band sound and a substantial reference to the Yemenite vocal tradition. Argov's major breakthrough came in 1980, when his song 'Perah Begani' ('Flower In My Garden') won first prize in a national competition for Oriental music. Argov's rise coincided with an opening of Israeli Radio's airwaves to the previously scorned Oriental rock, but Argov remained resolutely untamed. In 1987 his drug use led to a prison sentence, during the course of which he was found dead in his cell: the official explanation of suicide caused a degree of controversy and led to a posthumous boom in his popularity.

The second major Oriental rock star was **Haim Moshe**, also of Yemenite extraction, whose first hit was 'A'avat Hayay' in 1980, but who is best known for his version of the Samir Shukri song 'Linda, Linda', a song he actually recorded at home with a rhythm box and a guitar to fill a last-minute gap on the B-side of the record, but which rapidly became hugely popular. Other prominent exponents of the genre are **Jacki Makayten**, of half-Libyan, half-Yemenite origin, whose biggest hit was 'Mean Tezet' ('Flirt'); **Eli Luzon**, an albino singer and keyboard player of Tunisian origin, famed for 'Ezou Medina' ('What A Country'); and **Boaz Sharabi**, a gentler, more Western-folk-influenced stylist.

Two major female stars work in the Oriental style, although **Ofra Haza**, who is most famously identified with Yemenite songs outside Israel, is in reality a Western-style light-pop singer who has made one excursion into the Yemenite repertoire. Ofra Haza started her career as a child actress and singer and her attractive voice, vivacity and beauty brought her rapid middle-of-the-road success, culminating in a second place in the 1983 Eurovision Song Contest with a song called 'Hi', believed not to have been written by the Rabbi Shalom Shabazi. It was to the two-hundred-year-old poetry of Shabazi that Haza turned, however, for her 1985 album 'Yemenite Songs', which featured modern rock settings while retaining interesting touches such as the traditional oil-can percussion, used in Yemen because the Jewish community were forbidden the use of drums.

In 1990, **Zuava**, another beautiful young Oriental singer of oriental origin, shot to fame with her song 'Salamat' ('Greetings'), which she followed a year later with the equally successful 'Tipat Maza' ('A Touch of Luck'). Zuava is of Moroccan origin, and sings in both Arabic and Hebrew.

The most famous star of the Greek strand in Oriental rock is **Yehuda Poliker**, the son of two Greek Jews who met on the boat taking them to Palestine in 1946, having escaped the Nazi death camps. Poliker left the rock group **Benzine** in the mid-1980s and began to experiment with bouzouki and rembetika-influenced vocals in his music. A major influence on him was the traditional rembetika (see **Greece**) artiste **Aris San**, who occupies a position in relation to Israeli Greek music akin to that of Aharon Amram to Yemenite.

Yehuda Poliker's first solo album 'Enayim Sheli' ('These Eyes of Mine') was a great hit, selling 60,000 copies. In 1988 he followed it with 'Afar Ve Avak' ('Cinders and Dust'), a dramatic co-production with his manager and artistic collaborator **Yakov Gilad** on the theme of the Shoah ('Holocaust'). Poliker's powerful songs and strong seven-man group, including two Greeks, make him one of the most interesting of modern Israeli artistes.

Israel: Discography

Klezmorim East Side Wedding (Arhoolie ARH 3006)
Piamenta Brothers Simon Tov Mazal Tov (Ness Music HC 805)
Zohar Argov Greatest Hits (Acum CDR 010)
Zohar Argov Floods of Tears (BM Records 1007)
Haim Moshe Greatest Hits (Ness Music RV 001)
Eli Luzon Greatest Hits (Ness Music 1050)
Ofra Haza Yemenite Songs (Globestyle ORB 006)
Zuava Tipat Mazal (Ness Music CD)
Yehuda Poliker These Eyes of Mine (Cobalt COB 360 220)

TURKEY

The historical background of Turkish music is complicated: as the country's position between Europe and the Middle East indicates, many influences have met, mingled, competed and superseded one another throughout the large country over the centuries. These include the martial pipes and drums of the musical wing of the Janissary mercenary soldier corps; on their demise, a large number of gypsy entertainers who are still common; the asik style of the age-old Anatolian troubadours; the music accompanying the eighteenth-century dancing boys; the türkü style of rural folk song nowadays drawn upon for inspiration by young groups; the Ottoman light classical style şarki with its use of traditional instruments qanun (zither), 'oud (Arabic lute), saz (long-necked plucked stringed instrument) and ney (flute): all of these have left their mark.

A number of parallel popular genres have emerged in modern Turkey. The first is a modernised version of the şarki semiclassical art music, lightened, Westernised and glamorised for modern record and concert consumption. Its earliest exponent was the female singer **Müzeyyen Senar** and, as performed by serious conservatory-trained musicians such as **Emel Sayin** and the flamboyant but still serious, in musical terms, **Zeki Müren** and **Bulent Ersoy** (see below under Arabesk), it still retains a substantial audience.

A variant in the late 1960s was the work of artistes such as **Zülfür Livaneli**, a singer and saz player and film director whose politically conscious songwriting and sophisticated incorporation of Western instrumentation into an essentially Turkish sound have often led to comparison with his friend and collaborator, the Greek popular composer Mikis Theodorakis. Other occupants of this category merge with the associated genre of political-folk protest song, often Kurdish: an example is **Cem Karaca**.

There is, of course, a strong current consisting simply of Turkish language songs in a purely Western pop, disco or rock style; examples are **Ajda Pekkan, Sezen Aksu, Aşkin Nur Yengi** and **Baris Manca**.

It is important to note that many Turkish popular artistes do not restrict themselves to one genre: a light classical art-music singer may include Western songs or Arabesks (see below) in his repertoire, while assorted individual creations include items such as **Cengiz Coşkuner**'s extremely successful electric modernisation of the gypsy fife and drum sound used to accompany dancing-girl shows in Istanbul's Sulukule gypsy district.

Perhaps the most striking development in the 1980s has been the rise of the Arabesk. Arabic and Turkish music have long interacted with each other but latterly the Arabesk style has positively boomed, to the distaste of the Turkish cultural establishment who regard it as cheap, melodramatic and inferior. Arabesk is indeed much associated with the lower classes and with the Eastern Mediterranean areas, especially the city of Adana near the Syrian border. At the same time, however, like the blues, rembetika, raï and all the other low-life musics become lately fashionable, its rise was partly occasioned by a number of trained art-music artistes who took it up. A minor but significant part of its appeal to the intellectual world must be the way in which it overlaps another interesting area of Turkish cultural and entertainment life, that of homosexuality in general and transsexuality in particualr. A distinct air of camp attends Arabesk, which is of course most compatible with the melodramatic, self-indulgent, doomladen lyrics, rattling tambourine and derbouka rhythms, swirling Oriental violins and ornamental saz or 'oud lines. One of the major Arabesk stars, **Zeki Müren**, is flamboyantly homosexual, while another, **Bulent Ersoy**, is sensationally transsexual. It is interesting that both these artistes are intellectual, musically educated art singers, while the other principal category of Arabesk star, musically uneducated, 'redneck' Easterners are, for the most part, working-class macho. (In the view of Arabesk-haters, the genre's espousal by 'classic' singers, who often release cassettes with art music on one side and Arabesk on the other, simply reflects their inability to avoid cashing in on a craze which came to dominate the cassette market.) The ambivalent position of Arabesk — most educated, Eurocentric young people despise it — is reflected in the fact that Turkish television and radio still shun it, and it remains a music associated with the popular 'gazino' cafés and cabarets and the sound systems of taxis.

The first recording to be described explicitly, both by its author and the critics, as Arabesk, was **Orhan Gencebay**'s 1967 cassette 'Bir Teselli Ver' ('Console

Me'). Gencebay, a classical singer, composer and player of the saz and the similar baglama, originated from the central Black Sea region of Turkey rather than the Arab-influenced East, and was therefore in every sense an 'outsider' popularising a form he had taken up. Gencebay remains immensely popular. He was followed in the early 1970s by **Ferdi Tayfur**, a film star from Adana, very much in the rough, untutored classic Arabesk mode. Other stars of the redneck school include **Mülüm Gürses**, whose dramatic songs ('Dertliler Neyhanesi' – 'Café Of The Broken-Hearted'; 'Hüzünlü Günler' – 'Sad Days') have made him a master of a sort of turbocharged country and western world of remorse, loneliness and alcohol. The leading Arabesk star from this background, however, is **Ibrahim Tatlises**, a former building worker from the Kurdish region of Urfa. Tatlises started as a singer of folk music, especially the türkü genre, but reached his present massive fame via such high-energy Arabesk classics as his late 1980s 'Fosforlu Cevriyem' ('Haughty Courtesans').

Arabesk stars in the category of Gencebay, in the sense of being converts, as it were, from an art-music background, included Zeki Müren (see above), whose first Arabesk cassette was the wonderfully melodramtic 'Kahir Mektubu' ('Sobbing Letter') and whose 'Helal Olsum' ('May It Be Permitted') was one of the biggest hits of the late 1980s; **Mustapha Topaloglu**, the author of the celebrated 'Cukulata'; and Bulent Ersoy, who merits an entire chapter to himself (and, as of 1980, herself). Ersoy was classically trained in Istanbul, and embarked on a highly successful art-music career before embracing Arabesk and, more controversially, undergoing sex-change surgery in 1980. Banned from performing in Turkey, Ersoy moved to Germany for a number of years and made a successful non-Arabesk, austere, classically inclined cassette, 'Konseri' ('Concert'), which may have helped towards the lifting of the ban in 1988. On her return to Turkey she plunged anew into Arabesk with the cassette 'Süskün Dünya' ('Quiet World'). Tranquillity has not been a feature of Ersoy's life since her return to public performance, however. In 1989, a drunk and semi-deranged member of the ultraright-wing Grey Wolves paramilitary group shot and seriously injured her on stage in an Adana nightclub when she refused to sing a nationalist song on request. Ersoy survived to continue performing and launch another controversy by announcing her engagement.

The female singer **Bergen**, one of Arabesk's biggest woman stars, led a similarly lurid public life until her demise in 1990. Bergen made her name singing in the clubs of the south east, and acquired her entirely justifiable sobriquet 'The Woman of Grief' after an assault with car-battery acid by her jealous fiancé lost her an eye. She carried on, and triumphed in 1988 with major hit songs 'Yiller Assetmez' ('The Years Do Not Return') and 'Onu Dayak Tanrim' ('Let Him Burn In Flames of Love, O God') before dying of gunshot wounds after a second attack by the released former fiancé.

A development of the Arabesk boom was the arrival on the scene of a series of young teenage singers, many of whom prefixed their names with the word 'Kucuk', meaning roughly 'little', rather in the manner of the 'Chebs' of raï music (see **Algeria**). The leaders of this field were the female singer **Kucuk Ceylan**, whose great hit 'Seni Sevmeyen Ölsün' ('Let The One Who Doesn't Love You Perish') was adopted by Prime Minister Turgut Ozal's party as an election signature tune, and **Kucuk Emrah**, the begetter of 'Sevdim' ('I Loved'), who, with the onset of his twenties, has now discarded the 'Kucuk'.

The nineties have seen signs of a slowing down of the Arabesk boom, or at least a revival of other forms eclipsed by it. One such form is the ozgün genre, which combines a return to folk roots with a left-wing political consciousness which appeals typically to radical university students and socialist youth. One of its stars is the former Arabesk singer **Ahmet Kaya**, whose guitar-backed settings of texts, such as 'An Gelir' ('The Moment Will Come'), by the banned Communist poet Nazim Hikmet, are immensely popular.

Other artistes in this field include the singer **Fatih Kisaparmak**, whose hit 'Kilim' (about the traditional Kilim carpet) well illustrates the strand of folkloric, traditionalist, artisan feeling running through the genre; and the groups **Grup Yorum** and **Yeni Türkü**, both of whom are strongly indentified with university-centred left-wing political protest.

Finally, the ozgün genre overlaps that of Kurdish folk-based protest music which, until an alleged easing of restrictions after the Gulf War, was banned, as was the Kurdish language itself. Principal artistes such as the female singer **Selda**, or the male star **Shivan Perer**, therefore, were obliged either to exercise extreme caution to avoid punishment, or go into exile. Shivan Perer eventually opted for the latter after exceeding the implicit bounds of an 'Eastern Evening' (the phrase 'Kurdish Evening' being unacceptable) concert in Ankara's Guney Park in the early 1970s by singing in full a fiery and patriotic Kurdish poem.

Turkey: Discography

Emel Sayin Sevdalilar (Turkuola CD 8000)
Miscellaneous (inc. Tatlises, Manco, Müren The Best of Turkey (Sonodisc CD 8649)
Livaneli Gokyuzu Herkesindir (Destan MS 006)
Ibrahim Tatlises Fosforlu Cevriyem (Bayar CD 80020)
Ahmet Kaya Resitaller 2 (Destan MS/CD 014)
Selda Ozgurluk (Bayar CD 80007)

IRAN

The revolution which overthrew the Shah and ushered in the strict Islamic regime of Ayatollah Khomeini in 1979 put paid to the development of popular music inside Iran. Both for its religious unacceptability and its associations with the decadent Westernised old regime, pop was immediately suppressed and some musicians suffered jailing and beating. After the revolution Iranian popular music reorganised in the expatriate communities of Los Angeles and, to a lesser extent, London.

During the Shah's reign, however, popular music flourished, helped by a well-established and highly Americanised recording industry and media. Iranian television, nowadays charged exclusively with the propagation of Islam, was originally founded by the Iranian Pepsi-Cola franchisee in 1958, making Iran, along with Thailand, one of the two earliest developing countries to set up commercial TV networks.

The genre which blends Western pop and rock styles with traditional Persian musical traits — 6/8 time, an emphasis on poetry of lyrics and on melody as opposed to harmony — is generally referred to as jazz, and its earliest star, sometimes dubbed the Sultanijazz — the King of Jazz — is **Viguen**, the Iranian Elvis Presley, who is still deploying his (now white) Elvis quiff on stage in Europe and Los Angeles, his base since 1969. Viguen's earliest models were Sinatra and Nat King Cole and he was discovered by the head of Iranian Radio, who overheard him singing to a group of friends on a seaside picnic. Viguen's first big hit, 'Mahtab' ('Moonlight'), in 1954, was followed by a string of songs which became household names to all Iranians. 'Shahdumad' is still played at many of the country's weddings, and latterly 'Ahwazekhan' ('The Singer') has become a standard. Though still popular, Viguen has slipped into a rather sterile and glossy showbiz formula in recent years.

The second great name of Iranian pop is **Gougoush**, a charismatic and glamorous female star in the mould of Diana Ross who, in her heyday in the late 1960s and the 1970s, was reputed to earn £4,000 a performance in plush Tehran cabarets such as the Bokhara and the Shokufeynow, where members of the country's 'thousand families' — the social and business élite — would congregate. A child star, daughter of an Azerbaijani comedian father, Gougoush was famous for her emotional delivery and her choice of songs — 'Ghessey Vafa' ('The Story of Love'), 'Garibe Ashena' ('Familiar Stranger') and 'Jaddeh' ('The Road') were among her most famous — often written by top lyricist **Iraj Janati-Atai** and arranged by the masterly **Varoudjian**. Gougoush refused to join the exodus to the West after the fall of the Shah and now lives, silenced, in retirement in Tehran, having been left respectfully unmolested by the new regime.

While the jazz style was, and is, very Westernised, a more traditional Persian popular genre does exist which also exhibits Arabic shading, typified by singers such as **Haideh** and **Moin** (see below). Haideh was the younger sister of a successful female artiste, **Mahasti**, whom she overtook in popularity with her great hit 'Sal' ('Year') in the early 1970s; she continued her career in Los Angeles after 1979 and died there in 1990.

The early 1970s saw a new wave of Iranian popular music come into existence, influenced by the Western rock revolution of the Beatles, Rolling Stones, etc. Groups began to be formed in Tehran — the **Black Cats**, **Takhalha** ('The Aces'), **Ojoubeha** ('The Incredible Ones') — a number of them performing in the Kuchini nightclub. The most significant formation of this period, which lasted until the revolution, was the Black Cats, several members of which went on to major solo careers. The group itself was briefly re-formed in London after 1979, but without any success.

The most important sometime Black Cat was the singer-guitarist **Farhad**, who affected a Dylanesque cigarette between the strings of his guitar-head, and put to music high-quality texts of the new post-1940s school of Iranian poets such as **Ahmad Shamlou**. Farhad's most famous songs – 'Joumeh' ('Friday') and its linked sequel 'Haftehghokesteri' ('The Grey Week') flirted with veiled political protest against the Shah's regime. Post-revolution Farhad stayed in Tehran, silenced of course, where he is rumoured to have become religious.

Two other Black Cats are now mainstays of the Los Angeles Iranian music business. The singer-songwriter and bandleader **Shahram** was known originally for his incorporation of a Latin American feel into standard Persian 6/8 time music, with brass punctuation in the arrangements. A minor star before the revolution, he is now influential and famous, with substantial involvement in the Los Angeles TV and recording industry. His former Black Cat colleague **Ebi**, famous for the song 'Mahyeh Tangeh Boulour' ('Fish In A Crystal Bowl'), has also flourished, his powerful voice and relatively serious songs helping to maintain his reputation as an Iranian Peter Gabriel.

Other Los Angeles singers in the jazz line include the big star **Daryoush**, who shares Ebi's reputation as a serious artiste rather than a lightweight entertainer, performing quality songs by lyricists such as the great **Iraj Janati-Atai**. His dramatic, somewhat mournful tones are notably associated with the politically allusive songs 'Bombast' ('Dead End') and 'Bouyegandom' (The Smell Of Wheat'). Originally regarded as something of a Daryoush imitator, the similar performer **Sattar** has, as a result of continual touring, become more and more successful, with an uneven repertoire of songs, the most famous of which are 'Gole Ponhe' (the name of a flowering herb) and 'Assal' ('Honey').

One major artiste in the more traditional, less Westernised line established by Haideh is working out of Los Angeles, and is immensely popular. **Moin** is noted for the exceptional range and control of his voice, and for his dramatic, Arabic-tinged, rendition of songs such as 'Yeki Ra Doust Midaram' ('I Love Someone').

A not inconsiderable Iranian music scene exists in London. Its most notable stylists are **Faramarz Aslani**, a singer and guitarist in the mould of Daryoush; **Toufan**, a former star guitarist with the backing orchestra of Gougoush who lost everything in the revolution but has, with considerable effect, worked to forge a quality new Iranian sound since; and **Kouch**, a duo comprising the singer, guitarist and keyboard player **Cyrus Khajavi** and the violinist, keyboard and santoor player **Farzad Khavand**, whose debut cassette 'Baran' ('The Journey') combined a promising set of songs by **Khajavi** with Iranian folk songs, all set to tasteful modern fusionist arrangements.

Within Iran, pop and rock remains strictly forbidden, but not all music is extinct. Classical styles, represented notably by the composer and performer **Shadjarian**, are flourishing and, if only for lack of any alternative, a return of interest in pure folk music has occurred.

Iran: Discography

Viguen Viguen (Taraneh K7 198)
Kooch Baran (Kooch K7)

INDIA

Numerous regional folk styles and two distinct art-music traditions — Hindustani in the north and Karnatic in the south — make the Indian musical world complex. However, a broad, urban popular style has arisen which appeals to the whole nation and to the widespread diaspora which includes large, long-established communities in Britain, the Caribbean and East Africa, and newer or less permanent ones in the Middle East and many other parts of the world.

Although this is changing, the most important category of Indian popular music for many decades has been film music. The Indian film industry, the second largest in the world, based since the 1940s in Bombay and Madras, churns out hundreds of brilliantly colourful fantasies a year, films which still bear traces of their parentage in the old Ramayana theatre epics. Narrative, song and dance are jumbled together, and characters may zoom abruptly to a new location in mid-song or join a suddenly materialising Busby Berkeley chorus for an elaborate set piece. From the first sound movie, *Alam Ara*, in 1931 musical directors, composers and soundtrack singers (the actors generally mimed) rapidly outstripped the actors in importance as the songs became the chief attraction for the audiences. The basic recipe for a successful film became one or two stars, six songs and three dances. The songs would be ghazals, the light semiclassical love couplets based on old Persian poetry, or qawwals, Muslim devotional song (see **Pakistan**), in which case the normal all-male religious harmonium- and tabla-backed style was dropped in favour of romantic lyrics, Western instruments and women singers duetting from opposite sides of the screen on which, unusually, the backing musicians were shown.

In the earliest 'talkies', the actors did their own singing and the first star, and model for a whole generation of film singers, was **Kunda Lal Saigal**, who adopted an improvisatory classical style, in spite of his lack of a classical music training, and sold many recordings of his hit film songs ('Devdas', in 1945, was the most successful) before his death in 1946.

In the 1940s, actor-singers became a minority, and the Golden Age of the great 'playback singers' arrived. Three names, **Mohammed Rafi**, **Lata Mangeshkar** and **Asha Bosle** dominated this period, and the latter two were still at the top in 1990. Rafi's forte was his extreme versatility: he could sing in numerous languages and was equally adept at comedy or tragedy. Although a Muslim, he stayed in India after partition, when many of his co-religionists moved to the newly created Islamic-majority Pakistan, and his modest, likeable public persona, as well as his distinctive renditions of huge hits such as

'Chaudwin Ka Chaand' ('Like The Moon'), made him a national hero who has never been equalled by subsequent male playback stars.

Lata Mangeshkar and Asha Bosle are both daughters of a famous early actor-singer, **Dinanath Mangeshkar** (a third sister, **Usha Mangeshkar**, also sings but is less famous). Lata studied classical music in Bombay and made her film song debut in 1946 in the production *Aap Ki Seva Mein*. Over forty years, and 25,000 recorded songs later, her famously girlish voice was still putting the songs into the mouth of the sixteen-year-old heroine of the 1990 hit movie *Heena*. Slight in stature, serious, reserved and private, Lata Mangeshkar is also a composer and arranger, and a popular international concert performer: her recitals are austere, refined occasions very much in the classical style, unlike those of her sister, Asha Bosle, who is a more flamboyant, show-business figure, still bearing a trace of an image of rebelliousness she acquired by choosing her own husband instead of accepting a parental choice. Asha Bosle started her film singing career in 1948 with *Chunariya* and made her reputation singing light-hearted romantic roles in a series of 1960s films for the director O.P. Nayar. In the late 1980s she broadened her scope with triumphant classical interpretations, notably in the film *Umrao Jaan*, and now ventures into the rock bhangra style (see below) in collaboration with the top bhangra group **Alaap**. Other great stars of this period included the female singer **Geeta Dutt**, wife of the director Guru Dutt, noted for her low, sexy voice, and the male singer **Mukesh**, whose sung role in the Raj Kapoor film *Shree 4.20* gave rise to the universally known song 'Mira Joota Hai Japani' ('My shoes are English, My hat is Russian . . . but my heart is Indian'), and who died of a heart attack on stage during a concert.

Younger Bombay playback singers who have come up in the 1980s include **Shabbir Kumar**, **Bhupinder Singh** and, above all, **Suresh Wadkar**, who made his name singing the part of Rishi Kapoor, son of the great actor Raj Kapoor, in one of the first films to feature modern teenagers in a love story. Top new Madras singers are **Yesudas** and **Janaki**. One modern actor-singer, **Amithab Bachchan**, is a huge star in his own right, transcending the compartmentalised roles of the film industry. A new development at the end of the decade was the first penetration of the top rock bhangra artistes, exponents of a genre created outside India, into the Bombay industry, in the shape of singers **Channi**, from the group **Alaap**, and **Malkit Singh**, from **Golden Star**.

In the 1970s, the market for popular music unconnected with films, previously very minor, assumed major importance. The two genres to benefit were the old Moghul styles, qawwali and the ghazal, especially the latter. Qawwali music, with its fierce Muslim spirituality, is very much a Pakistani speciality though certain Indian singers, notably **Mohammed Rafi** and **Manadey**, were noted exponents. By the late 1980s, in smart Delhi hotels, Moghul-era themed restaurants, or concert halls, a new set of sophisticated ghazal singers were very much in fashion. The ghazal, originally Persian romantic poetry, had been performed through the film era by singers such as **Saigal** and **Begum Akhtar** in an increasingly musical and popular form, but the dramatic modernisation of the seventies was initiated by the husband-and-wife team of **Jagjit and Chitra**

Singh, whose album 'The Unforgettables' used modern, easy-listening accompaniments and simple current Hindi lyrics to make the formerly rarefied art music accessible to a new mass audience. At the same time, their contrasting characters – he a Sikh, of simple tastes, she Bengali, glamorous and sophisticated – made them highly visible in the media, as did elements of their ill-starred personal lives, such as the death of their only son in a motorbike accident. Two of the most famous singers of the ghazal boom, **Mehdi Hassan** and **Gulam Ali,** are Pakistani. Other top Indian artistes include **Anup Jalota,** the son of the Hindustani classical musician Purshottam Jalota, who first performed in London to small private audiences in 1977 and by 1990 had over fifty records to his credit and was able to attract 9,000 people to Wembley Conference Centre; **Pankaj Udhas,** whose serene, white-shawled, seated figure is also an enormous concert draw, and whose records sell hugely (his most famous song is 'Chiti Aye' – 'Letter Coming' – of appeal to all diaspora Asians and their relatives at home), and his brother **Nirmal Udhas.**

Standing apart from the ghazal mainstream is the British Asian singer **Najma Akhtar,** whose successful assault on the world music market has resulted in her achieving greater fame with non-Asian audiences in Britain, Europe and, especially, Japan than with Asian audiences. Najma, whose father had interests in Indian film distribution in Britain, took a degree in chemical engineering at London University, won the Asian Song Contest in Birmingham in 1984, and in 1987 released 'Qareeb', an album of ghazals which attracted considerable media attention and led to her becoming a regular performer at European festivals.

During the 1980s other British Asian artistes worked in a roughly pop fusion vein. The Pakistan-born, London-resident brother-and-sister duo of **Nazia** and **Zoheb Hassan** scored a massive hit with their 'Disco Deewane', basically a disco tune with Hindi lyrics and an unusually polished 24-track production. The young TV actress, dancer and singer **Sheila Chandra** scored an early crossover hit with the group **Monsoon,** in the form of their 1982 UK Top Ten hit 'Ever So Lonely': Chandra went on to make experimental 'Indipop' solo albums. The major contribution of British Asians to the popular music sphere, however, was the rock form of bhangra music. Bhangra, with its distinctive accompanying dance, is a regional traditional style, played on the dhol and dholak drums in the Punjab at bhasaki – New Year – and at harvest time. Bhangra is traditionally danced by men, and its boisterous, hedonistic, slang lyrics make it an attractive entertainment even to non-Punjabis. Pop-bhangra grew up in the late 1970s and early 1980s in the big British Asian communities of Southall in London, the Midlands and, to a lesser extent, Bradford. Groups of amateur or semiprofessional musicians had long been in demand to play at weddings and other celebrations, and little by little their repertoire of film songs and traditional rhythms, including bhangra, began to be adapted to modern instruments – synthesizers, drum machines, etc. – as well as the traditional percussion. The first group to record an album of new electric bhangra was the ten-piece Southall-based Alaap, who opened the floodgates to a rapidly growing stream of new competitors. Alaap's British success soon spread to the Asian subcontinent and by the mid-1980s the band had acquired a huge following with old and young audiences. In 1987, the duets of Asha Bosle and lead singer Channi on the album 'Chham Chham Nachdi Phiran', recorded in Southall, imparted major new mainstream status to bhangra. Alaap's style retains a substantial traditional base, unlike some later bands – a feature which is shared by the groups **Premi** and **Apna Sangeet**, an exciting showband whose virtuoso dancer **Kuljit Bhamra** helped make them the top Asian band of 1987.

The mid-1980s saw a new wave of bhangra groups, harder, more percussive and more influenced by house and other Western dance musics. The two leaders of this trend were **Holle Holle**, led by a former Alaap singer, **Manjeet Kondal**, whose eponymous debut record remains a party standard; and the ten-member **Heera**: both Holle Holle and Heera were assisted by the arranger-producer **Deepak Khazanchi**. The domination of these groups, all from London, was challenged by Midlands bands, notably **DCS**, led by producer-arranger and, later, radio presenter **Danny Choranji**, and by **Azaad**.

A third wave of young bhangra groups included the stylish and inventive **Sahotas**, from Wolverhampton; **Pardesi**, whose 'Pump Up The Bhangra' was a huge hit; the Coventry group **Anaamika**; **Shava Shava**; and Golden Star, featuring the well-known Punjabi singer Malkit Singh, who moved to Britain to enter the bhangra fray. By 1990 hundreds of groups were in competition for the booming record market, and the UK still remained way ahead of the subcontinent both in producers and consumers of bhangra. Several female singers have entered the male world of bhangra singing. Some, such as **Kamaljit Neeru**, perform bhangra itself; others, notably **Mala**, invent female dance variations, in Mala's case the dance 'Gidha'.

India: Discography

Lata Mangeshkar The Legend (EMI India PMLP 1180)
Various (inc. Mangeshkar, Bosle, Rafi, Mukesh) Golden Voices From the Silver Screen, Vols. 1–3 (Globestyle ORB 054, 056, 059)
Suresh Wadkar The Golden Voice of (Sirocco CBS 015)
Jagjit and Chitra Singh Black Magic (ABC LP 0001)
Nirmal Udhas Greatest Hits Vols. 1 and 2 (Sirocco 011, 012)
Najma Atish (Triple Earth terra 108)
Asha Bosle and Alaap Chham Chham Nachdi Phiran (Multitone MUT 1121)
Sheila Chandra Roots and Wings (Indipop SCHCD 5)
Holle Holle Wicked and Wild (Arishma ARI 1006)
DCS Bhangra's Gonna Get You (Multitone MUT 1126)
The Sahotas Aaja (Multitone MUT 1102)
Various Compilasian (Indipop INDCD 1)

PAKISTAN

As a predominantly Muslim state, Pakistan has a much more austere cultural life than India. Historically, strict Islamic practice forbade music and such musicians as there were belonged to the inherited caste of Mirasis. Although the profession is now more open, dance and music are very restricted by comparison with India. Partly for this reason, and partly because it was already well established in India's commercial centres, the film industry is not strong in Pakistan (although its strait-laced television dramas are highly respected in the subcontinent). Indian film music, however, is as popular in Pakistan as in its home country.

The ghazal light classical form flourished in Pakistan; **Noor Jehan** is the equivalent and equal of Lata Mangeshkar (see **India**), while the male singers **Mehdi Hassan** and **Ghulam Ali** were leading lights in the ghazal revival of the 1970s and 1980s.

Noor Jehan rose to fame as a playback singer in the 1940s, before the partition of India and creation of Pakistan; she made her name with soundtracks for great film successes such as *Anmol Ghari* and *Jugnu*, but on partition chose to live in Pakistan. Unlike the retiring Lata Mangeshkar, Noor Jehan is flamboyant and dramatic, much married and fond of gorgeous dresses and elaborate make-up. While Lata Mangeshkar's concerts are serious affairs, seated and with smoking banned, Jehan's are wild and emotional, with spectators rushing to the stage to shower her with money. Mangeshkar's voice still appeals to Indians and Pakistanis of all ages, but Jehan's distinctive tones are now appreciated by a declining, older, mainly Pakistani audience.

In the early 1960s, **Mehdi Hassan**, a classically trained singer from an old family of Moghul court musicians, embarked on a ghazal singing career that rapidly made him number one in the subcontinent. Hassan's greatest successes were his versions of the poetry of the great writer **Faiz Ahmed Faiz**, who died in the mid-1980s; famous examples were 'Galoon Main Rung Bhuray' ('The Early Morning Breeze Through The Garden . . .') and 'Janeh Bahara' ('Life And Soul Of Spring'). Mehdi Hassan also achieved great success as a film singer, and was greeted as a visiting monarch on his first trip to the Bombay studios in the early 1970s.

By the late 1970s, Mehdi Hassan was eclipsed by the second great Pakistani ghazal singer, **Ghulam Ali**, another classical artiste who had studied with the famous maestro **Ustad Barkat Ali Khan**. Ghulam Ali, a simple reserved man by comparison with the mercurial Mehdi Hassan, rose to fame with his rendition of 'Raat Din Ansoon Bahana' ('I Remember Crying Night and Day') by the nineteenth-century poet Moman, and went on to score major film-song hits such as 'Yedil Yepagil Dil Mirah' ('This Crazy Heart of Mine').

Mehdi Hassan entered the 1990s as the top ghazal singer; among his male rivals is the London-based but internationally travelling **Asad Amanat Ali Khan**, whose father was also a famous singer, noted for his interpretation of the poem 'Inshagi Ab Kooch Kuro' ('Inshagi, Let's Move On'), in which the late poet Inshagi prepared himself for his imminent death.

Top modern female ghazal singers include **Farida Khanum**, the sister-in-law of the eminent writer Agha Hashar; **Iqbal Bano**, an important film singer; **Tina Sani**, a young artiste who sings folk and Western disco material as well as ghazals based on the poetry of Faiz Ahmed Faiz; and the mother-and-daughter duo **Malika Pukhraj** and **Tahira Syed**.

One field in which Pakistani artistes remain supreme is qawwali singing, which is the devotional music of the Sufi branch of Islam, a tradition related to the Persian-based cult of dervishes. Like dervish dancing, qawwali music's original function is to induce a state of ecstatic contemplation of the greatness of Allah. It does this by the repetition and improvisation of religious poetry, some verses dating back as far as the thirteenth-century master **Amir Khusrow**. Qawwali is normally performed by parties of up to a dozen, one or two improvising lead voices backed by a chorus of several more, with hand-pumped harmoniums, tablas, dholak bass drums and synchronised flamenco-style hand-clapping. A degree of secularisation of qawwali has taken place, helped by a 1980s film-industry craze for including qawwali scenes (with women singers). As a result, the more progressive performers may now include love songs and humorous monologues in their repertoires.

Of the three major stars of qawwali, the **Sabri Brothers**, led by the charismatic former army sergeant and member of the Karachi Drama Society, **Ghulam Farid Sabri**, are the most traditional performers. Ghulam Sabri and his singing co-star and brother **Maqbool Sabri** come from an old family of East Punjab singers, and their eight fellow group members are mainly younger members of the same extended family. Given the theatricality of the henna-locked kohl-eyed Ghulam Farid Sabri, it is not surprising to learn that he has a useful sideline in fruitily villainous voice-overs for films. In addition to their numerous cassettes, the Sabri Brothers have, while touring with the WOMAD organisation, recorded one British album, 'Ya Habib' at Real World Studios.

While the Sabris' music is relatively conservative, the qawwali of **Nusrat Fateh Ali Khan** is resolutely innovative. Nusrat learned music from his father **Ustad Fateh Ali Khan**, also a famous singer, and became a singer on his father's death in 1964. With the retirement of the group's leader, his cousin **Mujahid Mubarak Ali Khan**, in 1971, Nusrat took over leadership and rapidly established himself as the most exciting new voice in the country, winning the Khusrow Festival, qawwal's top prize, in 1976. Apart from his extraordinary quicksilver scat-singing voice, Nusrat's music distinguished itself for its appeal to a common, non-learned audience, with texts concerning love, alcohol and other profane subjects, sung in modern Urdu or Punjabi as well as the normal, classical Urdu only semicomprehensible to ordinary people. As Nusrat's group began to attract increasing numbers of Western world music aficionados in the mid-1980s, he began to experiment with Western fusions, the culmination of which was his 1990 album 'Mustt Mustt', recorded at Peter Gabriel's Real World Studios and featuring Gabriel's rhythm tracks and contributions by the ex-Sting bassist Darryl Johnson, the guitarist and producer Michael Brook and the remixing talents of the young Bristol dance producers Massive Attack; the result was curious and not unpleasant.

The third major contemporary qawwali star is **Aziz Mian**, a poet and self-taught musician from a non-musical background, whose performances include lengthy extemporised stories, some of them humorous, tied together by Mian's gruff, fierce, dramatic voice. Mian's qawwal 'I come To You Mohamed' was the first such song composed in English.

In addition to ghazals and qawwali music, Pakistani music features a range of more or less popularised folk styles. The music of Sind province, containing the great port of Karachi as well as a very large number of Sufi shrines, is particularly rich and its greatest exponent, the young female singer **Abida Parveen**, an all-round artiste also excelling in ghazals and Westernised pop, is one of Pakistan's top popular singers. Abida Parveen's father was a musician and proprietor of a music school, and she was still in her teens when she was discovered and featured on Hyderabad Radio by the producer Sheikh Ghulam Hussain, who later became her husband and manager.

At the age of 26, Abida Parveen became the youngest artiste ever to be awarded the Presidential Pride of Performance medal and she subsequently toured Europe and the Middle East. She is a particularly noted interpreter of the religious folk style known as 'loake geet' (people's song'), as well as the religious poetry, known as wai, of the great Sufi mystic Shah Abdul Latif.

Another prominent performer of Sha Abdul Latif's body of music is **Allan Fakir**, an actor and singer who has successfully adapted the Sufi poet's wai songs for a modern audience by increasing and enlivening the tempos, helped by his considerable gifts as a comic actor, mimic and dancer.

From the North-West Frontier province bordering Afghanistan, two substantial Peshto folk-based artistes have achieved fame outside their region. The female singer **Zarsanga** is a member of a nomadic hill tribe and performs a rabab (lute), harmonium and tabla-backed wedding music, the choruses of which can be marked by mass rifle-firing from her audience; she also toured Europe in 1990.

Her countryman **Fazad-E-Malik Akif** is quite another matter, a lawyer and intellectual with a naturally fine voice who took up singing at college. He now supports himself by his legal practice while making regular TV and concert performances and recording very successful cassettes for his home audience and the large numbers of Peshto expatriates in the Middle East. Akif's speciality is updated Peshto folk, using electric guitar, synthesizer and conga as well as rabab.

In the Pakistani Punjab, rock bhangra music does not flourish as it does in the Indian Punjab and Britain because of the relative intolerance of modern dance and the rock-music image; there are however Punjabi folk-pop singers of considerable fame, notably **Shaukat Ali** and **Alam Lohar**.

Finally, Pakistan has a considerable Western-style pop scene, though its Urdu lyrics tend to be its only non-Western features. In the early 1980s, the sister and brother Nazia and Zoheb Hassan recorded an album, 'Disco Deewane', while at college in London, which created a tremendous impact among Indians and Pakistanis around the world. Nazia Hassan's fame was extended by her role in the hit film *Qurbani* ('Fate'), but the duo's popularity was overshadowed by the bhangra boom of the late 1980s.

Among the top pop groups in Pakistan are the **Jupiter Group**, the **Live Wires**, the **Strikers**, the **Nite People**, the group led by top actor and singer **Hasan Jahangir**, and the **Vital Signs**, a group of former engineers and doctors who scored a huge hit in the late 1980s with 'Dil Dil Pakistan, Jaan Jaan Pakistan' ('Heart, Heart, Life, Life, Pakistan').

Pakistan: Discography

Noor Jehan Greatest Hits (Sirocco CD 014)
Mehdi Hassan Ghazals (Sirocco CD 001)
Ghulam Ali Very Best Original Ghazals (Sirocco CD 006)
Farida Khanum Supreme Collection (Sirocco CD 041)
The Sabri Brothers Greatest Hits (Sirocco CD 045)
The Sabri Brothers Ya Habib (Real World RW 12)
Nusrat Fateh Ali Khan Greatest Hits Vols. 1 & 2 (Sirocco CD 007 & 008)
Nusrat Fateh Ali Khan Mustt Mustt (Real World RW 15)
Abida Parveen The Inimitable (Sirocco CD 023)
Nazia and Zoheb Hassan Young Tarang (Sirocco CD 019)
Vital Signs Vital Signs (Sirocco CD 015)

SRI LANKA

Sri Lankan music and culture is based on that of its huge and close northern neighbour India. The two ethnicities of the island, Tamils and Sinhalese, tend to follow their respective Indian sister communities, but to different extents, so that while Sri Lankan Tamils are closely connected to Indian Tamil culture and Southern Indian karnatic music, Sri Lanka's Sinhalese majority has an affinity with Northern Indian Hindustani music, but a considerable impetus also for independence from it. Hindustani music, particularly film music, has been boosted in the country by two factors in recent decades: the first is the Sinhalese-dominated government's desire to counter the growth of Tamil arts among the independence-minded minority group: the second was Radio Ceylon's Indian film music-dominated output of the 1950s, a policy encouraged by the financial incentives from Indian advertisers, displeased at Indian State Radio's boycott of film music during that period.

Sri Lanka does have another more original musical genre, however, which appeals to both Sinhalese and Tamils. The style known as baila is very popular at village level, where it is played for dancing at weddings with the assembled company joining in on handclaps, and improvised percussion on household utensils. Baila, which in its modern commercial form is played on electric guitars, drums and synthesizers, is related to a similar older form, Kaffrina, more usually played on acoustic guitars and violins, and possessed of certain African characteristics. Both styles are probably derived from the music of visiting early Portuguese sailors, and as such have a strong family resemblance to other Portuguese derived styles such as Indonesian kroncong. Baila, which has a competitive, verbal duelling offshoot, wada baila, is widely distributed on bootleg cassettes; its main stars are the older singer **Wali Bastian** and, since the 1970s, **Anton John**.

THE FAR EAST AND PACIFIC

INTRODUCTION

Right throughout the Far East you'll find Filipino entertainers in great demand. In all the five-star hotels of the region, it's Filipinos who provide the music. This is partly because the Filipinos are among the most musical and music-loving peoples of the region. Everywhere you go in the Philippines you hear music. In Japan, for example, you don't really hear music outside its normal place, such as on the radio. But in the Philippines it's a part of everyday life. Street vendors sing a song about the excellence of their goods; in the country the people you pass washing in a stream will be singing; a cook in his kitchen, a laundrywoman, they're always singing − anything from pure old folk music to Western pop songs. It's as though they're full of music and even when things are bad, instead of becoming depressed and quiet, they sing to forget their problems.

In addition to this natural desire to sing, Filipinos seem to have a talent for picking up a tune easily and learning it. Also, they are good at languages; the Filipino tongue adapts easily to many different languages − English, Spanish, French, Japanese − and a good Filipino musician can very quickly and accurately copy a song after hearing it only once or twice.

The disadvantage of this is that the musicians are not always very original. If all you do is copy, and you don't bring any originality to your interpretation, it's not very worthwhile artistically. In fact this was a problem for me when

I started my career − I had my own unique style, but I used to do other people's songs. Even if I did a song by Cat Stevens or James Taylor or Neil Young, though, I always used my own style and because of this I was always getting complaints. They'd say, 'You're no good, you don't sound like (whoever it was whose song I was singing)', and I'd reply, 'But I'm not the guy, I'm a different guy!' I never won many competitions because of this.

One Western musical style which was adopted everywhere in the East was country and western. You found it everywhere − and still do in many countries. Australia and New Zealand made country and western their own, with lyrics speaking of their own situation; Malaysia has many country singers; my own country, too. One of my first musical memories was the singing of Fred Panopio, who is still a big star in the Philippines. He's a C & W singer who sings in Tagalog about local themes and stories. I remember one of his early good songs was 'Pitung Gatang' − it means 'Seven Litres' and it refers to a street in Manila which was a bit like the Bronx in New York − the title refers to the fact that you'd buy rice by the litre there.

Of course, the Far East doesn't simply copy Western styles. The different regions have their own musical traditions, and many styles of popular music have developed from folk musics. Indonesia, Malaysia and other countries have done this well. In Japan, too, there is a lot of interest to preserve traditional styles. There are also Japanese musicians like Boro, who does very good research into musics of other nearby countries like the Philippines.

Traditional music in the Philippines survives, but many of the old instrumental styles are in danger of dying out now. Not so much the songs, but the traditional instruments which used to accompany them. One of my earliest memories of music is of the folk songs I heard − and sang − at home. When I was five, my parents used to encourage me to sing for our visitors. The songs I sang then were Filipino folk tunes which at one time would have been accompanied by guitar, but tuned to an open tuning, and often with only five instead of six strings, and traditional instruments like the nose flute and the kulintang. These are the instruments which are so hard to find now. There are many artistes today, including me, who would love to feature nose flute in their modern arrangements, but you just can't find the players. The new generation was never taught to play.

The same with the kulintang. This is a Muslim instrument, a set of small gongs with a very penetrating sound. I've used it on my records, but it's very hard to find a kulintang now in Manila. Nobody's making them any more, and the people who do have a set aren't selling them. A very good friend of mine, a former mayor of the city of Davao, has a beautiful set, perfectly pitched, which he's let me play. I begged him to sell it me, but he couldn't, it was a gift from his tribe, the Datu. The situation in the Philippines is much worse than in certain other countries in the region, which have kept their traditional instrument-making much more alive. The gamelans of Java and Bali, for instance, are still produced regularly and Japanese and even Chinese traditional instruments are available much more easily than Filipino ones.

I hope I'll have a good kulintang set before long, though. Another political friend, a senator from Mindanao, has promised to get me a set by finding the different gongs one by one. This political connection, by the way, is another interesting point about Filipino popular music which makes it different from other countries in the Far East (although the King of Thailand is a keen jazz fan and used to play saxophone regularly). Since music is so popular in my country, politicians have always used it to appeal to the people. If you've got a good name and you can belt out a song, you're halfway to being accepted as a politician. That was why the Marcoses did their famous singing routines, and why other politicians before them did the same, for example President Magsaysay in the 1950s, whose nickname and campaign song was 'Mambo Mambo Magsaysay'. Cory Aquino was the first politician to break with this tradition − she's never tried to pretend to be a singer.

In fact, it was one of my songs − or at least, my version of an older song − that was Cory Aquino's rallying hymn during her 1986 election campaign. The song was 'Bayan Ko' ('My Homeland'), a 1930s kundiman song which I reworked in a modern style. When I first began to perform it there were many raised eyebrows − why had I changed such a famous old song? But now my version is totally accepted.

My style was very influential in the Far East − many singers followed the same path of taking Western rock and folk styles and adapting local music and lyrics to them. There were even singers who copied my look − one Thai guy in particular with long hair and a hat just like mine. Now there are young singers from Japan and Hong Kong copying all the latest Western pop and disco styles. In general, the East is keen to be modern in its pop music, but there is also a good number of singers and musicians who try to incorporate older traditions.

FREDDIE AGUILAR

CHINA

Three basic elements mix and conflict in Chinese popular music: traditional instrumental pieces played on a variety of flutes and bowed and plucked stringed instruments, often painting simple tone pictures, for example of galloping horses on a steppe or moonlight on a rippling pond; Western styles from romantic orchestral to rock; and the martial or political songs imposed in varying degrees under the Communist government.

Pre-revolutionary Shanghai, the commercial capital, contained the clearest early forms in which both of the latter influences were particularly strong. The Western influence, diffused through the 1930s world of cabarets, nightclubs and brothels, manifested itself in 'yellow music', louche, romantic songs with Chinese melodies and Western string arrangements. Key exponents of this style included the prolific songwriter **Li Chin-hui** and the female singing star **Chou Shuang**, who made songs such as 'When Will You Return' and 'The Four Seasons', which are popular to this day.

At the same time, Shanghai was a centre of militant trade unionism and of the growing Communist movement which was associated with the nationalist cause against Japanese and Western domination. This movement gave rise to the revolutionary songs which combined inspiring political lyrics, mass choirs, and a mixture of Chinese folk and Western elements, the latter from Protestant hymns, martial brass bands and Russian revolutionary songs. The composers **Nie Er** ('The March of the Volunteers') and **Xian Xinghai** ('Yellow River Cantata') are outstanding practitioners of this form.

After the 1949 revolution which brought Mao Tse-tung to power, popular music changed somewhat but nevertheless flourished for the first seventeen years. Mao's Marxist-Leninist-based aesthetic and cultural policies regarded music as an important tool in the development of a socialist society, but the propagandising role of song this implied was not at all at odds either with Confucianism, which always regarded music as behaviour-modifying, or with previous Chinese rulers' habits of regulating court musics. Experimental schemes in communal composing and sending professional music-makers to live and work in rural communes were set up, and a revival and modernisation of folk music was embarked upon. There was, however, no very harsh suppression of Western music, which was studied as actively as Chinese music, and a wide range of styles, including recreational and dance music, were permitted. Thus, in addition to the mass choirs and orchestras singing Western-scored, Russian-influenced hymns to the glory of the revolution, 'soft music' also flourished. A prime exponent was the singer **Guo Lan-Ying**, whose initial success stemmed from coming from Mao's home province and power base, and who made such songs as 'The Waves Of Hung Lake' nationally famous.

The advent of the Cultural Revolution in 1966, when Mao launched his brutish Red Guards into the eradication of everything in society except a drear, spartan, radical communist system, put paid to most forms of popular music until Mao's death in 1976. Dance halls were closed, popular festivals banned for their past association with a feudal system, and intellectuals and artists killed or put to work in the fields. The narrow range of music permitted was a body of five 'model operas' and three 'model ballets', expressing microscopic variations on a theme of implacable revolutionary fervour and repeated endlessly on television and radio, and settings of extracts from Mao's *Little Red Book* to music.

Mao's death, and the return to power of the dismissed moderate Deng Xiaoping, relieved the artistic desolation. The despised model operas disappeared and a whole range of popular musics became current, diffused by a reorganised recording industry in which the state monopoly record company was augmented by dozens of newly permitted profit-making cooperative record producers, and by many new regional radio stations. One of the principal styles to become established very rapidly was the light Westernised ballad singing of Hong Kong and Taiwan artistes such as **Deng Li-Chun**, also known as **Teresa Tang** (see

Taiwan), who became a favourite in mainland China. A spate of similar Chinese singers was led by **Li Gu Yi**, a former Hunan opera star whose best-known songs include 'The Ship Needs A Pilot', a Cultural Revolution tract with the lyrics changed to introduce a love theme.

A number of new romantic singers came forward as a result of a series of talent-spotting 'New Star Concerts' in the early 1980s. Among them was **Su Chow Ming**, who scored a major hit with 'The Night Of The Military Harbour' before being officially criticised for alleged immorality, at which point she left the country to study in France. A second female star who suffered from what appeared to be official ambivalence towards the new Westernised pop was **Chung Lin**, who was also publicly criticised but, in a manifestation of the new mood of relative freedom, survived with the assistance of a number of senior members of the musical establishment, who defended her.

In addition to Hong Kong-style pop, Chinese rock and disco boomed in the 1980s. A crop of discotheques, ranging from tiny bars to major dance halls, sprang up, catering for both young professionals and the new liumang class of alternatively minded denim clad youth. A curious aspect of the disco craze in the late 1980s was the return to fashion of the five model operas, in disco-ised versions. This trend was further accentuated after the 1989 Tiananmen Square repression, as a sense of nostalgia set in for the idealism and democracy Mao had once, to a certain extent, represented.

A significant contribution to the late 1980s democratisation movement was made by Chinese rock musicians, of whom the two most famous are **Cui Jian** and **Hou Dejian**. Both had severe restrictions imposed on their activities after the Tiananmen Square massacre.

Cui Jian became a rock singer, composer and guitarist via a musical background (his mother was a dancer, his father director of a military band), and brief employment as trumpeter in the Beijing orchestra. In 1988 he recorded his first album of Western rock songs with Chinese lyrics and musical adornments. His songs, while not openly rebellious, were subversive in expressing a sense of frustrated desire for self-expression and personal development, while his band's performance often made strong visual points. The song 'A Piece Of Red Cloth', for example, was performed by the musicians wearing red scarves as blindfolds or gags. The album's most successful song 'Nothing To My Name', with its jangling Byrds guitar and breathy flute arrangement, became a huge hit and was covered throughout the country. In the aftermath of the repression of 4 June 1989, rock concerts were banned. Cui briefly circumvented the ban by undertaking a tour to raise funds for the next Asian Games, but after episodes of 'V for Victory' signalling from audiences, the concerts were stopped in midseries.

The second major Chinese rock star, Hou Dejian, was born in Taiwan but moved to the mainland in 1983. Songs such as 'Descendant Of The Dragon' rapidly made him famous throughout the region and enabled him to live ostentatiously, by Beijing standards, with a Mercedes and sizable flat to himself. Hou was a prominent exponent of the updated rural music from the poor, barren northern Shan-shi province which became a sort of blues-equivalent among young Chinese in the mid-1980s. His role in the democracy movement was controversial: after briefly joining the hunger strike in Tiananmen Square just before the repression, he was prominent in negotiating an end to the violence, took refuge for two and a half months in the Australian Embassy and emerged to a much reduced level of activity after publicly stating he had seen no killing on the fateful day.

Another popular rock-linked trend in the mid-1980s was the so-called 'prison music' developed by the young film actor and singer **Chi Zhi Qiang**, who was imprisoned for sexual misdemeanours and on his release recorded the highly successful 'Tear Of Regret', which seemed to strike a chord in a society with an increasing crime rate and substantial numbers of prisoners.

A number of Chinese musicians operate outside the Republic of China. In the UK, the **Guo Brothers**, **Yi** and **Yue**, two classically trained instrumentalists, have worked in a range of formats since their arrival in 1974. Guo Yi plays sheng, a portable mouth-blown organ, of which he was a prominent soloist with the Peking Film Orchestra, while the flautist Guo Yue is a former member of the Chinese Army Orchestra. Both formidable musicians, the Guos worked their way up from busking in London's Covent Garden to participating in the creation of the score to Bertolucci's film *The Last Emperor* and making solo albums such as 'Yuan', on the Virgin-owned Real World label.

Also UK based, the young female singer and composer **Liu Sola** creates rock-based multi-influenced music, including a rock opera, *Blue Sky Green Sea*, a number of pop cassettes which have been successful in the Far Eastern market, and collaborations with English groups such as Durutti Column. A graduate of the Beijing Central Conservatoire of Music, Liu is also a published novelist of some repute.

China: Discography

Miscellaneous My Motherland (HUGO HRP 9012)
The Guo Brothers Yuan (Real World RW 11)

HONG KONG

Until the arrival of **Sam Hoy** in the 1970s, Hong Kong's popular music consisted almost entirely of English-language lyrics coupled with 90% Western melodies and arrangements. Hoy began to sing Cantonese folk songs and later new pop songs in Cantonese, and set the scene for the 1970s and 1980s generation of 'Cantopop' singers, whose music is still highly Westernised.

Two major stars lead a field of dozens of lesser entertainers. The top female singer **Anita Mui** started as a child star, having come from a poor family with show-business connections (her elder sister is also a singer). Her repertoire consists of a mixture of covers of Western hits, Cantonese versions of successful Japanese songs, particularly those of the singer Masahiko Hondo, and some original pieces of which the most famous is her big hit 'Bad Girl'. Very much a Madonna-follower, Mui appealed at first to teenagers. Her appeal is boosted by her 'multiple faces' image, meaning she is photographed constantly in a succession of exotic and fairly kitsch outfits. Her film debut in the 1989 ghost drama *Rouge* considerably broadened her appeal.

Mui's male equivalent is the slightly older **Allan Tam**, whose career began singing in English with the group the **Winners**, and whose success is based on Cantonese covers of songs by the Japanese singer Mayumi Itsuwa.

Among a small number of less glossily showbiz figures, the singer **Danny Summer** is prominent for his political lyrics; his 1989 songs 'Pursuit', 'You've Called Up My Soul' and 'Mama I've Done Nothing Wrong' were the most prominent examples of protest by the Hong Kong popular music world at the atrocities of Tiananmen Square.

Hong Kong: Discography

Anita Mui Crazy Love (CAL 04 1039)

TAIWAN

A large body of popular tunes survives in Taiwan from the period before 1945 when the island was under Japanese occupation. Because of the suppression of indigenous song, melodies such as the famous 'Waiting For Spring' were diffused by word of mouth in popular clubs and concert halls and are not associated with any particular singers.

Much the most famous singer of modern Taiwan is the star **Teresa Tang**, also known by her non-Westernised name **Deng Li-Chun**, who is hugely popular throughout the region and resides mainly in Japan. Slightly older than the Hong Kong star Anita Mui, Tang's appeal lies in her glossy mellifluous Cantonisation of essentially Western pop ballads, which she adorns sparingly with traditional flutes and other instruments. Her most successful song is the Japanese-authored 'Small Town Story'.

In the 1980s, several more rock-oriented artistes started performing, also influenced by the 1970s campus folk-song movement which had arisen in opposition to the Western gloss of local pop. **Tsai Chin**, the most popular female exponent, is a radio personality and occasional film actress (her husband is a director), whose husky voice made her first record, 'Your Tenderness', a major hit.

The male singer **Luo Da-Yu** is a former hospital radiologist who, in 1980, started to make interesting rock records, the best tracks combining a Cantonese melodic feel with brushes of sound colour in the form of a massed Chinese choir, a bamboo flute or a traditional violin adding drama to a rock backing. Luo's most famous hits are the two records, separated by a decade, 'Love Song In 1980' and 'Love Song In 1990'. His political lyrics are also notable; in more than one song, including 'Mid-Queens Road', he has criticised the Chinese and British governments over their arrangement for the handover of Hong Kong to China in 1997.

In the aftermath of the Tiananmen Square massacre in Beijing in 1989, a number of Taiwanese artistes recorded songs commenting on events. One of the most prominent was the singer and composer **Ryang Hongzoo**, whose song 'Open Wound Of History' was featured on a cassette 'Historical Gain' co-published by four leading Taiwan record companies immediately after the event. Also featured was the well-known **Judy Wong**'s 'Belief', a popular Japanese television serial theme tune.

Taiwan: Discography

Teresa Tang Untitled (Polydor 831 874 – 1)
Various Historical Gain (EMI K7)

JAPAN

At first glance, there might appear to be little truly vernacular popular music in Japan. The market is highly stratified and derivative. Young girls listen to saccharine girl 'idols', older women listen to different, older idols, businessmen listen to enka at weekends, etc. Most of the pop-rock record market is occupied by Japanese versions of Western genres. At the end of the 1980s one of the most popular groups was the **Blue Hearts**, a Ramones-style heavy-rock outfit. For the huge teenybopper market, a continually changing succession of idols – junior, Oriental Kylie Minogues – record an endless supply of bright, syrupy pop ditties, many of them featuring bizarrely meaningless Japlish catch phrases which could have been written by a computer after uncomprehending analysis of a hundred Western pop hits. An example is the adaptation of the Monkees' song by a Monkees-simulacrum group called the **Timers**: 'Hey hey we're the Timers, and we're just Timing around . . .'

The longer-lasting and more substantial of these artistes both lead and echo Japanese youth mores. **Yumi Matsutoya** has stayed at the top for over a decade with marginally less juvenile songs, such as 'Sugar Town' ('it's the town for goodbye'). During this period she has shifted her lyrics from describing love tangles, jealousy and passion to an emphasis on platonic, idealised love and fidelity. The advertising industry can have a major influence on the success of a song – **Myuki Nakajima**'s recording of 'Ashita' ('Tomorrow') became a huge hit after it was used in a telephone company TV commercial. The saccharine tone of the songs is sometimes mitigated by what the Japanese often refer to as 'depressing' or 'gloomy' lyrics which deal with a sort of Buddhist-modified angst about life in general.

It is worth noting that Japanese versions exist of a much wider range of musics than pop-rock. The Japanese have had their own blues boom. In the 1950s, a craze for French chanson was fuelled by visits from all the Paris stars but also by home-grown artistes such as **Yoshiko Ishii**, who is still performing her repertoire taken from the work of musicians from Brel to Barbara. Both in Japan and in Seville, dozens of young Japanese study and practise flamenco, and the all-Japanese salsa band **Orquesta de la Luz**, who sing in Spanish without understanding their songs, have been convincing enough to top the Latin charts in the United States.

There are groups roughly within the pop-rock sphere who incorporate Japanese elements to a greater or lesser extent. Some, such as **Kabuki Rocks**, do so mainly by wearing kimonos, on stage. Others, for example **Tama**, have incorporated traditional instruments, or even non-musical objects such as the big wooden bowl known as an 'oke', into their acts, but usually only on a token level.

One reason for the almost total annexation of Japanese youth music by Western styles is the formalisation and ossification of Japanese folk musics, which were at once overlooked in the twentieth-century rush to modernise, standardised into a central core termed 'minyo' and made the preserve of a large body of professional performers and teachers, the Minyo Association, who pass the music on to their pupils as a static, ceremonial art. Vital roots minyo persisted in certain rural communities, however, and the 1980s have seen several rock-oriented musicians create fusions based on regional folk musics, notably those of the extreme north, Hokkaido, and the extreme south, Okinawa (see below).

One of Japan's best-known progressive rock artistes, **Ryuchi Sakamoto**, is now using traditional instruments (mainly the banjo like shamisen) and vocalists in his work, but in the context of a sort of 'world soup' sound composed of West African and Latin American percussion, Indian jazz violin and New York minimalist rock feeling. Sakamoto's former Japanese group, the **Yellow Magic Orchestra**, now defunct, was originally formed in the late 1970s to play synthesized techno-pop in the style of Tangerine Dream and Kraftwerk, and were highly successful in this field, with numerous Japanese hits in the early 1980s. In 1987 Ryuchi Sakamoto formed the first of his **Neo Geo Ensembles**, which combine elements described above with odd touches such as a snatch of Wolof language vocal by Senegalese star Youssou N'Dour or a guest appearance by Iggy Pop. Sakamoto also flourished as a film score composer (Bertolucci's *The Last Emperor* and *The Sheltering Sky*) and occasional actor. Sakamoto's one-time wife and musical collaborator **Akiko Yano** also works internationally, primarily in America, and creates music which, though mainly Western jazz-rock in feel, sometimes uses traditional Japanese instrumentation and melody.

The Japanese inclination towards technology is also well represented by the star keyboard player and New Age composer **Kitaro**, who has collaborated over a decade and a half with numerous American rock practitioners including the Grateful Dead. Kitaro now produces highly successful instrumental albums, some of which, like his 1990 'Kojiki', take as their theme Japanese folklore and legends and incorporate ancient Japanese percussion and other traditional instruments. Kitaro's music is, however, mainly derivative of 1970s rock composers such as Jean-Michel Jarre and Mike Oldfield, with vapid sub-Wagnerian overtones. A further influence on Kitaro must be the older pop orchestral composer **Katsuhisa Hattori**, whose travelogue-style mood music (typical titles: 'Legend of a Comet', 'Elegie', 'Tivoli Gardens') has little of Kitaro's spiritual pretensions but all of his blandness.

One significantly Japanese popular music does still flourish, but mainly among an older audience, rather akin to that of country and western in the United States. The enka style, while almost universally derided by fashionable young Japanese, is still heard throughout the country, not least in the karaoke bars, where it is the principal music. There, at the end of a long day's hard work, Japanese businessmen go to drink and smoke (tobacco) away their cares, and to take the microphone to star through the lyrics while a backing track plays one or other of the hundreds of enka classics. Enka (the two syllables composing the word mean respectively 'public speech' and 'song') came into existence around the beginning of the century, from a mixture of Buddhist chants, shamisen-backed Kabuki narratives, Japanese folk music and the newly penetrating influence of Western music. Western instruments – guitar, organ, saxophone, strings – provide the main accompaniment nowadays, and the Western influences absorbed have progressed to include 1950s and 1960s ballad singers, but nothing newer. The songs are sad to maudlin, usually concerning broken, doomed or illicit love affairs, and contain an unvarying inventory of images, including cigarette smoke in an empty room, a ring dropped in a glass, a single flower blooming in winter and so on. The vocal style is melodramatic and minor key, and a soblike vibrato known as kobushi is often employed. The greatest enka star of recent years, **Hibari Misora**, died in 1989, but her best-known song 'Kanashii Sake' is well established as one of the famous songs of the postwar decades. The remaining stars are mostly in their forties or fifties. Few new young enka singers are entering the profession and its future looks shaky, although Hibari Misora's death sparked the beginnings of a retro movement and her record sales boomed posthumously. Leading singers now include **Shin'ichi Mori**, known for his rough deep voice and gloomy songs; **Saburo Kitajama**, an older male singer noted for male-honour-oriented lyrics, appearances in Yakuza gangster films and rumoured real-life connections with the Yakuza; **Sachiko Kobayashi**, a female artiste with a powerful vibrato; **Takashi Hosokawa**, whose flopping career was recently revitalised by a successful divergence into television comedy.

Of the Japanese artistes attempting to create fusions of rock dynamics and performance with traditional regional minyo folk styles, the most important movement centres on the southern island of Okinawa. Okinawa, long occupied by the US Army, was only returned to Japan in 1970. Its inhabitants are more Polynesian than the rest of Japan and are felt by mainland Japanese to be different, 'more emotional and outspoken'. Okinawan pop usually incorporates shamisen and traditional percussion, and is often played to an up-tempo, lumpy beat. One of the earliest groups to incorporate an Okinawan influence was **Sandii and the Sunsets**, at least one of whose members had Okinawan blood and who incorporated an Okinawan feel, along with techno-pop elements, on a series of albums – 'Heat Scale', 'Immigrants', 'Viva Lava Liva', 'Banzai Baby' – in the mid-1980s. The band has toured abroad, and has played concerts in Britain.

The most influential Okinawan rock musician is undoubtedly **Kina Shoukichi**, the son of the famous traditional musician **Syouei Kina**. Shoukichi, shamisen player, singer and songwriter, produced his first song, 'Haisai Ojisan' at the age of sixteen – it is now virtually a standard. After diversions into gambling and running nightclubs, Shoukichi spent a year and a half in prison for drug offences, during which time he discovered radical politics and ecology and acquired a veneration for Bob Marley and John Lennon, and a concomitant attraction to the idea of the rock star as messiah. In the late 1970s he formed his band **Champloose** with his three sisters as vocalists and a line-up of shamisen, koto (harp), kokyu (traditional fiddle), Okinawa drums, keyboards and bass guitar. In 1980 he met Ry Cooder, who played guitar on the Hawaii-recorded album 'Bloodlines', which included Shoukichi's song 'Hana' ('Flowers'). 'Hana' was subsequently covered by groups throughout the Far East. Champloose's 1990 album 'Niraikani Paradise' also had a reggae feel.

Two other younger groups operate in the Okinawan rock field. In 1987 the **Rinkenband**, led by **Teruya Rinken**, recorded an album, 'Arigaton', combining synthesizer and drum machine with Okinawan feel, while **Shang Shang Typhoon**, a young Tokyo group led by a shamisen and banjo player stage-named **Red Dragon**, created a significant stir in 1990 with a heavily Okinawan-influenced world music sound also combining reggae, Hawaiian guitar, African percussion and other currently fashionable elements.

Finally, **Takio Ito**, a singer from the northernmost island of Hokkaido, who had studied and was qualified to teach formal minyo singing, formed in 1984 a group of two shamisens, two wood flutes, two Japanese percussion sets and Western drumkit, named the **Takio Band**, to play updated versions of the old fishermen's songs of his region. The band's first album 'Takio' also features sympathetic keyboard parts by the jazz pianist **Masahiko Satoh**.

Japan: Discography

Ryuchi Sakamoto Beauty (Virgin CD VUS 14)
Akiko Yano Akiko Yano (Elektra Nonesuch 79205)
Hibari Misora Kawa No Nagare No Yo Ni (Nihon Columbia/Cataloguing in Japanese)
Shin 'ichi Mori Yubi-Wa (Victor/Cataloguing in Japanese)

Kina Shoukichi and Champloose Niraikani Paradise (Toshiba EMI 6270)
Kina Shoukichi and Champloose Bloodlines (Polydor H25 P20307)
Shang Shang Typhoon Shang Shang Typhoon (CBS-Sony ESCB 1140)
Takio Band Takio (CBS-Sony CD32 DH 5123)

SOUTH KOREA

Korean popular music is essentially based on that of Japan, although the interaction is in reality more complex than this; cultures absorbed by Japanese merchants on the 'silk route' through Korea into the continent have imparted significant ingredients to Japanese culture itself.

Nonetheless, the earliest Korean 'pop music' this century, the 1920s form known as kagok, came from Japan. It incorporated sentimental lyrics, Western minor-key harmonies and instrumental adornments and was an earlier forerunner of the Korean equivalent of Japanese enka. Enka, known as 'yuhaengga' in its Korean form (although many people simply know it as 'light music') is immensely popular in Korea. As in Japan, however, it is invariably scorned by intellectuals (even if 'classical' musicians will cheerily join in a chorus after work, as it were).

In the 1960s and 1970s, yuhaengga merged with a generally Western-influenced pop style, in which the principal Western stars of the period – Cliff Richard, etc. – were reproduced, Korean style, for domestic consumption. Backing was usually by electric guitars and organs, and passages of Western songs were frequently borrowed whole. The most enduring practitioner of this period, who is still popular, is **Yimé Ja**. More recently, the most successful artistes have been the younger female singer **Lee Sun-hui**, who is extremely popular among college students, and her male equivalent **Pyon Chin-sop**, whose greatest hit of 1990 incorporated a jazzy piano introduction and a substantial quote from Gershwin's 'Rhapsody in Blue'.

Two other styles command a more intellectual following. Korean heavy-rock bands appeal to an élite student audience, and a much larger following attaches to the modern folk-poetry artistes who sprang up with the protest-liberation movement in the universities during the 1970s. The leaders of this style were **Kim Min-gi** and **Kim Young-dong**. The latter, particularly, is still a very substantial figure, with half a dozen albums to his name. Several of these are in the folk-pop vein, but one is of Buddhist meditation music and was in fact a huge seller. Young-dong was a classical musician who turned away from the exclusive and élite coteries of Korean classical music towards film, folk and, ultimately, popular music. The artistic movement surrounding the music and poetry of artistes such as Young-dong and a newer exponent, **Kim Su-ch'ol**, is, occasionally, referred to as the 'Third Group'.

Other major stars of youth music include the punningly named **Seoul Sisters**, and **Choyong P'il**, whose biggest hit of the late 1980s, 'Han Obaengnyon' ('Five

Hundred Years'), asked his beloved why she had kept him waiting 'for five hundred years'.

Outside the country, the impressive and powerful four-man vocal and traditional percussion group **Samulnori** have acted as rare ambassadors of Korean culture.

South Korea: Discography

Samulnori Record of Changes (CMP Records CD 3002)

NORTH KOREA

The iron Stalinist dictatorship of Kim Il Sung has, unsurprisingly, not optimised conditions for sex and drugs and rock and roll.

The occasional government-run performance groups to be sent outside the country, for example to China, tend to feature either revolutionary lyrics grafted on to antiquated yuhaengga-style music or Chinese-style revolutionary operettas.

The last reported significant revisions to instrumentation date from the early 1960s.

The only regular, known penetration of this rigidly enclosed society is by the exiled but pro-North Korean avant-garde classical composer **Ysang Yun**, who returns annually from Germany for a special festival in his honour.

THAILAND

In addition to Buddhist devotional music, traditional semiclassical art music, ballet music and the Thai-lyric Western pop known as sakon, Thailand possesses several strong indigenous-based popular genres, as well as a monarch, **King Bhumipol**, noted for his jazz saxophone playing and composition; for many years, the King's music was aired on a weekly radio show.

Two major and contrasting Thai popular styles are named after their respective audiences: luk tung, meaning 'provincial people', and luk krung, meaning 'metropolitan people'. Luk tung is associated with an uneducated country audience (the term can also mean 'uncouth', 'uncivilised') while luk krung appeals to urban university students.

Luk krung is influenced by Western pop and rock but pursues its own separate development, with phases favouring female singers succeeding trends for male singers, then groups superseding both, and so on. A large number of semiprofessional singers come and go from the public spotlight.

The father of modern luk krung is **Winai Panturang**, whose most famous song 'Baur Pong' ('Lotus Flower', or 'Young Girl') is still popular. The major solo star of the 1980s has been **Jumras Sawate Taporn**, creator of the successful album 'Nok Chao Pobin' ('Flying Bird'), while the most popular group is **Char Tree**, whose major hit has been 'Rug Krung Rag' ('First Love'). Certain luk krung groups are noted for their left-wing antigovernment lyrics. The most famous of these is **Carabow**, whose 1987 album 'Made in Thailand' attacks via double meanings and veiled references the corruption and inequality it considers to be fostered by the establishment. Another similar group is **Caravan**, composed of former students of Bangkok's Tamasart University, the Oxford or Cambridge of Thailand and a centre of Communist thought.

Luk tung is a gaudy, vital entertainment performed by big travelling troupes led by a star singer and consisting of dozens of dancing girls, a band of mainly Western instruments − electric guitar, brass − and quite possibly midgets, clowns and other vaudeville elements. Frequently the luk tung show takes place on the site of a travelling fairground. In comparison with delicate and decorous Thai classical song luk tung is down to earth and unrestrained. Its themes are the problems of impoverished country life, the loss of a sweetheart gone to the city, etc. The worlds of luk tung and Thai boxing overlap to a point; both are infiltrated by organised crime so that a degree of sensationalism attaches to certain luk tung stars, who can earn a great deal of money and support flamboyant lifestyles.

A prime example is the dynasty of the king of luk tung, **Surapon Sumbatcharon**, who shot to fame in the early 1960s with a succession of songs culminating in the famous 'Sib Hok Pee Hang Kwam Lang' ('Sixteen Years of Memories'). Surapon was as famous for his prolific love life as for his music, and it was generally believed that it was a discarded mistress who paid the gangsters to shoot him dead.

Surapon's son, **Surachai Sumbatcharon**, followed in his father's footsteps with considerable success, but without ever rivalling his father's fame. Surachai adopted a number of his father's songs as well as performing new compositions of his own such as 'Fon Ja' ('Cry For Rain'), a hit during a drought period when rain dances would have been a feature of rural life. In 1980 Surachai suffered a series of unsuccessful, unexplained attacks on his life which impelled him to retire, firstly to monastic life, and secondly to Birmingham, England, for two years before returning with the cassette 'Wai Chi Wit Pom Turt' ('Please Leave My Life Alone'), since when his popularity has waned slightly.

Other prominent luk tung singers are **Come Pee Saing Tong**, known for 'Rong Hi Gup Daurn' ('Cry With The Moon'); **Sayun Sunnya**, who sang 'Lam Tay Sataurn' ('Moving Earth'); and **Son Pat Sonsupun**, whose best-known song is 'Nam Ta I Num' ('Tears of a Young Man').

The folk music of the northeastern rice-growing region, Isan, flourishes both in traditional acoustic form and with amplified versions of the traditional instruments such as kaen, a large bamboo tube mouth organ, and pin, a three-stringed guitar. It also overlaps with popular music, both by the amount of radio airplay it receives and the extent to which it is drawn upon by a new young generation of rock singers. The central feature of the Isan style is the lam song form, performed by mawlam, masters of lam, who continually expand the repertoire of ancient songs, which includes courting songs, comic duets between male and female singers and stories of the life of the Buddha. Well-known performers include **Saman Hongsa**, whose fifty-strong troupe of musicians and dancers, known as the **Diamond of the Golden Peninsula**, has been built up over thirty years. Hongsa is a member of the group **Isan Slété** ('The Flower of Isan'), which also features the musicologist and performer **Dr Jarvenchai Chonpairot**, and which in 1989 recorded an excellent album, 'Songs And Music From North-East Thailand', for the UK label Globestyle.

Thailand: Discography

Isan Slété Songs and Music from North-East Thailand (Globestyle ORBD 051)

CAMBODIA

Unlike its large neighbour Vietnam, Cambodia did not produce a modernised and indigenous popular music form of its own. Furthermore, its classical court dance and music was almost wiped out during the horrific 1975–79 rule of the Pol Pot regime, whose campaign to eradicate all traces of pre-revolutionary culture extended to killing most of the country's artistes and destroying all written records of the centuries-old theatrical representations of the Hindu epics. During the 1980s, however, the tradition was successfully pieced together again. A key figure was the court costume maker **Em Theay**, the only person left alive with knowledge of the elaborate costumes and whose memory was also a major repository of the thousands of traditional songs used in the performances. By 1990, the re-formed and renamed **Cambodia National Dance Troupe** was ready to undertake a European tour, demonstrating their delicate and beautiful art. Meanwhile, the shattered but reviving artistic community has begun to produce groups playing modernised traditional dance music on electric instruments usually donated by the Vietnamese. These groups include the National Dance Troupe's own off-shoot group **Machan**, who play songs both in .the slow rombong dance rhythm and the faster sarawan, on electric guitar, keyboards and drums, mainly for wedding parties; the national radio group **Vi Siu Chie** who broadcast similar music four times a week; and **Mahapté**, a group composed of members of the police force. None of these groups have recorded yet.

VIETNAM

In its cai luong song form, Vietnam possesses a highly original and largely intact popular music which, although its following among the younger audience is strongly threatened by Western pop, is surviving and even producing interesting and original hybrids. Cai luong, literally 'reformed theatre', evolved in the early decades of the twentieth century from a mixture of older classical and folk theatres as an entertainment for the new middle class of Saigon. Most of the performance of a cai luong piece consists of song, so that cai luong stars are, in effect, singing stars. Although Western styles from tango and bolero through to rock intersperse cai luong soundtracks, purely Vietnamese pieces, played on tranh zithers, nguyet lutes and nhi fiddles, are in the majority. Latterly guitars, often electric, modified to produce extravagantly bent notes and much vibrato and known as octavianas, have become essential instruments. Of the various set musical modes available to the cai luong composer, vong co is the most common; the two terms are sometimes used interchangeably. In the past the themes of cai luong lyrics tended to include a modern, anti-Confucian idea of personal freedom and individualism, during the French occupation a veiled anti-colonialism and, since the Communist reunification of North and South, politically 'correct' themes relating to the new society.

Stars of cai luong inside Vietnam include the top female singer **Bach Tuyet** and her male counterpart **Ut Tar On**. A number of top performers have left the country and now operate in the large Vietnamese communities of California and Paris. The top Paris-based composer and performer **Tran Van Hai** left Vietnam as a child to study in France, where he has remained ever since. **Huu Phuoc**, a top male singer, defected to the West in the late 1980s during a government-sponsored concert visit to Paris and later moved to California, where he continues both to perform in a purely traditional style and to mix electric guitar judiciously and subtly with traditional instruments on popular cassettes such as his 1990 'Mot Cuoc Doi' ('One Lifetime').

THE PHILIPPINES

Filipinos are generally acknowledged to be the entertainers of Southeast Asia, though this is less a sign of a distinctive national popular music than of a facility for interpreting middle-of-the-road American pop-rock. Booked through agencies in Singapore and Hong Kong, Filipino pop groups play in five-star hotel lounges from Tokyo to Jakarta. In addition to their international repertoire, they can draw on a large number of Western-style songs with lyrics in tagalog, the Filipino metropolitan lingua franca. A typical top four of indigenous songs for such groups might consist of 'Kapantay Ay Langit', the great hit by **Pilita Corrales** (see below), 'Bayan Ko', an old patriotic 'kundiman', 'Anak', the best-known song of the rock singer **Freddie Aguilar** (see below) and, above all, the most famous Filipino light ballad 'Dahil Sayo' ('Because of You'), the sugary torch song beloved of Imelda Marcos, who used to sing it in public with her husband, the late President Ferdinand Marcos. Filipino politicians are as fond as the rest of the country of sentimental pop (see Freddie Aguilar's **Introduction** to this section). Most modern Filipino music is played on Western instruments: local traditional instruments have not made any significant impact on new music. Occasional rare exceptions, such as the beauty queen **Gemma Cruz's** incorporation of nose flute on one excursion into recording, or Aguilar's use of the kulintang gongs on certain songs, prove the rule.

The style regarded as most typically Filipino, though its modern manifestation still sounds very Western, is kundiman, a genre dating from the 1920s and 1930s which has both classical and popular forms and which is showing signs of a return to fashion, without having ever entirely gone away. Traditional kundiman instrumentation is Spanish guitar, acoustic bass, the mandolin-like rondalia and, sometimes, violin. Kundiman songs such as the top 1930s artiste **Diomedes Naturan's** 'Three Dahlias' have long featured in the repertoire of a wide range of Filipino entertainers, from the crossover opera singer **Silvia Latorre** down, but in recent years the king of kundiman has been **Ruben Tagalog**.

For years Tagalog, always dressed in the white silk traditional barong tagalog jacket, starred in the weekly TV show *Harana with Ruben Tagalog*, which featured the kundiman subgenre harana, meaning 'serenade', typified by Tagalog's big hit 'O Ilaw' ('A Light'). The singer **Vic Manrique Jr**, was a close second to Tagalog in popularity.

The most famous postwar Filipina singer has been **Pilita Corrales**, referred to by a string of miscellaneous titles such as the 'Ambassadress of Song' and the 'Queen of Asian Song'. Corrales was responsible for the massive fame of the syrupy Marcosian anthem 'Dahil Sayo' and for innumerable hit songs which have become standards, among them 'Rosas Pandang' ('Rose Tree') and 'Kapantay Ay Langit' ('My Love Is As High As The Sky'). A colourful figure, Corrales was born a half-Spanish mestiza on the island of Cebu, and her marriage to a movie star and subsequently to a Mexican ballad singer, and her daughter **Jackie Lou Blanco's** less successful show-business career are the subjects of much gossip.

A number of older singers have echoed the styles and images of top Western stars, among them **Rico J. Puno** and **Basil Valdez** (echoing the Sinatra to Presley generation) and **José Maria Chan** (a Cliff Richard equivalent). Country and western has also been extremely popular in the Philippines; its chief exponent is the veteran − but still popular − star **Fred Panopio**, whose career was made singing the theme songs of movies by the massively popular actor **Fernando Po Jr**. Panopio was one of the earliest artistes to sing C & W songs in tagalog, and his hits, notably 'Tatlumbaraha' ('Three Cards') and 'Pitung Gatang' ('Seven Litres', a tale of the tough, low-life area of Manila where you'd go to buy rice by the litre) are extremely well known. Another top C & W artiste is the female singer **Coritha**.

While the above singers continued to be popular, the 1970s saw the rise of a new generation of rock-influenced artistes singing in tagalog, sometimes with a mixture of English. One of the earliest was the 'Pinoy Rock' star **Joey 'Pepe' Smith**, but the top name is **Freddie Aguilar**. Aguilar's earliest venture in music-making was copying songs such as 'House of the Rising Sun', in its Animals version; he first came to public attention as a result of coming a totally unexpected second with a song, 'Anak' ('Child') he entered in the 1978 Metro Manila Popular Music Festival, without any hopes for its success. 'Anak' became a great hit and was followed by a succession of others, including 'Magdalena' which, like 'Anak', entered several European hit parades, and 'Bayan Ko' ('My Homeland'), a sort of folk-rock reworking of an old kundiman number. Aguilar became closely involved in Cory Aquino's opposition to the Marcos regime, and his version of 'Bayan Ko' was the Aquino campaign anthem in the 1986 election, while his earlier 'Katarungang' ('Justice') was a prominent anti-Marcos protest song.

The most prominent group of the 1980s has been the **Apu Hiking Society**, a trio of male singers led by the popular composer **Jim Paredes**, whose works include a rock opera based on the life of the national hero José Rizal. The Apu Hiking Society are noted for a modern rock-ballad style, a slickly choreographed stage and TV show, and a succession of middle-of-the-road hit songs including 'Panalangin' ('My Prayer'), 'Ewan' ('I Don't Know') and the 1990 'Barkada' ('Gang', or 'Group').

Other popular groups include the **Asin**, Freddie Aguilar's former group, a light sixties-sounding folk-rock outfit who had a number one hit in 1980 with 'Masdan Mo Ang Kapaligiran' ('Look Around The City'); another Aguilar off-shoot band **Kayu Manggi** (the 'Brown Race'); and a rock group, the **Sino Band**.

One of the most successful popular composers is **Ryan Cayabyab**, who has composed rock ballet music, a modern Filipino mass and pop hits such as 'Kay Gandang Ating Musika' ('Our Beautiful Music'), performed by **Haji Alejandro**.

The Philippines: Discography

Freddie Aguilar Child of the Revolution (Classic 2 Records CD 001)

MALAYSIA

The father of Malay pop, the late **P. Ramlee**, started the 'pop yeh yeh' boom of the 1960s which consisted of 95% Western music with Malay language lyrics, and the country's recorded and broadcast youth music has been similarly derivative ever since. Ramlee, who was made 'Tan Sir', in effect knighted, by his government, achieved great fame as an actor starring in films such as *Ali Baba Bujang Lapuk* and *Madu Tiga*, sometimes with his wife, the actress and singer **Saloma**, and many of his songs, such as 'Getaran Jiwa' ('Palpitating Soul') and 'Bunyi Gitar' ('The Sound Of The Guitar'), became the subject of a retro boom in the late 1980s, with new young singers such as **Sheila Majid** (see below) rerecording them. Certain original singers from this period are therefore experiencing rejuvenated careers: these include the unrelated **A. Ramlie**, whose 1967 hit 'Oh Fatima' recorded with the **Rhythm Boys**, was the prelude to a succession of cabaret-style hits such as 'Kenangan Mengusik Jiwa' ('Haunting Memories') and 'Buah Hati Ku Sayang' ('My Sweetheart').

In the late 1970s and early 1980s, the focus of the music changed to rock (as played by the **Alley Cats**), heavy metal (dozens of identical bands, led by **Black Rose**) or international cabaret (**Anita Sarawak**). Certain artistes such as **Sharifah Aini** laced their music with dangdut, which retained a considerable level of lower-class popularity (see **Indonesia**). One or two dangdut artistes made inroads into the media; a heartening example was the eccentric **Dr Sam Rasputin**, whose haircut – the nearest a Malay could get to dreadlocks – and granny glasses attracted as much attention as his records, most important of which are 'Dangdut Reggae' and 'Oh Sayang' ('Oh Darling'). A modern singer notable for upholding the cause of dangdut is **Aishah**, whose eponymous 1991 album is a good example of the genre.

The kroncong style from adjacent Indonesia also exists in Malaysia, and as the retro-traditional trend has taken hold a number of Malay pop stars, including **Sudirman** (see below) and Sharifah Aini have recorded medium-paced, crooning kroncong numbers accompanied by accordion, real or synthesized.

Internationally, Malaysia's most visible stars are Sudirman and Sheila Majid. The former, a lawyer by training, specialises in large, theatrical outdoor rock concerts, some of them major traffic-jamming events in Kuala Lumpur, during which he wraps himself in the national flag to sing syrupy patriotic numbers.

Prior to her retro phase, Sheila Majid's main influences were lightweight cabaret-oriented rock and jazz, typified by her great hit 'Tiru Macam Saya' ('Follow Me'). 'Leyenda', her tribute album to P. Ramlee, has been a tremendous hit.

A potentially interesting development is the growth of the 'balada nusantara', a type of song combining traditional tunes with a pop-ballad style, of which the songwriters **Manan Ngah** and **Fauzi Marzuki** are the main practitioners.

Malaysia: Discography

Various Album Melayu Deli II (EMI Malaysia K7)
Sudirman Pilhan Sentimental Emas (EMI Malaysia K7)
Sheila Majid Leyenda (EMI Malaysia K7)

SINGAPORE

The hypercommercial and internationally minded society of Singapore is not one in which roots-rock music would be expected to flourish, and indeed the Singapore pop scene is almost totally derivative of Western music. The principal rock star **Dick Lee**, however, injects a certain amount of local colour into his lyrics, which are half English, half Singapore Chinese and which sometimes (an example is 'Fried Rice Paradise') incorporate local slang. A few of Lee's songs, such as 'Rasa Sayang', also referred to as 'Feel Good', are based on traditional folk tunes. Lee often sings with the female star **Jacintha Abishenagan**; his most recent album is the 1990 'Mad Chinaman'. There is also a Mandarin Chinese musical scene in Singapore, mainly associated with the Chinese immigrant population. The music is referred to as 'sing yao' and its chief exponent is the male singer **Han Yu**.

INDONESIA

Indonesia has one of the richest popular music scenes of the region, and includes styles such as jaipongan which retain totally indigenous instrumentation. The style most commonly associated with the country is gamelan, although this is not a popular music but rather a quite rarefied manifestation of kerewitan classical music. While many hotel lounges retain small (as little as five-piece) tourist-oriented gamelans, and large groups of up to thirty players still play at state and private ceremonies, the music is not current listening in the capital, Jakarta. Such innovations of arrangement and performance as exist, for example under the auspices of Java's prestigious STSI Performing Arts Academy, are very much in the realm of art music.

The islands of Bali and Java are the centres of gamelan. The Balinese style is faster, livelier and nowadays more and more tourist-associated, while the slow, stately Javanese tradition is still linked strongly to the palaces of the royal cities of Yogyakarta, with its rousing martial drum and trumpet-augmented gamelan, and Surakarta.

The bronze gongs and chimes collectively known as a gamelan were first forged in Central Java in the seventh century, and the city of Surakarta still contains four family-run gamelan foundries, supplying up to 3,000 gamelan musicians in Java.

The STSI Academy, under its director, the composer **Dr Sri Hastanto**, has developed a modernised style of gamelan music. Its chief characteristics are shortened pieces, and heightened dynamism via more stresses and volume changes; traditional gamelan is slow, dreamy and serene. This new style is highly influential; a rare wayang dance performance combined with gamelan accompaniment staged in Jakarta by the newspaper *Compas* to celebrate its 25th anniversary in 1990 was notable for lasting a mere two and a half hours instead of the more usual eight. The now symbolic royal courts still support the gamelan tradition. In June 1990 the wedding of the Crown Prince Mangkoenagoro IX of Surakarta (in civilian life a hotel manager) was celebrated by a specially commissioned new bedoyo mystical dance accompanied by the playing of a composition by **Sri Hastanto** on the great two-hundred-year-old double gamelan of the palace. It was a magnificent and stirring occasion.

Of the Indonesian popular styles the oldest, kroncong, has acquired a semiclassical status while fading out of fashion with the younger generation. It is still widespread, however, and interesting, as its development and status are very similar, for example, to that of the Argentinian tango. The roots of kroncong are among the Portuguese merchants and sailors who frequented Indonesian ports in the sixteenth and seventeenth centuries, bringing with them multiple influences from the Chinese, African and European populations with whom they mixed. By the nineteenth century, kroncong had developed into a Portuguese-based low-life music, popular in the kampung working-class districts of Jakarta and associated with drinking, womanising, knife-wielding dandies known as 'buaya' (crocodiles) or 'jagos' (roosters), very similar to the Greek manges hoodlums of Piraeus rembetika music. In the 1920s and 1930s, partly through its use in Indonesian films, kroncong became respectable and during the Dutch and Japanese occupations it became associated with patriotism and authentic Indonesian culture; it retains this 'national music' cachet today and is often played on formal occasions. Kroncong is named after the ukelele-like instrument which, along with guitars, violins and sometimes flute, cello or light percussion, forms part of the kroncong ''asli' (traditional or classical kroncong) ensemble. A whole range of kroncong derivatives – kroncong stamboul, connected with a form of theatre, kroncong langgam jawi, rhythmically different and associated with regional folk influences – grew out of kroncong 'asli, whose most famous performers were the singers **Tan Ceng Bok**, **Vivi Young**, **Anne Landow**, **Netty**, **Surip Mataroda** and **Sam Saimun**. In the 1960s and 1970s pop kroncong developed, with guitars, Western percussion and keyboards augmenting or ousting the traditional instrumentation and adding a substantial hint of the more ersatz end of Nashville to the sound. Chief modern exponents are **Toto Salmon**, **Sundari Soekocoh**, **Mus Mulyadi** and two major all-round female artistes, **Waldjinah** and the younger, glamorous **Hetty Koes Endang**, who include kroncong, both 'asli and pop, in a wide-ranging repertoire.

If kroncong is a respectable popular music associated with National Day ceremonies and establishment receptions, dangdut is quite the reverse, regarded by many intellectual Indonesians as kampung music, listened to by becak (bicycle rickshaw) drivers and the delinquent youth. Dangdut is extremely popular, however, filling vast open-air concert areas with many thousands of dancing young people, something no kroncong singer or gamelan could do. 'Dangdut' is an onomatopoeic word describing the sound of the Indian tabla drum which dominates the music. In addition to the Indian influence, also notable in the dangdut film genre, the principal external component is Arab, an important element of the orkes melayu style which flourished in Malaysia and Indonesian Sumatra in the 1940s and 1950s. During the nationalistic Sukarno regime in the 1950s and 1960s, orkes melayu, along with kroncong, was officially encouraged as an 'authentic' music, and with the reopening of Indonesia to Western influence after the Suharto coup in 1965, orkes melayu began to mix with Indian and Western pop, and later with rock. The result was dangdut. Its chief creator and populariser was **Rhoma Irama**, whose music the term was first used to describe in the mid-1970s. Irama was a dynamic performer and entrepreneur from a poor background and with his group **Sonata** he transformed dangdut into a craze, with songs such as his 'Pena Saram' selling massively. Irama soon moved into films, inspiring a spate of colourful dance and romance-laden rags-to-riches fables but also, following Irama's pilgrimage to Mecca, several moral tales warning against alcohol and the pursuit of worldly success and denouncing poverty and corruption. A prime example is the 1980 film *Perjuangan Dan Do'a* ('Struggle and Prayer'). Other top dangdut singers are **Elvy Sukesih**, a noted exponent of the mildly pelvic-thrusting dance performed in groups by dozens of teenage boys at dangdut concerts, and a large number of young performers including **Heidy Diana, Titiek Sandhora, Titiek Nur, Ali Usman** and **Mansyur**.

The jaipongan style, and its accompanying dance, also grew out of the Sukarno-launched authenticity movement of the 1960s, when a young composer, arranger and producer named **Gugum Gumbira Tirasondjaja**, from a prominent family in Bandung, the capital of the West Javanese region of Sunda, updated a traditional rural village song and dance style, ketuk tilu. Ketuk tilu featured a female singer and dancer known as a ronggeng, originally a prostitute and still retaining an aura of licentiousness, who would dance with men from the audience to the backing of a small group of gamelan-like gongs, chimes and rebab spike-violins led by a prominent and dynamic kendang hand-drummer. Gugum Gumbira began to experiment with the ketuk tilu formula, speeding up the rhythm, inventing a new dance by adding vaguely twist and rock-and-roll movements to the traditional languorous ronggeng's steps, and then recording the new music on cassettes whose covers, as in Western pop, featured the singer prominently. The new style rapidly acquired a name, jaipongan, like dangdut based onomatopoeically on the sound of the music, in this case the characteristic percussive cries and exclamations the band members emit to punctuate the music. In the late 1970s jaipongan became a craze throughout Bandung and Sunda in general, and eventually conquered the capital, Jakarta. Sundanese restaurants featured jaipongan dancing and numerous dance schools sprang up to teach the new young middle-class enthusiasts, much as in the Sevillanas boom in Spain. By 1980, having survived a brief backlash against the alleged immorality of the dance, jaipongan was featured on national TV and, though the craze had passed by the end of the decade, this genre remains popular and still unsullied by synthesizers or drum machines. The best-known group is the **Jugala Group,** named after Gugum Gumbira's cassette company, who often back the star, female singer **Euis Komariah,** Gugum Gumbira's wife and a classically trained singer and music teacher. The ensemble rerecorded a number of their best songs in 1989 for the excellent UK album 'Jaipongan Java', on Globestyle. Other important singers are **Daun Pulus, Tati Saleh, Dede Winingsih, Karawang** and the **Suwauda Group.**

The rise of jaipongan prompted the restoration of an associated Sundanese style, degung, also featuring a small quasi-gamelan group and a singer, but playing in a more serene, chamber-music style. A fine example is the Globestyle album 'The Sound of Sunda', companion volume to 'Jaipongan Java', again featuring Euis Komariah and the Jugala Group with another male singer, **Yus Wiradiredja.**

Several other traditional styles have modern versions: the anklung tuned bamboo percussion groups of Java occasionally perform and record a modern repertoire; the Sumatran style known as batak has its offshoot, pop batak, best represented by the group **Banabon Plus,** who tour outside the country, mainly in luxury hotel lounges; the tarling style of the Cerebon region has a popular modern form accompanied by another allegedly erotic dance − two good exponents are the singer **Yoyo** and the bandleader **Wati.**

Finally, a wide range of Indonesian-modified Western pop exists including the intellectual rock style of the former leader Sukarno's son **Guruh Sukarno,** which features occasional passages of gamelan and the sentimental pop sunda of artistes such as **Detty Kurnia.**

Indonesia: Discography

Waldjinah, Mulyadi and others Seleksi Kroncong (Fajar K7)

Hetty Koes Endang Hati Yang Luka − Pop Kroncong (AA Records K7 060)

Euis Komariah with the Jugala Orchestra Jaipongan Java (Globestyle ORB 057)

Euis Komariah and Yus Wiradiredja The Sound of Sunda (Globestyle ORB 060)

Various Music of Indonesia Vol. 2 (Kroncong, Dangdut & Langgam Java) (Smithsonian Folkways SF 40056)

HAWAII

The music of the original inhabitants of the Hawaiian islands is all but lost; it appears to have consisted of rhythmical chanting, with percussive accompaniment from a variety of gourds, rattles, conch shells, etc. The modern Hawaiian sound was born of contact with the successive waves of outsiders to arrive after first European contact in 1778. Protestant church choirs brought harmony singing, Portuguese sailors introduced the little braguinha, which the

Hawaiians renamed 'jumping flea' (ukelele) and Mexican labourers and sailors introduced the Spanish guitar. These elements blended with certain Hawaiian musical proclivities – a feeling for sunny, major-chord harmonies, a preference for lyrics about the beauty of the land ranging from the passionate and semimystical to the mawkish – with two characteristic instrumental innovations, the steel guitar and the slack key guitar, and with a mysterious love of falsetto singing and yodelling.

The steel, or Hawaiian, guitar is almost certainly a genuine Hawaiian invention. It is usually credited to **Joseph Kekuku** who, in the 1890s, began playing an ordinary acoustic guitar flat on his lap using a steel comb, to slide on the strings, and metal finger-picks. Subsequent refining of the style increased the height of the strings above the fretboard and added pedals controlling tone and volume to create the instrument later taken up by country and western performers. Following its great American, and then world, boom in the 1920s and 30s, the king of the acoustic Hawaiian guitar was **Sol Hoopii**; other top players of his era included **Frank Ferara**, **King Benny Nawahi**, **Jim and Bob**, known as **The Genial Hawaiians**, and **Tau Moe**, star of **Madame Riviere's Hawaiians**. The slack key, or ki ho'alu, guitar style consists of a conventional acoustic guitar retuned to a lower, open pitch. Its best known stylist was **Gabby Pahinui**, who died in 1980 after his rediscovery during the 1970s Hawaiian renaissance (see below).

The new Western hybrid Hawaiian music flourished firstly under the aegis of King Kamehameha V, who imported the German bandleader **Heinrich Berger** to create a royal band in the late nineteenth century, and later under the influence of his successor King David Kalakaua, who maintained the high level of royal patronage of popular music and dance which still exists today.

In 1915, shortly after the United States had annexed Hawaii, **George E.K. Awai's Royal Hawaiian Quartet** performed at the San Francisco Panama-Pacific International Exposition, starting a craze for Hawaiian music which swept the world. In the USA, radio programmes such as the popular *Hawaii Calls* diffused the music which was rapidly taken up by Hollywood (in Bing Crosby's 1937 film *Waikiki Wedding*) and Tin Pan Alley. By the 1930s the 'hapa haole' (half-white) song, with its half or wholly English lyrics, had taken over and was turning the music into a parody, sometimes an insulting one, of itself: Al Jolson's gobbledegook 'Yaaka Hula Hickey Dula' or Harry Owen's insinuating 'Princess Poo-Poo-ly Has Plenty Papaya' are cases in point. The tourism boom and the mushrooming hotels and nightclubs of Wai-ki-ki accelerated the vulgarisation. Talented singers such as **Alfred Apaka** were reduced to commercialising their repertoire in establishments like the Huala Rumba or the Hawaiian Village Hotel. On Apaka's death in 1959, the year of the incorporation of the new State of Hawaii into the American Union, the singer **Don Ho** became the islands' top artiste, and so he stayed, performing 'I'll Remember You' Hawaii style and inviting tourists on stage to hula at Duke Kahanamoku's club. It was at this time that Hawaiian music reached its nadir of relevance to the islands' youth, who now had the Beatles, the Rolling Stones and Dylan to look to.

As elsewhere in the world, the 1970s saw a dramatic revival of interest in Hawaii in traditional dress, dance, religion and, especially, song. Musically, the movement had two aspects: a rediscovery of those old traditional artistes still performing and the arrival of a new generation of young, back-to-roots innovators. A strong working-class, pure Hawaiian, unsophisticated audience had continued to support numbers of authentic performers and now they began to be increasingly sought out by a young generation dissatisfied with the commercialisation and cultural smothering of the islands by the dominant American tourist-based business population. In 1966, the radio station KCCN began to broadcast exclusively Hawaiian music 24 hours a day, concentrating at first on the old stars and soon introducing a range of new young artistes. The most important rediscovery was the slack-key guitarist and singer **Philip 'Gabby' Pahinui**, who had had considerable success in the 1940s and 1950s playing traditional music mixed with jazz, but who had subsequently been reduced to manual labour to support his substantial capacity for alcohol. Pahinui was taken up by the young musician **Peter Moon**, who studied his guitar techniques and guided his career into a successful relaunch, recording with his own new **Gabby Band** and, at one point, with Ry Cooder. Pahinui died of a heart attack in 1980, on the crest of his new-found wave. Other old performers to experience rejuvenated demand included **Auntie Genoa Keawe**; another virtuoso slack-key guitarist, **Raymond Kane**; a singer, composer, ukelele player and former bandleader **Andy Cummings**; and a younger but well-established group who combined authentic old material with skilfully crafted new songs in the old ku a'aina or grass-roots style, the **Sons of Hawaii**. The Sons of Hawaii were crucial in spreading the new-old music of the 1970s and 1980s and songs such as their leader **Eddy Kamae**'s 'E Ku'u Morning Dew' became massively popular and were immediately incorporated into the repertoires of the islands' serious entertainers.

The most important of the new young groups was the **Sunday Manoa**, formed in 1969 by Peter Moon and including two of Gabby Pahinui's sons, **Cyril** and **Bla**. Moon, educated on the American mainland, brought a rock sensibility to a mixture which also included slack-key guitar and ancient percussion devices such as shark-skin drums, gourd rattles and stone castanets. Their early 1970s album 'Cracked Seed' sold a remarkable 30,000 copies within Hawaii. The Sunday Manoa split up in the late 1970s, and its founder went on to form the **Peter Moon Band** and to play a key role in the creation of the annual Kanikapila festival of traditional Hawaiian music at the University of Hawaii.

In addition to the resurgence of interest in national culture, which, by the 1980s, saw hundreds of traditional hula teachers and competitors, the new music was very much linked to political movement protesting at the erosion of Hawaiian society, and at the islands' environmental destruction. **George Helm**, a major singer and activist who coined the phrase 'Hawaiian Soul' to describe his songs, drowned at sea while protesting against the use of the small island of Kahoolawe as a bombing range by the US Navy.

Another important member of the Hawaiian renaissance music movement was the group the **Mahaka Sons of Ni'ihan**, a group whose name refers both to a poor, native Hawaiian suburb of Honolulu (Mahaka) and a small, unmodernised island (Ni'ihan), and whose tremendous success is due in part to their sweet, four-part harmony singing.

The end of the 1980s saw the Hawaiian renaissance become the islands' mainstream entertainment, with the hula craze still booming and the new music, purveyed by top groups such as the **Cazimero Brothers**, former members of The Sunday Manoa, available in many tourist clubs and hotels. New fusions of American rock and pop with slack-key guitars are also meeting with success: a prime example is the big hit 'Honolulu City Lights' by **Keola** and **Kapono Beamer**.

Hawaii: Discography

Miscellaneous Steel Guitar Masters 1928–34 (Rounder 1052)
Various (inc. Raymond Kane, Genoa Keawe, Mahaka Sons of Ni'ihan) Hawaiian Rainbow (Rounder 6018)
Peter Moon Band Hawaiian Soul (Panini PC 1012)

AUSTRALIA

Even more than the United States, Australia is a young country with a population composed of immigrants of dozens of different nationalities, and an indigenous population which came near to cultural, and indeed physical, extinction. The popular music scene therefore consists of pockets of performers of everything from Greek rembetika to Chilean political song, a heavily American-derived mainstream scene, and, happily, a flourishing movement of new aboriginal music.

In the 1930s, the old bush songs and ballads of English and Irish origin gradually gave way to a craze for the Australianised country and western which persists today. Hillbilly singers such as **Tex Morton, Buddy Williams** and, above all, **Slim Dusty** achieved great success in the 1950s and 1960s. Slim Dusty (né Gordon Kirkpatrick, a bush farmer's son who taught himself to yodel by listening to 'cowboy' records) is still the country's top-selling artiste and his song 'A Pub With No Beer' is seen by many people, for better or worse, as a quintessentially Australian musical artefact. In the 1970s and 1980s, Australian rock bands flourished, especially in the pubs and clubs of Melbourne where dozens of groups, some, such as Split Enz and Men At Work, to become nationally famous honed their skills competing for the attention of young drinkers. Virtually all their music, even that of more distinctive bands such as **Midnight Oil**, is, however, indistinguishable from its American model.

Aboriginal rock-pop grew up in the late 1970s and in the 1980s, nurtured by the climate of rehabilitation of all aspects of the culture of the downtrodden and dispossessed original inhabitants of the huge country. A key institution formally engaged in the field was, and is, the Centre for Aboriginal Studies In Music (CASM) of Adelaide University, whose alumni include important movers in the aboriginal rock milieu. Such music, it must be said, is more rock than aboriginal, no body of modernised popular music having had a chance to develop from the ancient clap-stick percussion, chanting and basic wind instruments of aboriginal music. Particularly in its main area of use, the northern region around Darwin, the didjeridoo is often incorporated into the new rock groups, and many groups sing in tribal languages such as Pitjanjatjara, Warlpiri, Numbrindi and Papunya; otherwise main influences are rock, country and western, reggae and church choral music. These influences spring naturally from the circumstances in which young aborigines have in recent decades found themselves. Their background has generally been one of extreme disadvantage – menial jobs, blatant contempt and prejudice from the white population, despair drowned in alcohol, petty brushes with the law. In true rock-and-roll style, music or sport have been two possible paths to escape from poverty. Musical influences, via the radio which until quite recently was the only medium accessible to parts of the outback, would be redneck country and western (giving rise to a range of aborigine versions including the 'prison songs' of artistes such as **Roger Knox** and **Mac Silva**), the religious music brought by Irish or German mission priests (the inspiration for the 'desert choirs' such as the **Lajamanu Choir**, the **Kintore Gospel Band**, the **Nyirripi Gospel Band** and the **Yirrara Girls' Choir**) or the rock and reggae favoured by radical circles around institutions such as CASM. It is possible to divide current professional or, at least, serious amateur aboriginal rock bands, up to a hundred in number, into three broad regional styles; the northern area around Darwin, where a tropical feel augments the rock and country mix, and where the didjeridoo is most featured; the great central desert around Alice Springs, home of the influential and active Central Australian Aboriginal Media Association recording and management enterprise, whose style features more traces of country and gospel; and the western area around Broome, where reggae has its greatest penetration.

The first aboriginal rock group to achieve major prominence was **No Fixed Address** whose leader, the drummer and didjeridoo player **Bart Willoughby**, was a former CASM student. They played internationally before breaking up in the late 1980s. Subsequent leaders of the field have been the **Warumpi Band**, who scored a national hit with 'Out Of Jail', described by one critic as 'Chuck Berry with didjeridoos', before also breaking up; **Yothu Yindi**, a prime exponent of the Darwin tropical sound; **Coloured Stone**, a New South Wales quartet led by the brothers **Bruce** and **Buna Laurie**; and, most important of all, **Scrap Metal**, who entered the 1990s as the genre's major hope for international stardom. Scrap Metal was formed in the late 1970s in the small, isolated coastal town of Broome, home of former British Conservative Party Chairman Lord McAlpine's new exclusive resort and of the active Broome Musicians Aboriginal Corporation. Consisting of five musicians of mixed French, Filipino, Scottish, Japanese, Indonesian and local Yawru aboriginal blood, Scrap Metal are led by the brothers **Alan** and **Steve Pigram** and by the guitarist **Johnny Albert** (the latter two CASM graduates). Years of local gigs led to a successful national tour supporting Midnight Oil in 1987, followed by a major LP release, 'Broken Down Man', on Polygram in 1988 and a follow-up, 'Scrap Metal', in 1990. The group, all family men, elected to remain in Broome and overcame some of the logistical problems of running a national business several thousand kilometres from the capital by doing an unusual sponsorship deal with Australian and British Telecom, thereby obtaining free telephone-line time to run their electronic mail and other communications operations.

Other aboriginal bands and artistes include the **Areyonga Desert Tigers**; **Black Iron**; **Blekbala Mujik**; **Dharrwar Band**; **Koori Youth**; **Poison Whiskey**; **Archie Roach**; the **Titkikala Desert Oaks Bands**; the **Wairuk Band** and **Wedgetail Eagle**.

Australia: Discography

Various (inc. Roger Knox) Koori Classic, The Aboriginal Prison Song Collection (ENREC ENL 044)
Coloured Stone Black Rock From The Red Centre (Rounder 5022)
Various From The Bush (CAAMA Music CD 214)
Scrap Metal Broken Down Man (ABC Records, Broome, W. Australia)
Scrap Metal Scrap Metal (ABC Records, Broome, W. Australia)

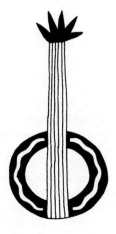

THE
CARIBBEAN

INTRODUCTION

I was born in a fishing village called Emmerton a few hundred yards from Kensington Oval. Kensington Oval is perhaps the most famous place in Barbados. It is here that such world-renowned cricketers as Frank Worrel, Wes Hall and the world's greatest ever cricketer, Sir Garfield (Gary) Sobers, call home. My first appearance on stage, long before taking up calypso, was as a six-year-old in the National Village Choir Christmas Competition. What makes that debut so memorable for me is the feeling of pure joy that erupted from all the fishermen, tailors, masons, carpenters and dock workers who made up the majority of our menfolk, when the final tally of points was announced and we came out winners. In those days the village choir had to sing a carol of their choice, as well as a song selected by the Committee which the City Council had put together. Needless to say, Kensington Oval would be packed with people from all the wonderful villages which made up Barbados at that time. Unfortunately, most of those villages have been turned into parks and terraces now, which means middle class and upper-middle class. It also means the disappearance of the greatest breeding ground for musical talent in Barbados.

There were no such luxuries as electricity, gas, television or even running water in our homes or villages back then, but music was always with us in great abundance. I have a number of strong memories of my boyhood. I recall people always sharing what little food we managed to obtain – roast breadfruit, fish and sweet potato were a major part of our diet. And I recall the music of the tuk band, consisting of a kettle drum, a bass drum, both made from sheep or goat skins, and a home-made flute.

The tuk bands had their equivalents all over the Caribbean — simple instruments usually made by the people that played them in the villages. A little of the sound of these bands came from the French or the English military bands and so on. But most of all, that tuk band music came to us via Mother Africa and histories of the region talk about the pulsating rhythm of the drums at plantation feasts, with dancing that was in almost complete contrast to what Europeans were accustomed to seeing.

Reggae, its parents the Jamaican blue beat and ska, those intoxicating Cuban-Afro rhythms, and Brazilian samba have all influenced Barbados's calypso music, yet the roots of the African drum, indisputably dominating all these varieties of music, play no lesser role in Barbados calypso. It is the link from which no rhythm music can be separated.

Many of the slaves that came to Barbados came out of Ghana, Sierra Leone, Nigeria and other West African countries. Barbados was the first stop in the slave trade. There the slaves were broken, then shipped on to the rest of the West Indies and the United States of America, with many ending up on plantations in the Carolinas and Virginia. The first houses in the State of Virginia were built by Barbadians.

The slaves took with them the drum, and around the same time the drum was banned in Barbados the plantation slaveowners also banned it in the USA. This ban lasted throughout the life of slavery but did not stop the slaves singing to make their work seem less burdensome, and their songs have been passed on to us in the form of Negro spirituals. So there is a strong connection between Barbados and the USA in jazz, Negro spirituals and hymns, which are the forerunners of modern-day calypso. All we have to do is add that African drum.

The musical development of Barbados is useful as a guide to the same sort of process which happened throughout the Caribbean, but there are some Barbadian artistes who are of interest in their own right, as major influences. When the musical history of Barbados is written, for example, the name of Jackie Opel must certainly be there in the number-one spot.

Jackie Opel formed a group called the Happy Jacks when he was not more than fourteen or fifteen years old. They would pass by our house at night just before bedtime, singing these songs in three-part harmony so sweetly that, long after they were probably sleeping, I would lay awake there, still mesmerised by their amazing talents. Think of a guy with the phrasing ability of Stevie Wonder, blended magnificently with the high vocal range of Jackie Wilson, who could dance like James Brown, and you begin to see Jackie Opel emerge. Yet with all that talent, he had to dive for coins in the Shippings (the name we gave to the makeshift harbour Barbados had at the time).

Jackie Opel emigrated to Jamaica in the sixties and there helped to change the music of that super musical country for ever. He topped the Jamaica charts with such blockbusters as 'Eternal Love' and 'Cry Me A River', still regarded as two of the finest pieces of work ever to come out of Jamaica. The late great Robert Nesta 'Bob' Marley is on record as having said that Jackie Opel was way ahead of his time.

Nowadays, the Caribbean has such a richness of music, well recorded so you can hear it all over the world, and big stars from Trinidad and Jamaica and Martinique or Guadeloupe are world stars. But that wasn't so when I was a boy.

Until 1965, the only radio station in Barbados was the British Wireless box called Rediffusion. Rediffusion brought us BBC Sports, news, a programme entitled *Music To Remember* (which is still aired today) and a steady diet of Frank Sinatra, Nat King Cole, Pat Boone, Elvis Presley and the other artistes who dominated the 1950s and 1960s. West Indian or Caribbean music? Forget it.

Apart from an hour on Wednesday or Thursday night, there was no music played which we could say came from our region; nevertheless that hour was looked forward to by the village people like water by a very thirsty man.

Sparrow, Kitchener and Lord Melody (who wrote such songs as 'Mama Looka Boo Boo' for Harry Belafonte) were given the most airplay and rightly so, for in the history of calypso music there is no threesome that can match them.

In Emmerton there was just one Rediffusion box, in the village shop, and I would spend the majority of my non-school hours swallowing every note and chord I could hear, and then singing the great calypsonians' work to anybody who would listen. The old fishermen would give me roast corn or pennies to sing, and that really is how I started. That led to my first National Pop and Calypso Competition in 1965, my first big hit 'Heart Transplant', my time in New York in the theatre, later on my meeting with superstar Eddie Grant, who is still my producer and arranger and best friend. And though the details might be different from here to there, that sort of background is fairly typical of most of the great music coming out of the Caribbean today.

ANTHONY CARTER, 'THE MIGHTY GABBY'

JAMAICA

Jamaican music stands apart from that of the rest of the Anglophone Caribbean, although reggae and its successors are immensely influential internationally. Jamaica has no strong carnival tradition to link it to the Trinidad circuit, although its newly created carnival (founded 1990), interestingly, features mainly Trinidadian soca music, a fact of some controversy among reggae lovers. Jamaica's early and lengthy British colonial status was a major factor in the island's comparative lack of a continuing African musical heritage, though the traditional burru drumming preserved the link with the mother continent. Rastafarianism of course emphasises African cultural connections, and reggae has taken strong root throughout Africa. London, traditionally the second centre of Jamaican music, was challenged in the 1980s by New York, with a large and musically active Jamaican population.

In the 1940s, the nearest thing to a Jamaican popular style was mento, a calypso-like folk music with a gentle, lilting melody and topical, sometimes mildly bawdy, lyrics. A number of groups continue to play in this style, mainly in tourist hotels, and in 1989 one group, the **Jolly Boys**, were taken up by a holidaying New York record producer, issued an album, 'Pop 'n' Mento', and toured Europe. Led by septuagenarian banjo player **Moses Dean**, the Jolly Boys, who played for Errol Flynn's parties at his Port Antonio house, attracted a substantial amount of attention with numbers such as 'Big Bamboo' and 'Don't Touch Me Tomato'.

In the late 1950s, Jamaican interpretation of the popular American rhythm and blues sound resulted in the birth of ska, a street music of poor Kingston-dwellers played on electric guitars, drumkit and, usually, a small brass section. Ska's distinctive feature was its choppy syncopated beat, emphasised by clipped guitar and piano chords on the second and fourth beats of the bar. Ska's main practitioners included the **Skatalites**, a studio band which included the influential musicians **Rolando Alphonso** on tenor sax and **Jackie Mittoo** on keyboards; **Desmond Dekker** and his band the **Aces**, whose records '007' and 'The Israelites' were British hits in the late 1960s; and numerous configurations of musicians later to achieve wider fame as members of groups such as the **Maytals**, the **Wailers** and the **Ethiopians**. In 1964, the white Jamaican entrepreneur Chris Blackwell founded Island Records, subsequently of great importance in the international propagation of Jamaican music, and scored an international hit with the ska-rhythm 'My Boy Lollipop' by **Millie Small**. Ska transmuted into rock steady, a slightly heavier, less busy version of what was essentially the same rhythm, in which the reggae characteristics of a spare, lazy but powerful drumbeat and a heavy, prominent bass-guitar part were beginning to assert themselves. The new style was named after the Alton Ellis hit 'Get Ready to Rock Steady' and other prominent artistes included singers such as **Prince Buster**, writer of the famous 'Judge Dread' and groups such as the **Cables**.

An important Jamaican phenomenon from the 1950s onwards was the popularity of the sound systems, portable sets of record decks and huge banks of speakers which played in dance halls or yards to paying customers. These began by playing imported American rhythm and blues records, but certain top sound system proprietors began to record their own exclusive discs on cheap equipment and thus, in effect, to found the modern Jamaican recording industry of which the earliest products were intended purely for the use of the sound systems which produced them. Another enduring Jamaican phenomenon, the DJ who is a performing star in his own right, dates from the earliest sound systems. The DJs would keep up a stream of shouted banter through their systems, exhorting punters to pay up and come into their yards; gradually the patter itself became central and the tradition of 'toasting' or 'chatting' was born. Early sound-system proprietors often attached ironic titles to their names, like old plantation bosses, and competition between top systems was fierce, with violence a continual possibility from the 'rude boy' street groups which provided the clientele and the workforce. Leading early sound systems were run by **King Tubby, Duke Reid** and **Clement 'Sir Coxsone' Dodd**, the latter rapidly becoming the most serious ska producer when he started to market to the public the hottest of his 'Downbeat' system's discs.

Around the end of the 1960s, the bass-heavy rock steady sound slowed down, grew heavier still, and began to be recorded on newly arriving multitrack equipment with the capacity for a limited range of effects. It also acquired the name reggae, of uncertain origin (**Frederick Hibbert, 'Toots'** of The Maytals, wrote 'Do the Reggay', the first widely played song to use the term). The new music began to come to the attention of the outside world; an important early populariser was the 1963 film *The Harder They Come*, which transposed the true Bonnie and Clyde story of a young Jamaican gangster to the reggae milieu, with the singing star **Jimmy Cliff** in the title role. Jimmy Cliff became the first international reggae star, and went on to spread the music in a hugely successful tour of Africa. The cult of Rastafarianism by now had come to exert considerable influence on reggae musicians and thus the music. Rastafarianism comes from a mixture of Old Testament prophecy and Caribbean back-to-Africa thinking. It identifies the former Africans of Jamaica, now displaced to 'Babylon', with a promised future in Ethiopia led, until his overthrow, by the Emperor Haile Selassie I, Conquering Lion of the Tribe of Judah, and formerly known as Ras Tafari Makonnen. Rastafarianism, with its trademark dreadlocks and reverence for the use of ganja, converted many, but by no means all, Jamaican musicians in the 1960s and 1970s. One musical effect was the introduction of the African-based burru drums into one strand of the reggae sound. Another was the tone of messianic fervour it imparted to the lyrics, especially when these began also to deal with the frustrations, poverty and violence of life in slum areas such as Kingston's Trenchtown. This messianic quality was enormously important in the rise to fame of reggae's first and only international reggae star, **Bob Marley**. Marley, the son of an English father and Jamaican mother, grew up in Trenchtown, and began playing and singing in 1960 at the age of fifteen with his friends **Bunny Livingston** (later to adopt the name **Bunny Wailer**) and **Peter McIntosh** (who subsequently abbreviated his surname to **Tosh**). The trio eventually insinuated themselves into the studios of 'Sir Coxsone' Dodd and made a single, 'Simmer Down', in 1963, backed by the Skatalites, under the name, given by Dodd, of the **Wailing Wailers**. In 1966 Marley married his wife Rita and espoused Rastafarianism. In the late 1960s the group, now the **Wailers**, recorded with producer **Lee Perry** (see below), whose house group, the **Upsetters**, eventually contributed two new Wailers, **Aston 'Family Man' Barrett** and his brother **Carlton**. In 1971, having travelled to Europe with the American singer **Johnny Nash** (who had scored European and US reggae hits with 'I Can See Clearly Now' and Marley's 'Stir It Up', the Wailers, in dire straits financially, approached Chris Blackwell in London, who gave them £8,000 to go home and make a record for his Island label. The result was the brilliant 'Catch A Fire', with its striking and sophisticated arrangements and stylish 'Zippo lighter' novelty cover, the Wailers' breakthrough to international stardom. The following ten years saw a succession of major hits − 'Burning', 'Natty Dread', 'Rastaman Vibrations', 'Exodus' and, lastly, 'Uprising' before Marley's death from cancer in 1981. Bunny Wailer, having left the group, proceeded to make a successful solo career with albums such as 'Blackheart Man', as did Peter Tosh, who scored hits with 'Legalize It' and 'Bush Doctor' before being shot dead by robbers at his Kingston home. Marley's son **Ziggy** followed in his father's shoes in the mid-1980s, forming a group, the **Melody Makers**, in which he deployed a singing voice remarkably similar to his father's, and achieving some success with records such as 'Conscious Party' and 'One Bright Day'.

Among the numerous other successful artistes of the 1970s and early 1980s, classic reggae's boom years, were Toots and the Maytals, whose irresistibly bouncy 'Funky Kingston' and 'Reggae Got Soul' followed the Wailers as early Island hit albums; Lee Perry, an eccentric, inventive producer, arranger and singer, veteran of Sir Coxsone's sound system, who produced hundreds of tracks for other artistes and many for his own group, the Upsetters; the duo of bassist **Robbie Shakespeare** and drummer **Sly Dunbar**, whose musicianship and production skills made them internationally sought after in the late 1970s; **Gregory Isaacs**, a smooth-voiced crooner whose career took off again spectacularly in the late 1980s with the earliest techno-reggae (see below) hit 'Rumours'; **Burning Spear**, a powerful and intense rasta singer whose 'Marcus Garvey' and 'Dry and Heavy' albums became classics; and **Augustus Pablo, Freddie McGregor, Jacob Miller, Sugar Minott, Dennis Brown, Marcia Griffiths**, the **Gladiators**, the **Abyssinians, Ras Michael and the Sons of Negus** and the **Mighty Diamonds**. British-based groups included **Aswad**, who reached number one in the British charts in 1988 with 'Don't Turn Around'; **Steel Pulse** and **Black Uhuru**.

The reggae boom years saw two parallel genres, one minor, one major. The minor one was the rise of a small group of reggae or 'dub' poets, led by the British **Linton Kwesi Johnson** and **Benjamin Zephaniah** and the Jamaican **Mutabaruka**, who recited their verse either with or without a reggae backing. The major trend was the rise of the DJs, also known as toasters, successors of the original sound-system self-publicists, who developed the art of calling out a stream of improvised lyrics over a specially recorded backing track − often the 'dub' version, minus lyrics, found on the B-side of a record − and in some cases over the record itself, competing and interacting with the vocalist. Chief among these performers were **I. Roy, U. Roy, Dennis Alcapone**, and **Big Youth**, whose 'Dread Locks Dread' was one of the best albums of the 1970s.

With the death of Bob Marley, live reggae went into something of a decline. In the UK, the Jamaican market was dominated by the softer, non-political, non-rasta style of 'lovers' rock', while at home, the DJs tightened their hold on the scene, with the development of the 'dancehall' sound. A new crop of DJs, sporting macho, Western or kung-fu oriented names like **Clint Eastwood**,

Josey Wales, Dillinger and **Ninjaman,** and geometric razor-cuts rather than dreadlocks, took over and their 'chatting' became increasingly crudely concerned with sex. First master of the sexual bragadoccio style known as 'slackness' was the albino DJ **Yellowman,** né Winston Foster, who made dozens of successful records alone and with rapping partners like **Fathead** and **Sister Nancy** between his discovery in 1980 and his signing to Columbia Records in 1984. Yellowman's early hits – 'Soldier Take Over', 'One Yellowman Inna Yard' and others – still featured live bands, including substantial brass sections, which he reproduced in full-scale stage shows. By the second half of the 1980s, however, most record producers were using sampled backing tracks from existing discs, often older classic reggae from the 1970s, as a base upon which to place the DJ's or singer's voice. The move to artificially created dancehall peaked in the creation of 'digital dancehall', or 'digi', in which a voice, a computerised keyboard and a drum machine were the only ingredients. The mid-1980s saw an increasing merging of the audiences for black American hip-hop music, in which the rapping vocal style was, in any event, a distinct throwback to the Jamaican-originated 1950s sound-system DJs, and for dance hall reggae, which began to be referred to as 'ragga', for 'ragamuffin', music, in acknowledgement of its young audience of latter-day rude boys in Kingston, Brooklyn or Brixton. An atmosphere of violence and banditry continued to attend dancehall events: in Kingston it became the practice to fire guns ('lickshots') in the air to salute a good performance by a DJ – at which the crowd would shout out 'Pum! Pum!' in boisterous agreement with the mark of respect. This led to periodic police clampdowns and raids on sound systems, while Jamaican radio stations have also tried periodically to ban slackness from the airwaves in favour of the non-obscene, non-violent 'reality' lyrics also forming part of the DJ repertoire.

At the beginning of the 1990s, the top DJ, and a master of slackness (his most famous early hit was 'Wicked In Bed'; a later song 'Dem Bow' was a scarcely concealed reference to fellatio) was **Shabba Ranks,** the first new DJ to sign with a major label (Epic) in 1991. Rexton Gordon, as he was christened, took his stage name from a joint reference to the husband of the Queen of Sheba and a notorious Kingston bandit, and, as Shabba Ranks, scored his first big hit in Jamaica in 1988 with 'Can't Do The Work', and went on to impose his rough, tough persona on the market. He had an eye for effective self-publicity such as arriving at the 1989 'Reggae Sunsplash' concert by helicopter. The dancehall/DJ recording scene in Jamaica continues to be as fluid and informal as the 1950s ska scene, with top DJs and singers continually teaming up for one-off records or performances; Shabba Ranks has been no exception. Other top DJs include Ninjaman, Shabba Ranks' chief rival; **Cocoa Tea; Cutty Ranks; Home T; Papa San; Red Dragon; Daddy Lizard; Johnny P.; Lieutenant Stitchie; Tiger; Lloyd Lovindeer** and **Charlie Chaplin.**

In addition to the rapper DJs, 1990s Jamaican music features numbers of reggae singers who either perform in duets with DJs, or as soloists in the other principal new trend often referred to as techno-reggae. Techno-reggae is, above all, the creation of the long-standing Kingston producer **Augustus 'Gussie' Clarke**, who spent twenty years quietly producing quality classic reggae records by artistes such as **Big Youth** before opening a new, selectively-equipped studio, the Music Works, in 1988 and starting to put out a hugely successful series of records combining the latest digital techniques with carefully chosen and arranged songs and quality singers. Clarke's first big hit was 'Rumours', which revitalised the flagging career of older singer **Gregory Isaacs**; his second transformed the image of the rather staid, if successful, female singer **J.C. Lodge** with the song 'Telephone Love', which became a huge hit in Jamaica and America. Other top singers to have benefited from the production experience of Gussie Clarke and his protégé **Mikey Bennett** are **Nadine Sutherland**; the duo of **Brian** and **Tony Gold** and **Karl Meeks**.

Finally, a number of successful artistes have come forward via channels connected with neither ragga dance hall nor techno-reggae. These include New York-based reggae singers such as **Sister Carol** and **Shelley Thunder**, graduates of Jamaica's North Coast cabaret circuit such as **Marcia Griffiths** and **Karen Smith**, and exponents of the softer, soul-influenced 'New Jamaican Lovers' Music', such as the group **Kotch**.

Jamaica: Discography

The Jolly Boys Pop 'n' Mento (First Warning)
Various (inc. the Skatalites, etc.) Intensified and More Intensified (Island 162 539 524 and 597)
Various Soul Defenders At Studio One (Heartbeat HB 66)
Bob Marley and the Wailers 11 major albums, from Catch a Fire to Uprising (reissued on Island Records 422 846200–846211)
Lee Perry and the Upsetters Super Ape (Island 162 539 417)
Gregory Isaacs Night Nurse (Island 162 539 721)
Various (a wide range of top 1970s reggae classics, inc. U. Roy, Gregory Isaacs, the Mighty Diamonds) All-Time Reggae Classics series (Virgin Frontline 9001–9013)
Various Turn It Over (Island 510 908-2)
Various (inc. Tiger, Brian and **Tony Gold)** Ram Dancehall (Mango 162 539 853)

TRINIDAD

Trinidad is still the leading calypso and soca nation, and the source of the majority of the artistes whose records supply the large expatriate communities in Brooklyn, Miami, Toronto and London. Trinidadian music is in fact quite complex, a result of the island's ethnic mix. A neglected Spanish possession for centuries, before passing briefly to France and finally to Britain in 1797, Trinidad still has a Spanish and Venezuelan-linked string-based music, parang, now making a minor comeback, and French patois was replaced by English in song lyrics only at the beginning of this century. The large Indian population, who arrived after the abolition of slavery in 1838, has its own music, based on tassa drumming, which again is very much alive; non-Indian artistes such as the black singer and dancer **Raymond Cameo** have taken up Indian-based music, even to the extent of learning Hindi.

Calypso sprang from the African traditions of the slaves; the word may come from 'kaiso', which is an alternative term, taken from the similar West African Hausa word meaning, roughly, 'Bravo!' The slave work-gangs were spurred on by singers from among them, who exalted their own teams and scorned competitive gangs, and 'picong' verbal duels between singers became an institution which still features in modern calypso. The kalenda stick-fight also played its part. During slavery, the nascent carnival had allowed the black population brief licence to dress up (masquerade) as comic versions of their masters and mock the ruling élite. After emancipation, the euphoric slaves took to roaming the streets in carnival bands armed with poui fighting sticks, supported by chantwells (prototype calypsonians) who traded insults in song prior to the actual battle. The kalenda gangs and carnival's other major musical feature, their accompanying big bands of African drummers, were banned at the end of the nineteenth century, and higher-class Trinidadians began to enter the carnival-song fray, accompanying their music with Venezuelan-style guitar and cuatro bands, while the poor blacks resorted to tuned lengths of bamboo percussion known as 'tamboo bamboo', early forerunners of the steel bands.

In the first two decades of the twentieth century, calypso acquired all of its main features. The singers took extravagantly boastful names reminiscent of the old chantwell ethos – **Attila the Hun**, the **Roaring Lion** – and sang, by now universally in English, often commenting humorously, indeed scurrilously, on current events and sometimes retaining a level of double entendre or hidden meaning from the days when the songs were the only way of criticising the masters with impunity. As calypso started to take on a life independent of carnival, groups of calypsonians began to perform in tents as syndicates and to charge admission, and gradually an early form of business sponsorship crept in; for example, the Toddy chocolate-drink company would support the Toddy Syndicate tent in exchange for advertising.

In the 1930s, calypso spread to the United States. The American bandleader Paul Whiteman had a hit with a calypso, 'Sly Mongoose', and in 1934, top calypsonians Attila the Hun and the Roaring Lion went to New York to record for Decca, where they were fêted by Bing Crosby and Rudy Vallee, who featured Lion's 'Ugly Woman' on national radio. For its part, calypso's instrumentation began to adapt under the influence of New Orleans Jazz, acquiring brass sections or guitar, bass and violin that reflected a mixture of parang and American 'folk' styles.

World War II strengthened the American links, with large numbers of GIs based in Trinidad, a presence viewed with ambivalence by islanders who saw their money as a corrupting influence. 'Rum and Coca Cola', Lord Invader's pointed comment on some Trinidadian women's response ('Both mother and daughter/Working for the Yankee dollar'), was, ironically, made into a major hit in the USA by the white Andrews Sisters; Invader had to take the American artistes to court to obtain composer's royalties.

As late as the 1940s, calypsonians had been subject to a considerable degree of censorship, with the British Colonial Secretary empowered to ban any record and a licence required to sing in a calypso tent. Attila the Hun, the greatest of the early calypsonians, had his song on the subject 'The Banning of Records' itself banned in 1938. Attila fought back extra-musically: in 1950 he successfully stood for election to the Legislative Council, a position he used to ameliorate calypso conditions. Attila died in 1962 leaving dozens of famous songs, including 'Women Will Rule The World', 'Good Will Flyers' and 'Roosevelt in Trinidad', as well as a book, *Attila's Kaiso: A Short History of Calypso*.

With the greatly increased international audience in the 1940s and 1950s a new school of calypsonians, the so-called young brigade, began to switch the lyrical emphasis of their songs away from community-level politics and gossip and towards more international issues and the universally comprehensible subject of sex. The greatest of the young brigade, and one of the all-time top calypsonians, was **Lord Kitchener**, who is still making an album a year in his seventies. After early success in Attila's calypso tent with songs such as 'Tie Tongue Mopsy' and 'Double Ten', Kitchener emigrated to London in 1948 where he was among the first wave of Britain's West Indian arrivals and was filmed for the newsreels singing 'London Is The Place For Me' as he disembarked from a transatlantic steamer. The following four decades saw him score a huge hit, 'Nora', in West Africa, where he toured in the 1950s, enlist Princess Margaret as a fan during his performances in the Soho calypso club the Sunset, and win the Calypso Monarch competition (for best individual singer) and Road March of the Year (for most crowd-pleasing dance song) of the Trinidad Carnival on numerous occasions. In 1978, at the age of 57, he scored the first international hit in the new soca style with 'Sugar Bum Bum'.

The 1970s saw two major developments in Trinidadian music. Firstly, women began to participate in the carnival competitions; the title 'Calypso King' was changed to 'Calypso Monarch'. Secondly, soca was born, the product, as its name suggests, of a mixture of soul feeling and calypso, with the former's tougher, more electric bass, guitar, drums and brass hardening the arrangement. The calypsonians **Maestro** and **Lord Shorty**, along with the arranger **Pelham Goddard**, are generally credited with the earliest soca records. Lord Shorty (Garfield Blackman) started his career in the early 1960s with 'Long Mango' and 'Sixteen Commandments' and recorded a series of songs filled with sexual innuendo ('Lesson In Love', 'Love Man'), which were followed in 1973 by his first soca 'Soul Calypso Music'. In 1981, after producing hits by his younger daughter **Abbi Blackman** and son **O.C. Blackman**, he became a Rastafarian, moved his family to a remote country settlement, changed his name to **Ras**

Shorty I and with thirteen of his children formed a band, the **Love Circle**, with whom he began to record a new gospel-influenced 'healing' music he called jamoo. His 25th anniversary as a singer was commemorated by the live LP 'Watch Out My Children'.

An early embracer of soca was the **Mighty Sparrow**, probably the greatest calypso artiste in the world, whose records, from 'Pussycat Party' in 1979 onwards, were frequently in the new style. Sparrow was born Slinger Francisco in Grenada and moved to Port of Spain as a child; he became a professional calypsonian in 1955. His numerous early songs (such as 'William the Conqueror') in support of Dr Eric Williams' People's National Movement party marked a major shift of calypso from a critical to a supportive role vis à vis the government. In 1958, Sparrow's 'Calypso Carnival' was the first calypso LP. The ensuing three decades have seen the international show-business success of Sparrow, with an unending stream of songs on such topics as the 1983 break-in to Queen Elizabeth's bedroom by an unhinged Londoner ('Philip My Dear'), and a record-breaking run of wins in both Calypso Monarch and Road March competitions in three successive years. Sparrow is now a successful businessman with a sports club, Sparrow's Hideaway, outside Port of Spain and a continuing output of hit songs every carnival.

Other successful calypsonians of Sparrow's generation are **Calypso Rose**, the first female Calypso Monarch and Road March winner in 1978 with 'Her Majesty' and 'I Thank Thee', now somewhat internationalised by her residence in New York; **Shadow**, whose 1974 Road March winner and runner-up 'Bass Man' and 'Ah Come Out To Play' ended Kitchener's and Sparrow's decade-long domination of the title.

The late 1960s saw the advent of a newly politicised lyrical direction in calypso, influenced by the Black Power Movement, Bob Marley, and so on. Its chief proponents were the **Mighty Chalkdust**, a schoolteacher, and **Black Stalin**. Chalkdust survived government attempts to silence him by forbidding him to accept non-teaching work and dominated late 1970s calypso-writing with songs such as 'Ah 'Fraid Karl', but his career slumped in the 1980s as public taste switched to purely dance and party-oriented soca lyrics. Black Stalin, on the other hand, cannily modified his work to take account of new trends and remained hugely popular, winning the Calypso Monarch 1991 competition with his well-planned duo of songs, the out-and-out dance number 'Black Man Feelin' To Party' and the more thoughtful 'Look On The Brighter Side'.

If the 1980s were increasingly dominated by 'Hot Hot Hot' style party lyrics, thoughtful writers were by no means absent. **David Rudder**, one of the biggest stars of the late 1980s, is as much known for his quality lyrics − his 1986 hit 'The Hammer', in memory of the steel-pan tuner Rudolph Charles, is a fine example − as for his eloquence and erudition on the subject of calypso, and his rejection of the burlesque aspects of the form (he refuses to take a calypsonian name for example). Rudder's general orientation is, in fact, more rock than calypso, and his background is not in the pure calypsonian tradition so much as in the allied but distinct field of big bands or brass bands, the eight-to-twelve-strong guitar, percussion and brass groups who play for dances and whose repertoire includes calypso and soca but also other rock-pop styles. After early pop work with the **Solutions**, a Motown cover band, and then playing calypso with Kitchener, David Rudder joined the brass band **Charlie's Roots** in 1980 as a temporary replacement for their singer **Christopher Herbert**, a.k.a. **'Tambu'**, a member of the **Trinidad Police Band**. (Tambu continued to perform and rejoined Charlie's Roots shortly afterwards; he is still extremely popular.) Charlie's Roots, with their arranger and keyboard-player Pelham Goddard, dominated the 1980s band scene and Rudder's 1986 Calypso Monarch and Road March double win marked the high point of his career.

The other top calypsonians at the beginning of the 1990s were **Gypsy**, **Baron** and **Super Blue**. Gypsy's reputation as one of the best live entertainers rests on his expertise in 'extempo' – improvisatory – calypso. He rose to major fame in 1986 with 'The Sinking Ship', his attack on the mishandling of the Trinidadian economy, and continued with big dance hits such as 'Bad Behaviour', 'Kingston On Fire' and his 1991 'Jump Jump'. Baron's forte is his mellifluous delivery; he is not a great writer. After early success in the 1970s, he faded for some years before coming back very strongly in 1983 with 'Feelin' It'. Super Blue, a former fisherman, burst on to the scene in 1980 as **Blue Boy** but lapsed into a New York-based, drug-impeded career hiatus for two years before changing his name and making a terrific comeback with 'Ploom Ploom' (1990) and 'Get Something And Wave' (1991), which won him that year's Road March title. Popular second-rank artistes include **Cro Cro**, **Denyse Plummer**, **Sugar Aloes**, **Crazy** and **Duke**.

Other important features of the 1980s and 1990s soca scene are the two other members of the trio of ubiquitous top arrangers, the Trinidad-based **Leston Paul** and the New York-based **Frankie ('The Right Hon.') McIntosh**, up-and-coming younger arrangers **Nappy Mayes** and **Beaver Henderson**, and two more top big bands, the young, multiracial **Second Image**, and **Taxi**. The latter, particularly, led by guitarist **Robin Imamshah**, had a massive hit throughout the Caribbean with their 1991 carnival song, 'Dollar', written by new star vocalist **Colin Lucas**.

Calypso/soca is not the only distinctive musical style associated with Trinidad: the joyful trill of the steel band is the island's other contribution. The orchestra of steel oil drums with surfaces beaten into concave tuned 'keys' originated in an improvised kitchen pots-and-pans descendant of the tamboo bamboo bands, which has in turn superseded the banned kalenda drum groups of early carnival. Steel drum, or 'pan', bands boomed after World War II and innovative bandleaders such as **Winston 'Spree' Simon** began to arrange everything from calypso to Chopin for pans. In 1951 the newly formed government-sponsored **Trinidad and Tobago All Steel Percussion Orchestra** represented the islands at the Festival of Britain, to a rapturous reception from Londoners. Soon afterwards, the 'Panorama' steel band competition became an essential part of carnival music, along with the Calypso Monarch and Carnival King and Queen costume competitions. During the months of lead-up to Carnival, the country's two hundred and fifty steel bands practise in their panyards for the lengthy eliminating competitions. Top bands are sponsored by commercial enterprises such as the Amoco oil company (the **Renegades**), Witco tobacco group (the **Desperados**, Panorama winners in 1991) or fast-food chain Bermudez (**Phase Two Pan Groove**, top arranger **Len 'Boogsie' Sharpe**'s band).

Trinidad: Discography

Various (inc. Tiger, Atilla, Lion, etc.) Calypso Ladies (Interstate HTCD 06)
Sparrow More Sparrow More (West Indies Records 2020)
Black Stalin Roots Rock Soca (Rounder CD 5038)
Various Wind Your Waist (Shanachie 64034)
David Rudder & Charlie's Roots Haiti (COTT Music CR 008)
David Rudder The Power & The Glory (West Indies Records CR 010)
Tambu The Journey (West Indies Records CR 09)
Taxi Dollar (Hot Vinyl HVT 63)

BARBADOS

The mid-1970s saw the beginning of a period of cultural development in Barbados which in ten years propelled the island's music from also-ran status to the front rank, along with Trinidad and Antigua, of the calypso/soca producing nations.

The 1960s had seen a profusion of small-time club and hotel entertainers, many of them including calypsos in a repertoire which also took in pop, soul, rock and roll and ballads. Very few of them recorded to any significant extent; of those who did, two achieved some prominence. The first of these was **Jackie Opel**, whose powerful voice interpreted to considerable effect rock and pop standards of the period, and who also popularised a sort of early soca-variant rhythm, peculiar to Barbados, known as spouge. Jackie Opel's career, sadly, was terminated at an early stage by a fatal car crash, but the second of the late-1960s star acts was still going strong twenty years later.

The **Merrymen**, five white Bajans (as Barbados inhabitants are known), produced a rather limp cabaret folk-calypso-pop mix which nonetheless enabled them to build a successful touring career in the USA, Canada and Britain, record 26 albums and score a number of substantial hit songs, notably the perennial 'Big Bamboo'. The Merrymen continue to entertain tourists at venues such as the Plantation Restaurant dinner show, for which they have adapted their act to include new soca features and assorted other trends. (A second-generation version of the Merrymen, **Spice**, led by Merrymen founder **Emile Straker**'s son **Dean**, now performs roughly the same function, twenty years updated, mixing rather bland Caribbean rhythms with rock.)

In terms of pure calypso, Barbados in the late 1960s could probably count eight or nine amateurs and no large-scale mechanism for nurturing new professional practitioners. Part of the reason for this was the absence of any equivalent of Trinidad's carnival tradition, which supported the substantial seasonal calypso industry. The nearest parallel, the festival celebrating the end of the sugar harvest in May and June, was fast dying out as the sugar crop became less important.

From 1974 onwards, this state of affairs changed as the Crop-Over Festival was founded. At first a rather artificial government-organised tourist attraction, it gradually grew into a genuine popular carnival equivalent, each August attracting considerable numbers of expatriate Bajans home from Britain, the USA and Canada. By the late 1980s, the pool of amateur and (a few) professional calypsonians had grown to well over a hundred and the quality of their music was very high, arguably better overall than Trinidad's. Musically, Crop-Over is organised in a manner roughly similar to Trinidad's carnival, with ten or more calypso 'tents' (which are really nightclubs, public halls or warehouses) each featuring a regular bill of up to a dozen calypsonians performing two or three numbers each with a house band, during the three or four weeks leading up to Pic O De Crop Calypso Final in the National Stadium. The best calypsonian is adjudged Calypso Monarch and the most popular song on the streets is elected Tune O De Crop, the Barbados equivalent of the Trinidadian Road March of the Year.

Musically, Bajan calypso (Bajans tend to favour the older term even though the music is clearly soca) is harder, rougher and bouncier than its Trinidadian equivalent. Lyrically, it has retained a high level of humour and topicality in the song texts, which are often bracingly scurrilous.

The songwriter **Sach Moore**, nowadays retired but still a prominent calypso commentator, was the earliest of Barbados' serious calypsonians, recording the first Bajan calypsos in the early 1970s. This period, however, was dominated by two performers, the **Mighty Gabby** and **Romeo**, both of whom are performing strongly today.

Gabby, as he has been known since the 'Mighty' was rendered redundant by his fame, is the doyen of Bajan calypsonians and is generally regarded as the island's most gifted exponent. He first came to prominence when he won the 1968 Barbados Calypso Competition (a low-key predecessor of the Crop-Over Pic O De Crop event) with his song 'Heart Transplant', a feat he repeated the following year with 'Family Planning'. By the mid-1970s, Gabby was writing prolifically, both folk songs and calypsos, immersing himself in the works of the new Caribbean literary movement (whose ranks included the Bajan writers George Lamming and Edward Braithwaite) and getting involved in theatre (in 1975 taking over the lead role of Barbados Theatre Workshop of New York City's production *Under The Duppie Parasol*). In 1982, Gabby's huge hit song 'Jack' revolutionised Bajan calypso with its inventive lyrics, tough modern bass line and polished melody. 'Jack', which was recorded live in one of the Crop-Over tents, was the spark which ignited the interest of the Guyanese-born, long-term London resident rock star **Eddie Grant**, who had recently moved to Barbados to set up his Ice record company and recording studio at Bayley's Plantation, in St Philip. Grant began to produce and arrange Gabby's records, boosting the bass guitar part more towards a reggae volume and generally achieving a crisper, modern sound. In 1981, Gabby had played in Britain, the USA, Canada, Cuba, Germany and Colombia and by 1989 his status was such that like an elder statesman he ruled himself out of competition at Crop-Over, though his song 'Chicken 'n' Ram' was heard everywhere throughout August of that year.

The second artiste taken up by Eddie Grant was the dance king **Grynner**, a former building worker whose eccentric stentorian voice, lively lyrics and sense of a catchy melody enabled him in 1990 to notch up a double hat trick – winning the Road March competition six years running. Grynner's 1990 winning song, 'Get Out De Way', which warns all other calypsonians to get out de way as 'de ugly man', i.e. Grynner, 'is de only man who music we want to hear', was written by Gabby. Eddie Grant played several instruments on the backing track, as he does also on Gabby records.

The third great name of eighties Bajan calypso is **Red Plastic Bag** who, unlike Gabby and Grynner, still holds down a full-time non-musical job as a clerk at Caribbean Air Cargo's airport office. Along with **John King**, another of the top half-dozen singers, RPB (alternatively 'De Bag'), as he is generally known, comes from the calypso hotbed district of St Philip. He won his first Calypso Monarch title in 1982 and repeated the feat in 1984 with the famous 'Mr Harding Can't Burn' and in 1989 with 'Pluck It'. RPB's forte is lyrical cleverness and clarity and performing expertise.

Among several dozen substantial second-rank calypsonians, the following deserve mention: **Ras Iley**, a young Rasta performer who scored a major success in 1987 with 'Spring Gardens On Fire'; **Adonijah**, a London-educated journalist, also a Rasta, whose 1981 'Rock In Ethiopia' was a big hit; **Commander**, whose 1989 hit 'Bring Back the Spouge' did exactly what its title suggested and reprised the 1970s Barbados soca-variant spouge which had lost most of its mass popularity; **Rita, Marcee** and **Miss B.**, three leading female calypsonians; **Charles Lewis**, a minor name in Barbados who scored a major hit in Europe in 1990 with 'Soca Dance' with the help of a clever marketing move in the wake of the Lambada craze.

In addition to calypso and soca, reggae and dub styles are of course popular in Barbados. The spread of Rastafarianism, which is prevalent on the wilder north coast closest to Africa, was boosted by the arrival from Jamaica in 1975 of the Rasta group **Ras Boanerges and the Sons of Thunder**. As Barbados is relatively conservative and antagonistic to drug use, Rastas have a fairly hard time and are by no means proliferating, although the sect is well established on the island.

Barbados: Discography

Jackie Opel The Memorable Jackie Opel (West Indies Records WO15)
Red Plastic Bag De Heat Is On (Bayfield Records BF020)
Red Plastic Bag Red Hot Soca (Bayfield Records BF023)
Gabby Across The Board (Ice Records ICE 89 12021)
Grynner The Road March King (Ice Records ICE 89)
Gabby, Grynner, Square One Illegal Tender (Ice Records 204)

THE WINDWARD ISLANDS

St Lucia, like Dominica, has a joint English and French colonial background which manifests itself in the great popularity of zouk as well as of soca-calypso. In addition the acoustic 'shak shak' bands, centred on the gourd maracca of that name, are still popular. Top St Lucian calypsonians are the **Parrot,** a long-standing favourite, and the younger **Invader,** whose hits 'Walk and Wine', 'Bend Down Low' and 'Sit On It' have been popular throughout the region. Secondary calypsonians are **Pep, Educator, Tricky,** the **General** and **Short Pants.**

Dominica was more heavily influenced by the Haitian merengue and compas rhythms and Martiniquan cadence and subsequently zouk than by calypso, though French and English-derived forms merged in the 1970s to form 'cadence-lypso', as purveyed by top groups **Exile One,** the **Swinging Stars,** the **Gaylords,** the **Grammacks** and the female singer **Ophelia Olivacé.** The 1980s saw this quite substantial regional music fade in the face of reggae and zouk from the exterior. At the same time, however, the local 'jing ping' style, a derivative of the shak shak bands featuring basic percussion, accordion, flutes and other semi-improvised instruments, regained popularity and a number of groups – the **Giraudel Jing Ping Band,** the **Paix Bouche Cultural Troupe** and the **Dominican Folk Singers** – were revived or formed. In 1990, Gordon Henderson, a former member of The Grammacks, brought together jing ping, cadence and other style elements on his album 'Le Mariage'.

St Vincent boasts two soca singers who have scored major Caribbean hits. **Becket's** two-decade career has included a pioneering signing with the major US record company Casablanca in the 1970s, a lengthy fall from the top ranks of calypsonians and a triumphant return with his huge 1991 hit 'Teaser' from the album 'Gal A Rush Me'. **Vincent Soso** has scored major hits with 'Rude Girl Posse' and 'I Don't Mind'.

Grenada has a healthy local calypso scene (main singers are **Ajamo, Black Wizard, Scrunter, Squeezy** and **Randy Isaacs**), but no larger-scale stars.

Windward Islands: Discography

Becket Gal A Rush Me (Cocoa Records 0090)

THE LEEWARD ISLANDS

Antigua has a strong calypso-soca scene and a large and flourishing carnival; its music is generally regarded as having the fastest tempo of the soca nations. **King Short Shirt** is Antigua's longest-standing calypsonian. In 1988 he won the Calypso Monarch competition for the fourteenth time, and stood down from subsequent competition to devote more time to running his beach bar and glass-bottomed cruise-boat business. The other three top calypsonians are **Obstinate**, **Swallow** and **King Progress**. Obstinate, known regionally for his song 'Elephant Walk', worked for a number of years in the Virgin Islands and returned to Antigua in 1982 to win the Calypso Monarchy three years in succession before retiring undefeated from the competition. Swallow first became Calypso Monarch in 1973, since when he has scored a string of hits, notably 'Pepper Sauce' and 'Doctor'. Latterly, he has spent more time in the United States than at home. King Progress, a customs officer in non-musical life, has benefited from the absence or withdrawal of the big three singers on a number of occasions, notably in 1984 when he won the Calypso Monarch title with a pair of songs, 'Madness' and 'You Getting It'. Other calypsonians include **Douglas**, **Lion** and **Zero**, whose 'Like A Prayer' won him the Monarchy in 1990. Aside from the calypsonians, Antigua's top soca-rock group, the **Burning Flames**, have achieved major regional fame. Led by the brothers **Clarence 'Oungku' Edwards** and **Toriano 'Onyan' Edwards**, the group backed **Arrow** for some time before developing their rock/Central American/Antigua soca mix with songs such as 'Sweet Little Island Girl', and winning Road March of the Year in 1989 with 'Congo Man', which featured with the excellent mid-paced soul number 'Chook and Dig' on their 1990 album 'Mek E Bark'.

The little island of **Montserrat** boasts one major international star, **Alphonsus Cassell**, better known as **Arrow**, whose 1983 recording of his song 'Hot Hot Hot' became a party anthem all over the world, even ending up as theme tune of the Mexico City soccer World Cup. Arrow started singing at school and by 1971 had won the Calypso Monarch of Montserrat competition. A series of successful releases – 'On Target' in 1974, 'Instant Knockout' in 1981 and 'Double Trouble' in 1982 – built up to the massive 'Hot Hot Hot', which transformed Arrow from a local calypsonian into an internationally minded artiste, a process already encouraged by the late 1970s ruling confining participation in the Trinidad Carnival competition to native Trinidadians. In 1988 Arrow signed to the British Island Records label and released an album 'Knock 'Em Dead', followed in 1989 by 'O La Soca' and in 1990 by 'Soca Dance Party'. Arrow's speciality is fast, high-energy formulaic dance soca with little originality or wit in terms of lyrics, and a well-calculated use of other Caribbean rhythms, including zouk, so as to appeal to as large an audience as possible.

The Leeward Islands: Discography

King Short Shirt Leroy (A & B Records, Antigua, no catalogue number)
The Burning Flames Mek E Bark (Dr G. Production BF 0008)
Arrow Hot Hot Hot (Arrow 019)
Arrow Soca Dance Party (Island 162 539 878)

THE VIRGIN ISLANDS AND THE BAHAMAS

Neither of these groups of islands, both culturally dominated by the United States, have local musics of the strength of soca, but both possess and preserve their own styles. **St Croix**, like other Virgin Islands, has its 'scratch bands', named after the guiro scraper-percussion, known locally as a squash, central to the sound. Scratch bands mixed calypso with Dominican merengue and musical traces of the island's former French, British and Danish settlers. Until the 1970s, they were unamplified and led by flute and guitar. In the 1970s, musicians such as **Sylvester McIntosh**, a.k.a. **Blinky**, leader of **Blinky and the Roadmasters**, introduced saxophone and electric guitars and bass, and scratch bands began to draw a new, younger audience. The Roadmasters, so named because a number of the band's early members were road-maintenance workers, play a large repertoire of traditional and new songs at local nightclubs and parties, and have visited the United States twice, in 1988 and 1989, during which time they recorded an album for Rounder Records.

The **Bahamas** possess a strong original blues heritage, imported during the mid-nineteenth century by slaves escaping to the emancipated islands from the southern states of the USA. The best-known blues performer outside the islands is **Joseph Spence**, whose eccentric, highly mannered singing and unique acoustic guitar playing were recorded by the great blues archivist Samuel Charles in the 1960s and whose songs have been covered by Ry Cooder. The Bahamas' African percussion heritage is found in the drum, cowbell, conch shell and whistle-bands participating in Junkanoo, the Christmas-New Year carnival equivalent. Other regional musics, including calypso, merengue, Latin jazz and soul-funk, have contributed to a range of modern popular sounds. The 1960s and 1970s saw artistes such as the **Fred Munnings Orchestra**, the **Eloise Trio**, **Count Bernadino** and **Peanuts Taylor** come to prominence. Two major record hits, **Ronnie Butler**'s 'Burma Road' and the **Beginning of the End**'s 'Funky Nassau', made the British Top Ten in 1975. Ronnie Butler made a comeback in 1990, when a new crop of artistes began revitalising the Bahamian recording scene. Chief names are **Eugene**, whose single 'Da Girl Look Good' was a huge hit; **KB**, whose album 'Kicking Bahamian' was also a massive seller; and the band **High Voltage**, whose guitarist **Fred Ferguson** is also the most important and creative new independent producer.

Bahamas: Discography

Blinky and the Roadmasters Crucian Scratch Band Music (Rounder 5047)

CUBA

Twentieth-century Cuban music has been immensely influential internationally; in the 1930s Cuban bands played in Paris and New York; in the 1950s and 1960s Cuban son was of critical importance in Africa's burgeoning musical modernisation, while the words 'mambo' and 'cha-cha-cha' infiltrated song titles from Cairo to Manila; in the 1970s the US-nurtured salsa boom was entirely based on Cuban models. The island's political and cultural isolation since the 1959 Castro revolution, the subsequent US trade and communications embargo and the departure for the USA of many top musicians, have meant that, except in the field of jazz, modern Cuban bands are marginalised in terms of popularity throughout Latin America, as opposed to its domestic following. If Cuba no longer leads the way commercially, however, the country still has a wealth of excellent music-makers.

The basic ingredients of Cuban music are the same as in other Spanish-colonised islands: Spain provided the ten-line decima verse form still used in some songs, the ornamented bel canto vocal style, the harmony, and the stringed instruments (guitar and little six-string tres). African slaves provided the drums, the call and response vocal style, some melodic lines and the open-ended song form. African culture is particularly strong in Cuba, partly because of the relative tolerance by the Spanish of their slaves' customs, unlike the repressive British and North American practice, partly because of the large numbers of slaves imported and the long duration of the trade – which lasted as late as the 1870s. Cuba's African population came mainly from the Congo and the Yoruba-populated areas, and the santería religion, in which Christian saints double with Yoruba deities for worship (a famous song example is Santa Barbara and the god Chango), is widely practised, as well as musically significant (the three big wooden bata drums used in sacred santería music also feature in Afro-Cuban secular groups).

The most purely African style in Cuba is the rumba, a drum-and-vocal form whose name was incorrectly applied to the quite different, son-based dance music which became popular in the USA in the 1930s. The rumba originated in the early 1900s in the province of Matanzas, and until the 1950s was an entirely private, informal music performed by the participants at local fiestas. Although conga drums, metal shakers and 'cata' slit-tube percussion are used today, in the past sets of wooden boxes were often used in the poor black communities where the rumba flourished. The rumba is essentially a dance – to be precise, a generic term for a set of three dances, the yambu, the columbia and the guaguanco – involving not-quite-touching pelvic thrusting, 'vacunado', by the man towards his female partner. The songs, wailed out by a solo vocalist and a small chorus, may concern daily life and its problems but often deal, too, with santería-linked themes or African tribal lore whose meaning is secret except to small numbers of initiates. Professional rumba groups are usually composed of former Matanzas port workers who take up the activity on retirement. The most important group and the first to become professional is **Los Muñequitos de Matanzas**, an eleven-man ensemble who sometimes play with the solo son vocalist **Carlos Embale**. In their forty-year career the Muñequitos have made only two records (one of which was released in Europe in 1990 by UK label Globestyle). A second major formation is **Yoruba Andabo**, featuring singer **Pancho Quinto**. A weekly Saturday public rumba concert in Havana, the Sabado de la Rumba, attracts entire families and also a good many musicological tourists.

The first major multi-instrument popular music in Cuba was the contradanza, which originated in French country dance and probably arrived with the large Haitian immigration in the mid-nineteenth century, and which transmuted into the habañera. Its successor was the danzon, played by the bands known as charangas Francesas, consisting of piano, bass, percussion, two violins and a flute. The danzon lasted into the 1950s before being replaced in the repertoire of the charangas by the cha-cha-cha. The cha-cha-cha, which flourished in the United States, is generally credited as the invention of the violinist **Enrique Jorrín**, who added a light vocal chorus to the shuffling instrumental arrangement of the danzon and added further elements of the other great Cuban dance genre, the son. The top Cuban cha-cha-cha band was the **Orquesta Aragon**, led by virtuoso flautist **Richard Egües**, which scored hits with dozens of songs including 'El Bodeguero', 'Guajira Para Ti' and 'Que Viva El Cha Cha Cha', and which is still playing in Havana forty years after its formation. In the USA, Cuban émigré musicians such as **José Fajardo** (see **North America**) specialised in the cha-cha-cha, while it also entered the 1950s repertoire of the star New York-based bands of **Machito**, **Tito Puente**, **Tito Rodriguez** and **Perez Prado**, who had brought the mambo to its international prominence. Mambo, a rather vague term, described a Cuban-originated style, tinged with jazz from the big-band era, and featuring the trumpet, saxophone and trombone associated with the conjunto formation rather than with the string-and-flute charanga line-up. Cuban-based bands most closely associated with the mambo, which faded in the 1960s, were those of **Arsenio Rodriguez** and **Beny Moré** (see below).

The most influential Cuban popular style was, and is, son, an Afro-Hispanic hybrid which originated in the eastern, rural region of Cuba. Son has many variants, but its essential features are the syncopated rhythm (clave) played on the heavy wooden sticks known as claves, the soulful lead vocal, ideally improvised, and the exciting chanted, usually male, 'montuno', or chorus. Early son was played by sextets, septets or conjuntos, featuring trumpets rather than violins; bass, claves, bongos, other percussion including maraccas, congas, or shallow, stick-played timbales; and guitar or tres. The first star national son group to emerge after the music spread to Havana in the 1920s was the **Sexteto Habanero**, who were joined in 1927 by the **Septeto Nacional** under the direction of its founder **Ignacio Piñeiro**. The Septeto Nacional, now led by singer **Carlos Embale**, is still playing today. In the 1940s, the blind tres player and bandleader Arsenio Rodriguez introduced an expanded trumpet section playing tight unison arrangements and a more African, rumba-influenced percussion feel; this style was immensely popular in Cuba and New York where it became, in effect, the progenitor of salsa. Arsenio Rodriguez died in poverty in California in 1970, seven years after the death of the other major Cuban sonero (son singer) and bandleader of the 1950s, the great Beny Moré. Moré, nicknamed **El Barbaro del Ritmo** (Rhythm Barbarian), and the subject of tribute albums from dozens of top Latin artistes since his death, worked in Perez Prado's band before founding his own **Banda Gigante** in Havana in 1953, and proceeding to record many successful songs including 'Yiri Yiri Bon', 'Maracaibo Oriental', 'Cienfuegos' and 'Corazon Rebelde'. Both Arsenio Rodriguez and Beny Moré retain virtually national hero status in Cuba, with weekly radio shows devoted to their music. Other major Cuban son performers of the 1950s include the **Sonora Matancera**, **Celia Cruz** (see **North America**) and **Celina Gonzalez**, a contemporary of Cruz's, and an equally accomplished singer, though she sang in a campesina (country) style while Cruz's American residence led her more and more in a sophisticated, jazz-tinged direction. Celina Gonzalez, who sang as a duo with her husband **Reutilio** until his death in 1971, brings to her music influences from the country styles punto Cubano and son guajiro (guajiro, meaning countryside, as in the famous Cuban anthem 'Guajira Guantanamera' – 'Country Girl from Guantanamo'). She continues to be extremely popular, performing her large repertoire of songs ('Santa Barbara', 'Yo Soy El Punto Cubano', 'Mi Tierra Es Asi') with her son **Lazaro** on her own daily radio programme.

In listing the current top Cuban bands, it is helpful to diverge to describe two highly influential groups at the opposite end of the popular music spectrum to son, namely that closest to jazz. Afro-Latin music and jazz have long overlapped, particularly with regard to percussion from the Latin side (for example, the music of the great rumbero **Chano Pozo** with Dizzy Gillespie). The 1970s and 1980s saw a series of particularly eclectic and inventive Havana conservatoire-trained musicians create intellectual jazz-rock-son fusions of great influence. One of the most important is the group **Irakere**, led by the pianist **Chucho Valdes**, who draw deeply on sacred bata drumming as part of their sophisticated and internationally successful sound. Further along the spectrum towards the pop-country-son end is **Los Van Van**, whose music nonetheless contains a strong element of jazz feeling. Los Van Van were formed in 1969 by leader **Juan Formell** who chose the charanga violin and flute format, later adding a trombone section, synthesizer and syn-drum. Formell christened Van

Van's mixture of modernised son and rock 'songo', and the group's continued live performances, plus top-selling records such as 'Sandunguera', 'Muevete' and 'La Titimania' (the latter licensed to Europe by Island Records) made them one of the most popular groups of the 1980s. Among other top groups roughly in the jazz-rock-progressive sphere are **Sintesis**, who combine Pink Floyd-style rock with elements of Afro-Cuban lore; **Mezela**, who mix nueva trova-influenced, socially concerned lyrics with elements of rock, jazz and assorted Caribbean rhythms; and **Opus 13**, an Irakere-style group very popular at jazz festivals.

Chief among the more traditional son-based dance groups is the **Orquesta Revé**, led by 60-year-old timbales player **Elio Revé** who led numerous bands, mainly in charanga formation, before breaking through to major success with his latest group in 1983. Revé's music is rough, vital, more popular with a lower-class, black audience than an intellectual, Hispanic-oriented one, and based on the very African 'son changui' of his native province of Guantanamo. Revé's music, with its hallmark bata drumming (by his brother **Odelquis**) and the nasal 'old woman's voice' singing of singer **Rafael Padrino**, was well represented by the 1989 Virgin Real World compilation of his greatest hits, 'La Explosion del Momento'. Other top Cuban dance bands are **N.G. La Banda**, the initials standing for 'nueva generacion', led by former Irakere members **José-Luis Cortez** and **Herman Velazco**; **Dan Den**, led by former Orquesta Revé pianist and arranger **Juan-Carlos Alfonso**, whose first post-Revé album 'Siempre Hay Un Ojo' was a huge hit in 1989; **Adalberto Y Su Son**, led by the virtuoso tres player and singer **Pancho Amat**; the **Original de Manzanillo**, an impeccable traditional-style charanga led by the sonero **Candido Fabré**, reputed to be one of the best vocal improvisers in the world; **Sierra Maestra**, a young group playing in the old Septeto Nacional style; and the **Orquesta Ritmo Oriental**, a long-standing traditional charanga whose best songs such as 'Nena, Asi No Se Vale' were big hits in the 1970s.

In addition to the dance and rhythm musics described so far, Cuba continues to be a strong producer and consumer of styles descended more from the lyrical and romantic guitar-backed solo or duo song tradition found throughout Latin America and derived from a mixture of Spanish canciones and Italian operatic arias. In Cuba this romantic ballad style expressed itself firstly in the trova songs of composers such as **Sindo Garay** and **Pepe Sanchez**, and in the 1940s and 1950s transmuted into the two similar styles of bolero, with its slight Afro-Latin colouring, and 'filin' (feeling), a more American-influenced and schmaltzy ballad style. Both bolero and filin continue to be popular with older Cubans, though no sign of a retro fashion has developed among the young; an annual bolero festival takes place in Havana while the capital has two nightclubs, El Pico Blanco and El Rincon del Filin, devoted to filin. The two 'Kings of Filin', **Cesar Portilla de la Luz** and **José Antonio Mendez** (who wrote the famous 'La Gloria Eres Tu') died in the late 1980s, leaving the genre in the hands of singers such as **Marta Valdez**.

In the early 1970s, the so-called 'nueva' (new) trova form, a Cuban version of the protest-linked 'new song' movement found all over Latin America, rose to great popularity. Nueva trova mixed the general style of the Bob Dylan-Joan Baez movement ('poetic' protest lyrics as opposed to love songs, informal clothes as opposed to stage outfits, etc.) with the new eclectic rock sounds of the Beatles generation to produce music with distinct similarities to American soft rock. (Many of the nueva trova musicians went on to form bland 'progressive' jazz-rock groups in the 1980s.) The most famous nueva trovadores internationally, **Silvio Rodriguez** and **Pablo Milanes**, became so as a result of having newly finished solo records ready to contract to multinational companies during their first tour of Spain after Franco's death in 1976. Their fellow tour artiste, the equally popular **Sara Gonzalez**, had no recording available and never made up her lost lead in the international market. While Silvio Gonzalez's generally pro-regime, anti-imperialist songs such as 'Sueño Con Serpientes' and 'Canción Urgente Para Nicaragua' became standards, a new generation of trovadores, led by **Santiago Feliu**, **Carlos Varela** and **Frank Delgado**, are continuing to advance the form.

Cuba: Discography

Los Muñequitos de Matanzas The Rumba Originals (Globestyle ORB 053)
Various A Carnival of Cuban Music (Rounder 5049)
Beny Moré El Barbaro Del Ritmo (Nuevos Medios 67369 AX)
Celina Gonzalez Fiesta Guajira (World Circuit WCB 006)
Orquesta Ritmo Oriental La Ritmo Oriental te Esta Llamando (Globestyle ORB 034)
Los Van Van Songo (Island 162 539 825)
Various Sabroso - Havana Hits (Earthworks EWV 11)
Orquesta Revé La Explosion Del Momento (Real World 4)
Sylvio Rodriguez Cuban Classics (WEA 7599 264801)

PUERTO RICO

Puerto Rico's modern dance music was dominated stylistically by the son and its variant, the guaracha of Cuba, with which Puerto Rico shares its Afro-Hispanic background. Cuba's aesthetic advantage, however, was counter-balanced by the socialist island's post-revolutionary isolation from the USA and Puerto Rico's very different status as a US 'Overseas Commonwealth Territory', so that in the 1970s and 1980s Puerto Rico, not Cuba, was the joint centre of salsa development with New York. The movement of musicians of Puerto Rican origin between the overlapping scenes of their island, New York and Miami is so continual that certain artistes whose reputations were made mainly through their US-based work are treated here under 'North America: Latin', which section should be consulted in conjunction with this section.

Puerto Rico possesses its own versions of Afro-Hispanic musics of varying types. The danza was a nineteenth-century equivalent of the Cuban danzon; the seis is a largely Hispanic song form closely connected with the decima stanza at the basis of Cuban country music; the plena is a colloquial, narrative song, slightly reminiscent of the calypso, accompanying a couple dance; and the bomba is a heavily African, percussion-backed equivalent of Cuba's rumba, and also accompanies a couple dance in which the man moves separately from the woman, often interacting with the requinto drummer's improvisation. The plena featured prominently in the repertoire of the jíbaro (country) artistes of the 1930s and 1940s, played by ensembles using pandereta tambourine, congas, bongos, güiro scraper, guitar and the little four (latterly five) double-string guitar called a cuatro, similar to Cuba's tres. The most famous performer of plenas in the 1930s was the band of **Manuel Jimenez**, '**El Canario**', whose prolific recording career included his own compositions such as 'La Nieve De los Años' ('Snow of the Years'), 'Por Primera Vez' ('For the First Time'), and 'Sentir Gitano' ('Gypsy Feeling'). El Canario was the first to augment a Puerto Rican band with piano, bass and brass, leading to a bifurcation in direction between a more modern, New York-inclined, brass-scored music, taken up by **Cesar Concepcion**'s band in the 1940s and **Rafael Cortijo**'s (see below) in the 1950s, and a simple string-based jíbaro sound, purveyed through the same period by artistes such as **Ernestina Reyes**, 'La Calandria', **Flor Morales Ramos** 'Ramito' and, later, **Pedro Padilla**.

In the 1940s and 1950s Puerto Rican urban bands began to merge into the New York pan-Latin melting pot which, along with Cuban charanga and conjunto styles (see **Cuba**) and big-band jazz, gave rise to the successive waves of so-called rumba, mambo and cha-cha-cha. Early Puerto Rican stars of this genre were the **Morales** brothers, especially bandleader and composer **Noro Morales**, and the great mambo interpreter **Tito Rodriguez** (see **North America: Latin**). The musician who did most to preserve Puerto Rican flavour was, however, the bandleader and percussionist **Rafael Cortijo**.

Cortijo was born in the coastal village of Loiza Aldea, a centre of African-based musical tradition, and he was responsible for bringing back to fashion both classic plenas of El Canario and new ones of his own, and bombas, for which he augmented his standard brass-led band with traditional drums. Cortijo's sound, as typified on numbers such as 'El Bombon de Elena', 'Micaela' and 'Chongolo', was an eclectic mix of rootsy, black feeling, Puerto Rican as opposed to Cuban touches – for example, female voices rather than male in the 'coro' ('chorus') – and avant-garde features such as his exceptionally early use of rock-style guitar solos. Cortijo's most outstanding work featured the brilliant, husky-voiced sonero **Ismael Rivera**, and his band served as a training ground for young musicians such as **Rafael Ithier** and **Roberto Roena** (see below). Cortijo died in New York in 1983.

Pianist **Ithier** and six fellow Cortijo musicians formed **El Gran Combo de Puerto Rico** in 1962 with the aim of building on the dark soulful Cortijo sound so as to create a slicker dance band of wider appeal. After some resistance, a song, 'Akangana', from the group's second LP became a huge island hit; El Gran Combo went on to develop a rich, tight sound featuring a trombone-boosted brass section playing over Ithier's distinctive rolling keyboard vamps and, until his departure in 1977, the soaring voice of star vocalist **Andy Montanez**. By the 1980s, hits such as 'Ojos Chinos' ('Chinese Eyes') and 'Jala Jala' had made El Gran Combo easily Puerto Rico's top band, a position they consolidated with continual top-quality performances and polished LPs such as the 1989 'Amame' ('Love Me'), a return to the rhythmic son form after a spell of several years of softer material.

One other major band of 1950s vintage continued to perform into the 1990s as inventively and successfully as ever. **La Sonora Ponceña** named themselves after Ponce, their town of origin, on achieving a measure of international fame (while still a purely local band they had been called **La Orquesta Internacional**). Founded by **Enrique 'Quique' Lucca**, and led since the mid-1970s by his son, the multi-instrumentalist, piano star and virtuoso arranger **Papo Lucca**, the Sonora Ponceña features a smooth, rich front line of four impeccable singers and a four-trumpet brass section, demonstrated on albums from the 1978 'Explorando' to 'Back To Work' of ten years later.

Two other Puerto Rican artistes of almost equal longevity remain popular. The singer **Cheo Feliciano** started his career in New York, where he performed with everyone from Tito Rodriguez to **Eddie Palmieri**, and carved himself a considerable reputation as a warm-voiced romantic singer of bolero and salsa. The timbalero and bandleader **Willie Rosario** studied journalism in New York and worked as a newsreader before deciding, under the influence of Tito Rodriguez' performances at the legendary Palladium dance hall (see **North America: Latin**) that he must take up music. Since 1972 based in Puerto Rico, Rosario's high-quality band, featuring a four-trumpet and baritone sax brass section, has acted as launching pad for a succession of young singers including **Gilberto Santa Rosa, Tony Vega** and his current cantantes **Primi Cruz** and **Bernie Perez**.

Puerto Rican artistes were prominent in the New York-led salsa boom of the 1970s when the Cuban son-based pan-Latin mix took on a rock flavouring and again began to appeal to a crossover audience after a decade and a half out of fashion with young Anglos. Top names included **Bobby Valentin**, a bass-player, trumpeter and bandleader who played with Charlie Palmieri on arrival in New York in the 1960s and went on to make a string of his own records including the classic 1973 'Soy Boricua' ('I Am A Puerto Rican') before founding his own Bronco record label in Puerto Rico in 1974; **Roberto Roena**, a top bongo player and noted dancer who worked frequently with his band the **Apollo Sound** and experimented with rhythms such as the Puerto Rican soca adaptation 'zuky'; **Luis 'Perico' Ortiz**, a virtuoso trumpeter and eclectic, experimental, conservatoire-educated arranger responsible for dozens of top collaborations and recordings of his own; **Tommy Olivencia**, another trumpeter and producer whose tutelage has helped the careers of **Frankie Ruiz** and **Eddie Santiago** (see below), the young salsa romantica stars; and **Yomo Toro**, a cuatro player whose mastery of an instrument uncommon in 1970s New York made him a much sought-after session player and led to a contract with Island Records to produce solo albums such as the traditionally based 'Funky Jíbaro' and the Latin-rock fusion 'Gracias' in the 1990s.

The most famous Puerto Rican star of the 1970s and 1980s, however, was the charismatic and brilliant singer **Hector Lavoe**, who in the 1960s teamed up with the young **Willie Colon** (see **North America: Latin**) in the latter's first band, became a leading light of the Fania All Stars-led salsa boom of the 1970s, and became hugely popular for his emotional, ghetto-attuned lyrics and high, fluid improvisatory singing. After early success with songs such as 'El Todopoderoso' ('The All-Powerful') and 'Rompe Saraguey' ('Break the Spell'), problems with drugs and illness and the murder of his son led to a two-year silence. This was broken in 1978 by the brilliant album 'La Comedia', featuring his greatest hit 'El Cantante' ('The Singer'). The 1980s saw Lavoe's tragic personal life continue as a suicide attempt in 1988 left him temporarily paralysed and, obviously, again out of action.

The 1970s saw the bomba and plena become a scarcely perceptible ingredient of the general salsa canon. Native Puerto Rican music fared no better in the 1980s as salsa itself was challenged by the Dominican merengue rhythm (see **Dominican Republic**). Merengue bands swamped the Puerto Rican music market and it was not until the emergence of the new salsa romantica style that the New York-Miami-Puerto Rico axis fought back. Salsa romantica, or 'salsa erotica', depending on the strength of its lyrics, consists essentially of more or less sexy lyrics ('Desnudate Mujer' ('Undress, Woman') and 'Devoráme Otra Vez' ('Devour Me Once More') were two of the greatest hit songs of the late 1980s), crooned by presentable young romantic singers over a soft, relaxed salsa backing which some would describe as bland; one older salsero refers to the genre as 'salsa monga' – 'limp salsa'. The first star of salsa romantica was New Jersey-born **Frankie Ruiz** (see **North America**), followed by **Lalo Rodriguez**, a singer who has risen through the ranks of bands, including Eddie Palmieri's, and scored a massive pan-Latin American hit in 1988 with 'Devoráme Otra Vez'. At the end of the decade, however, the most successful artiste was the young singer **Eddie Santiago**, who started his career in 1984 with the minor Puerto Rican conjunto **Chaney** and went solo two years later, developing a smooth, four-trombone band sound (he avoided trumpets so as not to drown his rather quiet voice). His first LP yielded the major hits 'Tu Me Quemas' ('You Burn Me Up') and 'Que Locura Enamorarme De Ti' ('What Madness To Fall In Love With You'), which he followed up with further successes either in his lyrically explicit style ('Insatiable', etc.), or his purely romantic one ('Lluvia' – 'Rain').

Puerto Rico: Discography

Various (inc. Canario) The Music of Puerto Rico (Harlequin HQ 2075)
Cortijo y su Combo No Title (Sonodisc TRLP 5130)

Ismael Rivera Sonero No. 1 (Sonodisc CLP 164X)
El Gran Combo Sus 15 Grandes Hits (Gema GO31)
Willie Rosario Viva Rosario (Bronco 21019L)
Bobby Valentin Como Nunca (Bronco B2504)
Hector Lavoe El Cantante (Charly/Caliente CD 205)
Frankie Ruiz Voy Pa' Encima (TH Rodven CD 2453)

DOMINICAN REPUBLIC

The music of the Dominican Republic, which occupies the eastern two thirds of the island of Hispaniola (the western part is Haiti), is important as much for its exportability to the two million Dominicans in the USA as for its home audience. In the 1980s the boom in popularity of the Dominican merengue dance rhythm eclipsed salsa, and in **Juan-Luis Guerra** and his group **4:40** the early 1990s saw a Dominican artiste dominate the Latin American world.

As in most of the Hispanic-influenced nations, Dominican popular music is divided between dance music and romantic music. Romantic music was typically represented in the 1940s and 1950s by the bolero (see **Cuba**), which later gave way to the balada. A more roots-level strand of Dominican romantic song transmuted itself into the bachata form, however (see below).

In terms of dance music, the merengue is the Dominican Republic's national style. A fast, galloping 2/4 rhythm, it is very different from the mellower Haitian meringue and from other 'merengues' on the Latin American continent. Its distinctive features are the rumbling tambora drum, played horizontally with a stick at one end and a hand to adjust tension at the other, the metal guira scraper and, in its modern version, the exciting breakneck saxophone arpeggio-choruses known as jaleos which punctuate the songs.

The origins of the merengue are in the usual Latin-Caribbean mix of African slave and Spanish colonial musics; in the nineteenth century it was a popular dance music, played on tambora, guira, guitar and tres. By the twentieth century accordion had replaced guitar, and this form of traditional country merengue still exists, particularly in the northern Cibao area where it is known as merengue tipico Cibaeño, or sometimes as merengue 'perico ripiado', literally 'ripped parrot', a nickname rich in allusions – the rough squawking accordion and rasping guira, 'perico' as slang for a prostitute, 'ripiado' meaning 'dirt poor', 'ripping the parrot' meaning to cut loose with alcohol and women . . .

Both ripiao and the smoother, modern pop merengue are features of the annual merengue festivals in the island's capital, Santo Domingo, and in New York, but merengue ripiao is not well represented in the record market. Its main exponents are **Cieguito de Nagua**, a seven-man group named after its blind leader ('Cieguito' is the dimunitive of 'ciego', meaning blind); **Bartolo Gonzalez Pereyra**, featuring strong sax-and-accordion breaks; **Francisco Ulloa**, a virtuoso accordionist with a 1987 British LP release on Globestyle; **Agapito Pascual**, who plays a modernised ripiao style with bass, guitar and keyboards augmenting the traditional instruments, and two star female accordionists, **Fefita La Grande** and **Maria Diaz**. Other artistes include **Diogenes Jiminez, El Cieguito Jacagua, La India** and **Rafaelito Roman**.

The development of the modern pop merengue, and its dominance over all other Dominican folk styles, was greatly helped by the dictator Rafael Trujillo, president from 1930 until his assassination in 1961, a man of peasant stock who loved the music and commissioned arrangers and big bands to polish and refine it so as to make it a national music acceptable to the bourgeoisie. The merengue declined briefly after Trujillo's death, but bounced back as a new generation of bandleaders speeded up the tempo and introduced the powerful new brass versions of the old accordion jaleos. The most successful of the new merengueros was **Johnny Ventura**, a dynamic singer and bandleader whose background in arranging for the more Cuban-based salsa bands of the 1970s made him ideally suited to create rich exciting brass parts for his group the **Combo Show**. Ventura's visual flair – he choreographed and dressed his musicians meticulously – and his business sense – with his manager William Liriano he built a prosperous touring and recording organisation – were as impressive as his musicianship. After major hit records, including 'Protesta De Los Feos' ('Protest of the Ugly Ones') (1974), 'La Que Te Gusta' ('What You Like') (1981). 'El Lloron' ('The Cry-Baby') (1983) and 'El Señor Del Merengue' (1986), he began to slow down his musical career in favour of politics, in the late 1980s becoming a member of the Chamber of Deputies.

Ventura's rise was rapidly followed by that of another brilliant musician, businessman and showman, **Wilfrido Vargas**. The man later responsible for the alleged 'Wilfridisation' of the merengue was born in 1949 to musician parents, learnt music at school, was the precocious first trumpet of his home district of Altamira's municipal band at age eleven and set up his first group **Los Beduinos** for a nightclub residency on losing his job as a postman at age sixteen. Vargas rapidly expanded the band into a polished merengue outfit and began to incorporate into his arrangements elements of soca and zouk, as well as innovations such as synthesizers and rapping in English on his records 'El Jardinero' ('The Gardener') (1984) and 'El Baile' (1986), which featured one totally synthesized track, 'La Loteria'. Vargas' 1978 album 'Punto y Aparte!' ('New Chapter') launched his major hit-making career, which included pan-Latin American smashes such as 'El Africano' in 1984.

Wilfrido Vargas' business empire rapidly extended to the formation and management of a series of other groups, some composed of salaried employees of his organisation, some formed for specific recording projects and others, all with varying degrees of autonomy. **Los Hijos del Rey** were the first, followed by **Los Kenton, Los Nietos del Rey, Jossie Esteban y la Patrulla 15** (who scored a major hit with 'Acariciame' – 'Caress Me' – in 1987), **La Orquesta Liberacion, The New York Band**, and the teen-oriented **Altamira Banda Show**. Vargas' most successful creation, however, was the all-woman group **Las Chicas**

del Can, meaning roughly 'the party girls', consisting of a dozen or so professional female musicians dressed in sexy stage gear – black lace shorts, gold high heels, etc. Although rumours that male session musicians played their instruments for them abounded, the Chicas, centred on the leader and trumpet player **Maria Acosta** and the vocalists **Miriam Cruz** and **Eunice Betances**, put on an enjoyable live act and good songs (chosen by Vargas) such as 'Juana la Cubana' and 'Pepe', made albums such as 'Caribe' (1989) successful throughout Latin America. A number of other all-female groups in the mould of Las Chicas del Can have sprung up in Santo Domingo, chief among them **La Media Naranja** and **Las Chicas del País**.

Along with Ventura and Vargas, the third major merengue musician of the 1980s was **Cuco Valoy**, who began his career singing primarily Cuban pre-salsa material with his brother Martin in a duo known as **Los Ahijados** before switching to merengue with his new band **La Tribu**, also known for a period as **Los Virtuosos**, in the mid-1980s. Noted for his relaxed and soulful singing, subtle sense of rhythm, and rumoured mystical streak, Valoy has released a number of excellent albums including 'El Brujo' ('The Wizard'), 'Mejor Que Nunca' ('Better Than Ever') and 'Con Sabar Del Tropico' ('Tropical Flavour'). His son, **Ramon Orlando Valoy**, is also active as a singer.

Other prominent merengue artistes include **Sergio Vargas**, **The Cocoband**, **Los Hermanos Rosario**, **Conjunto Quisqueya**, **Fernandito Villalona**, and the New York-based **Millie y los Vecinos** and **La Gran Manzana**. By the 1990s, however, the merengue boom has slowed somewhat.

In the 1970s and 1980s, while the merengue continued with its status as national music and enjoyed its international fame, an emerging Dominican style known as bachata was becoming immensely popular with a lower-class, unsophisticated audience. The term 'bachata', regarded as an invalid label by some Santo Domingo commentators, originally referred to an informal get-together in a country back yard at which simple guitar and guira music would be played. A wide variety of styles, including the merengue, would be drawn upon, but it was the romantic songs – the boleros and baladas – which formed the line of descent to the bachata. Early performers in this style included **José Manuel Calderon**, **Luis Segura**, **Oscar Olmos** and **Leonardo Paniagua**. During the 1960s and 1970s, as more and more country people moved to the poor quarters of Santo Domingo in search of work, the little neighbourhood 'colmado' shops and the male-frequented bars, in some cases serving as meeting places for prostitutes, became the principal places where bachata could be heard on record or on the radio; the new commercial station Radio Guarachita, with a high bachata and guitar-music content aimed its programming successfully at the Dominican campesino class. The lyrics of the bachatas diversified, becoming more ribald and colloquial, full of broad double meanings and references to sex; but also becoming more sociopolitical, and frequently bewailing the hardships and betrayals of life. The latter category gave rise to an alternative tag of 'musica de amargue', or music of bitterness, and it has been argued that this is a sub genre distinct from bachata. In the 1980s, in the hands of young singers such as **Tony Santos, Julio Angel** and **Blas Duran**, the bachata progressed musically, speeding up its tempo, evolving into a dance and in some instances incorporating electric guitars and other modern instruments. Latterly, a certain overlap with the merengue field has occurred – merengueros such as Cuco Valoy and Wilfrido Vargas have adapted bachatas to their style. In the person of Juan Luis Guerra, however, the bachata style and elements of merengue have merged with a sophisticated and eclectic rock sensibility to create a new sound of huge international Latin American appeal.

Guerra was born in 1957 of a Spanish mother and Dominican father, entered the University of Santo Domingo to study Arts and Philosophy, left and enrolled at the Berklee College of Music in Boston, where he was given grounding in theory and composition and added a love of jazz and progressive rock to his enthusiasms for the music of the Caribbean and its African heritage. Taking the softer, melodic aspects of the bachata, a toned-down, cooler merengue rhythm, smooth mixed male and female vocal backing harmonies and, above all, a fine sense of a catchy melody, Guerra and his group 4:40 created the 1985 album 'Acarreo Y Mudanza' ('Moves and Changes'), which was a minor hit, followed in 1989 by his big breakthrough, 'Ojala Que Llueva Cafe' ('If Only It Would Rain Coffee'), which was a hit throughout Latin America. 4:40's sound was perfectly suited to a smart, urban middle-class Latin audience and 'Bachata Rosa', his follow-up album a year later, was a similarly huge hit. The advent of **Grupo Canaveral**, a new group very much in the 4:40 style indicates the growing extent of Guerra's influence in the early 1990s.

Dominican Republic: Discography

Luis Kalaff El Rey Del Merengue (Seeco SCLP 9241)
Francisco Ulloa Merengue! (Globestyle ORB 020)
Johnny Ventura Si Vuelvo A Nacer (CBS 999)
Wilfrido Vargas Animation (Sonografica 10241)
Wilfrido Vargas Siempre Wilfrido (Sonagrafica 10293)
Las Chicas del Can Caribe (Cosmo Records WV 10003)
Cocoband Pero Con Coco! (Kubaney CDK 304-2)
Juan Luis Guerra y 4:40 Bachata Rosa (Karen KLP 136)
Various Pura Bachata (Kubaney 0244-2)

MARTINIQUE AND GUADELOUPE

Both major islands of the French Antilles are full overseas départements of France – just as French administratively as the Alpes-Maritimes or the Ile de France – and a large Antillean population lives in the 'metropole', as the mainland is known: Paris alone contains 200,000 Antilleans, equivalent to just under half the combined population of the two islands. Antillean music is strongly influenced by French mainstream pop, while modern zouk artistes operate between Paris or the two island capitals, Martinique's Fort de France and Guadeloupe's Pointe à Pitre. The influence is of course mutual. Zouk has penetrated mainstream French pop to such an extent that the 1990 French Eurovision Song Contest representative was the glamorous Guadeloupean singer **Joelle Ursull**.

Antillean music can be regarded as one entity, although the two islands have distinct characters – Guadeloupe is politically more separatist and musically more roots and African percussion-oriented than bigger, suaver Martinique. The islands' African heritage manifests itself in the modern use of the traditional drums known as gwo ka, a big, congalike log drum, and ti bois, a small, horizontally supported hollow tube. In addition to French, the French-derived creole language, similar to that of Haiti, is spoken on both islands; French-based words are transcribed phonetically according to their local pronunication, e.g. 'gwo', from 'gros' ('big'), 'ka', from 'caisse' ('drum'), ''ti', from 'petit' ('small'), 'bois' ('wood'). The fashion for Creole orthography has latterly extended to French personal names, e.g. Janklod is often substituted for Jean-Claude.

The earliest Antillean music to come to the attention of the outside world was the biguine, or beguine, a Martiniquan fusion of nineteenth-century French ballroom dance steps and African rhythms. In the 1920s, the nascent Parisian population of Antillean ex-soldiers remaining after World War I service in Europe nurtured bands such as that of the great **Alexandre Stellio**, a virtuoso clarinetist and composer whose New Orleans jazz-influenced ensembles shared honours with early Cuban bands in Paris dance halls such as the Bal Nègre. (It was through mediation of the Spanish-Cuban bandleader **Xavier Cugat** in the 1930s, incidentally, that Cole Porter was inspired to write his famous 'Begin the Beguine', which is, in fact, more a bolero.)

Stellio's **Orchestre Antillais** and other groups such as the **Orchestre Créole Delvi** and the **Kaukira Boys** were succeeded in the 1950s by a crop of similar orchestras, led by another clarinetist, **Sam Castandet's Orchestre Antillais**, whose residence at the Canne A Sucre ballroom was long a feature of Montparnasse nightlife. When in the islands bands of this period, which also included those of **Robert Mavounzy** and **Abel Beauregard**, and the **Orchestre Créole** of star songstress **Moune de Rivel**, played at the semiopen-air nightclubs known as paillottes (thatched huts), whose boom years were the late 1950s. In Martinique, popular paillottes such as the **Miramar**, the **Escale** and the **Terpsichora** featured a mixture of biguine, tango, bolero and waltz and gradually incorporated US-French pop. This style lasted until the early 1960s when the last major practitioner, the group **Star Dust** (whose members' sons were to form the popular zouk band **Taxi Creole** twenty-five years later), stopped playing.

The music which swept the islands from 1963 onwards was Haitian compas direct, as played by **Jean-Baptiste Nemours** and **Weber Sicot**; it was purveyed both by Haitian bands resident in Martinique, such as **Gary French's Tropicana** and **Les Gais Troubadours**, and by local orchestras – **Los Caribes**, **El Typico** and, above all, the **Ensemble Abricot**. When the Haitian compas direct orchestras gave way to the mini-jazz groups in the 1970s, the musicians of Martinique and Gaudeloupe followed, as they did at the end of the decade when, under the influence of expanded Haitian bands such as **Tabou Combo**, the Antillean groups **Les Leopards, Gentelemen, Operation '78** and, most importantly, **Les Vikings** in Guadeloupe, and **La Perfecta** in Martinique began to play the bouncy, guitar and sax-led dance style known as cadence. Perfecta and the Vikings led the cadence scene until its eclipse in the early 1980s by the new zouk sound, which was largely the invention of the Vikings' bass guitarist and composer **Pierre-Edouard Decimus**.

Decimus, a seasoned and perceptive arranger with a wide knowledge of Caribbean rhythm, decided to programme a drum machine to produce a thumping, disco-related version of the gwo ka sound. To this, he added his brother George's bass and the catchy metallic guitar riffing of fellow Guadeloupean **Jacob Devarieux**, a rock guitarist making a successful session career in Paris after some years living in West Africa. The trio called their loosely constituted studio group **Kassav** (creole for cassava, or manioc, used in the Antilles and Africa to make flour), and in 1979 scored hits with their first record, 'Love And Ka Dance' and three subsequent releases in the following three years. The term 'zouk', meaning a party, often paying like Jamaican 'blues parties', rapidly came to describe Kassav's new hard sound. By 1983 Kassav had become a live band, augmented by the Guadeloupean vocalist **Patrick Saint Eloi** and drummer **Claude Vemur** and the Martiniquan star singers **Jean-Philippe Marthely** and **Jocelyne Béroard** and keyboard player **Jean-Claude Naimro**, whose synthesized accordion parts became an intermittent and distinctive feature of Kassav records. The final touches were supplied by a duo of girl dancers and a brass section consisting of four French trumpeters and the Algerian trombonist **Hamid Belhocine** (whose father **Abderrahmane**, incidentally, is an eminent Arabo-Andalous musician in Algiers). From the early 1980s onwards, Kassav produced a stream of albums to satisfy the Antillean appetite for a fast turnover of music; a considerable number of them were attributed to individual members of the group for variety, such as Jocelyne Béroard's huge 1986 hit 'Siwo'. Devarieux and Decimus' 'Zouk-la Se Sel Medikaman Nou Ni' ('Zouk is the only medicine we have'), from their 1984 album 'Ye Lé Lé', was the song that exploded Kassav throughout the Antilles and, subsequently, Africa, selling 100,000 copies. Through the mid-1980s, Kassav's sound was immensely influential on African music, particularly Cameroonian and, to a lesser extent, Zairean, as well as on other Caribbean islands such as the Dominican Republic and Trinidad. In 1987 Kassav, by now capable of filling the massive Parisian Zenith concert-hangar for five consecutive nights every year, signed to CBS, leaving the small record label of Fort de France-based entrepreneur George Debs, with whom they had started. In 1990 members of Kassav, along with a number of other top Antillean artistes, formed the supergroup **Le Grand Mechant Zouk** and recorded a live album at the Zenith.

The Debs family, Syrian-Lebanese traders by origin, are important organisational figures in the short history of zouk. **Henry Debs,** of Guadeloupe, and his brother **George,** of Martinique, are both prominent and competing producers, while a cousin, **Assad Debs,** runs a major distribution business in Paris. Henry Debs, reportedly not pleased that the originally Guadeloupean Kassav had gone to his brother George, retaliated by signing a trio, **Zouk Machine,** who became the second mainstream zouk stars. Zouk Machine were formed in 1986 by two former members of the group **Experience 7,** who perceived a gap in the market for a sexy young female singing trio in the style of American pop-soul groups such as The Supremes. In 1988, the group's album, 'Maldon', was a big Antillean success, repeated two years later in France where the record went to number one in the album charts. Also in 1990, Joelle Ursull, a founder member of Zouk Machine who had left to go solo two years previously, became the first black performer to represent France in the Eurovision Song Contest. She performed a Serge Gainsborough song, 'White and Black Blues', and came second; the song went on to enter the French hit parade. Ursull, a former Miss Guadeloupe and model with Lanvin and Ricci, had worked as a dancer before joining Zouk Machine and in 1988 scored a considerable success with 'Myel', her first solo album.

By the beginning of the 1990s, French Antillean music had three broad tendencies. The first, zouk, after its mid-1980s Kassav-led, hard, fast phase, often referred to as 'zouk-béton' ('concrete zouk'), had softened into the slower, more romantic and melodic zouk-love, an equivalent of Jamaican lovers' rock, and developed into a somewhat anaemic and amorphous zouk-pop purveyed by a large number of artistes. Prominent among the dozens of names are **Eric Virgal,** a Martiniquan crooner responsible for the great 1970s hit 'Stanislas' and the 1980s 'Sublime'; **Ronald Rubinel,** an experienced keyboard player and singer who has guested on records by numerous African and Antillean artistes; Rubinel's companion, the singer **Edith Lefel; Francky Vincent,** a Guadeloupean singer noted for his sexually suggestive lyrics; **J.M. Harmony,** led by the Martiniquan **Joel Zabulon; Sakiyo,** led by ubiquitous session bass-guitarist **Michel Alibo; Zaza,** a dynamic entertainer and the daughter of **LouLou Boislaville,** famous founder artiste of the **Ballets Martiniquais; Simon Jurad, Eric Brouta, Michel Linerol** and **Frederic Caracas,** all of whom record individually and participate in innumerable other projects; **Djo Dezormo,** whose anti-EEC 'Voici Le Loup' was the great hit of the 1990 Martinique Carnival; **Pier Rosier** and his group **Gazolinn;** and the glamorous **Tanya St Val.**

A second tendency was the reinterpretation of traditional Antillean rhythms such as the biguine and the mazurka. This direction was first explored in the 1970s with great success by the Martinique group **Malavoi,** whose ten members, variously teachers and civil servants, started out playing for local Fort de France dances and soon progressed to researching and interpreting their musical patrimony with a line-up of four violins, bass, percussion, keyboards and brass. Led by violinist **Mano Césaire** and keyboardist **Paulo Rosine,** and featuring the popular and charismatic crooner **Ralph Thamar,** Malavoi achieved considerable success in France and Japan in the 1980s, releasing a series of subtle albums, notably 'La Case A Lucie' and 'Jou Ouvé'. In 1988 Ralph Thamar left to pursue a solo career, releasing the light, jazzy album 'Exil', and was replaced in Malavoi by the young singer **Pipo Gertrude**. Two other traditionalists to enjoy major new success in the early 1990s have been the singer **Max Ransay**, former member of Los Caribes and Les Leopards in the 1960s, who made an impressive comeback at the 1988 Carnival performing spirited biguines and cadences, scoring hits with records such as 'La Route Chanflô' and 'Au Secours!', and the banjo player **Kali** (né Jean-Marc Monnerville) a former member of the rock group **6th Continent**, whose simple lilting reprises of old Stellio biguines and other traditional tunes made his LPs 'Racines' (Vols. I and II) best sellers. Another prominent musician in the traditionalist area is the clarinetist **Michel Godzom**.

The third and final tendency of French Antillean popular music is also a roots re-exploration, but of a more African nature. Its chief exponent is the traditional flute player and singer **Eugène Mona**, who performs his raucous, primitive music with an ensemble of drums including a foot-damped bélé instrument and wild 'sha sha' maracas made from pebble-filled mosquito-repellant canisters. A more modernised version of the same sound, including the 'chouval bois' fairground music, is produced by the **Groupe Tumpak**, led by singer-percussionist **Marcé**, and by the smiliar group of **Dédé Saint Prix**. The traditional bamboo flute player **Max Cilla**, an early exponent of this music, has played throughout Europe and the USA, and composed for theatre and cinema (Euzhan Palcy's *Rue Case-Nègres*).

Martinique and Guadeloupe: Discography

Various (inc. Stellio) Au Bal Antillais (1920s biguines, etc.) (Folklyric 9050)
Various (inc. Castendet) Antillaisement Votre (1950s biguines, etc.) (EMI France 2534062)
Les Vikings Vikings Guadeloupe (3A Prods 3A121)
Various Dance! Cadence! (Globestyle ORB 0002)
Kassav Zouk is the Only Medicine we Have (Greensleeves GREZ 2001)
Kassav Majestik Zouk (CBS 4654941)
Jocelyne Béroard Siwo (Sonodisc GD 36)
Joelle Ursull Myel (CBS 4624331)
Various (inc. Zaza, M. Ransay, E. Virgal) Zoukollection Vols. II, III (Cocosound 88014, 88033)
Kali Racines Vol. II (Cocosound 88034)
Dédé Saint Prix Mi Sé Sa (Mango 162 539 813)
Malavoi Jou Ouvé (WEA 723 689)

HAITI

The varying circumstances and fortunes of this small country, which occupies the western third of the island of Hispaniola, which it shares with the Dominican Republic, have meant that the fortunes of its music have also shifted. In the 1960s, Haitian compas was highly influential on the other Francophone Caribbean islands, but the poverty and political violence of the 1980s meant that musical activity was drastically limited. The slave rebellion in 1801 which made Haiti, under its first leader Toussaint L'Ouverture, the earliest nation to achieve independence from its European (French) coloniser, contributed to the continued strength of African culture. This is most famously typified by the vitality of the voodoo religion, in which all-night ceremonies led by houngan priests call up the spirits of ancestors and of gods such as Shango and Ogun to the continual rhythm of a changing battery of drummers. The voodoo drum ensembles have been occasionally borrowed by Haitian popular music, as has the marching drum beat of the 'rara' carnival processions which shuffle through the streets, preceded by a band 'kolonel', cracking his ceremonial whip to purify the spiritual space in front of the band.

Of the hybrid Euro-African musics, the carabinier was the earliest substantial dance style, giving way by the end of the nineteenth century to the meringue, a slower version of the Dominican merengue, and one which used guitars more than accordions. The development which boosted Haitian meringue to regional prominence was its adaptation in the 1950s to a Cuban-North American big-band instrumentation, principally by the orchestras of Jean-Baptiste Nemours and Weber Sicot. Nemours coined the term 'compas direct' for his sound, which dominated the late 1950s and early 1960s; one of his top numbers of this period, 'Tchoul No. 3', was included in the 1990 compilation album 'Konbit' (see discography). Nemours' closest rival was the bandleader Weber Sicot, who applied the term 'cadence' to his similar music. A third band, the **Super Jazz des Jeunes** of St Aude, experimented with the inclusion of traditional instruments, particularly the 'vaccines' – blown tubes of bamboo – prefiguring the voodoo-jazz style of the 1980s.

Although in the 1960s Haitian music moved away from the early compas sound, two big bands continue to purvey this marvellous music. Both are based in the run-down second city of Cap Haitien, where they have carved a small retro-compas empire. **Orchestra Septentrional**, originally formed in the late 1940s around a Cuban-style guitar trio led by **Pierre-Louis Ulrick**, added a seven-piece brass section and a star singer, **Roger Colas**, developed its own version of compas direct called rit boul difè ('ball of fire' in créole) and acquired the consequent sobriquet 'Boule de Feu du Cap'.

The **Orchestra Tropicana** (Cuban-influenced and named after the famous Havana nightclub) was formed in the mid-1960s by a Cuban wrestler, **Basil Copti**, to play a compas-pachanga repertoire. Tropicana's alleged hick origins led to derisive nicknames such as 'okes pat kanna' ('duck foot orchestra') and 'okes gwo zorey' ('big ears orchestra'); nonetheless, like Septentrional, it remains popular. Both bands have opened their own club and restaurant complexes and both released successful albums (Septentrional's called 'Bwa Kayiman' and Tropicana's, 'Fok Sa Change') in 1989.

In the 1960s, the general trend of Haitian music changed. Under the influence of the Euro-American pop groups, big bands dwindled and a new variety of 'mini-jazz' groups replaced them. These groups used rock to modify slightly the compas, but also used an important new influence, the burgeoning Central African guitar sound brought back by the substantial number of young Haitian teachers who went to work in newly independent Zaire. The Zairean group **Ryco Jazz**, who based themselves for a time in Haiti, were also important diffusers of the sound.

Not all mini-jazz groups remained small; some, such as **Tabou Combo**, reacquired substantial brass sections under the influence of black American groups such as Earth Wind and Fire. The 1960s also saw the big wave of Haitian emigration to the USA and Canada, and as a result Haitian groups were increasingly to be found playing, recording and even living in New York, Miami or Montreal. Throughout the 1970s and into the 1980s the mini-jazz groups continued to be Haiti's chief popular music expression. Chief among these was the internationally successful, and now Brooklyn-based, Tabou Combo. Other top groups and artistes were **Gesner Henry**, better known by his stage name **Coupé Cloué**, a top bandleader who remained one of the few entertainers to operate continually through the political violence of the late 1980s; the **Magnum Band**; the **Mini All Stars**, a mainly US-based studio group; **D. P. Express**, whose album 'David' was one of the 1980s' top records in Haiti, composed of former members of the early mini-jazz group **Difficiles de Petionville**; the Miami-based **Skah Shah**; the **Frères Dejean** and **Schleu-Schleu**.

In the 1980s, a new sound challenged the bubbling guitars, buoyant rhythm and gentle melodies of the mini-jazz compas. Sometimes known as 'voodoo-jazz' or 'nouvel jenerasyon' ('new generation'), it used a mixture of American funk-rock and angular, African-sounding melodies, traditional rara or voodoo drums, electric guitars and synthesizers, and lyrics which were frequently political. One of its earliest exponents was the group **Aziyan**, led by a New York-based guitarist **Alix Pascal**; but the first substantial populariser of the sound was **Boukman Eksperyans**, a ten-member group named after the slave leader Boukman who helped launch the Haitian revolution in 1804. Assisted by the American producer and hotelier Richard Morse of the Oloffson Hotel, Boukman Eksperyans developed a repertoire typified by songs such as 'Wet Chenn' ('Remove the Chains'), which won the annual Haitian Konkou Mizik (Music Competition) in 1989 and appeared on the group's first European album, on the Island label, in 1991. Other leading new-generation bands include **Zeklé**, led by the **Widmaier** brothers, key arrangers of the new sound; **Sanba Yo**, whose rara-dominated hit song 'Vaksiné!' (Vaccinate!') was so named because of its function as a UNICEF-commissioned health jingle and not because of its inclusion of a bass-guitar part mimicking the traditional vaccines bamboo trumpets; **Sakad**, a New York-based group represented, like Sanba Yo, on the 'Konbit' album (see discography); **Masterdji**, a rara-rapper; **Djakout Mizik**; and the **Frères Parent, Clarke** and **Alain**, a duo of blind, Brooklyn-based singers much influenced by reggae, who collaborated with the Neville Brothers on 'Konbit'.

Current Haitian pop also includes solo performers of acoustic guitar-backed, local-melody protest song, of whom the most famous is **Manno Charlemagne**, and French-American-influenced light jazz-rock-ballad singers, led by **Emmeline Michel**. Michel, a former student at Detroit Jazz Center and wife of the influential producer **Ralph Boncy**, has achieved considerable success, due partly to her combination of beauty and vivacity reminiscent of the Martiniquan zouk belle, Joelle Ursull.

Haiti: Discography

Nemours, Jean-Baptiste 25th Anniversary (Seeco 9334)
Orchestre Septentrional Bwa Kayiman (Maxnell MH 001)
Tabou Combo Aux Antilles (Zafem TCLP 8056)
Coupé Cloué Madam Marcel (Sonodisc ESP 17902)
Various Konbit, Burning Rhythms Of Haiti (A&M SP 5281)
Boukman Eksperyans Vodou Adjae (Mango 162 539 899)
Emmeline Michel Flanm (Cobalt COB 760239)

THE NETHERLANDS ANTILLES (Including Surinam)

The territories of the Dutch colonial heritage in this region consist of two groups of islands — the northern trio of Saba, Sint Eustatius and Sint Maarten, the southern trio of Aruba, Bonaire and Curaçao (all autonomous regions of the Kingdom of the Netherlands) — and the independent South American mainland state of Surinam. Of the miniscule first group, mixed English and Spanish-language calypso is one prominent musical form, with the **Mighty Dow** its main exponent. Another is zouk, played by groups such as the **Rebels** from St Martin, the French half of the island whose other division is St Maarten.

The second group of islands, Aruba, Bonaire and Curaçao, lie close to the Venezuelan coast and their musical culture thus has both African elements and Hispanic influence brought from the nearby mainland. The racial mix is, in fact, highly complex with Portuguese, Indian and, of course, Dutch strongly represented. Papiamento, the creole language spoken in the islands, originated with Portuguese Jewish immigrants in the seventeenth century, but contains words from a dialect known as Guéné, which probably refers directly to Guinea, a past general term for West Africa.

African-derived traditional instruments still in use in the islands include the tambú drum and the matrimonial, a set of cymbals attached to a board; the Spanish string tradition is represented by the cuarta, a small guitar equivalent to the cuatro found elsewhere in Latin America. All modern Caribbean dance rhythms are popular, particularly merengue, salsa antilleana, soca and reggae; the islands' own beat, however, represented at carnival (like that of nearby Trinidad, in February) is the tumba.

As in the case of the French Antilles and Paris, Dutch Antillean musicians tend to work as much in Amsterdam and Rotterdam as at home, while most of the records are pressed in Caracas or Miami. Top Curaçao acts are **Harry Zimmerman**, **Dizzy and the Playboys** and the groups **Doble 'R'** and **Era**. In addition to the tumba, Aruba possesses a fast 'Aruban waltz' made highly popular by the island's 'national anthem' composer **Padu del Caribe**. Aruba's main contemporary artistes are the female singers **Sharon Rose** and **Dhaddy Brokke**; the big bands **Time**, **Papito y su Doble Sabor** and **Pride**; and the smaller groups **Supermania** and the **Trio Huasteca**. In addition, the Aruban musician **Hildward Croes**, former leader of the group **Criptus Confession**, is a prominent session arranger in the Dominican Republic, having worked with merengue stars Wilfrido Vargas and Juan-Luis Guerra.

The same mixture of Spanish and African immigration influenced Surinam, but the large Asian population, mainly Indian and Indonesian, has had a considerable effect on Surinam's music. Groups such as the **Twinkle Stars**, **Sukru Sani**, the **Draverboys** and **Trafassie** reflect this mix, creating multihybrids such as zouk records with Hindi lyrics or, in the case of Trafassie, songs which begin in English, and move through the Surinam creole known as Negro English or Taki Taki to end in Hindi.

SOUTH AMERICA

INTRODUCTION

I think it's fair to say that my credentials as a spokesman for Latin American music are as good as anyone's. To begin with, I'm Brazilian and Brazil, the continent's largest country, contains in itself virtually all of the individual characteristics that have gone into the melting pot of Latin American music as a whole. Secondly, as a musician and composer, I've always been deliberately eclectic, using elements of many different styles and not just Brazilian styles. This was in fact a central tenet of the movement I co-founded at the beginning of my career, the Tropicalia movement as we called it. 'We' means myself and friends and fellow artistes, such as Gaetano Veloso, Gal Costa and Jose-Carlos Capeinan living in the city of Sao Paolo at the time.

Brazil in the early 1960s was very much like London, Paris, New York or Los Angeles – there was an atmosphere of experimentation, of freedom, of counterculture and Brazilians, being already of cosmopolitan, mixed ancestry, are very open to change and fusion. (The military dictatorship following the coup of 1964 stopped things for a while, but couldn't fundamentally change Brazilians' nature.) We had in our minds very much the theories of Brazilian modernist thinkers such as the poet Oswald de Andrade, who put forward in the 1920s the idea of Brazil as a sort of creative consumer and regurgitator of the world's cultures. Musically, a major source of inspiration for me was the work of the Beatles with George Martin on songs such as 'A Day In The

Life' from the Sergeant Pepper album, with its cinematic lyrics and bold imaginative arrangements.

Experience of a broad spectrum of styles to draw upon as a songwriter was not a problem for me. I grew up in the Northeast, partly in the sertäo, the interior, and partly in the port city of Salvador de Bahía (a city, incidentally, whose council I now serve on). In the interior, my family lived in a small town of only 800 people, the population of some of the hotels I spend so much time in nowadays, but the range of music available was tremendous – the polkas and schottisches of Italian and German farmers, Portuguese fado, Duke Ellington, Miles Davis, Chet Baker, Cuban music – Celia Cruz and Perez Prado's mambos – Mexican boleros, classical music, Sicilian and Neapolitan songs and, of course, the forros – the local cowboy music. This is less black music, more mixed, as you find all over the continent in the cattle and farming areas, but in Salvador you get the deep African music, as you do all down the Atlantic-Caribbean coast from Panama south. My discovery, or rediscovery, of Afro-Brazilian music as an ingredient of my songs came later. I was immensely moved and inspired by my visit to the FESTAC Black Arts Festival in Nigeria in 1977 – 40,000 black writers, musicians, poets, playwrights, dancers from all over Africa and the whole diaspora. This was an impressive demonstration of Africa's contribution to Latin American culture – there were major delegations from Brazil, Colombia, Venezuela, all discussing negritude, racism, the fight for independence. Back in Salvador, I continued with renewed enthusiasm on my work with the Filhos de Gandhi afoxé group and incorporated both African rhythms and reggae in my music. Both of these elements have subsequently become widespread throughout the new Latin American popular musics, particularly on the Atlantic coast.

These are the essential ingredients of Latin American popular music, then: European, mainly Spanish or Portuguese, and African. The least prominent ingredient is that of the original Indian inhabitants of the region, although it is there and, of course, pockets of intact Indian culture, including music, exist in the forests of Venezuela, Colombia and Brazil or high in the Andes. But that's another story, and perhaps another book.

GILBERTO GIL

MEXICO

The popular music of Mexico, the world's largest Spanish-speaking country, is dominated by its Hispanic colonial past; Aztec and Mayan music is a matter for archaeological speculation and the black slave heritage is confined to minor elements of certain regional forms, for example the Veracruz son. While Spanish, particularly Andalucian, influences – zapateado heel-tapping steps, stringed instruments, melody – predominate, Italian bel canto and operatic singing has also had a powerful effect on the development of Mexico's strong ballad tradition.

Among the wide variety of regional Spanish-influenced folk styles, three different varieties of the son dance music are important roots or components of modern popular genres. All feature combinations of guitar, guitarrón (acoustic bass guitar), vihuela (small round-bodied guitar), violin and harp. The son jalisense, from Jalisco state, is at the origin of the mariachi repertoire.

The trumpet-augmented mariachi (traceable linguistically to 'marriage') groups who nowadays congregate in the evenings in Mexico City's Garibaldi Square looking for work, spread throughout the country in the 1920s and their charro (cowboy) costume of embroidered trousers and sombrero came to represent the Mexican tourist equivalent of the British Coldstream Guardsman outside Buckingham Palace. Mariachis originally backed slow songs, especially serenades, as well as dance music and, although clichéd, their services are still in popular demand. Top mariachi bands such as the **Vargas de Tecalitlán** sell large numbers of records and can overlap the youth pop market: an example is the **Mariachi Oro y Plata de Pepe Chavez**, who have backed the young romantic singer **Fernando Allende**.

The son jarocho, from the Veracruz region, played on a wide variety of small guitars, is notable for its vivacity and the relative complexity of its rhythm. The Richie Valens hit song 'La Bamba' is based on a son jarocho.

Finally, the son huasteca, from the region of that name, and also commonly referred to as the huapango, is a particularly strong, living traditional music still played by small groups in bars and at fiestas throughout the region. The huapango tradition includes virtuoso violin solos and also the improvised verse competitions known as topadas in which rival trovadores — a top practitioner is **Guillermo Velasquez** of the group **Los Leones de la Sierra** — try to outdo each other in wit and topicality.

The huapango, in commercialised 'composed' form, was a major element of the repertoire of the most important, widely disseminated and nationally popular music of the 1920s through to the 1950s, the music of great vocal trios such as **Los Panchos, Los Calaveras** and **Los Hermanos Martinez Gil**. The other element was the non-dance form, the slow, romantic canción developed under the influence of Italian song in the nineteenth and early twentieth centuries, and of which a substantial subgenre was the bolero.

The pan-Latin bolero, which also flourished in Cuba, became a speciality of Mexican male canción singers such as **Pedro Infante, Jorge Negrete** and **Pedro Vargas**, and composers, of whom the doyen was the great **Agustin Lara** of 'Noches de Veracruz' ('Veracruz Nights') and 'Palabras de Mujer' ('Woman's Words'). One of the top boleristas of the 1950s, **Lucho Gatica**, Chilean born and a dentist by profession, achieved great fame with songs such as 'El Reloj' ('The Clock') and Lara's 'Solamente Una Vez' ('Only Once'), not only in Mexico but also in Spain. This link between the two countries was to continue with later romantic artistes such as Spain's Julio Iglesias and Mexico's **José José**. In 1990 Lucho Gatica made a Madrid comeback amid signs that the retro fashion for older Spanish song forms such as the tonadilla (see **Spain**) might be extending to the bolero. The 1960s and 1970s, meanwhile, saw the bolero superseded by the romantic balada, Spanish in language but otherwise increasingly similar to its Euro-American-international counterparts. Mexico, nonetheless, also excelled at this form, with singers such as José José and composers such as **Juan Gabriel** conquering the world Spanish-speaking market.

The 1920s and 1930s saw the development of the canción ranchera form parallel to, and different from, the bolero and balada tradition, which started as peasant and cowboy entertainment, developed into a commercialised popular form, and as performed by singer-actor stars in dozens of stylised films, swept the country in the 1940s. Like country and western in the USA, ranchera music appealed primarily to a lower-class non-intellectual audience. It was, and is, played either by mariachi bands or by conjuntos featuring guitar, the acoustic bass guitar known as bajo sexto and, increasingly, accordion. This last formation is the typical configuration of the norteño group, a style which originated in the northern border region with Texas, similar to but not identical with Tex-Mex music (see **North America: Texas** for further details), and which became popular throughout Mexico in the 1960s and 1970s. Like Texas, the norteño border regions received considerable numbers of German and Czech immigrants and their accordion waltzes and polkas became a major part of the region's music. A second important part of the traditional norteño repertoire is the corrido, a rollicking narrative song, in the past concerned with the exploits of prominent figures such as the revolutionary hero Pancho Villa and nowadays dealing with all aspects of border life. Popular norteño artistes include **Chayito Valdez**, **Ramon Ayala** and **Los Tigres del Norte**, while a sort of modernised synthetic ranchera is also part of the repertoire of Mexico's top group **Los Bukis**, a six-piece led by the singer-composer **Mario Antonio Solis**, whose records regularly sell a million copies. Norteño groups and 'tropical' artistes such as **Rico Tovar**, also feature the Panamanian-Colombia cumbía dance rhythm, extremely popular in Mexico.

Mexico: Discography

Vargas de Tecalitlán El Mariachi (Phonogram 842 1202)
Various Antología del Son de Mexico 6 vols. from different
  regions (Musica Tradicional, Mexico MT01–MT06)
Music of Mexico Vol. 1: Son Jarocho Vol. 2: Son Huasteco (Arhoolie
  ARH 3008 & 3009)
Lucho Gatica Bolero Es . . . (EMI 180 7944 571)
Los Tigres del Norte Triunfo Solido (Musivisa MUPR 8002)
Los Tigres del Norte Para Adoloridos (Musivisa MUPR 8004)
Los Bukis Si Me Recuerdas (Musivisa LUNS 420)

COLOMBIA

Colombia possesses an extremely rich popular music scene; Colombian musicians excel in the field of Cuban-derived pan-Latin salsa and produce magnificent distinctive dance music in a variety of local styles, notably the cumbia. Though probably first found in neighbouring Panama, the cumbia has become something of a national dance in Colombia. Events such as the big carnival in Barranquilla and the Caribbean Music Festival in the beautiful old colonial city of Cartagena are important showcases for talent throughout the region.

Along with a number of similar rhythms and dances − the porro, the chandé, the bullerengue, the gaita, the mapalé and the puya − the cumbia is a rhythm of the Atlantic-Caribbean coast and in its modern form is often subsumed under a general heading 'musica tropical', a blend which, in the hands of practitioners such as **Joe Arroyo** (see below) can also include elements of soca, merengue and other adjacent non-Colombian styles. Originally known as the cumbiamba, the cumbia is a dance of black, probably West African slave origin and, as played by fishermen or banana plantation workers on traditional percussion and cane flutes to accompany a candle-wielding dance, had a slow, heavy, shuffling beat. In the 1940s and 1950s this was speeded up as modern bands adapted the rhythm for popular urban consumption.

A key figure in the development of Colombian music was **Antonio Fuentes**, a Cartagena engineer, musician and composer who founded the radio station Emisoras Fuentes in the 1930s and produced the first Colombian-pressed record, 'Pollo Pelongo' by **Raphael Campo Miranda**, in 1945. His company, Discos Fuentes, went on to launch numerous top artistes and, in 1990, pioneer the intensive European distribution of Colombian music via a licensing deal with Island Records. The 1950s and early 1960s saw an upsurge of tropical bands, and bandleaders, often with large brass sections augmenting a line-up which included guitars, accordions and mixed Afro-Latin percussion. Notable among them were **Pacho Galan**, who directed the house orchestra of Fuentes radio and helped create the craze for the merengue-cumbia hybrid, merecumbé; **Pedro Laza y sus Pelayeros**, whose wonderful sidling 'Navidad Negra' ('Black Christmas') is a classic of big-band cumbia arrangement; **Los Corraleros de Majagual**, a folksy, accordion-dominated group of huge importance which has employed dozens of top musicians including the prolific composer and bandleader **Calixto Ochoa**; **Guillermo Buitrago**, the earliest idol of postwar tropical music, who died at the age of 23; **Peregoyo y su Combo Vacana**, who created some of the most soulful and exciting tropical music of the 1960s before breaking up in the 1970s; **Los Diplomaticos** and **Los Trovadores de Baru**.

The band from this period which has endured most successfully is **La Sonora Dinamita**, formed in 1960 by the singer and composer **Lucho Argain**, which has stayed at the top with a combination of simple, catchy songs, often lyrically suggestive in the manner of their often-covered 'El Africano', and a distinctive sound featuring bright piano and brass riffs. Joint musical director of Sonora Dinamita is the bassist and arranger **Julio Ernesto Estrada**, stage-named **Fruko** because of his resemblance to a character in an advertisement for a canned-fruit brand of that name. Fruko also runs his own extremely popular band, **Fruko y sus Tesos**, featuring the top sonero **Wilson Gil**, also known as **Saoko**. The 1970s and 1980s saw the rise of many new cumbia-tropical artistes: **Rodolfo Aicardi**, a singer who appears with a vocal group **Los Hispanos** and the band **La Tipica R A 7** (Rodolfo Aicardi Seven, of whom there are nine), and attracted much media attention in Europe when his hit 'La Colegiala' ('The Schoolgirl') was used in a TV advert for Nescafé; the **Latin Brothers**, a dynamic salsa-and-tropical outfit originally formed as a studio band under the direction of Fruko, now also an excellent live act featuring the singer **Piper Pimienta Diaz**; **Los Graduados**, starring the comedy-inclined singer **Gustavo Quintero**; **Los Nemus del Pacifico** ('The Gods of the Pacific'), an intense country-sounding roots salsa band from the poor, black Choco Pacific hinterland, led by the deep, rough voice of **Alexis Murillo**; **Los Tupamaros**, a polished salsa-oriented twelve-man band, some members of which also operate as **La Fuerza Mayor**.

In addition to the cumbia and tropical-oriented groups, who may occasionally include salsa in their repertoire, there is a further category of primarily salsa groups who may do the occasional cumbia. The centre of Colombian salsa is the city of Cali, home of the immensely popular, influential and talented **Grupo Niche**, a young band led by the singer-arranger-percussionist-songwriter **Jairo Varela**, and named after the derogatory slang term 'niche' for a city shanty-dweller. Niche's dynamic early 1980s sound, well represented on LPs such as 'No Hay Quinto Malo' and 'Me Huele A Matrimonio', was in the later part of the decade softened slightly into the fashionable 'romantica' genre.

Also primarily a salsero, though highly eclectic in his influences, and the inventor of the term 'son caribeño' to describe his hybrid 1980s sound, is the hugely popular **Joe Arroyo**, a Cartagena singer who worked with Fruko y sus Tesos for ten years before forming his own band **La Verdad** ('The Truth') in 1981. He went on to score great pan-Latin hits with albums such as 'Rebellion', 'Fuego En Mi Mente' (Fire In My Mind'), 'En Accion' ('In Action') and 'La Guerra De Los Callados' ('The War Of The Silent'). Arroyo's popularity was such that in 1991 a special prize, the Super Congo, was created for him at the Barranquilla Carnival after he had won the normal top musical prize, the Congo de Oro (the Golden Congo) thirteen times. Other top salsa-based bands include the **Orquesta Guayacan**, led by former Niche arranger **Alexis Lozano**; **Los Titanes**, a smooth trombone-led band directed by top arranger **Alberto Barros**; **Grupo Clase** and **Grupo Contraste**, young groups active in the salsa romantica (see **Puerto Rico**) sphere, and **La Renovación de Cali**. Finally, the salsa-tropical tradition has produced a number of young groups experimenting with rap, house and dancehall-influenced sounds: these include the group **Clan Caribe** who produced the European dance hit 'La Chica De Los Ojos Cafe' ('Brown-Eyed Girl'). Chief driving force of this group was the young Choco-born singer

Yorthley 'Ley' Rivas, whose considerable talents have also been demonstrated in the groups **Kerube** and **Cariaco**.

Another important and distinct genre of modern Colombian music is vallenata, a rough, accordion-based country style more Spanish than African in origin, native to the cowboys and small farmers of the Northeastern La Guajira mountain region. Vallenata came into existence at the turn of the century, and its traditional instrumentation, in addition to accordion, is the guacharaca scraper, the caja vallenata hand-drum and, latterly, the bass guitar, played in a distinctive, vital, jumpy style. Vallenata has certain similarities with both Dominican merengue and Mexican norteña music, not least because of the prominent accordion role. For decades vallenata music was a redneck minority taste, but the 1960s saw a boom in the genre, brought about partly by the small size and consequent affordability of vallenato combos, partly by the arrival on the scene of a number of outstanding vallenato musicians such as the accordionist **Anibal Velasquez**, and partly by the strong connection between the vallenata region and the trade in drugs, particularly in marijuana. In the 1960s and 1970s, the marijuana growers and runners, mainly local and unsophisticated, were able to pour newly obtained wealth into their favourite music, and vallenato musicians often responded by singing the praises of the trade, the women and cars its profits bought, and the barons who led it and rewarded the singers. The decline of the marijuana trade and the substitution of cocaine, controlled by bigger, smarter urbanites from Bogotá and Medellín, somewhat hampered the rise of vallenata, but it is still popular and the annual vallenata festival in the town of Valledupar is hotly contested.

Top vallenata performers include the older, more traditional country accordionist **Nafer Duran**; the top singer **Diomedes Díaz**, known as the 'Cacique (Boss) of la Junta' (his home town), who teamed up in 1978 with the virtuoso accordionist **Nicolas 'Colacho' Mendoza**, famed for the facility with which he plays along with the vocal line of a song rather than simply filling in between phrases, as is more normal; the **Chiches Vallenatos**, two young 'romantic' artistes who scored major record hits with 'Ceniza Fría' ('Cold Ashes') and 'Lloro Un Amor' ('Tears of Lost Love'); **Los Embajadores Vallenatos**, another smooth young duo; **Binomio de Oro**, a top Bogotá group who incorporate vallenata music into a wider repertoire, with internationally successful results; **The Meriño Brothers**; and **Alejo Durán**, 'the Black Vallenato King'.

Colombia: Discography

Pacho Galan Epoca de Oro (Discos Fuentes D16069)
Peregoyo y su Combo Vacana Tropicalisimo (World Circuit WCB015)
Los Corraleros de Majagual Epoca De Oro (Discos Fuentes D10025)
Various Musica Tropical De Colombia (Discos Fuentes D10002)
Various Tropical Sounds Of Colombia (Mango MLPS 1058)
Joe Arroyo La Guerra De Los Callados (Discos Fuentes 201690)
The Latin Brothers En El Caribe (Discos Fuentes 201605)

Grupo Niche Me Huele A Matrimonio (Codiscos 298 21061)
Grupo Niche Cielo de Tambores (CBS 80508)
Los Titanes Sobredosis De Amor Y Salsa (Discos Fuentes D10042)
Various 15 Grandes Sucesos De Salsa (Discos Fuentes D10093)
La Sonora Dinamita 16 Grandes Exitos (Discos Fuentes 201601)
Fruko Y Sus Tesos Contento (Discos Fuentes 201590)
Los Tupamaros La Calle De La Rumba (Discos Fuentes D10114)
The Meriño Brothers ¡Vallenato Dynamos! (Globestyle ORB 049)
Diomedes Díaz and Nicolas Mendoza Cantando (Globestyle ORB 055)

VENEZUELA

While Venezuela, probably because of its oil wealth and the comparative size and financial importance of Caracas, is an important centre of Latin American recording and record publishing, it has not produced as many major record stars as Colombia, Cuba or Puerto Rico. On the other hand, the country possesses a wide variety of traditional musics and many excellent working dance groups. The racial and musical mix is Spanish, African and native Indian, but the latter is only of marginal influence in mainstream popular music.

The music most widely identified as Venezuela's national style is llanera (from the 'llanos', or 'plains'), sometimes referred to by the wider term 'musica criolla' (creole), and features the plains harp with its pronounced bass strings, guitars, cuatros, mandolins, tambora double-headed drums, charrasca scrapers and furruco friction drums. Such ensembles accompany the famous joropo couple dance, and still play in bars and dance halls in the cattle towns of the interior, as well as in country-themed restaurants in Caracas. In its most refined form, represented by the work of the great harpist and composer **Juan-Vicente Torrealba**, llanera music has the status of a light classical art music (recordings of Torrealba's 'Alma Llanera' have been made with symphony orchestras). In its modern popularised showbiz form, its status is rather similar to that of country and western – it is not a music for the fashionable young. Top performers are extremely popular, however; one of the best known and most prolific llanera singers is **Simon Díaz**, who presents a weekly children's TV show and composed the song 'Caballo Viejo', which was taken up first by the New York salsa artiste Roberto Torres and then transformed, via the addition of a new chorus, into The Gypsy Kings' international hit 'Bamboleo'. (Diaz is said to have written 'Caballo Viejo' – 'The Old Horse' – to a former Miss Venezuela explaining why he couldn't have an affair with her.) Other top criollo singers who perform llanera music along with other regional styles include **Reynaldo Armas, Reyna Lucero, Luis Lozada, Freddy Salcedo, Armando Martinez** and **Jesus Gonzalez**.

Certain young artistes, such as **Nelson Blanco** and his group **La Manga E'Coleo** have modernised and tropicalised what is basically a llanera sound. The group **Un Solo Pueblo** plays a hybrid music, incorporating traditional instruments into a line-up of guitars and synthesizers, and covering a variety of Venezuelan and Caribbean styles including Spanish-language calypsos. The 'calypso' is a speciality of the coastal region nearest to Trinidad, particularly of the town of El Callao, and formed the basis of a national hit in 1989, 'Woman del Callao', by the group **V H** (for Vista Hermosa, a district of the regional capital of Ciudad Bolivar). A third group, known equally as the Spanish **La Misma Gente** or English **The Same People**, work successfully in the calipso field with hit songs such as 'Sexy Maria'.

Within the mainstream popular sphere, Venezuela possesses numerous Latin rock singers – the most famous are **Yordano, Ilan Chester** and the group **Daiquiri** – and several top ballad artistes, notably **José-Luis Rodriguez, 'El Puma'**, as well as a number of dance bands playing either salsa or a whole range of currently popular pan-Latin rhythms particularly, in recent years, Dominican merengue. The derogatory term 'musica gallega' (signifying a Spanish immigrant, literally 'Galician') is sometimes applied to the unintellectual, unpretentious music of the dance bands, in the same way salsa is sometimes dismissed as niche's (slum-dweller's) music in smart circles. Nevertheless they remain immensely popular.

Three major dance bands founded in the 1950s continue to thrive in Caracas, performing throughout the year at private dances, touring regionally and recording, with a line-up of guitar, bass, several percussionists, half a dozen brass players and four of five singers.

The oldest, **Billo's Caracas Boys**, was formed in the 1940s by the Dominican bandleader **Luis Maria 'Billo' Frómeta**, who dominated the 1950s and 1960s with his tight, exciting arrangements of mambos, cumbias, guarachas, plenas and boleros, featuring a succession of star singers, notably **Cheo Garcia, Memo Morales, Felipe Pirela** and the young **'Puma'**, José-Luis Rodriguez. Billo's Caracas Boys, led since the death of Billo by his son **Charlie Frómeta**, are still popular, but less so than their former competitors, **Los Melodicos** and the **Porfi Jimenez Orquesta**.

The Melodicos were founded in 1958 by their current director **Renato Capriles**, who continues to run the large band (at a minimum, twenty-two members, including four saxophones, three trumpets and three trombones – all continually transported around the country in Mercedes coaches) like a well-planned business, with pension schemes, etc., for the musicians whose latest line-up in 1990 included the glamorous young singer **Liz Lisbeth**.

The third top big band is led by another Dominican-born musician, **Porfirio 'Porfi' Jimenez**, who arrived in Caracas as a trombonist with the **Rafael Minaya Orquesta** in 1953, founded his own band ten years later and took twenty hard-working years to move into the top rank, which he achieved with a string of record hits in the mid-1980s, notably the huge seller 'Culúcucú' in 1987. Jimenez leads his band, unusually, on bass trumpet, and features merengues, socas and whatever is currently in demand for dancing.

The 1970s and the advent of the Cuban-American salsa boom saw the arrival on the scene of the bandleader **Oscar D'Leon**, today Venezuela's top international salsero. Born Oscar León Simoza, D'Leon started his earliest bands with money he had saved working as a painter at General Motors, Caracas, and funded several years of music-making driving a taxi. D'Leon formed his first successful band, **La Dimension Latina**, in 1973, and led it for three years before moving on to form **Salsa Mayor** and **Oscar D'Leon y su Orquesta**. D'Leon makes much of his ability to sing, dance and play his trademark white Fender upright baby bass at the same time. His first hit song was 'Pensando en Ti' ('Thinking of You') with **Dimension Latina**, and numerous later successes include 'Lloraras' ('You'll Cry') from the 1979 album 'El Mas Grande' ('The Greatest'). D'Leon's current organisation features his sons **Richard**, as administrator, and **Yorman**, as choreographer; he has collaborated with numerous top American and Puerto Rican musicians over the years and his repertoire has been modified to include merengues, soca and any of the changing fashions, including salsa romanticá **(see Puerto Rico)**, which no working dance band can afford to ignore.

D'Leon's former band La Dimension Latina continues to be successful, winning awards such as a Congo de Oro (see **Colombia**) at Barranquilla Carnival in 1990, and remaining much in demand for its velvety four-trombone sound and smart presentation under the musical directorship of **Joséito Rodriguez**. Other top contemporary bands include: **Guaco**, a fourteen-member salsa group who toured Spain in 1990; **Los Vibraciones**; and **Bronko**. The Colombian-born singer **Pastor Lopez** and his cumbia-dominated repertoire are extremely popular.

Venezuela: Discography

Various The Music of Venezuela (Zu-Zazz 2018)
Various Los Grandes Del Llano (Sonografica 10270)
V H Vista Hermosa (Sonografica 10219)
Billo's Caracas Boys Eternamente Billo (Classic older material – 16 vols.) (Tucan Records, Caracas)
Billo's Caracas Boys Para Todas (Velvet Rodven 200289)
Los Melodicos ¡Distintos! (Velvet Rodven 102214)
Porfi Jimenez Culucucu (Sonografica 10176)
Oscar D'Leon El Mas Grande (TH Rodven)
La Dimension Latina Los Duenos Del Caribe (Velvet Rodven 102231)
Pastor Lopez Los Bonitas No Son Fieles (Velvet Rodven 102204)

The Andean Countries

The story of the development (or lack of development) of indigenous popular music in Bolivia, Peru, Ecuador and Chile is superficially simple but actually highly complex. Hispanic and native Indian cultures, the latter principally of the Quecha and Aymara-speaking groupings, are important ingredients. Until the 1960s, Indian culture was peasant-based and spurned by the urban upper classes. Indian instruments – the sikus or zampoñas panpipes, the quena flute, the bombo bass drum and the chajchas sheep-hoof bracelet-rattles – were played individually rather than in mixed ensembles, and for calendar-related ceremonial or work reasons. Such city-band versions as existed added Spanish instruments such as the guitar or mestizo (creolised) ones, notably the little guitarlike charango made from an armadillo's shell, but even the music of early virtuoso charango players such as the Bolivian **Mauro Nuñez** was still regarded as lower class. In the 1950s, a growing awareness of Indian culture on the part of students and other intellectuals turned gradually into a full-blooded and government-sponsored revival, but the dances and songs were often performed by urban, educated groups who created combinations of instruments never normally played together, and accentuated the solo role of certain instruments, gradually creating a new style. This process was furthered by the identification of traditional Andean music with the anticapitalist nueva cancion wave led by folk-protest singers such as the Chilean **Violeta Parra**. As this movement transcended national boundaries, so too did its Andean components, resulting in the gradual emergence of a sort of artificial pan-Andean sound, instead of numerous distinct regional sounds. At the same time, Indian dance and fiesta music was turning increasingly to brass bands, leaving traditional instruments to their original rural ceremonial role. Fragmentary examples of the process summarised in this simplified account can be seen in the following four entries.

PERU

As of the 1950s, the handful of Peruvian artistes seen outside the country played non-indigenous music. In the 1930s, Lima bandleader **Ciro Rimac** toured internationally with his **Rumbaland Muchachos** performing Afro-Cuban and Brazilian music, and in the 1950s the bizarre **Yma Sumac**, a variety singer from Lima with a four-octave vocal range, succeeded in representing herself internationally as an interpretress of Inca music while in fact singing mambos and cha-cha-chas.

At the same time, a popular music style was developing in rural towns and in the working-class suburbs of Lima to which increasing numbers of formerly peasant Indians and mestizos were moving. This new style was based on traditional dances such as the huayño, the huaylas, the pasacalle, the carnevalito and the muliza which, though formerly linked to specific events, had by now become recreational. Concerts took place in the 'coliseos', open-air concert arenas, and could attract thousands-strong audiences, while 45-rpm records of major stars achieved similarly impressive sales.

Performers included solo artistes singing and accompanying themselves on guitar or charango – notable examples are **Ernesto Sánchez Fajardo 'El Jilguero** (Goldfinch) **del Huascarán'** and **Raul Garcia**, a guitarist and interpreter of the folklore of the region of Ayacuchó; small charango, guitar and harp combos such as **Lira Paucina** or **Los Jilgueros de Hualcan**; and larger groups, known as orquestas típicas, playing saxophones, clarinets and accordions, the brass instruments adding a rough vitality to the plaintive music. Some of the best and earliest orquestas típicas came from the Mantaro Valley region around the town of Huancayo, home of the huaylas, a former local harvest dance featuring the Spanish-derived zapateado heel-tapping, which equalled the huayño in national popularity as a result of these performers' work. Top orquestas include **Los Tarumas de Tarma, Los Rebeldes de Huancayo, La Sensación del Mantaro, Los Bordones del Peru** and **Las Golondrinas**.

The most famous individual singer of this style died in the mid-1980s. Like most of his contemporaries, **Alberto Gil Mallma** adopted a stage name connected with the natural history of the region – **Picaflor de Los Andes** ('Hummingbird of the Andes'). Gil Mallma worked in the mines, drove lorries, served his singing apprenticeship in the crowded backstage corridors of the National Coliseum where dozens of aspiring singers would flock to Sunday concerts to practise and audition informally, and rose finally to national stardom with beautiful, high, intense laments such as his 'Aguas del Rio Rimac' ('Waters of the River Rimac') which was included on 'The Real Music of Peru', an excellent Globestyle Records collection of this style of music, in 1991. Other top singers include **El Gavilán Negro** ('The Black Sparrowhawk'); **Flor Pucariña** ('The Flower of Pucará'); **La Princesita de Yungay** ('The Little Princess of Yungay'); **El Gorrión Andino** ('The Andean Sparrow'); and **Sumac Tika** ('Beautiful Flower').

BOLIVIA

Bolivan artistes were, and are, central to the spread of the pan-Andean folk sound which started in the 1960s. The 1952 revolution and the installation of a progressive government had created a climate conducive to the rehabilitation of Indian and mestizo culture. In 1965 a folk-music peña (club), the Peña Naira, was opened in La Paz by **Ernesto Cavour**, a virtuoso charango player who also founded its house band, **Los Jairas**. Los Jairas, whose innovative line-up became the model for a whole new generation of conjuntos, also included the Swiss singer and bombo player **Gilbert Favré**. Favré's presence was highly influential: as a European musician he not only brought prestige to the idea of playing Indian music, but distinct connections with both the nascent European pseudo-Andean music of groups such as **Los Rhupay** who had played in Paris clubs in the 1950s, and with the Chilean political song movement of Violeta Parra, with whom he had a romantic liaison. Los Jairas became internationally famous with songs such as 'El Llanto De Mi Madre' ('My Mother's Lament') and 'El Condor Pasa' ('The Condor Passes') and were copied by numerous other groups such as **Los Payos**, **Los Charkas** and **Kollahuara**, all of whom featured llama-motif poncho stage costumes and quena or charango solos in their performances. At the same time, folk peñas mushroomed and became increasingly commercial.

In the 1970s a second wave of groups began to reappraise the complex Andean musical heritage, and various attempts were made to counter the pan-Andean concert aesthetic with increased authenticity. The group **Savia Andina** specialised in meticulous re-creation of a wide variety of distinct styles and eschewed the use of folkloric costumes. **Los Takipayas** incorporate humorous banter and anecdotes relating to Quecha life in their act, while **Kollamarka** played songs that were vignettes of peasant life. A different direction was pursued by the groups **Aymara**, who introduced the panpipes as a virtuoso solo instrument, and Wara, who added electric guitars to the mix.

In the 1980s four groups were prominent in bringing variants of the new pan-Andean sound to Europe via a succession of tours. **Rumillajta**, based in La Paz where they run a substantial workshop making traditional instruments, recorded five albums for the west of England-based Tumi South American crafts importer. Tumi's record label also publishes **Awatiñas**, a seven-member family group of Aymara origin whose songs 'Kullakita' and 'Guerrero Aymara' were both Bolivian number one hits in 1990; and **Inti-Raymi**. Finally, **Kjarkas**, a five-piece group formed and led by the brothers and prolific composers **Ulises** and **Gonzalo Hermosa**, met a spectacular version of a problem which has long plagued the new Andean folk groups — the tendency of the outside world to take their music at face value as an indistinguishable mass of non-attributable pan-Andean folk material — when the French group Kaoma used the melody from their 1981 song 'Llorando se Fue' ('She Left Crying') as a basis for their world hit 'Lambada Song', a usage which was recognised only after court action by the group.

ECUADOR

The more northern country of Ecuador has its own versions of the student/folk revival Andean sound in the form of groups such as **Huellas**, a quartet featuring charango, guitar, panpipes and the large kettle drum known as wankara, and **Guayanay**, a similar conjunto also including the little snail-shaped ceramic pipe known as an ocarina. Other groups, such as **Los Duques** and **Los Principes**, include Andean elements in a wider repertoire of dance rhythms such as danzantes, Sanjuanitos and pasacalles played on modern instruments, including electric guitar. Finally, slower rhythms such as the 'vals' ('waltz') and pasillo performed by romantic singers in the line of **Julio Jaramillo**, who died in 1978, continue to be popular.

CHILE

Along with Cuba, Chile, was, in the 1960s, one of the major centres of the politically radical folk-linked nueva cancion which owed much musically to Bob Dylan and Joan Baez. Its greatest practitioners, **Violeta Parra** and **Victor Jara**, were closely identified with the rise to power of President Salvador Allende. Both artistes were also prominent in incorporating versions of Chilean altiplano Indian music into their songs; although Indians did, and still do, form only a small minority of the nation's population, they were powerful symbols of oppression and exploitation and their music was also diametrically opposed to the commercial North American pop that was political anathema to the nueva cancion practitioners. These, however were, for the most part, middle-class intellectuals; their espousal of Indian culture was a political rather than a musicological statement and their experience of Andean music was rarely at first hand. Violeta Parra's folk-music centre La Carpa de la Reina, and the peña founded by her children **Isabel** and **Angel**, were very much in the mould of the pan-Andean Los Jairas movement of which Parra's friend Gilbert Favré was a founding spirit (see **Peru**). During Allende's short-lived presidency, Parra, Victor Jara (who was executed by the Pinochet regime after the 1973 coup) and the newly-formed quasi-Indian groups **Inti-Illimani** and **Quilapayun** operated as spokesmen and ambassadors for the socialist government. Inti-Illimani and Quilapayun, who were abroad at the time of the coup, continued to perform in exile. During the Pinochet years, an initial clampdown on Indian features in music (charangos and quenas were unofficially banned at one time) was succeeded by the approval of non-political country versions of folk dances such as cuecas and trotes by groups such as **Los Huasos Quincheros, Grupo Caituy, Los Pascuenses** and **Conjunto Rauquen**. The end of the 1980s and the semiretirement of Pinochet saw a movement roughly equivalent to Spain's post-Franco 'movida'. Chilean rock boomed, but so also did certain new Andean hybrids such as the 'Andean New Age' of **Los Jaivas**, a former politically engaged group resident for a decade in France.

The Andean Countries: Discography

Various (incl. Picaflor de Los Andes) Huayños And Huaylas, The Real Music Of Peru (Globestyle 064)

Various (incl. Jilguero del Huascarán) Mountain Music Of Peru (Arhoolie CD 320)

Awatiñas Authentic Andean Music (VHI Records 290388)

Rumillajta Wiracocha (Rumillajta Recordings RUMI 891)

Kjarkas Canto A La Mujer De Mi Pueblo (Tumi 010)

Violeta Parra Vols. 1 and 2 (EMI 103004 and 103013)

ARGENTINA

Buenos Aires and Montevideo, the port cities at the mouth of the river Plate, were the birthplaces of one of the world's most distinctive popular dances, the tango, which retains a good deal of life though it is in no sense a widespread popular dance any more. The origins of the tango are unclear. It may have a distant link with the African slave culture which contributed to the similar and earlier genre, the milonga. It is almost certainly not linked with the Andalucian flamenco tango, and the Cuban habanera of the nineteenth century is a highly possible ancestor.

Tango culture grew up in the arrabales – the slum suburbs – of Rio in the 1880s, where its milieu was the brothels and cafés frequented by the large numbers of former soldiers and unemployed immigrants, many of them of Spanish or Italian origin, who flooded into the city at this time. Tango society was male-dominated – in the absence of a female partner it was commonly danced by two men together – and machismo and violence were an integral part of its early ethos. The typical tango figure was the compadrito, a knife-wielding, womanising early wide boy, while the lyrics of the first songs, expressed in lunfardo slang dialect, invariably concerned the cruelty of life and fate, the faithlessness of women, and the bitter consolation of alcohol.

Turn-of-the-century tango groups were small, typically trios of violin, flute, guitar or harp. By this time the dance had already acquired its distinctive moves – the corte (sudden halt), the quebrada (twisting of the torso) and the refalada (gliding step). This 'old guard' tango was a low-class ruffian's dance, and it spread to Buenos Aires polite society only after it was taken up as an exotic import by Parisians in the first decade of the twentieth century.

It was in the second decade that the 'new guard' tango developed, shedding its disreputable associations and entering the concert halls and the new cabarets. The instrumentation changed, with larger groups incorporating piano, double bass and, above all, the bandoneon, the small accordion which had recently been invented by the German Heinrich Band as a cheap transportable substitute for organ in remote country churches. The early orquestas típicas – the **Novel**, the **Select**, the **Victor** and the groups of **Juan Maglio, Francisco Canaros, Roberto Firpo** and **Eduardo Arolos** – which now sprang up to perform the newly popular tango invariably featured up to four bandoneons.

In 1918, the great success of **Pascual Contrusi's** 'Mi Noche Triste', performed by **Carlos Gardel**, ushered in the era of tango-cancion: from now on, the song itself was of prime importance as a poetic entity rather than simply as background music for a dance. Important lyricists of the 1920s and 1930s included **Caledonia Flores, Enrique Cadicamo** and the great **Enrique Santos Discépolo**, known for the bitterness and power of songs such as 'Yira, Yira'. The top performers of this period were **Agustin Bardi, Gerardo Mattos Rodriguez, Juan Carlos Cobian** and, towering above all in popularity, **Carlos**

Gardel, the most famous tanguista of all time. Gardel, of humble French birth, but Argentine domiciled from an early age, started singing in a duo in 1913 and rapidly adapted to the new tango-cancion; his emotional delivery and glamorous, soigné appearance rapidly made him a massive star at home and in Europe and the United States, where he starred in films such as the 1934 *Tango On Broadway*. Gardel's early death in a Colombian air crash on the way home from Paris confirmed his status as a national hero; his Buenos Aires grave is still a place of pilgrimage where fans place lighted cigarettes between the fingers of their idol's statue.

The 1940s and 1950s saw a consolidation of the tango as mainstream entertainment even, in certain cases, verging on art music. The top bandleaders of this period were **Anibal Troilo** and **Osvaldo Pugliese**, although two other musicians of great importance were consolidating their reputations at the same time. The first was the pianist, composer and arranger **Horacio Salgan**, whose innovative blending of jazz and classical elements with tango culminated in 1975 in a forty-minute oratorio dedicated to Gardel. Salgan, with the electric guitarist **Ubaldo de Lío**, led the group which first performed at the newly opened Buenos Aires tango club El Viejo Almacén in 1969, and he is still considered one of tango's greatest artistes. The second innovator of this period was the virtuoso bandoneonist **Astor Piazzolla**, another classically trained musician who returned to tango in the mid-1950s after living in New York and Paris, where he studied composition with Nadia Boulanger, and composing for the Buenos Aires Philharmonic Orchestra. Piazzolla's pyrotechnic performances with his New Tango Quintets in the 1960s and 1970s, and brilliantly dramatic recordings such as 'Tango: Zero Hour' in 1986, were instrumental in reviving international interest in the form, though his style is far removed from the old rough tango of brothel days.

Interest in the tango reached a low point in the 1960s and early 1970s as rock swept the world, but a minor revival began in the late 1970s. In Paris, the newly opened and remarkably authentic tango café Les Trottoirs de Buenos Aires featured new artistes such as the **Cuarteto Cedron**, led by the singer and composer **Juan Cedron**. In 1983, also in Paris, the glossy but high-quality show *Tango Argentino* began a run of performances that in subsequent years was to continue in Europe, the USA and Japan. The show featured the **Sexteto Mayor**, formed in 1973 by bandoneonist and arranger **José Libertella** and **Luis Stazo** and counting among its collaborators numerous top Buenos Aires classical musicians. *Tango Argentino*'s singers were the star baritone **Raul Lavié**, the female stars **Elba Berón**, a former Anibal Troilo Orchestra singer, and **Jovita Luna**, and the younger singer **Alba Solés**.

In 1990s Buenos Aires, the tango is still regarded as a national music, and is danced – just – by ordinary porteños, as the citizens are known, in the dowdy old Club Croata or the plush Viejo Almacén, while the radio station FM Tango plays the music round the clock. Top extant tanguistas include **Roberto Goyeneche**, '**El Polaco**' ('the Pole'), an old-style self-taught singer with a classic, deep, tragic tango voice, veteran since the 1940s of all the top bands, including Troilo's and Salgan's, and probably now the best embodiment of the tango feeling; **Eladia Blazquez**, a female singer-composer-guitarist of Andalucian ancestry, and also a serious singer of folk and light classical song: **Nestor Marconi**, **Ernesto Baffa** and **Raul Garello**, top bandoneon players; the pianist-arranger-composer **Osvaldo Tarantino** and the singer **Susana Rinaldi**. The 1970s and 1980s saw a boom in Argentinian rock music, often referred to as 'rock nacional', which is also extremely popular in other Latin American countries. Rock nacional, while eclectic in its influences, usually draws on non-Argentinian sources – rock, reggae, punk, folk – but certain groups have incorporated tangos into the mix. Notable examples are the groups formed by **Luis Alberto Spinetta** – **Almendra**, in the late 1960s, and subsequently **Invisible**; the group **Alas**; and some of the music of Dylan-influenced **León Gieco**.

Tango is not, of course, the only music form native to Argentina. In the Litoral, the northern river region bordering Paraguay and southern Brazil, the chamamé, a distant cousin of the milonga and tango, is the most popular style. Chamamé, played on accordion or bandoneon, guitar and bass, also spread to the Buenos Aires districts inhabited by the Guarani-speaking workers – usually menial – who moved to the capital. The chamamé's most famous exponent is the accordionist **Raul Barboza**, while another country accordionist, **Renato Borghietti**, also features the style.

Argentina: Discography

Roberto Firpo y su Cuarteto Alma De Bohemia (El Bandoneon EBCD8)
Osvaldo Pugliese Orchestra Collection 1949 (El Bandoneon EBCD5)
Astor Piazzolla Tango: Zero Hour (Pangaea PEA 4611561)
Astor Piazzolla Concert A Vienne (Sonodisc ESP 8429)
Cuarteto Cedron De Argentina (Polydor 2480143)
Raul Barboza King of Chamamé (Erde 001)

BRAZIL

This huge country contains a correspondingly large popular music industry in which hundreds of major artists and numerous styles, substyles and combinations of styles form an organic whole particularly resistant to quick dissection. Nevertheless, the major national-racial ingredients of most Brazilian music are African and Portuguese, the latter influenced slightly by Italian melody and song style. The Portuguese colonial legacy consists of instruments – the guitar (known as violão) and guitar variants such as the little cavaquinho – and of the pervasive bittersweet quality of saudade, similar to that of fado (see **Portugal**), found in many of the songs. The African contributions – mainly from the Yoruba western tribelands, the Congo and the southern area of present-day Angola – are dance and percussion. Afro-Brazilian percussion is particularly varied and includes drums such as the big bass surdo marching drum of the samba schools, shakers such as the afoxé, the double-cowbell agogo and the distinctive, twanged bowlike berimbao, all of which, while traditional, feature also in modern popular music. Many of the African rhythms are connected with dance forms such as the batuques and baianos, or the Angolan-originated martial art/dance capoeira so successfully revived in the city of Salvador de Bahía today. Others are connected with the voodoo-equivalent Afro-Christian religious cults collectively known as macumba, of which the most famous is the Bahían candomblé.

The earliest national popular genres of Brazil were the African-based lundu which, like the later samba, had separate song and dance forms, and the modinha, which was modelled on Portuguese and Italian song. By the end of the nineteenth century these had faded from popularity, and the maxixe, Brazil's equivalent of the tango with the same rough origins transmuting into high fashion, was in full flow.

At the same time, Rio de Janeiro saw the flowering of the choro (from the verb 'chorar', 'to cry'), the capital's first major style of its own. Choro bands, playing flute, cavaquinho and guitars, were based on the black or mulatto barbershop trios of the 1850s. Their audiences were at first lower class, but gradually their repertoire merged with the piano waltzes of fashionable salons and a series of talented composers raised the choro to a new level of excellence and prestige. The father of the choro was **Ernesto Nazareth**, a cinema pianist whose compositions penetrated the art-music establishment to the extent that in 1922 he was invited, amid great controversy, to perform in the National Institute of Music. Its greatest exponent, however, was the legendary **Pixinguinha**, a flautist and saxophonist much influenced by jazz, whose band **Os Oito Batutas** did much to popularise Brazilian music in Paris in the 1920s. He died in 1973. Choro was displaced by samba, modern jazz and rock in the 1950s, 1960s and early 1970s, but in the mid-1970s returned briefly to fashion, as played by a handful of old traditional combos such as the **Conjunto Atlantico**, by popular samba musicians such as **Paulinho de Viola**, and by a rash of new specialist groups such as **Choro Roxo, Amigos do Choro** and **Os Carioquinhas**.

The samba, a style thought of as quintessentially Brazilian, evolved in Rio. It is associated above all with the capital and its carnival, but it probably originated in the much more African city of Salvador de Bahía; the earliest sambas were played at black get-togethers in the Rio houses of the 'tias Baianas' – the 'aunts from Bahía' – whose parlours provided a social life for the growing black population descending on Rio for work. Samba has two broad forms, the drum-based samba played and chanted en masse by the samba schools during Rio Carnival, and the samba-cancâo (sung samba) performed and recorded by small groups and singers. The sambas of the carnival are composed to be sung by the hundreds, or even thousands, of members of the school, with the rhythm thundered out by the hundreds of drummers of the school's batería and the entire army usually costumed according to the historical or mystical theme that is the subject of the 'samba de enredo' ('narrative'). The samba itself may well be written by a sambista who also performs individual samba-cancâo, for example, the great **Nelson Sargento** who lives in the favela of Mangueira and writes for its school, one of the oldest and best. Sambas de enredo have generally speeded up in recent decades, and big flashy rich schools such as the extraordinary Beija Flor, led by its extravagant director **Joâozinha Trinta**, are light years away from the relatively humble and solemnly paced outfits of the early carnivals.

The story of recorded, sung samba begins with the artiste **Ernesto dos Santos**, better known as **Donga**, who recorded the song 'Pelo Telefone' in 1917. Succeeding decades saw the form developed by Pixinguinha, top radio singers such as **Francisco Alves, Noel Rosa** and **Nelson Goncalves**, composers such as **Wilson Batista, Ismael Silva** and **Ary Barroso**, whose song 'Aquarela do Brasil' is virtually a national anthem, and by stars such as **Carmen Miranda**, whose fruit-laden headgear and appearances in 1940s Broadway musicals and Hollywood films such as *Down Argentine Way* in the 1940s earned her the tag 'the Brazilian Bombshell'.

The 1950s and 1960s saw pop samba flagging slightly, becoming increasingly 'sweet' and overlapping to a certain extent with the new bossa nova form, before a number of female stars led a strong revival. The first was **Clara Nunes**, whose blending of 'old guard' sambas and new songs by her poet husband **Paulo César Pinheiro** led to massive sales for records such as 'Alvorecer' and 'Claridade' before her career was tragically terminated in 1983 by a fatal reaction to anaesthetic during a minor operation. Clara Nunes was followed by the experienced and vivacious club performer **Alcione** and by **Beth Carvalho**, a white middle-class 'carioca' ('native of Rio') who took up and mastered samba in the early 1970s. Not only did she record a wide variety of excellent new songs but she searched out classic old material and performers, sponsored young unknown ones from the favelas, in the process acquiring a reputation as the most serious and committed sambista of the young generation. Important modern male samba practitioners include the composer and instrumentalist **Paulinho da Viola**, noted for his skilful blend of white modern and pop music with the African, old guard, and favela styles; the husky-voiced graduate of samba de enredo, **Martinho da Vila; Agepe**, the northeastern-born star of the commercial, romantic samba 'joia' ('gem') style; the composer and singer **Jair Rodrigues**; and **Roberto Ribiero**, a leader of the disco-oriented sambâo – 'big samba' – sound. In addition to the rise of new star sambistas, the 1970s and 1980s saw a rediscovery or, in some cases, a first discovery of a number of old traditional singers who for decades had been quietly performing in the favelas. One of these was the 70-year-old **Clementina de Jesus**, a performer of the old 'partido alto' style samba, who had worked as a cleaning lady for years before being discovered by the television show *Rosa de Ouro* ('Golden Rose') in 1965. Others included **Cartola**, the great composer and founder of the Mangueira samba school, who made his first record in 1974 aged 66; **Nelson Sargento**; and **Nelson Cavaquinho**. A further manifestation of the return to samba tradition is the recent rise of pagode music. The pagode, an impromptu party in the favelas, used to take place in the houses of the old tias; it later moved to the samba school premises outside carnival season, to cheap favela café-bars and, since the opening of Rio's Cacique de Ramos pagode around 1980, to big new popular dance hall-terraces. The music is live, informal roots samba, played by a host of new artistes, a number of whom, including **Arlindo Cruz**, **Almir Guineto**, **Zeca Pagodinho**, **Javelina Pérola Negra**, **Neguinho** and the top group **Fundo de Quintal**, are now recording and radio stars.

The late 1950s saw the creation of a new Rio-based style – bossa nova – which swept not only Brazil but the world. Essentially bossa nova was a mixture of samba-cancâo with American West Coast cool jazz; it was soft, minimal, sophisticated, prone to cocktail-lounge blandness and relied to a large extent on the polished lyrics of writers such as its first and greatest practitioner, **Vinicius de Moraes**. De Moraes, poet, musician, sometime diplomat, film censor and journalist, wrote the lyrics set to music by bossa nova's first star **Antonio Carlos 'Tom' Jobim**, a pianist and professional arranger. Unlike samba, bossa nova was an upper-class intellectual music – it had started in the smart café-bars of the Copacabana and Ipanema districts, and part of its eventual fall from popularity after the military coup of 1964 was due to a vague association in the minds of young people with the establishment and therefore the right-wing dictatorship. Bossa nova's main stars were **Jobim** and **de Moraes**, whose 'Chega De Saudade' and 'Desafinado' were worldwide hits and who also collaborated on the music for the film *Black Orpheus*; **João Gilberto**, a Bahían singer and guitarist whose perfectionist recording and extreme simplicity and naturalness of style made him a huge star and the individual most influential on subsequent Brazilian popular performers (in 1991 Gilberto's first record after a ten-year silence was awaited with acute interest by the country's musicians); Gilberto's wife **Astrid** whose English-language recording 'The Girl From Ipanema' was a big US hit in 1964; and lesser-known but highly influential early performers **Carlos Lyra**, **Toquinho** and **Nara Leâo**. In addition, numerous groups such as **Os Cariocas**, **Sergio Mendes' Sexteto Bossa Rio**, the **Conjunto de Roberto Menescal**, the **Tamba Trio** and the **Samba Canço Trio** specialised in bossa nova.

In the late 1960s and 1970s a whole range of popular artistes established careers performing in an eclectic style influenced by elements of bossa nova, samba, jazz, and Euro-American pop and rock: the term 'musica popular brasileiro', abbreviated to 'MPB', came to be applied to this broad tendency. Among the most eclectic and influential of the new performers were those associated with the movement known as tropicalia, led by the Bahían artistes **Gilberto Gil**, **Gaetano Veloso**, **Maria Bethania** and **Gal Costa**. Tropicalia's principal aesthetic aim, much influenced by the recordings of the Beatles with George Martin's ground-breaking orchestral arrangements, was to liberate the musical imagination, remove barriers between genres and create new fusions. Extra-musically, its ethos was much connected with the 1920s modernist movement and the 'Anthrophagic Manifesto' of the poet Oswald de Andrade, which advocated a sort of creative recycling by Brazilians of the best of world art. Tropicalia's prime movers were also active politically and in other spheres of intellectual life. Gilberto Gil, a doctor's son, took a degree in business administration before turning to music professionally under the influence, initially, of Joâo Gilberto. Early successes such as 'Domingo No Parque' and the samba 'Aquele Abraco' led to a weekly television show in 1968, but under a right-wing military government (this was the time of the American Black Power Movement), Gil's political liberalism earned him a short jail sentence, after which he moved to London until 1972. Gil's career has continued to expand and he is now also a politician, having become a city councillor in Salvador de Bahía in 1987. Gil has been particularly active in the re-Africanisation of Bahía (see below) and his later work features much reggae and African rhythm. Gaetano Veloso's career started at the same time as Gil's, whom he joined in exile in London; he is a restlessly experimental artiste, having recorded avant-garde albums of jumbled voices and found noise – 'Araça Azul' (1972) – as well as more conventional songs in his gentle sambista's voice, such as his most recent album 'Estrangeiro' (1989). Maria Bethania, Veloso's younger sister, preceded him as a recording artiste – her first LP came out in 1965 – and her smoky alto voice and dynamic live performance have made her one of Brazil's top female stars and the first to achieve sales of a million records ('Rosa Dos Vento' in 1971). Gal Costa, a former record-shop sales assistant with a naturally fine voice, began her career singing the songs of the young Gaetano Veloso, whom she met in 1964 and, along with Gilberto Gil and Maria Bethania, joined as a partner in the revue *Nos, Por Exemplo* ('Us, For Example') in Salvador's Vila Velha theatre. Costa's first LP, 'Domingo' was a duet with Veloso; the subsequent two decades have seen a string of well-received, high-quality LPs including 'Bem Bom' (1985) and 'Lua De Mel' (1987).

Of the many other MPB stars of this period, **Milton Nascimiento, Chico Buarque, Jorge Ben, Gonzaguinha, Joâo Bosco** and **Elis Regina** stand out.

Milton Nascimiento is probably Brazil's most eminent popular performer. Rio born, but resident mainly in Minas Gerais, and possessed of a magnificent soaring voice, he has written hundreds of songs, many concerned with political and environmental issues, and has recorded prolifically, often in the company of American jazz and rock musicians such as Wayne Shorter, Herbie Hancock and Pat Metheny, among whom his reputation is sky-high. Albums such as 'Native Dancer' and 'Milton' brought him fame in America in the 1970s. Chico Buarque, the scion of a prestigious literary and academic family, is a poet and composer responsible for countless sophisticated popular songs and a Kurt Weill-inspired opera, *Opera do Malandro*. Jorge Ben is a self-taught black carioca singer and guitarist whose combination of favela-linked lyrics, warm sambista's voice, rock and reggae-influenced guitar and a strong mystical streak led to hits such as 'Taj Mahal' and 'Charles Angel 45' in Brazil and Europe. Gonzaguinha, né Luis Gonzaga Junior, is the son of a famous northeastern musician (see below) who has forged his own Rio-based career singing of the lives of favela-dwellers. Joâo Bosco is an acoustic guitarist, singer and composer from the central region of Minas Gerais noted for his re-creation, as an intellectual white Brazilian, of black roots forms such as early samba. The top female star of this generation, Elis Regina, died of an accidental overdose of drugs and alcohol in 1982, at the height of a career which had started in the mid-1970s with a smash hit record, 'Arrastâo', written by Vinicius de Moraes, which rocketed her to fame after winning the top song prize at the Excelsior TV Festival. Other top female stars of this period include Fafa de Belém, Nazaré Pereira, Simone, Joyce, Leila Pinheiro and Marisa Monte, while male artistes include Djavan, Ivan Lins, Moraes Moreira, Beto Guedes, Wagner Tiso (the latter two associated with the Minas Gerais-based Club da Esquina movement led by Milton Nascimiento) and the extravagantly camp and theatrical Ney Matogrosso, former singer of the equally provocative group Secos e Molhados.

The 1970s and 1980s saw a phenomenon of great significance for Brazilian popular music: the revival of the African cultural tradition of Salvador de Bahía, Brazil's second city and once its colonial capital. This manifested itself in the boom in capoeira, in candomblé ceremonies and in the candomblé-related carnival bands known as afoxés, which had dwindled in importance in the 1960s. With the help of Gilberto Gil the oldest afoxé, the Filhos de Gandhi, was rebuilt with 3,000 members. In 1975, a new Africanised variant on the Rio-style samba schools was born in the form of the big percussion marching bands known as 'Afro-blocos', the first of which was the Yoruba-named Ile-Aiyé, which rapidly gained a membership of 2,000. Ile-Aiyé was followed by others – Ara Ketu, Muzenza and Olodum – who included in their repertoire of rhythms their invention samba-reggae: the black consciousness message of Bob Marley had a powerful effect on Salvador. The blocos acted as social centres and informal street research institutes into African culture and, soon, as performance groups for reduced-scale versions of their massed drum and voice music. Olodum, for example, began with great success to tour a twenty-member troupe throughout the year, playing compositions such as 'Madagascar Olodum' or 'Canta Paro O Senegal' which combined newly reinvented 'ancestral' rhythms with a somewhat imaginative lyrical reconstruction of a continent few of the members actually knew. (Olodum was the first group Paul Simon went to for backing tracks when recording the 1990 Brazilian-influenced album 'The Rhythm of the Saints'.) The Afro theme was soon taken up by a whole crop of young Bahían 'Afro-pop' artistes who proceeded to take the regional sound into the national record charts. Many of these had come up via the phenomenon of Bahían Carnival and the trios electricos, trucks fitted with huge sound systems booming out the music of the performers who paraded on top of them. Some of them, such as the group Reflexu's, produced rock-pop versions of Afro-bloco songs, in Reflexu's case those of Olodum. The most popular artistes of this movement were/are Luiz Caldas, Geronimo, Celso Bahía, the groups Novos Baianos and Chiclete Com Banana (the latter, named after an old Gilberto Gil song, blend Afro-pop with Kassav-style zouk to great effect) and, above all, the dynamic young singer Margareth Menezes. As a teenager Menezes sang in church choirs and theatre productions, and made her first national record, including the hit song 'Elegibo', named after an ancient Yoruba city, in 1988. In 1989 she was invited to join David Byrne's international 'Rei Momo' tour; the following year she toured ten French towns playing from the top of a trio electrico.

Bahía state is not the only region of northeast Brazil to exert a distinctive and powerful influence on the country's music. The hectic frevo and maracatú styles of the large city of Recife were a significant, if minor, part of the tropicalia mix, and the country style forro is currently very much in fashion again. Forro is the dance music of the wild sertâo scrubland, an area which also retains its troubadour-ballad tradition of songs about famous 'cangaceiros' – 'bandits' – such as the legendary Lampiâo, and the improvised rhyming competitions between repentista balladeers whose modern recording equivalents are artistes such as **Elomar** and **Geraldo Azevedo**.

Forro is traditionally played on sanfona (accordion), triangle and zabumba (bass drum); modern combos add electric guitars and bass. Its musical roots include European-derived dances such as the xote (based on the widespread schottische) and its continued popularity in sertâo dance halls and fiestas make it a little like a Latin American Cajun or Tex-Mex. Forro's greatest twentieth-century interpreter was **Luis Gonzaga**, famous for his supple humorous voice and his colourful, ornate, embroidered suede sertâo cowboy outfits. Gonzaga first came to national prominence in the 1940s when he moved to Rio and began to popularise a version of the African-linked baiâo rhythm. His great success turned the baiâo into a craze which at one point rivalled the samba, but in the 1960s his popularity waned. He retired to the sertâo-based forro public that always remained faithful until, in the 1970s, renewed interest from the tropicalistas brought him a new, young audience. Gonzaga's song 'Asa Branco' is now practically a northeastern anthem.

Gonzaga's chief rivals were the younger singers **Dominguinhas** and **Jackson de Pandeiro**, who wrote the song 'Chiclete Com Banana' made famous by Gilberto Gil. Other major artistes were **Genival Lacerda, Joâo do Vale, Marinalva, Pinto do Acordeon** and the **Trio Nordestino**. The 1970s saw a new crop of young modern northeasterners: **Raimundo Fagner** and **Antonio Carlos Belchior**, whose song 'Mucuripe', recorded by the great Elis Regina, was a key factor in the forro revival; **Nando Cordel**, who created the forro-and-merengue mix forrorengue; **Amelinha; Jorge de Altinho; Ricardo Bezerra; Robertinho de Recife; Beto Barbosa;** and **Elba Ramalho**. Of these, Elba Ramalho has created much the greatest national and international impression, with her beauty, vivacity and excellent voice. Ramalho, from a musical family, made her name in the serious side of popular music – her first major success was in Chico Buarque's *Opera do Malandro* – and in 1988 returned to her northeastern roots with the album 'Fruto', a big hit. Elba Ramalho has also been one of the main beneficiaries of the late 1980s lambada craze.

Conflicting accounts of the pedigree of the lambada have proliferated. Madagascar, Cuba and Amazonia are among alleged points of origin; what seems reasonably clear is that the modern dance in linked to a hybrid Caribbean-influenced form that has existed for many years along Brazil's northeastern coast, particularly the far northern area around the port of Belem.

In the mid-1980s a minor revival began in the popular dance halls of the northeast, gradually catching on in the cities, where lambateria bars began to open. In 1989, a small consortium of Paris record producers and film-makers decided to try to capitalise on the sexy clinging dance and hot rhythm. Backed by the soft-drinks company Orangina who featured the dance in an advert, and the TV company TFI, a single, based without attribution on the Bolivian song 'Llorando Se Fue' (see **Bolivia**), by the French studio group **Kaoma** became a smash summer hit across Europe. The resulting publicity in turn boosted the lambada in Brazil, where the boom had been stagnating, in the rest of Latin America and, indeed, the world, so that 1990 saw the Kaoma lambada tune covered by literally thousands of ensembles in hundreds of regional style variations.

In addition to Elba Ramalho, chief Brazilian lambada interpreters were **Beto Barbosa, Alipio Martins, Betto Douglas, José Orlando, Ditâo, Nonato Do Cavaquinho, Cheiro De Amor**, the older artistes **Carlos Santos**, and **Pinduca**. A good roots lambada group in **Vieira e Seu Conjunto**.

Brazil: Discography

Various (inc. Sargento) Brazil, Roots Samba (Rounder 5045)
Various O Samba – Brazil Classic 2 (Warner Bros 926 019)
Joâo Gilberto The Legendary (World Pacific CDP 7938912)
Various Brasil – Samba, Bossa Nova, Nordeste, Afro-Brazil (Excellent four-volume compilation) (Philips 845 301-4)
Martinho Da Vila O Canto Das Lavadeiras (CBS 177 196)
Gilberto Gil Brasil... Les Indispensables (WEA 9031717722)
Gilberto Gil O Eternho Deus Mu Danca (WEA 2292566202)
Elis Regina Elis (Philips 8122 1514)
Jorge Ben Benjor (WEA 2292 56619 2)
Milton Nascimiento Milton (A&M AMLH 64611)
Various Axe Brazil (World Pacific CDP 7950572)
Reflexu's Da Mae Africa (Mango 162 539 901)
Luis Gonzaga Danado De Bom (RCA Camden 1070453)
Various Brazil: Forro (Rounder 5044)
Vieira e seu Conjunto Lambada (Sterns 2001)
Os Paralamas Do Sucesso Arquivo (EMI 068 7956671)
Various Lambada Brazil (Polygram 841 580)

NORTH AMERICA

INTRODUCTION

Not all music from the United States is mass-produced corporate pop – far from it. Whilst many of the wide variety of regional styles that once flourished are having a hard time surviving, or have changed so much they are almost unrecognisable, one glorious survivor is Cajun music. Cajun has not only continued seemingly oblivious to external circumstance but is gaining more and more devotees around the world. I think my first glimpse of the possibilities of Cajun music was a single of Johnny Allen's 'Promised Land', which I bought in the late 70s, although it wasn't strictly Cajun at all. It introduced me to the excitement of the Louisiana country accordion sound, and later I started getting into real traditional Cajun like the Balfa Brothers. Louisiana was one of the first places I visited when I started musical travelling, which basically was when for the first time I had a bit of money from my radio and TV work. It suddenly dawned on me that there was nothing to stop me just getting up and going to where all this wonderful music was coming from. I'd already been near Louisiana around 1986 or 1987 – I was in Texas filming ZZ Top for *The Old Grey Whistle Test*, and I knew that Louisiana was only a couple of hours over the border. I didn't make it that time, but I did the following year and I've been a regular visitor since.

Cajuns are remarkable people. They first arrived in Louisiana in 1755 from Nova Scotia. The British were giving the French a bit of a smiting at the time.

The French-speaking Arcadians ('Cajun' is a perversion of 'Arcadian') refused to side with the British so their lands were taken, families were split up, put on to different boats and shoved out into the Atlantic.

Louisiana was where they settled. Hot, humid, swampy and bug-infested, no one else wanted to live there. They brought with them the wild fiddle music, driving two-steps and bleak, waltz-tempo ballads later to be supercharged with accordions. They also brought an ethic of hard work and an ideology of 'laissez les bons temps rouler' when the work was done. And they are still letting the good times roll – harder, faster, and more spontaneously than any group I have stayed with outside of Africa.

Few hillbilly string bands can be found a-pickin' and a-grinnin' in the hollows of the Appalachians, but dotted around Lafayette in the cluster of small towns and villages that is Cajun country, you get used to the sound of belching accordions and mad-dog singing from a back porch or the doorway of a bar.

For anyone with an appetite for romantic rural Americana Louisiana is a paradise, though it is not surprising the place has a 1950s look about it. This is the poorest state in the Union. Lafayette was a boom town until the bottom fell out of the oil market. The crawfish farmers, whose flooded fields flash and shimmer on the plains, are producing a budget staple food, not an expensive delicacy. Lafayette is, I found, the best base camp for Cajun country. The town has banks, restaurants, lots of bars with live music and a downtown diner the size of a ballroom, where they will not look at you askance if you order a huge chicken and sausage gumbo stew with saltine crackers, potato salad and cold Corona beer for breakfast.

Saturday morning should be spent in Fred's lounge, thirty miles north of Lafayette in Mamou. It is from Fred's at 9 a.m. that the local radio station, KVPI, begins its Saturday morning dance and radio broadcast with a live Cajun band. Between the waltzes and two-steps, J.C. Fontenot, the MC, reads the advertisements, in French, for feed mills, furniture stores and Jack Miller's Barbecue Sauce. When the dancing finishes in Fred's at lunchtime it resumes three doors down, beyond the barber shop, in the Casanova Lounge. Resident band last time I visited was Sherryl Cormier and All The Cajun Girls. Some of the Girls had beards.

In a community where they are still playing, enjoying, recording and buying a style of music that has remained virtually unchanged since it was first recorded in the late 1920s, the tremors of Beatlemania, it seems, are just being felt. Even the songs themselves are the same. The Cajun anthem 'Jolie Blonde' is one of the most requested songs at KVPI; it was back on the charts in the spring. Joseph Falcon first took it there in 1928.

Marc and Ann Savoy's Cajun jam in the front of their music store in Eunice, just down the road, is another wonderful way to waste a Saturday morning. Marc is one of 50 independent accordion makers in the area. He is a man with an iron resolve to defend Cajun identity, and he combines it with a contempt for mainstream American culture. 'No one ever went broke underestimating the taste of the American public', reads a notice above his workbench. It is open house on a Saturday morning to musicians, dancers and bystanders. Denis McGee, aged 96, a master fiddler and one of the first Cajuns to record, was, until a recent stroke, still playing at the Savoy's store on a Saturday.

In the evening, chow down in Mulate's Restaurant in Breaux Bridge. Once a week the resident band is led by the great fiddler Dewey Balfa. With his brothers Will and Rodney in the 1960s he led what was probably the greatest of all Cajun bands. Two-thirds of The Balfa Brothers were wiped out in a car crash in 1973. Nowadays Dewey drives the local school bus for a day job, but since the crash he has played in the movies *Southern Comfort* and *The Big Easy*.

Over at Prejeans Restaurant, north of Lafayette, on a Friday night D.L. Menard, the Cajun Hank Williams, fronts the house band. Couples waltz between courses of alligator steaks and pecan pie. When D.L. Menard is not playing to alligator eaters at Prejeans, you will find him in his rocking-chair factory, a tin shed next door to his wooden house in Erath. D.L. is one of the happiest, most warm-hearted people I have met, a superb guitarist (his nickname is 'The Cajun Rhythm Machine'), and a craftsman of beautiful traditional furniture. D.L. rarely stops laughing, and the whole of his face dances when he shouts his conversations in the thickest of Cajun accents. There is a cartoon character waiting to be created around him. D.L.'s friend is Eddie Lejeune, an accordionist supreme with the saddest, bleakest, high Cajun singing voice. Eddie is 35. He looks 50.

I spent an evening on the front porch with D.L. and Eddie. D.L.'s wife, Louella, cooked us the best gumbo in the whole of Louisiana, then sat back in her chair, smoked, smiled and watched her husband and his friend play like men possessed. And I rocked back and forth in one of D.L.'s chairs, my eyes prickling and watering with the intensity of Eddie's singing. The cold beer just held at bay the heat of the night and my head swam with snatches of Cajun tunes, names and legends of the local greats, long-dead friends and neighbours of D.L. and Louella, suddenly real people who, for me, had been just the characters in sleeve notes before they were brought to life in that kitchen.

Louisiana Cajun may be an exceptional example of living, flourishing, independent American roots music, but there are others. In the same state there is the Mardi Gras Indian tradition of New Orleans which is as strong as ever. Texan rock and the Mexican music of Texas and California are all rich and vital. On the whole I can't see myself running out of musical reasons to keep forking out for transatlantic plane tickets for a few years yet.

ANDY KERSHAW

The United States

GENERAL

Among US musical styles with a broad geographic base and a continued strong connection with a community, rather than industry, origin, two (blues and country in general having been excluded here on grounds outlined in the preface) stand out. One is old and one new; they are gospel and rap.

The intense and ecstatic lead vocal of gospel, set against a rich harmony chorus of anything from three to a hundred and three voices, sprang originally from the fundamentalist hymns and spirituals of Southern black church congregations. Gospel first moved into the general popular domain in the late nineteenth century via diluted versions of songs such as 'Swing Low Sweet Chariot' by groups including the **Fisk Jubilee Singers**. The 1930s saw more authentic black artists recording successfully, led by the important singer-composer **Thomas A. Dorsey** ('Georgia Tom'), who is credited with the invention of the term 'gospel song', as well as the performance, accompanied by piano rather than a cappella, of religious songs outside church. He discovered the great **Mahalia Jackson** who was, along with **Sister Rosetta Tharpe**, one of the earliest female stars of a hitherto predominantly male genre.

A profusion of successful groups and individuals arrived in the 1950s, a decade which began with the first Negro Gospel and Religious Music Festival at Carnegie Hall, starring Mahalia Jackson and the **Revd James Cleveland**, a rough-voiced singing preacher from a poor Chicago family, who went on to work with **Aretha Franklin** and **Quincy Jones** and began the 1990s, forty years after the Carnegie Hall concert, still among the top ten gospel artistes nationally. Other top artistes from the 1950s and 60s included the **Soul Stirrers**, whose lead singer at one time was **Sam Cooke**, the **Pilgrim Travellers, Dorothy Love Coates and the Original Gospel Harmonettes**, the **Swan Silvertones**, the **Dixie Hummingbirds**, the **Five Blind Boys** (and a similarly named group, the **Five Blind Boys of Alabama**), and the **Edwin Hawkins Singers**, whose 'Oh Happy Day' was a huge international hit in 1967.

Gospel from the 1940s and 1950s had a very strong influence on early rock and rollers, many of whom, particularly if black, came from a churchgoing background (**Little Richard**'s fame was based on his scandalous combination of the ecstatic spiritual vocal style with profane, indeed highly risqué, rock lyrics), and, above all, on the new soul singers, a number of whom (Sam Cooke, **Al Green**, Aretha Franklin) actually came from gospel backgrounds, and all of whom based their vocal style strongly on gospel singing.

The soul connection in turn reinfiltrated popular gospel style, as did R&B

and even later black music trends such as funk and rap, so that the contemporary gospel scene is an eclectic mix of classic singers such as James Cleveland, large traditional choirs such as the Mass Choirs of Mississippi, Los Angeles and Georgia, and a variety of slick modern acts such as the **Winans** and **Take Six**, whose music is only partially recognisable as gospel. There is in addition a whole range of so-called Christian music, often performed by white artistes, which is connected to gospel by religion but which is otherwise rock, light country or various shades of the pop spectrum. Gospel music has also been extremely influential outside the USA, and substantial gospel traditions exist from South Africa to Australia (the aboriginal 'desert choirs').

In a little over ten years, rap advanced from a marginal trend among black and Hispanic teenagers in New York City's rough outer boroughs to a huge mainstream sector of the US pop industry. Leading star **MC Hammer**'s third album 'Please Hammer Don't Hurt 'Em' topped the pop LP charts for 21 weeks in 1990, and its author is now as sought after as Michael Jackson once was as a hugely paid product endorser (Pepsi Cola, British Knight footwear). Rap was, in fact, the fastest growing sector of the commercial popular music industry between 1987 and 1990.

The music, which started as bass-heavy disco-beat with, firstly, mixed-in snatches of music from pairs of records on the DJ's turntables (classic James Brown a favourite) and, secondly, a stream of improvised and chanted street poetry, began to transfer to record at the end of the 1970s (**The Sugar Hill Gang**'s 'Rapper's Delight' was the genre's first hit in 1979). In the early 1980s, artistes such as **Grandmaster Flash** popularised the 'scratching' effect, created literally by scratching the stylus back and forth in the groove of a record. In 1984, the trio **Run DMC** became the first rap artistes to achieve gold record status; in 1987 the white group **The Beastie Boys** scored the first number one album in the national pop chart with 'Licensed to Ill', followed two years later by the black rapper **Tone Loc**'s 'Loc-Ed After Dark'. By this time, in the hands of the black **MC Hammer** and the white star **Vanilla Ice**, rap had moved into a homogenised showbiz formula a good distance from its ghetto roots. In other hands, however, it retained and intensified its original subversive, anti-Establishment, deliberately provocative image. This was to a large extent a matter of lyrical content, which focused on three areas. The first, and least contentious, was that of Afrocentricity, which had been a theme of early artistes such as **Afrika Bambaata**, was expanded upon by top mid-1980s act **Public Enemy** with releases such as 1990s' 'Fear of A Black Planet', and in the early 1990s formed an important strand in the work of groups such as **X-Clan** and the **Poor Righteous Teachers**. The second was sex, explicit, violent and misogynist treatments of which formed an increasing part of the repertoire of groups such **2 Live Crew**, whose performances of numbers from albums such as 'As Nasty As They Wanna Be' and the 1987 trendsetter '2 Live Crew Is What We Are' led to the group's trial (and acquittal) on obscenity charges in Florida. 2 Live Crew were prime subjects of the controversy over the labelling and censoring of allegedly obscene records. Interestingly, female groups, notably **Choice** and the Texas rappers **Hoes Wit Attitude**, began to record their own explicit sexual braggadoccio in the 1990s. The final areas employed to enrage bourgeois America were criminality, gangsterism and violence in general. While the New York-based rappers such as **LL Cool J**, **Big Danny Kane**, **Kool G. Rap** and **DJ Polo** cultivated an image of smooth, gold-chain-draped pimps and hustlers, West Coast artistes, echoing the notorious crack-gang wars of Los Angeles, dealt with outlaw violence, cop killing and other topics not, in fact, remote from the day-to-day experience of the ghettos. In 1990 this latter style gave rise to the tag 'gangsta rap', an area represented by artistes such as **Compton's Most Wanted**, **Above The Law**, **NWA**, **Ice T**, and **Ice Cube**, whose 1990 'Kill At Will' album was publicised by a poster of the surly-looking Mr Cube proffering a pistol to the camera lens.

The United States: General: Discography

Various Greatest Gospel Gems (Specialty SPCD 7206/2)
The Staple Singers Pray On (Charly 220)
The Swan Silvertones My Rock/Love Lifted Me (Specialty 7202/2)
Run-DMC Run DMC (Profile PRO 1401)
Ice Cube Kill At Will (Priority 7230)

LOUISIANA

The music-rich state of Louisiana, named after Louis XIV of France and a French possession until 1803, represents a point of entry into US music for both French and Caribbean influence: it is an interesting, if peripheral observation that fifty years after the death of the great New Orleans jazz composer **Jelly Roll Morton** (né Ferdinand Lamothe, of Haitian ancestry), the city's current top stars the **Neville Brothers** were recording with another set of musical siblings, the Frères Parent, from Haiti.

The Cajun country around Lafayette and Mamou, and the city of New Orleans are the most significant geographical centres of Louisiana music and the French legacy, although much diffused in New Orleans, is still strong in Cajun culture. The mutated French language used in Southern Louisiana survived government discouragement during Roosevelt's 'one people, one language' campaign of the 1930s and 1940s, and returned very much to favour as a result of the affirmation of ethnic traditions of the 1970s and 1980s.

White Cajun music was based on dances of European origin – waltzes, two-steps, mazurkas, contredanses – and played at first on violins and subsequently on diatonic accordions, augmented with acoustic guitar and petit fer (triangle). Its chief occasion was the Saturday-night dance known as a fais do do, from the French expression used to tell a child to go to sleep, so called because at the dance the sleeping village children would be put in the charge of an old woman.

Cajun was first popularised along with the earliest blues and 'hillbilly' recordings of the 1920s; a likely candidate for first Cajun record ever made is 'Allons A Lafayette' by **Joseph Falcon** and his wife **Cléoma** in 1928, which the duo followed with 'Jolie Blonde' (often also rendered as 'Jole Blon'). Both songs are still standards of the Cajun repertoire. Other important artistes of this period were **Leo Soileau, Dennis McGhee, Auguste Breaux** and **Angela Le June**.

The mid-1930s saw Cajun music at a low ebb, marginalised by the Anglophone linguistic assault and the encroachment of Western Swing (see **Texas**) and by country music. But after the war the tide turned, helped partly by country, the style which had recently eroded its support. The region's population was now augmented by an influx of Anglophone workers, who had come to work for the booming oil industry, providing a substantial audience for country singers. Stars such as **Hank Williams** began to visit Cajun country, guesting on the new local radio programme *Louisiana Hayride* at the same time and absorbing a Cajun repertoire. In 1949 'Jambalaya', the great Hank Williams's ode to crawfish and filé gumbo parties of the bayous, became a massive national hit and introduced the era of country-Cajun, popularised by artistes such as **Harry Choates**, who made 'Jole Blon' a hit again before dying, a youthful alcoholic, in police custody; and **Jimmy C. Newman**, the 'Alligator Man', a Grand Ole Opry favourite through the 1950s and 1960s, who from the late 1970s onwards, also worked with a progressive Cajun group, **Cajun Country**, featuring **Michael Doucet** (see below). While the crossover impetus flourished, and also gave birth to the similar hybrid, Swamp Pop, created by Cajun-country rock and rollers such as **Johnnie Allen, Shorty Le Blanc, Rob Bernard** and later **Cooky and the Cupcakes**, authentic Cajun was kept alive in its introverted heartland by artistes such as **Iry Lejeune, Nathan Abshire**, the **Balfa Brothers, Austin Pitre**, and **Joseph Falcon**, whose second wife **Theresa** played drums in his **Silver Bell String Band**. In addition, the rock wave of the 1960s had its Cajun overlap, notably personified by the fiddle-playing brothers **Doug and Rusty Kershaw** (Doug scored hits with 'Louisiana Man' and 'Diggy Liggy Lo'.

The 1970s and 1980s saw authentic Cajun returning to strength and acquiring an increasing international audience. In New Orleans, spicy Cajun cooking became the height of fashion as a result of chef Paul Prudhomme of K-Paul's restaurant; the musical equivalent was Mulate's, a small country bar-cum-restaurant in Breaux Bridge, taken over in 1980 by a young entrepreneur Kerry Bouffe. It was soon besieged by young New Orleans dwellers and then by tourists avidly seeking the Cajun music purveyed by the nightly succession of excellent new groups, above all **Beausoleil**. Beausoleil, led by **Michael Doucet**, a young university educated violin virtuoso and singer, is one of the leaders of the Cajun renaissance. Other key artistes include **Dewey Balfa**, violinist and sole survivor of the great 1950s Balfa Brothers trio, whose other members Rodney and Will died in a car accident in 1973; D.L. Menard, another older musician, nicknamed 'The Cajun Rhythm Machine' for his excellent guitar playing; Eddie Lejeune, acordionist and son of the late Star Iry; **Marc Savoy**, Eunice-based constructor, and expert player, of his Arcadien brand accordions; **Zachary Richard**, like Michael Doucet a former member of the seminal progressive Cajun group **Coteau**, known internationally for his Cajun-rock experimentation; **Joel Sonnier**, a former young accordion prodigy turned Nashville crooner and finally reborn Cajun. By 1990 the Cajun boom was so well established that the State of Louisiana declared the accordion its official instrument, while Mulate's numerous competitors and new attractions such as Vermilionville, a re-created Cajun-theme village near Lafayette, were catering to the tourist and convention markets.

At the beginning of the twentieth century relations between white Cajuns and their black neighbours, who were largely Francophone, Catholic and from free-born, not slave stock, were much closer than was normal in the South, and this closeness also applied to music. In the same year, 1928, as Joseph Falcon's pioneering 'Allons A Lafayette' record, the black accordionist and violinist Amadie Ardoin released his 'Valse de Guedon', which was stylistically almost identical. There is even visible in the traditional Cajun song canon an intermittent glimpse of an African root – the distinctive girl's name in the standard two-step 'Allons Danser, Colinda', for example. In the late 1930s, with the first sparks of antisegregationist protest inspiring a white backlash, a fissure developed between Cajun whites and blacks, symbolised tragically and dramatically by the murder of Amadie Ardoin at a dance in Eunice by Klu Klux Klansmen. An ugly thread of explicit racism entered Cajun lyrics – the singer **Happy Fats'** 'Dear Mr President' was an early example – of which traces still linger today. As if in response to the social conditions, black Cajun began to diverge, taking on elements of rhythm and blues, until in the early 1950s, the style known as zydeco was born. Zydeco, a linguistic deformation of 'les haricots', a nickname for poor blacks whose staple diet was haricot beans, mixed percussion, including the frottoir, a development of the washboard consisting of a corrugated metal vest, electric guitars, accordion and violins. The piano-accordionist **Clifton Chenier**, a musician's son, worked in Texan oil refineries before starting in 1954 the series of recordings, including his classic 'Squeeze Box Boogie', that made him the first 'King of Zydeco', and an international star until his death in 1987. Other stars of the genre include **Boozoo Chavis**, whose 1954 'Paper In My Shoe' was the earliest major zydeco hit; **Alphonse 'Bois Sec' Ardoin**, a cousin of Amadie; **Stanley Duval**, known as Buckwheat Zydeco, an influential artiste of the 1980s; **Alton Rubin**, also known as **Rockin' Dopsie**, a strongly R & B-influenced player; **Sidney Semien**, a.k.a. **Rockin' Sidney**, a bluesman and zydeco player whose 'My Toot Toot' was a national mainstream hit in 1986; the female singer **Queen Ida**; **Major Handy and The Wolf Couchons**; the new young artiste **Terrence Simien and the Mallet Playboys**; and **Wayne Toups**, the very popular leader of a tendency, which he has christened Zydecajun, to recombine the two branches of Cajun music.

In addition to zydeco, rural Louisiana developed a characteristic blues style, which came to be referred to as swamp blues. A key figure in its propagation was **J.D. (Jay) Miller**, who founded the small Crowley-based studio which recorded dozens of Cajun musicians, as well as all the top swamp blues artistes, who flourished in the 1950s and 1960s. Much influenced by Chicago harmonica and guitar star Jimmy Reed's lazy, trotting style, swamp blues artistes tended also to feature harmonica and a funky, loping rhythm. Top names at the peak of this genre were **Slim Harpo**, whose 'I'm A King Bee' was a central model for British rhythm and blues bands of the early Rolling Stones period, **Lightning Slim, Lazy Lester, Lonesome Sundown, Silas Hogan, Tabby Thomas** and **Kat and Her Kittens**. By the late 1980s, only the latter two artistes were still working the run-down blues bars of centres such as Baton Rouge, along with younger, but minor artistes such as **Clarence Edwards** and **Oscar Davis**.

The New Orleans based strand of popular Louisiana music is itself composed of several threads, including jazz, rhythm and blues, and soul, all of which fall outside the strict scope of this treatment, as do the city's top stars of 1990, the **Neville Brothers**, by virtue of their mainstream popular success. Nonetheless, the brothers, keyboard players **Art** and **Aaron**, saxophonist **Charles**, and percussionist **Cyril**, connect with many of the roots of New Orleans' distinctive sound: the 'second line' rhythm named after accompanying mourners whose outward funeral procession to the cemetery was sombre but whose return was joyful, with the band's drummers letting rip; the rolling piano style was descended from **Jelly Roll Morton** through the great 1950s artiste **Professor Longhair**, to **Antoine 'Fats' Domino** and **Huey 'Piano' Smith**, and thence to modern keyboard aces such as **Allen Toussaint**, composer-singer-arranger-proprietor of the important SeaSaint studios and linchpin of New Orleans music from the sixties onwards, and to Mac Rebennack. Rebennack is better known as **Dr John**, responsible for three decades of fine music including the voodoo-theme 'Gris Gris' in 1968 and the top ten hit 'Right Place Wrong Time' with the **Meters** in 1973. Other classic New Orleans popular artistes of the late 1950s to 1970s include **Irma Thomas, Lee Dorsey, Ernie K-Doe, Robert Parker, Earl King**, the rhythm and blues guitarist **Snooks Eaglin, Tommy Ridgely, the Dixie Cups**, who counted a Neville sister, **Athelga**, as a member, and the Meters, a Hammond organ, guitar, bass and drums group comprising Art Neville and the ubiquitous session players **Leo Nocentelli, Joseph Modeliste**, and **George Parker Jr**, who re-formed the group in 1990. At the beginning of the 1990s this area of music was also booming, with the Neville Brothers at the peak of their popularity, and numerous Neville sons and daughters entering the fray as members of the groups **Def Generation**, the **Uptown All-Stars**, and **Charmaine Neville and Friends**, while other young groups such as **Fred Le Blanc** and **Cowboy Mouth** made distinctive Southern rock music.

Two other subgenres of New Orleans music flourished in the 1980s, the first counting the ubiquitous Nevilles among its practitioners. The Mardi Gras Indian 'tribes' are groups of revellers, usually black, who parade dressed in lavishly embroidered, feathered and sequinned 'Red Indian' costumes at Carnival. The singing 'tribes', with names such as the **Wild Tchoupitoulas**, the **Golden Eagles** and the **Wild Magnolias**, are led by a chief, and back themselves with tambourines, cowbells and drums. In 1976, the **Wild Tchoupitoulas** recorded with the Meters and the Neville Brothers an extremely successful collection of songs by their 'chief', George Laudry, and the Nevilles. The record was produced by Allen Toussaint, and set a trend for the hitherto amateur, purely Carnival groups to perform periodically outside Carnival, and to record; both the **Golden Eagles** and the **Wild Magnolias** did this.

The second genre is the traditional brass band. Amateur brass bands or marching bands had long been a feature of New Orleans Carnival processions, as well as of an informal network of social clubs through which they would be available for old style funerals, parades and parties. By the 1970s, with serious jazz light years ahead in development, and rock, soul and R & B in favour for dancing, the brass bands were in decline. Their revival was started by the **Dirty Dozen Brass Band**, an eight-piece group who began to play a rumbustious mixture of old jazz with R & B riffs and snatches of mixed Caribbean rhythms on their trumpets, trombones, cornets, saxophones and sousaphone. The Dirty Dozen were rapidly followed by a succession of similar groups – the revitalised older band **Dejan's Olympic Brass Band**, the **Algiers Brass Band**, the dynamic young **ReBirth Brass Band** with their teenage prodigy trumpeter **Derrick Shezbie** – who packed neighbourhood dance bars such as the Glass House with enthusiastic dancers.

Louisiana: Discography

Various J'ai été au Bal Vols. I & II (Arhoolie AR 331 & 332)
Joseph Falcon Louisiana Cajun Music (Arhoolie F5005)
Nathan Abshire The Pinegrove Boys (Flywright Records FLY 19)
D.L. Menard No Matter Where You At, There You Are (Hannibal HN 1352)
Jimmy C. Newman The Alligator Man (Rounder 6039)
Zachary Richard Zack Attack (Arzed Records RZ 1009)
Clifton Chenier Live at St Mark's (Arhoolie AR 313)
Various Louisiana Swamp Blues (Flywright Records FLY 09)
Allen Toussaint Southern Nights (Reprise K 54021)
The Neville Brothers Yellow Moon (A & M AMA 5240)
The Wild Tchoupitoulas Untitled (Island 162 539 908)
The ReBirth Brass Band Rebirth Kickin' It Live! (Special Delivery SPD 1040)

TEXAS

Bigger than any country in Europe, the Lone Star State has one of the most distinctive and varied popular music scenes in the USA. Blues, country and rock all have strong Texan varieties. Top blues artistes included, in the 1920s, **Blind Lemon Jefferson**, **Blind Willie Johnson** and **Mance Lipscomb**, succeeded by **Sleepy John Estes**, **Lightning Hopkins**, and **T Bone Walker** (one of the earliest blues electric guitarists), and since the 1960s, **Albert Collins** and **Clarence 'Gatemouth' Brown**. White blues artistes from the rock wave of the 1960s included long-time Texas-resident **Johnny Winter** and his stylistic successor, 1980s star guitarist **Stevie Ray Vaughan**.

Texas country is itself multifaceted. The Western Swing style of the 1930s, which added elements of ragtime, swing and blues to the fiddle-combo line-up for which the State was already famous, was popularised by groups such as **Bob Wills and his Texas Playboys**, **Milton Brown and his Brownies**, and **Cliff Bruner's Texas Wanderers**, and is still found in the repertoire of the contemporary Austin-based group **Asleep At The Wheel**. The legacy of Western Swing was very much present in the lovely twin fiddle and piano honky-tonk style of great artistes such as **George Jones**, Texas's contribution to the 1950s and 1960s country charts. The 'outlaw movement' of the 1970s, which imparted a rough, informal rock feel to an excessively slick genre, was led by Texans **Willie Nelson** and **Waylon Jennings** (the latter a former Buddy Holly bassist), who made Austin, Texas, an alternative country capital to Nashville, Tennessee. Finally, talented singer-songwriters such as **Joe Ely**, **Butch Hancock** and **Jimmie Dale Gilmore**, who performed together in the 1970s cult group the **Flatlanders**, along with newer artistes such as **Lyle Lovett** and **Steve Earle**, are continuing to keep Texas a byword for authenticity in country music.

The Spanish language musics associated with the Mexican-origin Chicano residents of Texas (and adjacent California) are divisible into two styles, both booming at the beginning of the 1990s: firstly, the traditionally working-class, accordion-based small group 'conjunto' or 'norteña' music, often referred to as Tex-Mex; secondly, the less roots-based spectrum of pop styles, more centred round synthesizers and orchestras, known as Tejana, which appeals on the whole to a more affluent urban audience.

Conjunto music is closely linked to Mexican norteña (Southern Texas was part of Mexico until 1848), but not identical to it, the Texan style having led the way since the 1940s. The music originated in a mingling of German and Czech settlers' accordions, waltzes and polkas with Mexican corrido song-stories and other elements. Early stars in the 1920s and 1930s were the great singer **Lydia Mendoza**, and accordionists **Narciso Martinez** and **Pedro Ayala**. Towards the end of the period **Santiago Jimenez Sr**, father of one of today's top stars, **'Flaco' Jimenez**, and the group **Los Alegres de Teran**, became famous throughout Latin America.

In the 1940s, the modern conjunto line-up was established, adding drumkit and bass to the existing accordion and bajo sexto (twelve-string bass/rhythm guitar), and a new generation of star accordionists began to exploit the possibilities of amplification, bringing the accordion to the fore as a virtuoso feature of the music. These groups played in the cantinas (honky-tonk bars) and on the plataformas (outdoor dance-floors) of the chicano circuit of South

Texan small towns and barrios. Only later, in the 1960s and 1970s, did they penetrate first civic concert halls and cultural centres, and then the big Christmas and New Year dances of the Tejano upper classes.

The top names of this postwar generation, most of whom are still playing, were **Valerio Longoria, Tony de la Rosa, Paulino Bernal, Roberto Pulido, Ramon Ayala** and **Flaco Jimenez**, who started the late 1950s playing bajo sexto with his father Santiago Sr. Tony de la Rosa, noted for his accordion style, which featured continuous staccato as opposed to the more common intermittent flourishes, pioneered the new amplified conjunto sound and in the 1970s added brass to his line-up (his major hit 'Rio Rebelde' is from this period), while Valerio Longoria created a more sophisticated urban repertoire, including Mexican boleros and Colombian cumbias which he learnt by listening to short wave radio broadcasts from Colombia, and which became extremely popular in Mexico in the 1980s. Longoria is still active in the South Texas dancehall circuit, fronting a quartet which includes his sons Valerio Jr and Flavio on bajo sexto and alto sax, and his grandson, Valerio IV, on drums. It was Leonardo 'Flaco' Jimenez who brought Tex-Mex music to the attention of a new non-Chicano, international audience via his collaborations with the San Antonio rock-country star **Doug Sahm**, with the **Sir Douglas Quintet**, with Willy Nelson, and above all with roots stylist par excellence, Ry Cooder on the albums 'Chicken Skin Music' in 1976 and 'Showtime' in 1977. Jimenez' own hits include 'El Pantalon Blue Jean' and 'El Bingo'; in 1990 he formed a touring band, the **Texas Tornadoes**, with Doug Sahm, **Augie Meyers** and **Freddy Fender**, a San Benito-born country singer (real name Baldemar Huerta) who scored a series of hits in the mid 1970s with songs such as 'Wasted Days And Wasted Nights' and 'Vaya Con Dios'.

In addition to the pure conjunto stylists, a number of Texan country-rockers overlapped the Tex-Mex field in the 1970s and 1980s. They include **Domingo Samudio**, better known as **Sam the Sham** who, with his group **The Pharaohs**, recorded novelty 1960s hits 'Woolly Bully' and 'Lil' Red Riding Hood'; **Steve Jordan** (né Esteban), a roots rocker and speed accordionist whose twin trademarks are his black eyepatch and, since 1989, customised flat-button 'Steve Jordan Tex-Mex Rockordeon' created for him by top manufacturer Hohner; **Joe 'King' Carrasco**; and **The Trio San Antonio**. A number of women players, including **Chavela** of **Grupo Express**, **Lupita Rodela**, and **Eva Ybarra** are among second rank artistes. Finally, the top Los Angeles Chicano rock group **Los Lobos**, while not strictly Tex-Mex artistes, became famous for their hit versions of Mexican songs, notably the 1987 hit version of the old Richie Valens number 'La Bamba', which was based on the traditional son jarocho form. The following year their album 'La Pistola y El Corazon' consisted of Mexican sones, rancheras and waltzes played on traditional instruments which they had bought in cheap second-hand shops in the 1970s when they were still a garage band, and Mexican music meant nothing to most young Anglo-Californians.

The bifurcation between Tex-Mex conjunto music and musica Tejana dates from the 1940s, when certain Texas-based Mexican-origin big band leaders, notably **Beto Villa** and **Isidro Lopez**, added Mexican colour to their orchestras with the use of either accordions, or saxophones and trumpets playing norteña polka accordion parts. In the 1960s, new bandleaders developed the sound further. **Little Joe Hernandez** (now leader of **Little Joe y la Familia**) blended jazz into his sound while **Sunny and the Sunglows** added electric keyboards, synthesized strings and a wide selection of brass instruments. These artistes formed the vanguard of 'La Onda Chicana' – the 'Chicano wave' – of the 1970s when similar big bands were all the rage. The latest generation of Tejano artistes consists of a variety of groups and individuals who mix middle of the road pop, rock and country with synthesizer-based elements of polka, ranchera and conjunto sound. Leading artistes include the group **Mazz**, who produce a sort of synthesized Tex-Mex sound, **La Mafia, Inocencia, La Sombra, Little Joe y la Familia, Ram Herrera, Los Dinos** featuring singer **Selena, Patsy Torres, Laura Canales, Pio Trevino y Majic**, and **Ruben Ramos**.

While the conjunto style represents a Latin development of the accordion polkas brought to Texas by German and Czech immigrants, the Czech tradition itself is by no means extinct. In the 1920s and 1930s, the Baca family brass band recorded popular polkas and certain ensembles such as Adolph Hofner's, played Czech dance music along with Western Swing. Throughout the white farming area of Central Texas, Czech-polka bands still play at weddings and dancehalls and the numerous annual rodeos held in all towns of medium size and above. Senior bands include the **Czech Harvesters** and the **Vrazel Band**, which has been playing since 1953. There is, in addition, a lively polka-modernisation movement, represented notably by the **Brave Combo**, a Denton-based quartet featuring tuba, drums, washboard, guitar, accordion and various saxophones. Leader **Carl Finch** is also proprietor of Four Dots Records, a label whose artistes include **Schwantz Le Frantz**, the **Ducks, Hai Tex, Killbilly, Gregg Hansen** (author of 'D-Reg Music'), the **Potatoes** and **Little Jack Melody**.

The polka revival is not confined to Texas. San Francisco's late 1980s post-punk rock scene included the twelve-man **Polkacide**, whose stage costume at one point included lederhosen and spiked haircuts, while the traditional polka heartland is the Central European-settled region of the Midwest, with Chicago as its epicentre. Top bands include **Eddie Blazonczyk's Versatones** and **Joe Grushecky and the Houserockers**.

Finally, the polka, in its Tex-Mex adaptation, is a prime ingredient of the saxophone-based 'Chicken scratch' music found in North American Indian (native American) communities in southern Arizona.

Texas: Discography

Various (inc. Lydia Mendoza, Narciso Matinez and many more) Tex-Mex (Folkyric FL 9003 and onwards)
Valerio Longoria Caballo Viejo (Arhoolie 336)
Tony de la Rosa Asi Se Baila En Tejas (Rounder 6046)
Flaco Jimenez San Antonio Soul (Rounder 6042)

Joe King Carrasco Bandido Rock (Rounder 9012)
Los Lobos La Pistola y El Corazon (London 828 121–2)
Brave Combo Polkatharsis (Rounder 9009)
Joe Grushecky and the Houserockers Eponymous (Rounder 9020)

NEW YORK AND MIAMI

The most important component of US Latin American music has been until quite recently overwhelmingly Cuban. Cuban bandleaders were at the forefront of the so-called rumba craze of the 1930s, and the major exodus from Havana to the USA after the Cuban revolution in 1959 accentuated the influence. Even the substantial population of Puerto Ricans played essentially Cuban-style music. New York City has always been the major centre, with Miami, Los Angeles and Chicago in secondary roles. In the 1970s and 1980s, Miami, with its large population of Cubans and other Latinos, came increasingly to the fore, with the big Calle Ocho Festival a major annual showcase of talent.

The music scenes of the United States, Puerto Rico and Cuba have always overlapped, so that restricting a given musician to one or the other country is problematic: broadly, musicians in this section are either of US nationality or have had their greatest effect in the USA.

The first wave of Latin American music to achieve wide popularity was the misnamed rumba (for this and other terms such as charanga, conjunto, etc., see **Cuba**) of the 1930s, which was in fact more based on the Cuban son form. One of its first popularisers was the **Havana Casino Orchstra** of **Don Azpiazu**, whose version of 'El Manicero' ('The Peanut Vendor') was a crossover hit. The bandleader to find greatest national fame, however, was the Barcelona-born but Cuban-educated **Xavier Cugat,** who recorded with Bing Crosby and Frank Sinatra and appeared in dozens of films. The 1940s saw the major vogue for big-band Latin music, which in the 1950s developed into the mambo craze, essentially a mixture of the big band brass sound with Afro-Cuban percussion. Chief mambo purveyors, who packed out the legendary Palladium and Roseland ballrooms in New York, were the bands of **Frank Grillo,** known as **Machito,** who died in London in the 1980s while playing a season at Ronnie Scott's club; **Tito Puente,** a New York-born, Juilliard Music School-educated timbal virtuoso later associated with **Celia Cruz** and by 1990 the doyen of New York salsa; **Tito Rodriguez,** a Puerto Rican born timbalero, vibes player and singer, whose prolific jazz collaborations were cut short by his death from leukaemia in 1973; and **Perez Prado,** the Cuban-born recorder of the smash hit 'Cerazo Rosa' ('Cherry Pink and Apple Blossom White'), who came to personify the commercialised mambo to the non-Latino public.

Machito's, Puente's and Prado's groups, which in their use of trumpets nd trombones were more in a conjunto tradition than a charanga one, nonetheless also participated in the crossover craze, the cha-cha-cha, which followed the mambo. The cha-cha-cha, whose name was probably based either on the sound of shuffling feet or on that of the güiro scraper, was originated by Cuban charangas (featuring flute and violin as opposed to brass), notably the **Orquesta Aragon**, and popularised in the USA by the band of **José Fajardo**, who settled in the States shortly after playing for future President John F. Kennedy at a headline-making campaign concert at the Waldorf Astoria, New York.

The early 1960s was the heyday of the charanga style (although the cha-cha-cha craze was killed among young Anglos by dilution and the advent of rock and roll), with groups of this line-up formed by a new generation of great names: **Ray Barretto**, Brooklyn-born Puerto Rican conga player and bandleader who counted the 1963 Watusi fad among his many achievements and whose updated, brass-augmented **Charanga Moderna** set a new standard; **Charlie Palmieri**, a Puerto Rican-descended, New York-born pianist and bandleader whose **Charanga Duboney** was also a key group; **Johnny Pacheco**, a Dominican-born flautist who played with the Charanga Duboney before forming his own groups and co-founding Fania Records (see below); **Roberto Torres**, a Cuban-born percussionist and singer who founded the cooperative charanga **Orquesta Broadway** (which is still playing), before going on to create the influential SAR label and initiate the new charanga vallenata style in the 1980s.

By the mid-1960s, the charanga boom was over and a new, if short-lived, craze, the boogaloo, was gaining ground, played by artistes such as **Joe Cuba and his Sextet**, **Ricardo Ray**, **Joe Bataan**, a half-Filipino singer whose 1968 hit 'Subway Joe' typified the genre, and more established performers such as **Eddie Palmieri**, brother of Charlie. The boogaloo was a sort of mixture of mambo and R & B, with songs in English as well as Spanish, and prefigured the crossover genre Latin soul, into which it merged by the end of the decade.

The mid to late 1960s saw the charanga fall from fashion, superseded by a widespread return to a conjunto format closely based on that of the great Cuban Arsenio Rodriguez's bands – a format featuring trumpets, piano, bass, guitar and percussion. It was at this time that the term 'salsa', meaning 'hot chilli sauce', came to be used as a catch-all tag for the variety of new Latin musics being created, primarily in the centres of New York and Puerto Rico, but not Cuba (Cubans frequently resent the term as expropriation and renaming of 'their' son). The precise origin of the tag is impossible to locate with certainty, but strong cases are made out for 'Salsa Nova', a 1962 album by **Pupi Legarreta**, and, especially by Venezuelans, for 'Llegó la Salsa', a 1966 album by the Caracas artiste **Federico**.

Strongly associated with the new salsa of the 1970s was the record label Fania, founded in 1964 by Johnny Pacheco and the lawyer Jerry Masucci, whose policy of signing up-and-coming new talent rapidly made it the leading company of the decade. Among top artistes to have recorded for Fania are **Willie Colon**, a Bronx-born, Puerto Rican-descended singer, songwriter and bandleader whose early streetwise tough image (and similarly realist lyrics) gave way to a distinguished and multifaceted career at the top of his profession; **Larry Harlow**, a non-Latino New Yorker, Cuban music lover and multi-instrumentalist; **Cheo**

Feliciano (see **Puerto Rico**); **Ray Barretto; Mongo Santamaria**, a percussion wizard and successor of 1940s bongo virtuoso and Dizzy Gillespie collaborator **Chano Pozo; Hector Lavoe** (see **Puerto Rico**), a frequent singer with Willie Colon's bands; **Israel 'Cachao' Lopez**; and top arrangers such as **Louie Ramirez**.

The 1970s salsa boom also exalted to superstar status the Cuban-born singer **Celia Cruz**, whose 25-year career started with first prize in a Havana talent competition, and took in pre-revolutionary stints at the city's famous Tropicana nightclub and membership of the popular band **Sonora Matancera** with whom, on the pretext of a tour to Mexico, she abandoned Castro's Cuba in 1960 to work with top New York bandleaders such as **Tito Puente, Johnny Pacheco**, and later **Willie Colon**, and a starring role in *Hommy*, the Latino version of the rock opera *Tommy*.

The late 1970s saw a return to fashion of the charanga format with the creation of bands such as **Charanga 76**, featuring the subsequently famous duo of singers **Hansel Martinez** and **Raul Alfonso**, and **Charanga Casino**. The most successful artiste and producer of this movement, which peaked in the early 1980s, was the singer and bandleader Roberto Torres, whose SAR label produced a number of highly successful 'tipico' bands, which re-explored a Cuban son montuno style. Leading examples were the groups **Charanga de La 4, Charanga Colonial** and **SAR All-Stars**, and singers and musicians including **Alfredo 'Chocolate' Armenteros, Papaito, Alfredo Valdes Jr, La India de Oriente, Linda Leida**, and **Henry Fiol**, a half Puerto Rican, half Italian-American singer, bandleader, visual artist and sensitive and talented rediscoverer of the classic style of the old Cuban soneros. Torres' own highly successful recording during this period centred on the three LPs with the **Charanga Vallenata**, a combination of Cuban son with Colombian vallenato accordion played by **Jesus Hernandez**.

The mid-1980s saw salsa threatened in New York, as in Puerto Rico, by the massively successful Dominican merengue with its simple, catchy beat, irresistible brass choruses and numerous hungry young Dominican performers willing to work for low fees. Salsa's resurgence was led by the style known as salsa romantica, or erotica, depending on the explicitness of the generally steamy lyrics (see **Puerto Rico**). Musically, salsa romantica is smoother, quieter, more ballad-oriented and at its worst, both blander and more saccharine of music and clichéd of lyric. An early precursor of the style was the constantly innovative New York arranger and bandleader **Louie Ramirez**, whose work with the singer **Ray de la Paz** included Spanish baladas with a light, sweet salsaesque orchestration. Top romantica artistes include **Lalo Rodriguez** and **Eddie Santiago** (see **Puerto Rico**); **Frankie Ruiz**, a New Jersey-born singer who began performing with the Puerto Rican **Tommy Olivencia**'s band before successfully going solo with major hit albums in 1986 and 1987; **Jose Alberto 'El Canario'**, a Dominican-born former member of the Orchestra Típica 73, whose top-quality band and superior arrangements made albums such as 'Sueño Contigo' major successes; **Tito Allen**, a former singer with the bands of Ray

Barretto and Louie Ramirez; **Tito Nieves, Luis Enrique; Gilberto Santa Rosa;** and **Willie Chirino.**

In addition to the primarily Latin-American music described, the 1990 US Latino music scene covered a booming Spanish language but otherwise Western pop-rock scene, in the mould of **Gloria Estefan** and **Miami Sound Machine's** music, with an increasing tendency for non-Latin pop artistes such as Janet Jackson to include Spanish-lyric songs in order to boost their appeal to the Hispanic market. This tendency, curiously, was mirrored among salseros, by a trend harking back to the boogaloo days, to include English language songs in their repertoires. Spanish rap artistes, such as **Kid Frost** and **Mellow Man Ace,** also proliferated.

New York and Miami: Discography

Various A Carnival of Cuban Music (Rounder 5049)
Tito Puente The Mambo King (RMM CDT 80680)
Charlie Palmieri Gigante Hits (Alegre LPS 88957)
Joe Bataan Mr New York (Charly 166)
Willie Colon Legal Alien (CBS DCL 80351)
Celia Cruz The Brillante Best (Vaya VS 77)
Celia Cruz and Willie Colon Winners (Vaya JMVS 109)
Roberto Torres Y Sigo Criollo! (Manzana SML-3)
Henry Fiol Sonero (Earthworks EWV 19)
Luis Enrique Luces Del Alma (CBS DCL 804'/3)
Willy Chirino Acuarela del Caribe (CBS DIL 80228)
Tipica 73 En Cuba (Manzana FML 50)
Ruben Blades Caminando (Sony CD 80593)
Charanga Colonial Charanga Colonial (Neon NLP 103)

SELECTED INDEX